Viking Tales of Old Iceland 4

Original Texts, Translations, and Word Lists

Translated by
Matthew Leigh Embleton

Viking Tales of Old Iceland 4

The Tale of the Greenlanders (II) (The Tale of Einarr Sokkason) (*Old Norse*) 3
The Tale of the Greenlanders (II) (The Tale of Einarr Sokkason) (*Old Icelandic*) 61
The Tale of Hreiðarr the Fool (*Old Norse*) 124
The Tale of Hreiðarr the Fool (*Old Icelandic*) 180
The Tale of Star-Oddi's Dream (*Old Norse*) 240
The Tale of Star-Oddi's Dream (*Old Icelandic*) 304

Cover: Old Norse text over an outline of Iceland. Author's design.

The original Old Norse and Old Icelandic texts are in the public domain.
These translations ©2022 Matthew Leigh Embleton
©2025 Matthew Leigh Embleton (This Edition)

Acknowledgments

I have long been fascinated by languages and history, and I am very grateful to the special people in my life who have supported and encouraged me in my work. Thank you for believing in me. You know who you are.

Introduction

Old Norse is a North Germanic language spoken by inhabitants of Scandinavia from about the 7th to the 15th centuries. Old Icelandic is a variety of Old West Norse that emerged during the Norse settlement of Iceland in the second half of the 9th century. The rich tradition of Icelandic story telling survived by oral tradition over several centuries before being written down in the 13th Century. The Tales of Icelanders are known as Íslendingaþættir. The word 'þáttr' (plural: 'þættir') translates as a strand of rope or a yarn, comparable to the word 'yarn' in English sometimes used to refer to a story.

The texts are presented in Old Norse and Old Icelandic, in their original form, with a literal word-for-word line-by-line translation, and a Modern English translation, all side-by-side. In this way, it is possible to see and feel how the worked and how it has evolved. This book is designed to be of use and interest to anyone with a passion for the Old Norse or Old Icelandic language, Norse history, or languages and history in general.

The Tale of the Greenlanders (II) (The Tale of Einarr Sokkason) (*Old Norse*)

Old Norse	Literal	English
1	**1**	**1**
Sokki hét maðr ok var Þórisson.	Sokki was-named a-man and was Son-of-Thorri.	There was a man named Sokki, and he was the son of Thorri.
Hann bjó í Brattahlíð á Grænlandi.	He lived in Brattahlid in Greenland.	He lived in Brattahlid in Greenland.
Hann var mikils virðr ok vinsæll.	He was much respected and popular.	He was much respected and popular.
Einarr hét sonr hans ok var mannvænlegr maðr.	Einar was-named son his and was a-friendly man.	His son was named Einar and he was a friendly man.
Þeir feðgar áttu mikit vald á Grænlandi, ok váru þeir þar mjök fyrir mönnum.	They father-and-son had great power in Greenland, and were they there much foremost men.	The father and son had great power in Greenland and they were prominent men.
Einhverju sinni lét Sokki þings kveðja ok tjáði þat fyrir mönnum, at hann vildi, at landit væri eigi lengr byskupslaust, ok vildi, at allir landsmenn legðu sína muni til, at byskupsstóll væri efldr.	One-occasion they had Sokki assembly called and voiced that before the-men, that he willed, that the-land be no longer bishop-less, and willed, that all lands-men put themselves should to, a bishop's-seat to-be strengthened.	On one occasion Sokki had an assembly called and announced before the men that he wished that the land should no longer be without a bishop, and he wished that all the men of the land should contribute towards a bishop's seat to be established.
Bændr játtuðu því allir.	Farmers agreed accordingly all.	Accordingly the farmers agreed to this.
Sokki bað Einar, son sinn, fara þessa ferð til Nóregs, kvað hann vera sendiligstan mann þess erendis at fara.	Sokki bid Einar, son his, travel this journey to Norway, said he would-be to-be-sent man this errand to travel.	Sokki asked his son Einar to travel on a journey to Norway as the best man for this errand.
Hann kveðst fara mundu, sem hann vildi.	He said travel would, as he willed.	He said that he would travel as wished.
Einarr hafði með sér tannvöru mikla ok svörð at heimta sik fram við höfðingja.	Einar had with him walrus-tusks great and skins to carry himself from with chieftains.	Einar had great walrus tusks and skins with him to further his case with the chieftains.

The Tale of the Greenlanders (II) (The Tale of Einarr Sokkason) (Old Norse)

Old Norse	Literal	English
Þeir kómu við Nóreg.	They came to Norway.	They came to Norway.
Þá var Sigurðr Jórsalafari konungr at Nóregi.	Then was Sigurd Jerusalem-Traveller the-king of Norway.	Then Sigurd Jerusalem-farer was king of Norway.
Einarr kom á fund konungs ok heimti sik fram með fégjöfum ok tjáði síðan mál sitt ok erendi ok beiddi konung þar til fulltings, at hann næði slíku sem hann beiddi fyrir nauðsyn landsins.	Einar came to meeting the-king's and presented himself from with fee-gifts and spoke then matters his and errand and bid the-king there to help, that he get such as he bid for needs the-lands.	Einar came to have a meeting with the king and presented himself well with wealthy gifts on account of his errand, and asked the king to help him get that which his lands needed.
Konungr lét þeim þat víst betr henta.	The-king had them that certainly better suitable.	The king agreed that it would certainly be better suited.
Síðan kallaði konungr til sín þann mann, er Arnaldr hét.	Then called the-king to him then a-man, was Arnald named.	Then the king called to him a man who was named Arnald.
Hann var góðr klerkr ok vel til kennimanns fallinn.	He was good cleric and well to teaching fallen.	He was a good cleric and well fallen to teaching.
Konungr beiddi, at hann réðist til þessa vanda fyrir guðs sakir ok bænar hans, "ok mun ek senda þik til Danmarkar á fund Özurar erkibyskups í Lundi með mínum bréfum ok innsiglum".	The-king bid, that he deal to this problem for god's sake and prayers his, "and will I send you to Denmark to meet Ossur archbishop in Lund with my briefs and seals".	The king asked him to deal with this problem God's sake and his prayers, "And I will send you to Denmark to meet archbishop Ossur of Lund with my letters and seals".
Arnaldr kvaðst ófúss til at ráðast, fyrst fyrir sjálfs síns sakar, er hann væri lítt til fallinn, ok síðan at skilja við vini sína ok frændr, í þriðja stað at eiga við torsóttligt fólk.	Arnald said reluctant to that arrange, firstly for himself his sake, as he was little to weak, and then to part with friends his and kinsmen, and thirdly stand to not with difficult folk.	Arnald said that he was reluctant to arrange this, firstly for his sake because he was ill-fitted for it, and secondly to part with his friends and kinsmen, and thirdly he did not wish to have to talk to such difficult folk.
Konungr kvað hann því meira gott mundu eftir taka sem hann hefði meiri skapraun af mönnum.	The-king said he that more good would afterwards take as he had more temperament of men.	The king said that the more his difficulty at the hands of temperamental men, the greater his reward would be afterwards.

The Tale of the Greenlanders (II) (The Tale of Einarr Sokkason) (Old Norse)

Old Norse	Literal	English
Hann kveðst eigi nenna at skerast undan hans bæn, "en ef þess verðr auðit, at ek taka byskupsvígslu, þá vil ek, at Einarr sveri mér þess eið at halda ok fulltingja rétt byskupsstólsins ok eignum þeim, er guði eru gefnar, ok hegna þeim, er á ganga, ok sé varnarmaðr fyrir öllum hlutum staðarins".	He said not bothered to cutting away-from his prayers, "but if this becomes possible, that I take bishop's-appointment, then will I, that Einar swear to-me this oath to hold and fulfil rights bishop's-seat and owning them, the priest are given, and protected they, are to go, and being defender for all things the-place".	He said that he did not want the bother of cutting away from his prayers "but if it becomes possible that I take the appointment of bishop, then I wish Einar to swear to me this oath, to hold and fulfil the rights of the bishop's seat, and all that is given to the priest, and to be the protector and defender of all things to do with the bishop's seat".
Konungr kvað hann þat gera skyldu.	The-king said he that to-do should.	The king said that he should do this.
Einarr kvaðst mundu undir þat ganga.	Einar said would submit to go.	Einar said he would submit to going along with it.
Síðan fór byskupsefni á fund Özurar erkibyskups ok sagði honum sitt erendi með konungsbréfum.	Then travelled the-bishop-elect to meet Ossur archbishop and said to-him this errand with the-king's-brief.	Then the bishop-elect went to meet archbishop Ossur and told him of his errand with the king's letters.
Erkibyskup tók honum vel, ok reyndust hugi við.	The-archbishop took him well, and gave-him his-mind with.	The archbishop received him well and gave to him with his mind.
Ok er byskup sá, at þessi maðr var vel til tignar fallinn, vígði hann Arnald til byskups ok leysti hann vel af hendi.	And when the-bishop saw, that this man was well to position fallen, consecrated he Arnald to bishop and released him well of hand.	And when the bishop saw that this man was well given to the position he consecrated Arnald to bishop and parted with him warmly.
Síðan kom Arnaldr byskup til konungs, ok tók hann við honum vel.	Then came Arnald bishop to the-king, and took he with him well.	Then bishop Arnald went to the king and he received him well.
Einarr hafði haft með sér bjarndýri af Grænlandi ok gaf þat Sigurði konungi.	Einar had had with him a-bear from Greenland and gave it Sigurd the-king.	Einar had a bear with him from Greenland and gave it to Sigurd the king.
Fékk hann þar í mót sæmðir ok metorð af konungi.	Got he then to meet honour and esteem from the-king.	He then got honour and esteem from the king.
Síðan fóru þeir á einu skipi, byskup ok Einarr.	Then travelled they on one ship, the-bishop and Einar.	Then they travelled on a ship, the bishop and Einar.

The Tale of the Greenlanders (II) (The Tale of Einarr Sokkason) (Old Norse)

Old Norse	Literal	English
Á öðru skipi bjóst Arnbjörn Austmaðr ok norrænir menn með honum ok vildu ok fara út til Grænlands.	On another ship prepared Arnbjorn Eastern-man and Nordic men with him and willed also travel out to Greenland.	Prepared on another ship was Arnbjorn the Norwegian and other Norse men with him who wished to travel to Greenland.
Síðan létu þeir í haf, ok greiðist eigi byrrinn mjök í hag þeim, ok kómu þeir byskup ok Einarr í Holtavatnsós undir Eyjafjöllum á Íslandi.	Then had they to sea, and paying not bearing much of circumstances theirs, and came they bishop and Einar to Holtavatnsos under Eyjafjolls in Iceland.	Then they put to sea and the situation was not very favourable for them, and the bishop and Einar arrived in Holtavatnsós under the Eyjafjolls in Iceland.
Þá bjó Sæmundur inn fróði í Odda.	Then lived Saemund the learned in Odda.	Then Saemund the learned lived in Odda.
Hann fór á fund byskups ok bauð honum til sín um vetrinn.	He went to meet the-bishop and invited him to his about winter.	He went to see the bishop and invited him to stay with him for the winter.
Byskup þakkaði honum ok lézt þat þiggja mundu.	Bishop thanked him and had that accepted would.	The bishop thanked him and had accepted it.
Einarr var undir Eyjafjöllum um vetrinn.	Einar was under Eyjafjolls about winter.	Einar was under Eyjafjolls during the winter.
Þat er sagt, þá er byskup reið frá skipi ok menn hans, at þeir áðu á bæ nökkurum í Landeyjum ok sátu úti.	It is said, when that bishop rode from the-ship and men his, that they that to a-farm some in The-Landeys and sat outside.	It is said that when the bishop and his men got off the ship, they went to a farm in the Landeys and sat outside.
Þá gekk út kerling ein ok hafði ullkamb í hendi.	Then went out old-woman one and had wool-comb in hand.	Then an old woman walked out alone with a wool comb in her hand.
Hún gekk at einum manni ok mælti:	She went to one man and said:	She walked up to one man and said:
"Muntu festa, bokki, tindinn í kambi mínum?"	"Shall-you fix, buck, pin in comb mine?"	"Will you fix the pin in my comb, buck?"
Hann tók við ok kvaðst mundu at gera ok tók hnjóðhamar ór mal einum ok gerði at, ok líkaði kerlingu allvel.	He took with and said would to done and took hammer out-of the-matter one and did it, and liked the-old-woman all-well.	He took it over and said that he would do it, and he took a hammer off the ground and did it, and the old woman liked this very well,
En þat var byskup raunar,	And it was a-bishop actually,	and it was actually a bishop.

The Tale of the Greenlanders (II) (The Tale of Einarr Sokkason) (Old Norse)

Old Norse	Literal	English
hann var hagr vel, ok er því frá þessu sagt, at hann sýndi lítillæti sitt.	he was handy well, and was therefore from this said, that he showed humility his.	He was very handy and it is told from this of how he showed his humility.
Hann var í Odda um vetrinn, ok fór með þeim Sæmundi allvel.	He was in Odda about winter, and went with them Saemund all-well.	He was in Odda during the winter and got on very well with Saemund.
En til þeira Arnbjarnar spurðist ekki.	But to them Arnbjarn heard-of not.	But they did not hear of Arnbjarn.
Ætluðu þeir byskup, at hann mundi kominn til Grænlands.	Supposed they bishop, that he would come to Greenland.	They thought the bishop would come to Greenland.
Um sumarit eftir fóru þeir byskup ok Einarr af Íslandi ok kómu við Grænland í Eiríksfjörð, ok tóku menn við þeim allvel.	About summer after went they the-bishop and Einar from Iceland and came to Greenland in Eriksfjord, and took men with them all-well.	In the following summer, the bishop and Einar left Iceland and arrived at Greenland in Eriksfjord and were well received by the people.
Spurðu þeir þá enn ekki til Arnbjarnar, ok þótti þat undarligt, ok liðu svá nökkur sumur.	Heard-of they then but not to Arnbjarn, and thought that strange, and passed so some summers.	They still didn't hear about Arnbjarn and thought it was strange, and then a few summers passed.
Gerðist nú umræða mikil, at þeir muni týnzt hafa.	Became now discussed much, that they would lost have.	There was now much discussion that they must have been lost.
Byskup setti stól sinn í Görðum ok réðst þangat til.	Bishop set seat his in Gardar and ruled from-then to.	The bishop placed his chair in Gardar and ruled until then.
Var Einarr honum þá mestr styrkðarmaðr ok þeir feðgar.	Was Einar to-him then the-most supporter and they father-and-son.	Einar was his greatest supporter then, and they were father and son.
Þeir váru ok mest metnir af öllum landsmönnum af byskupi.	They were and most important of all lands-men of the-bishop.	They were and the most valued of all the countrymen by the bishop.

2

Sigurðr hét maðr ok var Njálsson, grænlenzkr maðr.	Sigurd was-named a-man and was Son-of-Njal, a-Greenlander man.	There was a man named Sigurd who was the son of Njal, a Greenlander man.
Hann fór oft á haustum til fangs í óbyggðir.	He travelled often out autumn to captivity in un-settled.	He often went in the fall to captivity in the wilderness.

The Tale of the Greenlanders (II) (The Tale of Einarr Sokkason) (Old Norse)

Old Norse	Literal	English
Hann var sægarpr mikill.	He was sea-champion much.	He was very much a champion of the sea.
Þeir váru fimmtán saman.	They were fifteen altogether.	There were fifteen of them together.
Þeir kómu um sumarit at jöklinum Hvítserk ok höfðu fundit nökkurar eldstóar manna ok enn nökkurn veiðiskap.	They came about summer to a-glacier Hvitserk and had-they found some fire-place men and still some hunting.	They came in the summer to the glacier Hvitserk and had found several small groups of men and still some hunting.
Þá mælti Sigurðr:	Then spoke Sigurd:	Then Sigurd said:
"Hvárs eruð þér fúsari, at hverfa aftr eða fara lengra?	"Which are you willing, to turn back or travel longer?	"Which are you more willing to go back or go further?
Er nú ekki sumars mikit eftir, en fang orðit lítit".	Is now not summer much remaining, but resources have-become little".	There isn't much left of the summer now, but the catch has become short".
Hásetar kváðust fúsari aftr at hverfa ok sögðu mannhættu mikla at fara um stórfjörðu undir jöklum.	The-crew said willing back to turn and said dangerous much to travel about large-fjords under glaciers.	The crew said they were more willing to turn back and said that it was very dangerous to go through a large fjord under glaciers.
Hann kvað þat satt, "en svá segir mér hugr um, at eftir muni it meira fangit, ef því náir".	He said that true, "but so says to-me mind about, that later would then more to-catch, if then getting".	He said it was true "but then my mind tells me that later the more will be caught if it is possible".
Þeir báðu hann ráða, kváðust lengi hans forsjá hlítt hafa ok þó vel gefizt.	They asked him advice, said long his foresight satisfactory had and though well given.	They asked him for advice, saying that they had been under his guardianship for a long time and that it had been successful.
Honum kveðst meira um at halda fram, ok svá var gert.	He said more about that to-hold from, and so was done.	He said that there was more to claim, and so it was done.
Steinþórr hét maðr, er á skipi þeira var.	Steinthor was-named a-man, was on ship theirs was.	A man on their ship was called Steinthor.
Hann tók til orða:	He took to words:	He spoke:
"Dreymði mik í nótt, Sigurðr",	"Dreamed me about the-night, Sigurd",	"I had a dream last night, Sigurd",

The Tale of the Greenlanders (II) (The Tale of Einarr Sokkason) (Old Norse)

Old Norse	Literal	English
sagði hann, "ok mun ek segja þér drauminn.	said he, "and will I say to-you the-dream.	he said, "and I will tell you the dream
Nú	Now	Now
er vér fórum á fjörðinn þennan inn mikla, þóttumst ek kominn í milli bjarga nökkurra ok æpa til bjargar mér".	when we travel to fjord then the much, thought I coming in between rescuing something and shouting to rescue me".	when we went to this great fjord, I thought I came between something to be rescued from, and shouting for my rescue".
Sigurðr kvað draum meðallagi góðan, "ok skyldir þú þar eigi björg undir fótum troða ok hitta eigi í þann einangr, at þú mættir eigi munni halda".	Sigurd said dream moderately good, "and should you there not rocks under feet tread and find not in that alone-going, that you might not mouth hold".	Sigurd said it was a moderately good dream "and you should not trample rocks under your feet there and you should not find yourself so alone that you could not keep your mouth shut".
Steinþórr var heldr æðimaðr í skaplyndi ok óforsjáll.	Steinthor was rather of-mind in temper and impulsive.	Steinthor was rather a hot-tempered and impulsive person.
Ok er þeir sækja inn á fjörðinn, þá mælti Sigurðr:	And when they sought in the fjord, then spoke Sigurd:	And when they entered the fjord, Sigurd said:
"Hvárt er sem mér sýnist, at skip sé inn á fjörðinn?"	"Whether is as to-me seems, that ship this in the fjord?"	"Does it seem to me that a ship is in the fjord?"
Þeir kváðu svá vera.	They said so being.	They said it was so.
Sigurðr kvað þat tíðendum mundu gegna,	Sigurd said that news would pass,	Sigurd said that this would bring great news.
heldu nú síðan inn at ok sá, at skipit var sett upp í einn árós ok gert fyrir ofan.	held now then in to and saw, the ship was sat up in a river-mouth and made for above.	Now they went inward and saw that the ship was set up in one estuary and made covered.
Þat var mikit hafskip.	It was a-great sea-going-ship.	It was a great sea-going ship.
Síðan gengu þeir á land ok sá skála ok tjald skammt frá.	Then went they to land and saw cabin and tent a-short-distance from.	Then they went ashore and saw a cabin and a tent nearby.
Þá mælti Sigurðr, at þeir mundu tjalda fyrst, "ok er nú liðit á dag, ok vil ek, at menn sé kyrrlátir ok varúðgir".	Then spoke Sigurd, that they would tent-up first, "and is now passed in the-day, and wish I, that men are still and cautious".	Then Sigurd said that they would camp first "and now it's late in the day and I want people to be quiet and careful".
Ok svá gerðu þeir.	And so done was.	And so it was done.

The Tale of the Greenlanders (II) (The Tale of Einarr Sokkason) (Old Norse)

Old Norse	Literal	English
Ok um morgininn ganga þeir ok sjást um.	And about morning went they and looked about.	And in the morning they went and looked about.
Þeir sjá stokk einn hjá sér, ok stóð í bolöx ok mannshræ hjá.	They saw a-log one beside them, and stood in the-trunk and human-body beside.	They saw a log by them and an axe in the butt and a human carcass.
Sigurðr kvað þann mann viðinn höggvit hafa ok hafa orðit vanmeginn af megri.	Sigurd said that the-man the-trees struck had and had become weak of meagre.	Sigurd said that the man had been striking trees and had become weak from hunger.
Síðan gengu þeir at skálanum ok sá þar annat mannshræ.	Then went they to the-cabin and saw there another dead-body.	Then they walked to the cabin and saw another corpse there.
Sigurðr kvað þann gengit hafa, meðan hann mátti, "ok munu þessir verit hafa þjónustumenn þeira, er í skálanum eru".	Sigurd said then walked had, as-long-as he might, "and would these been have servants-of they, who about the-cabin were".	Sigurd said that he had walked for as long as he could "and these will be the servants of who are in the cabin".
Öx lá ok hjá þessum.	Axe lay also beside these.	An axe lay beside these.
Þá mælti Sigurðr:	Then spoke Sigurd:	Then Sigurd said:
"Þat kalla ek ráð at rjúfa skálann ok láta leggja út daun af líkum þeim, er inni eru, ok ýldu, er lengi munu legit hafa,	"It call I decide to break-open the-hut and lay-out have out the-dead of bodies they, who in were, and decay, are long may laid have,	"This I call our plan, to break open the cabin and let the stench of the dead out, for the corpses will have been lying there for a long time.
ok varist menn fyrir at verða, því at þess er eigi lítil ván, at mönnum verði at því mein, er mjök er á mót eðli manna, þótt líkendi sé á því, at menn þessir muni oss ekki illt gera".	and weariness men for that be, because that this is not little hope, that men be that because-of disease, and much is to meet nature man's, though alike they-are that they, the men these should to-us not ill be-done".	And men be wary of it, because there is nothing more certain than men will be harmed by it, and it is very against human wellbeing, and though there are similarities, these men will not harm us".
Steinþórr kvað slíkt undarligt, at gera sér meira fyrir en þyrfti, ok gekk á hurðina, en þeir rufu skálann.	Steinthor said such strange, to do as more for than needed, and went to the-door, but they broke-up the-cabin.	Steinthor said that it was such a strange thing to do more than was necessary, and went to the door as they broke open the cabin.
Ok er Steinþórr gekk út, leit Sigurðr til hans ok mælti:	And when Steinthor went out, looked Sigurd to him and said:	And when Steinthor came out Sigurd got a look at him and said:

The Tale of the Greenlanders (II) (The Tale of Einarr Sokkason) (Old Norse)

Old Norse	Literal	English
"Allmjök er manninum brugðit".	"All-great is this-man upset".	"This man is greatly upset".
Hann tók þegar at æpa ok hlaupa, en þeir eftir félagar hans.	He took straightaway to shouting and running, but they followed companions his.	He started shouting and running away, but his companions followed him.
Hann hleypr síðan í hamarrifu nökkura, þar er engi mátti at honum komast, ok þar fekk hann bana.	He ran then into crags some, there where no-one might to him come, and there got he death.	He ran into some crags and became stuck between them so that no-one could get to him, and there he died.
Sigurðr kvað hann of berdreyman.	Sigurd said he of clear-dreams.	Sigurd said his dream was clearly true.
Síðan rufu þeir skálann ok gerðu eftir því, sem Sigurðr mælti, ok varð þeim ekki mein at.	Then tore-up they the-cabin and did following according, as Sigurd said, and came to-them not harm by.	Then they tore up the cabin and followed accordingly as Sigurd had told them, and no harm came to them.
Þeir sá þar í skálanum menn dauða ok fé mikit.	They saw there in the-cabin men dead and wealth much.	They saw dead people and a lot of money in the cabin.
Þá mælti Sigurðr:	Then said Sigurd:	Then Sigurd said:
"Þat sýnist mér ráð, at þér hleypið holdi af beinum þeira í heitukötlum þeira, er þeir hafa átt, ok er svá hægra til kirkju at færa.	"That seems to-me advisable, that you discharge flesh off bones theirs in boiling-cauldrons theirs, that they had had, and then so right to the-church to bring.	"It seems to me advisable that you get the flesh off their bones in their hot cauldrons that they have, and then move them to church.
Ok er þat líkast, at Arnbjörn muni hér verit hafa, því at skip þetta annat it fagra, er hér stendr á landi, hefi ek heyrt, at hann hafi átt".	And is that likely, that Arnbjorn should here been has, because that ship this other then the-fairest, is here standing about the-land, have I heard, that he had had".	And it seems likely that Arnbjorn will have been here, because this ship is one of the most beautiful that is standing on this land, I have heard that he had".
Þat var höfðaskip ok steint ok mikil gersemi.	It was a-headed-ship and stone-carving and much treasure.	It was a ship with a figurehead and stone-carving and great treasure.
Kaupskipit var brotit mjök neðan, ok kvaðst Sigurðr ætla, at þat mundi at engum nytjum verða.	Merchant-ship was broken much below, and said Sigurd suppose, that it would to no use be.	The merchant ship was broken below, and Sigurd said that it would be of no use.

The Tale of the Greenlanders (II) (The Tale of Einarr Sokkason) (Old Norse)

Old Norse	Literal	English
Þeir taka ór sauminn, en brenndu skipit ok höfðu hlaðna ferjuna ór óbyggðum, eftirbátinn ok höfðaskipit.	They took out-from the-seam, and burned the-ship and had loaded the-ferry out-of the-unsettled-land, the-after-boat and head-ship.	They took out everything from the seams and burned the ship and had loaded to ferry out of the unsettled land, the second boat, and the head ship.
Þeir kómu í byggðina ok fundu byskup í Görðum, ok sagði Sigurðr honum tíðendin ok fjárfundinn.	They came to the-settlement and found bishop in Gardar, and said Sigurd to-him the-news and wealth-finding.	They came to the settlement and found the bishop at Gardar, and Sigurd told him the news and of finding the wealth.
"Nú kann ek eigi annat at sjá",	"Now can I not anything-else to see",	"Now I can't see anything else",
sagði hann, "en þat fé þeira muni bezt komit, er beinum þeira fylgir, ok ef ek á á nökkuru ráð, þá vil ek, at svá sé".	said he, "but that wealth theirs would best come, that bones theirs followed, and if I of of some advice, then wish I, to so to-be".	he said, "but their money will be best served if their placed with their bones, and if I have any say, I want it to be so".
Byskup kvað hann vel hafa með farit ok vitrliga, ok þat mæltu allir.	Bishop said he well had with going and wise-like, and that said all.	The bishop said he had acted well and wisely, and everyone said so.
Mikit fé fylgði líkum þeira.	Much wealth followed bodies theirs.	A lot of money followed their corpses.
Byskup kvað gersemi mikla vera höfðaskipit.	Bishop said treasure much being head-ship.	The bishop said the great treasure was the head ship.
Sigurðr kvað ok þat sannligast, at þat færi til staðarins fyrir sálum þeira.	Sigurd said and it truthfully, that it going to the-place for souls theirs.	Sigurd said, and most truly, that it would go to the bishop's seat for the good of their souls.
Öðru fé skiptu þeir með sér, er fundit höfðu, at grænlenzkum lögum.	Other wealth divided they with themselves, as found had, to Greenlandic law.	They shared the other money they had found according to Greenlandic law.
Ok er þessi tíðendi kómu til Nóregs, þá spurði þat sá maðr, er Özurr hét ok var systursonr Arnbjarnar.	And when these tidings came to Norway, then learned that so man, was Ossur named and was sister's-son Arnbjarnar.	And when these tidings came to Norway, the man whose name was Ossur, who was Arnbjorn's sister's son, learned about it.
Ok	And	...and
fleiri menn váru þeir, er sína frændr höfðu misst á því skipi ok væntu til greiðslu um féit.	more men were they, in their kinsman had lost to because the-ship and expected to compensation about wealth.	there were more men on the ship that had lost their cousins and were expecting payment for the money.

The Tale of the Greenlanders (II) (The Tale of Einarr Sokkason) (Old Norse)

Old Norse	Literal	English
Þeir kómu í Eiríksfjörð, ok sóttu menn til fundar við þá ok slógu kaupum.	They came to Eriksfjord, and sought men to meet with then and strike a-deal.	They came to Eriksfjord and fetched people to meet them and make a deal.
Síðan tóku menn sér vistir.	Then took men themselves supplies.	Then people took supplies.
Özurr stýrimaðr fór í Garða til byskups ok var þar um vetrinn.	Ossur steersman went to Gardar to the-bishop and was there about winter.	Ossur the steersman went to Gardar to see the bishop and stayed there during the winter.
Í Vestribyggð var þá annat kaupskip.	In Vestribyggd was then another merchant-ship.	In the Western Settlement there was another merchant ship then.
Þar var Kolbeinn Þorljótsson, norrænn maðr.	There was Kolbein Son-of-Thorljot, Nordic man.	There was Kolbein Son-of-Thorljot, a Nordic man.
Inu þriðja skipi réð sá maðr, er Hermundr hét ok var Koðránsson, ok Þorgils, bróðir hans ok höfðu mikla sveit manna.	The third ship commanded so man, was Hermund named and was Son-of-Kodran, and Thorgils, brother his and had much company of-men.	The third ship was commanded by a man named Hermund, who was the son of Kodran, and his brother Thorgils, and they had a large force of men.

3

Um vetrinn kom Özurr at máli við byskup, at hann ætti þangat féván eftir Arnbjörn, frænda sinn, ok beiddi byskup þar gera greiða á bæði fyrir sína hönd ok annarra manna.	About winter came Ossur to discuss with the-bishop, that he had from-there fee-trust after Arnbjorn, kinsman his, and bid bishop there to-give assistance as asked for his hand and other men.	During the winter, Ossur discussed with the bishop that he had a trust there for his uncle Arnbjorn and asked the bishop there to give assistance both on his behalf and on other people's behalf.
Byskup kvaðst fé tekit hafa eftir grænlenzkum lögum eftir slíka atburði, kvaðst þetta ekki gert hafa með einræði sitt, kvað þat makligast, at þat fé færi þeim til sáluhjápar, er aflat höfðu, ok til þeirar kirkju, er bein þeira váru at grafin, sagði þat manndómsleysi at kalla nú til fjár þess.	The-bishop said wealth taken had after Greenlandic law after such events, said it not made had with self-will this, said that most, that it wealth go-to them to souls, who gain had, and to their church, where bones theirs were to in-the-grave, said that meanness to claim now to money this.	The bishop said that he had taken money according to Greenlandic laws after such events, he said that he had not done this with his decision-making, he said that it was most appropriate that the money should go to the souls they had earned and to the church where their bones were buried, he said it was mean to claim now to this money.

The Tale of the Greenlanders (II) (The Tale of Einarr Sokkason) (Old Norse)

Old Norse	Literal	English
Síðan vildi Özurr eigi vera í Görðum með byskupi ok fór til sveitunga sinna, ok héldu sik svá allir samt um vetrinn.	Then willed Ossur not to-be at Gardar with the-bishop and went to men-company his, and held him so all the-same about winter.	After that, Ossur did not want to stay in Gardar with the bishop and went to his companions, and they all stayed the winter anyway.
Um várit bjó Özurr mál til þings þeira Grænlendinga, ok var þat þing í Görðum.	About spring prepared Ossur a-case to the-assembly theirs Greenlanders, and was it assembly in Gardar.	In the spring, Ossur prepared a case for the assembly of the Greenlanders, and that meeting was held in Gardar.
Kom þar byskup ok Einarr Sokkason, ok höfðu þeir fjölmenni mikit.	Came there bishop and Einar Son-of-Sokki, and had they following-men many.	Bishop and Einar Sokkason came there and they had a lot of followers.
Özurr kom þar ok þeir skipverjar hans.	Ossur came there and they crew his.	Ossur and his crew arrived there.
Ok er dómr var settr, þá gekk Einarr at dómi með fjölmenni ok kveðst ætla, at þeim mundi erfitt at eiga við útlenda menn í Nóregi, ef svá skyldi þar.	And when judgement was set, then went Einar to the-court with many-people and said supposed, to them would difficult to have with foreign men in Norway, if so should there.	And when the sentence was passed, Einar went to the court with many people and said that they would find it difficult to deal with foreigners in Norway if it happened there.
"Viljum vér þau lög hafa, er hér ganga",	"Wish we then law have, that here going",	"We wish to have the law that goes here",
sagði Einarr.	said Einar.	said Einar.
Ok er dómrinn fór út, náðu Austmenn eigi málum fram at koma ok stukku frá.	And when the-judgement went out, reached Eastern-men not case from to come and went-away from.	And when the judgement came out, the Eastern-men could not progress forward and went away.
Nú líkar Özuri illa, þykkist hafa af óvirðing, en fé ekki, ok varð þat hans órræði, at hann ferr til, þar er skipit er þat it steinda, ok hjó ór tvau borð, sínu megin hvárt, upp frá kilinum.	Now likes Ossur ill, seems have of un-worthy, but wealth not, and became it his solution, that he went to, there where the-ship was that the stone-one, and struck out-of two boards, theirs sides each, up from the-keel.	Now Ossur did not like this and thought ill of it, because of the disrespect not the money, and so became his solution, that he went to where the ship was that had the stone and struck out two boards, one on each side, upwards from the keel.
Eftir þat fór hann til Vestribyggðar ok hitti þá Kolbein ok Ketil Kálfsson ok sagði þeim svá búit.	After that went he to Vestribyggd and met then Kolbein and Ketil Son-of-Kalf and said to-them so settled.	After that he went to Vestribyggd (The-Western-Settlement) and met Kolbein and Ketil Kalfsson and told them it was over.

The Tale of the Greenlanders (II) (The Tale of Einarr Sokkason) (Old Norse)

Old Norse	Literal	English
Kolbeinn kvað ósæmð til tekna, enda sagði hann órræðit ekki gott.	Kolbein said dishonourable to taken, and said he solution not good.	Kolbein said that it was taken as dishonourable and that the solution was not good.
Ketill mælti:	Ketil said:	Ketil said:
"Fýsa vil ek þik, at þú ráðist hingat til vár, því at ek hefi spurt fastmæli byskups ok Einars, en þú munt vanfærr at sitja fyrir tilstilli byskups, en framkvæmð Einars, ok verum heldr allir saman".	"Desire will I you, that you advise here until spring, because that I have learned opinion the-bishop's and Einar's, but you would unable to sit through guidance the-bishop's, but execution Einar's, and we rather all together".	"I want you to come here until spring, because I have learned the bishop's and Einar's opinion, and you will be unable to sit through the bishop's guidance, and Einar's actions and we should rather all stand together".
Hann kvað ok líkligast, at þat mundi af ráðast.	He said and likely, that it would of be-arranged.	He said that it was so, and it would likely be arranged.
Þar var í sveit með þeim kaupmönnum Ísa-Steingrímr.	There was in the-company with them trading-men Isa-Steingrim.	There was in the company of merchants with them a man named Isa-Steingrim.
Özurr fór þá aftr til Kiðjabergs.	Ossur went then back to Kidjaberg.	Ossur then went back to Kidjaberg.
Þar hafði hann áðr verit.	There had he before been.	He had been there before.
4	**4**	**4**
Byskup varð reiðr mjök, er hann spurði, at spillt var skipinu, ok kallar til sín Einar Sokkason ok mælti:	Bishop became angry much, when he learned, that damaged was the-ship, and called to him Einar Son-of-Sokki and said:	The Bishop became very-much angry when he learned of the damage that was done to the ship, and called Einar Sokkason before him and said:
"Nú er til þess at taka, er þú hézt með svardaga, er vér fórum af Nóregi, at refsa svívirðing staðarins ok hans eigna við þá, er þat gerðu.	"Now it to this that take, what you promised with oath, was we travelled from Norway, to punish disgrace of-the-place and its property with then, is it to-do.	"Now it is for you to take action as you promised by oath when we travelled from Norway, to punish the disgrace to this place and its property and those who did it.
Nú kalla ek Özurr hafa fyrirgert sér, er hann hefir spillt eign várri ok sýnt oss í öllum hlutum ópekkðarsvip.	Now call I Ossur have before-done himself, as he has damaged property ours and shown us to ill things ungraceful.	Now I announce that Ossur's life is forfeit, as he has damaged our property and shown us the most disgraceful ill.

The Tale of the Greenlanders (II) (The Tale of Einarr Sokkason) (Old Norse)

Old Norse	Literal	English
Nú er ekki at dyljast við, at mér líkar eigi svá búit ok ek kalla þik eiðrofa, ef kyrrt er".	Now is none to hiding with, that to-me like not so settled and I call you breach-of-oath, if still are".	Now there is no hiding that I do not like things as they so are, and I will call you in breach of oath if they still are".
Einarr svarar:	Einar answered:	Einar answered:
"Eigi er þetta vel gert, herra, en mæla munu þat sumir, at nökkur várkunn sé á við Özur, svá miklu sem hann er sviptr, þótt eigi sé vel í höndum haft, þá er þeir sá góða gripi, er frændr þeira höfðu átt, ok náðu eigi,	"Not is this well done, sir, but badly would that some, that some pity is to with Ossur, so much as he is deprived, though not is well in handling has, then is they saw good treasure, that kinsmen theirs had owned, and reached not,	"This is not a good thing to have done sir, but it would be bad for some may pity Ossur, for he has been deprived of so much, and it will not be handled well if they saw the good treasure that their kinsmen had owned and were unable to obtain it.
ok veit ek varla, hverju ek skal hér um heita".	and knowing I hardly, how I shall here about be-called".	And I hardly know how I shall call this.
Þeir skilðu fáliga, ok var reiðisvipr á byskupi.	They parted coolly, and was angry of the-bishop.	They parted coolly, and the bishop looked angry.
Ok þá er menn sóttu til kirkjumessu ok til veizlu á Langanes, var byskup þar ok Einarr at veizlunni.	And then when men sought to church-mass and to feast at Langanes, was the-bishop there and Einar at the-feast.	And when people went to church mass and to a feast at Langanes, the bishop was there and Einar was at the feast.
Margt fólk var komit til tíða, ok söng byskup messu.	Many folk were come to the-service, and sang the-bishop mass.	Many people had come and the bishop sang mass.
Þar var kominn Özurr ok stóð undir kirkju sunnan ok við kirkjuvegginn, ok talaði sá maðr við hann, er Brandr hét ok var Þórðarson, heimamaðr byskups.	There was come Ossur and standing under the-church to-the-south and with church-wall, and told so man with him, was Brand named and was Son-of-Thord, house-man the-bishop's.	Ossur had arrived there and was standing under the church to the south and by the church wall, and talking to the man with him whose name was Brand Thorisson, the bishop's houseman.
Þessi maðr bað Özur vægja til við byskup, "ok vænti ek",	This man bid Ossur make-peace to with the-bishop, "and expect I",	This man asked Ossur to make peace with the bishop, "and I expect",
sagði hann, "at þá muni vel duga, en nú agir við svá".	said he, "that then would well aided, but not desirable with so".	he said, "that all will be well, but it is not desirable as it is".

The Tale of the Greenlanders (II) (The Tale of Einarr Sokkason) (Old Norse)

Old Norse	Literal	English
Özurr kvaðst ekki fá þat af sér, svá illa sem við hann var búit,	Ossur said not get that of him, so ill as with he was settled,	Ossur said that he could not because of the ill with which it had been concluded.
ok áttu þeir nú um þetta at tala.	and have they now about this to spoke.	And they now spoke about this.
Þá gengu þeir byskup frá kirkju ok heim til húsa, ok var Einarr þar í göngu.	Then went they the-bishop from the-church and home to house, and was Einar there in going.	Then the bishop and the others went from the church to the house, and Einar went along.
Ok er þeir kómu fyrir skáladyrrnar, þá snerist Einarr frá fylgðinni ok gekk einn í brott til kirkjugarðsins ok tók öxi ór hendi tíðamanni einum ok gekk suðr um kirkjuna.	And as they came before the-door, then turned Einar from following and went alone to away to churchyard and took axe out-of hand worshippers one and went south around the-church.	And as they came to the door then Einar turned away from the followers and went away alone to the churchyard and took an axe out of the hand of one of the worshippers and went around to the south side of the church.
Özurr stóð þar ok studdist á öxi sína.	Ossur stood there and stood on axe his.	Ossur stood there leaning on his axe.
Einarr hjó hann þegar banahögg ok gekk inn eftir þat, ok váru þá borð uppi.	Einar struck him straight-away death-blow and went in after that, and were then the-tables up.	Einar struck him a death blow straight away and went inside by which time the tables were up.
Einarr steig undir borðit gegnt byskupi ok mælti ekki orð.	Einar stepped under the-table opposite the-bishop and spoke not a-word.	Einar took his seat at the table opposite the bishop and spoke not a word.
Síðan gekk hann Brandr Þórðarson í stofuna ok fyrir byskup ok mælti:	Then went he Brand Son-of-Thord in sitting-room and before bishop and said:	Then Brand Thordarson went into the sitting room before the bishop and said:
"Er nökkut tíðenda sagt yðr, herra?"	"Is some news told you, sir?"	"Has some news been told to you sir?"
Byskup kvaðst ekki spurt hafa, "eða hvat segir þú?"	Bishop said not learned had, "but what say you?"	The bishop said he had not heard "but what say you?"
Hann svarar:	He answered:	He answered:
"Sígast lét nú einn hér úti".	"Sinking laid now one here outside".	"Someone has dropped down laying dead here outside".
Byskup mælti:	Bishop spoke:	The bishop said:

The Tale of the Greenlanders (II) (The Tale of Einarr Sokkason) (Old Norse)

Old Norse	Literal	English
"Hverr veldr því, eða hverr er fyrir orðinn?"	"Who caused therefore, or who is before the-words?"	"Who causes it or who is behind the word?"
Brandr kvað þann nær, er frá kunni at segja.	Brand said then as-far, as from known to say.	Brand said someone as far away as him knew to say.
Byskup mælti:	Bishop said:	The bishop said:
"Veldr þú, Einarr, líftjóni Özurar?"	"Brought-about you, Einar, loss-of-life Ossur?"	"Did you bring about Ossur's loss of life, Einar?"
Hann svarar:	He answered:	He answered:
"Því veld ek víst".	"Because willed I certainly".	"This I willed certainly".
Byskup mælti:	The-bishop said:	The bishop said:
"Eigi eru slík verk góð, en þó er várkunn á".	"Not are-they such work good, but though is pity about".	"Such work is not good, but there is pity about it".
Brandr bað, at þvá skyldi líkinu ok syngja yfir.	Brand bid, that washed should the-body and sung over.	Brand asked that the body should be washed and a service sung over.
Byskup kvað mundu gefa tóm til þess.	Bishop said would give time to this.	The bishop said that there would be time to give to this,
Ok sátu menn undir borðum ok fóru at öllu tómliga, ok fekk byskup svá fremi menn til at syngja yfir líkinu, er Einarr bað þess ok kvað þat sama at gera þat með sæmð.	And sat people under the-tables and went to all time-like, and went bishop so provided men to that sing over the-body, as Einar bid this and said that same that to-do that with honour.	and the people sat at the tables taking their time, and so it went that the bishop provided men to sing over the body as Einar had asked, saying that it should be done with some honour.
Byskup kvaðst ætla, at þat mun réttara at grafa hann eigi at kirkju, "en þó við bæn þína skal hann hér jarða at þessi kirkju, at eigi er heimilisprestr".	The-bishop said supposed, to that would more-correct to grave him not at church, "but though with bidding yours shall he here earthed to this church, that not with local-priest".	The bishop supposed that it would be more correct not to bury him at a church "but because of your asking, he shall be buried at this church that does not have a resident priest".
Ok fekk hann eigi til fyrr kennimenn yfir at syngja en áðr var um lík búit.	And got he not to for priests over to sing but after was about the-body prepared.	And he did not get priests to sing over him as his body was being prepared.
Þá mælti Einarr:	Then said Einar:	Then Einar said:

The Tale of the Greenlanders (II) (The Tale of Einarr Sokkason) (Old Norse)

Old Norse	Literal	English
"Nú hafa orðit í stökki brögð ok ekki lítt af yðru tilstilli, en hér eiga þó hlut í ofsamenn miklir, ok get ek, at stórir úfar rísi á með oss".	"Now has-been become in blood-splattered chest and not little of your agency, but here not though part in overbearing-men much, and get I, that badly misfortune giants of with us".	"Now there has become bloodshed, in no small amount by your doing, and here are very powerful men, and I can tell that a great misfortune will be with us".
Byskup kvaðst vænta, at menn munu þessum ofsa af sér hrinda, en unna sæmðar fyrir mál þetta ok umdæmis, ef eigi væri með ofsa at gengit.	The-bishop said hoped, that people would this violence of themselves repel, but win honour for matter this and area, if not was with violence of going.	The bishop said that he hoped that the people who would bring this violence would be repelled, and that they would win honour in this matter as long as there was no violence.

5

Old Norse	Literal	English
Tíðendi þessi spurðust, ok fréttu þat kaupmenn.	News this heard-of, and found-out the trading-men.	News of this was heard of, and it was found out among the merchants.
Þá mælti Ketill Kálfsson:	Then said Ketil Son-of-Kalf:	Then Ketil Kalfsson said:
"Ekki fór fjarri getu minni, at honum mundi höfuðgjarnt verða".	"Not for far ability mine, that he would headstrong be".	"It is not outside of my ability if he would be headstrong".
Maðr hét Símon, frændi Özurar, mikill maðr ok sterkr.	Man was-named Simon, kinsman Ossur, great man and strong.	There was a man named Simon, a kinsman of Ossur, a great and strong man.
Ketill kvað vera mega, ef Símon fylgði atgervi sinni, at hann mun muna dráp Özurar, frænda síns.	Ketil said to-be may, of Simon follow plan his, that he would remember killing Of-Ossur, kinsman his.	Ketil said that if Simon followed his plan "that he would remember the killing of his kinsman Ossur".
Símon kvaðst þar eigi mundu ferlig orð um hafa.	Simon said that not would-be fair words about had.	Simon said that there would be no good words to be had about it.
Ketill lét búa skip þeira ok sendi menn á fund Kolbeins stýrimanns ok sagði honum tíðendin, "ok segið honum svá, at ek skal fara með máli á hendr Einari, því at mér eru kunnig grænlenzk lög, ok er ek búinn til við þá.	Ketil had prepared ship theirs and sent men to meet Kolbein steersman and said to-him the-news, "and say to-him so, that I shall travel with the-matter in hand Einar, because that to-me they-are known Greenlandic laws, and that I prepared to with them.	Ketil had prepared their ship and sent men to meet Kolbein the steersman and tell him the news "and say to him that I will prosecute Einar for the matter in hand, because the Greenlandic laws are known to me, and I am prepared to deal with them.

The Tale of the Greenlanders (II) (The Tale of Einarr Sokkason) (Old Norse)

Old Norse	Literal	English
Höfum vér ok mikinn liðskost, ef at oss kemst".	Have we-are and much force, of to us come".	We have a great advantage of company if it comes to us".
Símon kvaðst vilja Ketils ráðum fram fara.	Simon said wished-for Ketil's advice from going.	Simon said that he wished for Ketil's advice going forward.
Síðan fór hann ok hitti Kolbein, sagði honum vígit ok þar með orðsending Ketils ok þeir skyldu snúast til liðveizlu við þá ór Vestribyggð ok sækja til þings þeira Grænlendinga.	Then went he and found Kolbein, said to-him killing and there with word-sending Ketil's and they should return to support with then out-of Vestribyggd and seek to assembly theirs Greenland.	Then he went and found Kolbein, and told him of the killing, and that they should return to support them at Vestribyggd and attend the Greenland assembly.
Kolbeinn kvaðst koma mundu at vissu, ef hann mætti, ok kvaðst vilja, at Grænlendingum yrði þat eigi hagkeypi at drepa menn þeira.	Kolbein said come would to know, if he might, and said willed, to Greenland become that not good-bargain that killing men theirs.	Kolbein said that they would certainly come if he did and said that he wanted the Greenlanders to not have to kill their men.
Ketill tók þegar mál af Símoni ok fór með nökkura sveit manna, en sagði, at þeir kaupmenn skyldu halda skjótt eftir, "ok hafið varning með yðr".	Ketil took them the-matter of Simon and went with some company men, but said, that they trading-men should rather away afterwards, "and have wares with you".	Ketil immediately took the matter with Simon and went with a few men, but said that the merchants should leave quickly "and take your goods with you".
Kolbeinn fór þegar, er honum kómu þessi orð, bað ok félaga sína fara til þings ok kveðst þá hafa svá mikla sveit, at óvíst væri, at Grænlendingar sætu yfir hlut þeira.	Kolbein went straightaway, when he came these words, asked and companions his went to the-assembly and said then had so much company, that uncertain was, that Greenlanders reconcile over lot theirs.	Kolbein left as soon as these words came to him, and asked his companions to go to the assembly and declared that they had such a large force that it was uncertain that the Greenlanders would be able to handle their lot.
Nú hittust þeir Kolbeinn ok Ketill ok báru ráð sín saman.	Now found they Kolbein and Ketil and carried advice theirs together.	Now they met Kolbein and Ketil and discussed their advice.
Hvárrtveggi þeira var gildr maðr.	Each of-them was valid man.	Each of them was a valid man.
Nú fóru þeir, ok bægði þeim veðr, ok komast þó fram ok höfðu mikla sveit manna, en þó minni en þeir hugðu.	Now travelled they, and prevented them weather, and came though from and they-had large company of-men, but though less than they thought.	Now they travelled and the weather prevented them but they came through it, and they had a large company of men but less than they thought.

The Tale of the Greenlanders (II) (The Tale of Einarr Sokkason) (Old Norse)

Old Norse	Literal	English
Nú kómu menn til þings.	Now came men to the-assembly.	Now the men came to the assembly.
Sokki var þar kominn Þórisson.	Sokki was there coming Son-of-Thorri.	Sokki Thorisson came there too.
Hann var vitr maðr ok var þá gamall ok mjök tekinn til at gera um mál manna.	He was wise man and was then old and very taken to that doing about matters peoples'.	He was a wise man and was very old by then, and was often taken to dealing with peoples' matters.
Hann gengr á fund þeira Kolbeins ok Ketils ok kvaðst vilja leita um sættir.	He went to meet them Kolbein and Ketil and said willed seek about reconciliation.	He went to meet Kolbein and Ketil and said that he wished to seek reconciliation.
"Vil ek bjóðast til",	"Will I offer to",	"I wish to offer",
segir hann, "at gera í milli yðvar,	said he, "to make in between you,	he said, "to make this between you.
ok þótt mér sé meiri vandi á við Einar, son minn, þá skal þat þó um gera, er mér ok öðrum vitrum mönnum lízt nær sanni".	and though I him more custom to with Einar, son mine, then shall it though about be-done, that I and others wise men behold nearer the-truth".	And even though I have a bigger custom with Einar my son, it will still be about what I and other wise men think is closer to the truth".
Ketill kvaðst ætla, at þeir mundi málum fram halda til málsfyllingar, en fyrirkveðast eigi at taka sættir, "en þó er ört at gengit við oss, en höfum ekki vanizt því hér til at minnka várn hlut".	Ketil said intended, that they would the-matter from hold until the-matter-fulfilling, but refusing not to take reconciliation, "but though we-are swiftly to going with us, but have not custom as here to of decreased our lot".	Ketil said that they intended to take the matter to its conclusion, and refused to rule out a reconciliation "and though we are being treated swiftly, we are not accustomed to reducing our share".
Sokki kveðst ætla, at þeir munu eigi jafnt at vígi standa, ok kvað óvíst, at þeir fengi meiri sæmð, þó hann dæmði eigi.	Sokki said supposed, that they would not equal to battle stand, and said uncertain, that they would-get more honour, though he judged not.	Sokki said he supposed that they won't be equal if it came to a battle, and said it was uncertain that they would get any more honour though he would not judge the matter.
Kaupmenn gengu at dómi, ok hafði Ketill mál frammi á hönd Einari.	The-merchants went to court, and had Ketil the-case from in hand Einar.	The merchants went to court and Ketil had the case in hand from Einar.
Þat mælti Einarr:	This said Einar:	Then Einar said:
"Þat mun víða spyrjast, ef þeir bera oss hér málum"	"It will-be widely known-about, if they bear us here cases	"It will be widely known about if they bear this case here"

The Tale of the Greenlanders (II) (The Tale of Einarr Sokkason) (Old Norse)

Old Norse	Literal	English
ok gekk at dóminum ok hleypir upp, ok fengu þeir ekki haldit.	and went to the-court and released up, and got they not holding.	and went into the court and broke it up and they did not get their proceedings.
Þá mælti Sokki:	Then said Sokki:	Then Sokki said:
"Kostr skal enn þess, er ek bauð, at sættast ok gera ek um málit".	"Choice shall one this, that I asked-for, to reconcile and make I about the-case".	"The choice shall be one that I asked for to reconcile, and I shall make the case".
Ketill kveðst ætla, at þat mundi nú ekki verða, "er þú leggr til yfirbóta, þat er þó er inn sami ójafnaðr Einars um þetta mál",	Ketil said intended, that it would now not be, "but you propose to over-compensation, it that though is the same unequal Einar about that case",	Ketil said that he supposed that it would now not be "but to propose more compensation would be just as unequal to Einar in the case"
ok skilðu at því.	and separated to accordingly.	and they separated accordingly.
En því kómu kaupmenn eigi ór Vestribyggð til þings, at þá var andviðri, er þeir váru búnir með tveim skipum.	But then came the-merchants alone from Vestribyggd to the-assembly, that then were the-storm, that they were prepared with two ships.	But then came the merchants from Vestribyggd to the assembly that were in the storm and prepared with two ships.
En at miðju sumri skyldi sætt gera á Eiði.	But in the-middle of-summer should settled be in Eid.	But in the middle of summer a settlement should be made at Eid.
Þá kómu þeir kaupmenn vestan ok lögðu at við nes nökkut, ok hittust þeir þá allir saman ok áttu stefnur.	Then came they the-trading-men western and laid at with headland some, and met they then all together and had plans.	Then the merchants came from the west and laid at a certain headland, and they all met up and made their plans.
Þá mælti Kolbeinn, at eigi skyldi svá nær hafa gengit um sættirnar, ef þeir hefði allir samt verit, "en þat þykkir mér nú ráð, at vér farim allir til þessa fundar með slíkum föngum sem til eru".	Then said Kolbein, that not should so close have been about reconciliation, if they had all together been, "but it seems to-me now advisable, that we go all to this meeting with such resources as to they-are".	Then Kolbein said that it should not have been so close to a reconciliation if they had all been together "but it seems to me now advisable that we all go to this meeting with such resources as they are".
Ok svá var, at þeir fóru ok leyndust í leynivági einum skammt frá byskupsstólnum.	And so was, it they went and innermost in hidden-creek one a-short-distance from the-bishop's-seat.	And so it was that they went to the innermost of a certain hidden creek a short distance from the bishop's seat.

The Tale of the Greenlanders (II) (The Tale of Einarr Sokkason) (Old Norse)

Old Norse	Literal	English
Þat bar saman at byskupsstólinum, at hringði til hámessu, ok þat at Einarr Sokkason kom.	It bore together that the-bishop's-seat, that called to high-mass, and it that Einar Son-of-Sokki came.	And so it came together that the bishop's seat called a high mass, and Einar Sokkason arrived.
Ok er kaupmennirnir heyrðu þetta, þá sögðu þeir, at mikla skyldi gera virðing til Einars, at hringja skal í mót honum, ok kváðu slík mikil endemi ok urðu illa við.	And when the-trading-men heard that, then said they, that great should be-done worthiness to Einar, to call shall in meeting him, and saying such great unheard-of and became angry with.	And when the merchants heard that they said that it was paying a great honour to Einar to meet him in such a way, saying that it was a great unheard of, and they became angry with.
Kolbeinn mælti:	Kolbein said:	Kolbein said:
"Verðið eigi illa við þetta, því at svá mætti at berast, at þetta yrði at líkhringingu, áðr kveld kæmi".	"Become not ill with this, because that so might that bear, that this would to funeral-procession, before night comes".	"Do not become ill with this, because it might come to be that this will be a funeral procession before night comes".
Nú kómu þeir Einarr ok settust niðr í brekku einni.	Now came they Einar and sat down in the-slope alone.	Now came Einar and his men and sat down alone.
Sokki lét fram gripi til virðingar ok þá, er til gjalds váru ætlaðir.	Sokki laid-out from treasure to worthiness and then, when the payment was intended.	Sokki laid out treasures of value that were intended for payment.
Ketill mælti:	Ketil said:	Ketil said:
"Þat vil ek, at vit Hermundr Koðránsson virðim gripina".	"That will I, that with Hermund Son-of-Kodran worthiness treasure".	"I wish for Hermund Kodransson and I to value these treasures".
Sokki kvað svá vera skyldu.	Sokki said so being would.	Sokki said that it would be so.
Símon, frændi Özurar, sýndi á sér óþekkðarsvip ok reikaði hjá, meðan gripagjaldit var sett.	Simon, kinsman Of-Ossur, showed of himself dishonourable and wandered by, while the-artefact-fee was set.	Simon, a kinsman of Ossur, showed himself to be dishonourable and wandered by while the artefacts were being set.
Síðan var fram borin spangabrynja ein forn.	Then was from brought plate-mail one of-old.	Then an ancient plate mal was brought out.
Símon mælti þá:	Simon said then:	Then Simon said:
"Svívirðliga er slíkt boðit fyrir slíkan mann sem Özurr var",	"Disgracefully is such offering for such man as Ossur was",	"Such an offering is disgraceful for such a man as Ossur was"

The Tale of the Greenlanders (II) (The Tale of Einarr Sokkason) (Old Norse)

Old Norse	Literal	English
ok kastaði brynjunni á völlinn á burt ok gekk upp at þeim, er þeir sátu í brekkunni.	and cast the-armour on the-field and way and went up to them, as they sat on the-slope.	and he threw the armour away on the field and went up to them as they sat on the slope.
Ok er þat sá þeir Grænlendingar, þá spretta þeir upp ok horfðu forbrekkis ok í móti honum Símoni.	And when that saw they Greenlanders, then sprang they up and looked downhill and in facing him Simon.	And when the Greenlanders saw that, they sprang up and looked downhill at Simon and faced towards him.
Ok því næst gekk Kolbeinn upp hjá þeim, er þeir horfðu allir frá, ok slæst á bak þeim ok fór einn frá sínum mönnum,	And then next went Kolbein up beside them, when they looked all away-from, and slipped in back of-them and went alone from his men,	And then Kolbein went up beside them whey they all looked away and slipped behind them alone from his men.
ok var þat jafnsnemma, at hann komst á bak Einari ok hjó með öxi milli herða honum ok Einars öx kom í höfuð Símoni, ok fengu báðir banasár.	and was it equally-early, that he came to back Einar and struck with an-axe between shoulders his and Einar's axe came in head Simon's, and got both death-wounds.	And it was just as soon that he got behind Einar and cut him with an axe between his shoulders, and Einar's axe hit Simon in the head and both received mortal wounds.
Einarr mælti, er hann fell:	Einar said, when he fell:	Einar said when he fell:
"Slíks var at ván".	"Such was it expected".	"It was so as I expected".
Síðan hljóp Þórðr, fóstbróðir Einars, at Kolbeini ok vildi höggva hann, en Kolbeinn snaraðist við honum ok stakk fram öxarhyrnunni ok kom í barkann Þórði, ok hafði hann þegar bana.	Then ran Thord, foster-brother Einar's, to Kolbein and wanted to-strike him, but Kolbein caught-up with him and thrust from axe-horn and came in throat Thord's, and had he instantly killed.	Then Thord, Einar's foster brother, ran to Kolbein and wanted to cut him down, but Kolbein caught up with him and stuck out the axe horn and hit Thord in the throat, killing him instantly.
Síðan slær í bardaga með þeim.	Then struck to battle with them.	Then a battle was struck between them.
Byskup sat hjá Einari, ok andaðist hann í knjám honum.	Bishop sat beside Einar, and died he in knees his.	The bishop sat beside Einar and he died in his lap.
Steingrímr hét maðr, er þat mælti, at þeir skyldi gera svá vel at berjast eigi, ok gekk á milli með nökkura menn, en hvárirtveggja váru svá óðir, at Steingrímr var lagðr sverði í gegnum í þessi hríð.	Steingrim was-named a-man, who this said, that they should do so well to fight not, and went in between with some men, but either-side were so angry, that Steingrim was laid to-the-sword in through in this time.	There was a man named Steingrim who said that they would do well not to fight and went in between some of the men, but either side was so angry that Steingrim was laid to the sword through him in this time.

The Tale of the Greenlanders (II) (The Tale of Einarr Sokkason) (Old Norse)

Old Norse	Literal	English
Einarr andaðist uppi á brekkunni við búð Grænlendinga.	Einar died up on the-slope by booth The-Greenlanders'.	Einar died up on the slope by the Greenlanders' booth.
Ok nú urðu menn sárir mjök, ok kómust þeir Kolbeinn til skips með þrjá sína menn vegna ok fóru síðan yfir Einarsfjörð til Skjálgsbúða.	And now became men wounded much, and came they Kolbein to ships with three their men slain and went then over Einarsfjord to Skjalgsbud.	And now men became much wounded and Kolbein and his men came to their ships with three men killed and went over to Einarsfjord to Skjalgsbud.
Þar váru kaupskipin ok váru þá mjök í búnaði.	There were merchant-ships and were then much in preparations.	The merchant ships were there and they were very much prepared.
Kolbeinn kvað í hafa gerzt nökkura róstu, "ok vil ek ætla, at Grænlendingar uni nú ekki betr við en áðr".	Kolbein said that had done some uproar, "and will I suppose, that Greenlanders like now not better with than before".	Kolbein said that there had been some uproar "and I would like to say that the Greenlanders are now no better pleased than before".
Ketill mælti:	Ketil said:	Ketil said:
"Sannyrði gafst þér, Kolbeinn",	"True-words gave to-you, Kolbein",	"You gave true words Kolbein",
sagði hann, "at vér myndim heyra líkhringingina, áðr vér færim í brott, ok ætla ek, at hann Einarr sé dauðr borinn til kirkju".	said he, "that we would hear the-funeral-procession, before we travel to away, and suppose I, that he Einar is dead carried to the-church".	he said, "that we would hear the funeral procession before we travel away and I suppose that Einar who is dead will be carried to the church".
Kolbeinn kveðst heldr þannig hafa at stutt.	Kolbein said rather that-way had it supported.	Kolbein said that it was rather that way, that he had supported it.
Ketill mælti:	Ketil said:	Ketil said:
"Þess er ván, at Grænlendingar muni sækja á várn fund, ok kalla ek ráð, at menn haldi á búnaði sínum eftir föngum ok sé allir á skipum um nætr".	"This is expect, that The-Greenlanders will seek to ours meet, and call I advice, that men hold of equipment theirs after resources and are all to ships about night".	"It is expected that the Greenlanders will seek to meet us, and I advise that the men take hold of their equipment and resources and all stay on the ships overnight".
Ok svá gerðu þeir.	And so did they.	And so they did.

The Tale of the Greenlanders (II) (The Tale of Einarr Sokkason) (Old Norse)

Old Norse	Literal	English
Sokki harmaði mjök þessi tíðendi ok bað menn fulltingis at veita sér vígsgengi.	Sokki harmed much this news and asked men assistance to grant him in-battle.	Sokki was much harmed by this news and asked the men to grant him assistance in battle.

6

Hallr hét maðr.	Hall was-named man.	There was a man named Hall.
Hann bjó at Sólarfjöllum, vitr maðr ok góðr bóndi.	He lived at Solarfjoll, wise man and good farmer.	He lived at Solarfjoll, he was a wise man and a good farmer.
Hann var í liði með Sokka ok kom síðast með sínu liði.	He was in company with Sokki and came last with his team.	He was in company with Sokki and was the last to come to his team.
Hann mælti til Sokka:	He said to Sokki:	He said to Sokki:
"Ekki vænlig lízt mér þín ætlan, at leggja smáskipum at stórskipum við slíkan viðbúnað sem ek hygg, at þeir muni hafa,	"Not hopeful behold I your intention, to lay small-ships to large-ships with such preparation as I think, that they shall have,	"I am not hopeful of your intention to lay small ships against large ships with such preparations as I think they will have.
en ek veit eigi, hversu traust lið er þú hefir, en allir vaskir menn munu vel gefast, en hinir munu hlífast meir, ok verða höfuðsmenn fyrir þat uppgefnir, ok horfir þá enn þungligar várr málahlutr en áðr.	but I know not, how-so trust team is you have, but all brave men should well give, but others should protect more, and become head-men for that up-given, and where then but the-more-difficult our matter-lot than before.	But I don't know how strong a team you have, but all the good men will give well, but the others will be more careful, and the leaders will be exhausted because of it, and then our affairs will be even more difficult than before.
Nú sýnist mér ráð, ef menn skulu at leggja, at eiðar fari fram, at hverr maðr skyli annathvárt hér falla eða hafa sigr".	Now seems to-me advisable, if men shall to allow, that oath go from, to each man shall other-either here fall or have victory".	Now it seems to me that if men are to make an oath, each man shall either fall here or be victorious".
En við þessi orð Halls dignuðu menn mjök.	But with this word Hall's pride lessened much.	But at this word of Hall's, peoples' pride lessened much.
Sokki mælti:	Sokki said:	Sokki said:
"Eigi munum vér þó skilja við þetta, at ósett sé málunum".	"Not shall we though part with this, that unsettled is the-matter".	"However, we will not part with this, that things are not settled".

The Tale of the Greenlanders (II) (The Tale of Einarr Sokkason) (Old Norse)

Old Norse	Literal	English
Hallr kvaðst mundu leita um sættir milli þeira ok kallaði á kaupmenn ok mælti:	Hall said should seek about reconciliation between them and called the trading-men and spoke:	Hall said that they should seek reconciliation between them and called the merchants and spoke:
"Hvárt skal mér fritt at ganga á fund yðvarn?"	"Whether shall I peace to go to meet with-you?"	"Should I be at peace to go to a meeting with you?"
Þeir Kolbeinn ok Ketill svara, at honum skyldi fritt.	They Kolbein and Ketil answered, that to-him should-be peace.	Kolbein and his men answered that he should be at peace.
Síðan hitti hann þá ok lét nauðsyn, at málum væri sett eftir slík stórvirki.	Then met he then and had necessary, to matter should-be settled after such great-works.	Then he met them and made it necessary that matters should be settled after such great deeds.
Þeir kváðust nú búnir við hváru, sem aðrir vildi, kváðu af þeim landsmönnum allan þennan ójafnað staðit hafa, "en nú, er þú sýnir svá mikla góðgirnd, þá unum vér því, at þú gerir í milli vár".	They said now prepared with each, as other willed, saying of them lands-men all then un-equal stood have, "but now, are you showed so much good-will, then among us therefore, that you make to between us".	They said they were ready to do whatever others wanted, they said of those countrymen who have been through this uneven situation "but now you are showing so much kindness, we hope that you do among us".
Hann kvaðst eftir því gera mundu ok dæma, er honum sýndist réttligast, hversu sem hvárum líkaði.	He said after therefore be-done should and deemed, that to-him seemed correctness, how-so as each liked.	He said that he would do what he thought was the right thing to do, however everyone liked it.
Síðan var þetta fyrir Sokka borit.	Then was that for Sokki borne.	Then this was put before Sokki.
Hann kveðst ok mundu una umdæmi Halls.	He said and would content about-judgement Hall's.	He said that he would be content with Hall's judgement about it.
Kaupmenn skyldu um nætr at búnaði sínum vera ok kváðu Sokka ekki annat líka en þeir yrði í brottu sem fyrst, "en ef þeir seinka búnað sinn ok gera mér skapraun í því, þá er vís ván, at þeir skulu bótalausir, ef þeir verða teknir".	The-trading-men should about the-night to equipment theirs be and said Sokki not other like but they be to away as first, "but if they delay preparations theirs and make to-me temperament in because, then be aware hope, that they shall boat-lose, if they become taken".	The merchants had to make their preparations through the night and Sokki said that there was no other way except that they were to be away as soon as possible "but if they delay in their preparations and make to my temperament, then they shall lose their boat if they become taken".

The Tale of the Greenlanders (II) (The Tale of Einarr Sokkason) (Old Norse)

Old Norse	Literal	English
Nú skilðu þeir at því, ok var á sáttarfund kveðit.	Now separated they that accordingly, and were in peace-meeting declared.	Now they separated accordingly and a reconciliation meeting was declared.
Ketill mælti:	Ketil said:	Ketil said:
"Ekki horfir skjótliga búnaðr várr, en vistaföng þverra heldr, ok er þat mitt ráð at leita eftir vistunum, ok veit ek, hvar sá maðr býr, er mikinn mat á, ok kalla ek ráð at sækja eftir".	"Not looks shortly equipment ours, but resources running-out rather, and is it my advice to seek after provisions, and know I, where so man prepared, is much food to, and call I advice to seek after".	"It does not look like our equipment will be prepared shortly, and resources are running out, and it is my advice to seek provisions, and I know where there is a man who has much food, and I advise we seek him out".
Þeir kváðust þess albúnir.	They said this all-prepared.	They said they were all ready.
Síðan hlupu þeir upp eina nátt frá skipum, þrír tigir manna saman, allir vápnaðir, ok kómu at bænum, ok var þar autt allt.	Then ran they up one night from the-ship, three tens of-men together, all weaponed, and came to dwelling, and were there empty all.	They hurried up one night from the ship, and thirty men together, all armed, came to the dwelling but it was all empty.
Þórarinn hét bóndi sá, er þar bjó.	Thorarin was-named a-farmer that, was there settled.	Thorarin was the name of the farmer that was settled there.
Ketill mælti:	Ketil said:	Ketil said:
"Eigi hefir mitt ráð vel gefizt",	"Not has my advice well given",	"My advice has not given well"
ok fara síðan í brott frá bænum ok ofan á leið til skipa, ok var þar hrísótt, er þeir fóru.	and went then to away from the-dwelling and over to the-way to the-ships, and were there shrubs, where they went.	and then went away from the dwelling and over to the ships, and there were shrubs along where they went.
Þá mælti Ketill:	Then said Ketil:	Then Ketil said:
"Syfjar mik",	"Sleepy me",	"I feel sleepy",
sagði hann, "ok verð ek at sofa".	said he, "and deserve I to sleep".	he said, "and I deserve to sleep".
Þeir kváðu þat ekki mjök ráðligt.	They said that not much advisable.	They said that it was not advisable,
En þó lagðist hann niðr ok sofnaði, en þeir sátu yfir.	But though laid he down and slept, while they sat over.	but he laid down and slept while they sat and watched over.

The Tale of the Greenlanders (II) (The Tale of Einarr Sokkason) (Old Norse)

Old Norse	Literal	English
Litlu síðar vaknaði hann ok mælti:	Little later awoke he and said:	A little later he awoke and said:
"Margt hefir fyrir mik borit.	"Many have before me brought.	"Much has brought before me.
Hvat mun varða, þótt vér kippim upp hríslu þessi, er hér er undir höfði mér?"	What should happen, though we jerk up clump this, that here is under head mine?"	What would happen if we jerked up this clump that is here under my head?"
Þeir kippðu upp hríslunni, ok var þar undir jarðhús mikit.	They pulled up the-branch, and was there under earth-house great.	They pulled up the branches and under it was a great cave.
Ketill mælti:	Ketil said:	Ketil said:
"Vitum fyrst, hvat hér er fanga".	"Know-we first, what here is provisions".	"We should know first what provisions are here".
Þeir fundu þar sex tigi slátrgripa ok tólf vættir smjörs, skreið mikla.	They found there six tens carcasses and twelve weights of-butter, fish much.	They found sixty carcasses, twelve weights of butter, and a lot of fish.
"Vel er þat",	"Well is that",	"That is good",
sagði Ketill, "at ek hefi eigi villt upp borit fyrir yðr".	said Ketil, "that I have not wildly up presented for you".	said Ketil, "that I have not wildly brought up for you".
Nú fara þeir til skips með feng sinn.	Now went they to the-ships with provisions theirs.	Now they went to the ships with their provisions.
Nú líðr at sáttarfundinum, ok kómu hvárirtveggju til þess fundar, kaupmenn ok landsmenn.	Now passed to reconciliation-meeting, and came either-side to this meeting, trading-men and lands-men.	Now it passed to the reconciliation meeting, and both sides came to the meeting, the merchants and the landsmen.
Þá mælti Hallr:	Then said Hall:	Then Hall said:
"Sú er sáttargerð mín yðvar í milli, at ek vil, at á standist víg Özurar ok Einars, en fyrir manna mun skulu koma sekðir Austmanna, at þeir skulu hér ekki eiga vist né væri.	"So is settlement mine yours in between, that I will, to a to-stand slaying Ossur and Einar, but for men less would come penalty Eastern-men, that they shall here not own resources nor should-they.	"This is my settlement among you, that I wish for the killing of Ossur to stand for that of Einar, but for the loss of men, the Norwegians shall not be here nor shall they own resources here.

The Tale of the Greenlanders (II) (The Tale of Einarr Sokkason) (Old Norse)

Old Norse	Literal	English
Þau víg skulu ok jöfn vera, Steingríms bónda ok Símonar, Kráks Austmanns ok Þorfinns Grænlendings, Víghvats Austmanns ok Bjarna Grænlendings, Þóris ok Þórðar.	Those killings shall and even be, Steingrim's farmer and Simon, Krak The-Easterner and Thorfin The-Greenlander, Vighvats The-Easterner and Bjarn The-Greenlander, Thori and Thord.	Those killings shall be even, Steingrim the farmer and Simon, Krak the Easterner and Thorfin the Greenlander, Vighvats the Easterner and Bjarn the Greenlander, Thori and Thord.
Nú er einn óbættr várr maðr, er Þóarinn heitir, ómegðarmaðr.	Now that one uncompensated our man, that Thorarin is-named, poor-man.	Now one of our men is uncompensated, named Thorarin, a poor man.
Hann skal fé bæta".	He shall wealth be-compensated".	He shall be compensated with wealth".
Sokki hvat sér þungt gerðir líka ok svá öðrum Grænlendingum, er þannig fór um mannjafnað.	Sokki that himself unhappy made alike and so other Greenlanders, that that-way went about equal-man.	Sokki said that he was unhappy with how it was done that Greenlanders and the other men were equally paired in that way.
Hallr kvaðst ætla, at þar muni þó staðar nema hans ummæli.	Hall said intend, that there should though stand taking his about-matter.	Hall said he intended that it should though stand as he took the matter,
Ok við þat skilðu þeir.	And with that separated they.	and with that they separated.
Síðan rak ís at ok þakði alla fjörðu, ok hugðu Grænlendingar þá gott til, ef þeir mætti taka þá ok þeir færi eigi svá brott sem mælt var.	Then drifted ice to and covered all the-fjord, and thought The-Greenlanders then good to, of they might take then and they travel alone so away as told were.	Then ice drifted in and covered the whole fjord, and the Greenlanders thought it would be good if they could take them and they didn't go away as they were told.
En við þat sjálft at mánaðarmótit kom, þá rak í brott allan ísinn, ok gaf kaupmönnum brott af Grænlandi, ok skilðu við þat.	But with that itself to month's-end came, then drove to way all ice, and gave the-trading-men away of Greenland, and separated with it.	But as soon as the end of the month came, all the ice was swept away and the merchants left Greenland and parted with it.
Þeir kómu við Nóreg.	They came to Norway.	They came to Norway.

The Tale of the Greenlanders (II) (The Tale of Einarr Sokkason) (Old Norse)

Old Norse	Literal	English
Kolbeinn hafði haft einn hvítabjörn af Grænlandi ok fór með dýrit á fund Haralds konungs gilla ok gaf honum ok tjáði fyrir konungi, hversu þungs hlutar Grænlendingar váru af verðir, ok færði þá mjök í róg.	Kolbein had had one white-bear of Greenland and went with the-animal to meet Harald the-king residence and gave him and told for the-kind, how-so heavily lot The-Grænlanders were of being, and brought them much to slander.	Kolbein had had one white bear from Greenland and took the animal to King Harald's meeting and gave it to him and expressed to the king how much of a burden the Greenlanders were becoming and brought them into great slander.
En konungr spurði annat síðar, ok þótti honum Kolbeinn hafa fals fyrir sik borðit, ok kómu engi laun fyrir dýrit.	But the-king learned otherwise later, and thought he Kolbein had a-falsehood for him bore-up, and came no reward for the-animal.	But the king learned otherwise later and it seemed to him that Kolbein had borne up a falsehood for him and there was no reward for the animal.
Síðan hljóp Kolbeinn í flokk með Sigurði slembidjákn ok gekk inn at Haraldi konungi gilla ok veitti honum áverka.	Then ran Kolbein to grouped with Sigurd the-false-deacon and went in to Harald the-king residence and granted to-him a-wound.	Then Kolbein hurried to group with Sigurd the false deacon, and went into King Harald's residence and gave him a wound.
Ok síðan er þeir fóru fyrir Danmörk ok sigldu mjök, en Kolbeinn var á eftirbáti, en veðr hvasst, þá sleit frá bátinn, ok drukknaði Kolbeinn.	And then when they travelled to Denmark and sailed much, but Kolbein was in the-boat-behind, but weather stormy, then tore-up from the-boat, and drowned Kolbein.	And then when they travelled to Denmark their sail was carried much, but Kolbein was in the boat behind in stormy weather which then tore up the boat behind and Kolbein drowned.
En þeir Hermundr kómu til Íslands til ættjarða sinna.	But they The-Hermunds came to Iceland to homelands theirs.	But Hermund and the others came to Iceland, their homeland.
Ok lýkr þar þessi sögu.	And ends here this saga.	And here ends this saga.

Word List (Old Norse to English)

Word List (Old Norse to English)

Old Norse	English

A, a

aðrir	other
af	from, from, of, of, off
aflat	gain
aftr	back
agir	desirable
albúnir	all-prepared
alla	all
allan	all
allir	all, all
allmjök	all-great
allt	all
allvel	all-well, all-well
andaðist	died, died
andviðri	the-storm
annarra	other
annat	another, another, anything-else, other, otherwise
annathvárt	other-either
Arnald	Arnald (name)
Arnaldr	Arnald (name)
Arnbjarnar	Arnbjarn (name), Arnbjarnar (name)
Arnbjörn	Arnbjorn (name)
at	a, at, by, in, it, of, that, the, to
atburði	events
atgervi	plan
auðit	possible
austmaðr	Eastern-man
austmanna	Eastern-men
austmanns	the-Easterner
austmenn	Eastern-men
autt	empty

Á, á

á	a, about, and, as, at, in, of, on, out, that, the, to
áðr	after, before
áðu	that
árós	river-mouth
átt	had, owned
áttu	had, have
áverka	a-wound

Æ, æ

æðimaðr	of-mind
æpa	shouting
ætla	intend, intended, suppose, supposed
ætlaðir	intended
ætlan	intention
ætluðu	supposed
ætti	had
ættjarða	homelands

B, b

bað	asked, bid
báðir	both
báðu	asked
bæ	a-farm
bæði	asked
bægði	prevented
bæn	bidding, prayers
bænar	prayers
bændr	farmers
bænum	dwelling, the-dwelling
bæta	be-compensated
bak	back
bana	death, killed
banahögg	death-blow
banasár	death-wounds
bar	bore
bardaga	battle
barkann	throat
báru	carried
bátinn	the-boat
bauð	asked-for, invited
beiddi	bid

32

Word List (Old Norse to English)

Old Norse	English
bein	bones
beinum	bones
bera	bear
berast	bear
berdreyman	clear-dreams
berjast	fight
betr	better
bezt	best
bjarga	rescuing
bjargar	rescue
Bjarna	Bjarn (name)
bjarndýri	a-bear
bjó	lived, prepared, settled
bjóðast	offer
björg	rocks
bjóst	prepared
boðit	offering
bokki	buck
bolöx	the-trunk
bónda	farmer
bóndi	a-farmer, farmer
borð	boards, the-tables
borðit	bore-up, the-table
borðum	the-tables
borin	brought
borinn	carried
borit	borne, brought, presented
bótalausir	boat-lose
Brandr	Brand (name)
Brattahlíð	Brattahlid (place)
bréfum	briefs
brekku	the-slope
brekkunni	the-slope
brenndu	burned
bróðir	brother
brögð	chest
brotit	broken
brott	away, way
brottu	away
brugðit	upset
brynjunni	the-armour
búa	prepared
búð	booth
búinn	prepared
búit	prepared, settled
búnað	preparations
búnaði	equipment, preparations
búnaðr	equipment
búnir	prepared
burt	way
byggðina	the-settlement
býr	prepared
byrrinn	bearing
byskup	a-bishop, bishop, the-bishop
byskupi	the-bishop
byskups	bishop, the-bishop, the-bishop's
byskupsefni	the-bishop-elect
byskupslaust	bishop-less
byskupsstólinum	the-bishop's-seat
byskupsstóll	bishop's-seat
byskupsstólnum	the-bishop's-seat
byskupsstólsins	bishop's-seat
byskupsvígslu	bishop's-appointment

D, d

Old Norse	English
dæma	deemed
dæmði	judged
dag	the-day
Danmarkar	Denmark (place)
Danmörk	Denmark (place)
dauða	dead
dauðr	dead
daun	the-dead
dignuðu	pride
dómi	court, the-court
dóminum	the-court
dómr	judgement
dómrinn	the-judgement
dráp	killing
draum	dream
drauminn	the-dream
drepa	killing
dreymði	dreamed
drukknaði	drowned
duga	aided

Word List (Old Norse to English)

Old Norse	English
dyljast	hiding
dýrit	the-animal

E, e

Old Norse	English
eða	but, or
eðli	nature
ef	if, of
efldr	strengthened
eftir	after, afterwards, followed, following, later, remaining
eftirbáti	the-boat-behind
eftirbátinn	the-after-boat
eið	oath
eiðar	oath
Eiði	Eid (place)
eiðrofa	breach-of-oath
eiga	have, not, own
eigi	alone, no, not
eign	property
eigna	property
eignum	owning
ein	one
eina	one
einangr	alone-going
Einar	Einar (name)
Einari	Einar (name)
Einarr	Einar (name)
Einars	Einar (name), Einar's, Einar's (name)
Einarsfjörð	Einarsfjord (place)
einhverju	one-occasion
einn	a, alone, one
einni	alone
einræði	self-will
einu	one
einum	one
Eiríksfjörð	Eriksfjord (place)
ek	I
ekki	none, not
eldstóar	fire-place
en	and, but, than, while
enda	and
endemi	unheard-of

Old Norse	English
engi	no, no-one
engum	no
enn	but, one, still
er	and, are, as, be, but, in, is, it, that, the, then, was, we-are, what, when, where, who, with
erendi	errand
erendis	errand
erfitt	difficult
erkibyskup	the-archbishop
erkibyskups	archbishop
eru	are, are-they, they-are, were
eruð	are
Eyjafjöllum	Eyjafjolls (place)

F, f

Old Norse	English
fá	get
færa	bring
færði	brought
færi	going, go-to, travel
færim	travel
fagra	the-fairest
fáliga	coolly
falla	fall
fallinn	fallen, weak
fals	a-falsehood
fang	resources
fanga	provisions
fangit	to-catch
fangs	captivity
fara	going, travel, went, went
fari	go
farim	go
farit	going
fastmæli	opinion
fé	wealth
feðgar	father-and-son
fégjöfum	fee-gifts
féit	wealth
fekk	got, went

34

Word List (Old Norse to English)

Old Norse	English
fékk	got
félaga	companions
félagar	companions
fell	fell
feng	provisions
fengi	would-get
fengu	got
ferð	journey
ferjuna	the-ferry
ferlig	fair
ferr	went
festa	fix
féván	fee-trust
fimmtán	fifteen
fjár	money
fjárfundinn	wealth-finding
fjarri	far
fjölmenni	following-men, many-people
fjörðinn	fjord
fjörðu	the-fjord
fleiri	more
flokk	grouped
fólk	folk
föngum	resources
fór	for, travelled, went
forbrekkis	downhill
forn	of-old
forsjá	foresight
fóru	travelled, went
fórum	travel, travelled
fóstbróðir	foster-brother
fótum	feet
frá	away-from, from
frænda	kinsman
frændi	kinsman
frændr	kinsman, kinsmen
fram	from
framkvæmð	execution
frammi	from
fremi	provided
fréttu	found-out
fritt	peace
fróði	learned
fulltingis	assistance
fulltingja	fulfil
fulltings	help
fund	meet, meeting
fundar	meet, meeting
fundit	found
fundu	found
fúsari	willing
fylgði	follow, followed
fylgðinni	following
fylgir	followed
fyrir	before, for, foremost, through, to
fyrirgert	before-done
fyrirkveðast	refusing
fyrr	for
fyrst	first, firstly
fýsa	desire

G, g

Old Norse	English
gaf	gave
gafst	gave
gamall	old
ganga	go, going, went
garða	Gardar (place)
gefa	give
gefast	give
gefizt	given
gefnar	given
gegna	pass
gegnt	opposite
gegnum	through
gekk	went
gengit	been, going, walked
gengr	went
gengu	went
gera	be, be-done, do, doing, done, make, to-do, to-give
gerði	did
gerðir	made
gerðist	became
gerðu	did, done, to-do
gerir	make
gersemi	treasure
gert	done, made

Word List (Old Norse to English)

Old Norse	English
gerzt	done
get	get
getu	ability
gildr	valid
gilla	residence
gjalds	payment
góð	good
góða	good
góðan	good
góðgirnd	good-will
góðr	good
göngu	going
Görðum	Gardar (place)
gott	good
grænland	Greenland (place)
Grænlendinga	Greenland (place), Greenlanders (name), the-Greenlanders'
grænlendingar	Greenlanders (name), the-Greenlanders
grænlendings	the-Greenlander
Grænlendingum	Greenland (place), Greenlanders (name)
grænlenzk	Greenlandic (name)
grænlenzkr	a-Greenlander
grænlenzkum	Greenlandic (name)
grafa	grave
grafin	in-the-grave
greiða	assistance
greiðist	paying
greiðslu	compensation
gripagjaldit	the-artefact-fee
gripi	treasure
gripina	treasure
guði	priest
guðs	god's

H, h

Old Norse	English
hægra	right
haf	sea
hafa	had, has, has-been, have
hafði	had
hafi	had
hafið	have
hafskip	sea-going-ship
haft	had, has
hag	circumstances
hagkeypi	good-bargain
hagr	handy
halda	hold, rather, to-hold
haldi	hold
haldit	holding
Hallr	Hall (name)
halls	Hall's, Hall's (name)
hamarrifu	crags
hámessu	high-mass
hann	he, him
hans	him, his, its
haraldi	Harald (name)
haralds	Harald (name)
harmaði	harmed
hásetar	the-crew
haustum	autumn
hefði	had
hefi	have
hefir	has, have
hegna	protected
heim	home
heimamaðr	house-man
heimilisprestr	local-priest
heimta	carry
heimti	presented
heita	be-called
heitir	is-named
heitukötlum	boiling-cauldrons
heldr	rather
heldu	held
héldu	held
hendi	hand
hendr	hand
henta	suitable
hér	here
herða	shoulders
Hermundr	Hermund (name), the-Hermunds (name)
herra	sir
hét	named, was-named
heyra	hear
heyrðu	heard

Word List (Old Norse to English)

Old Norse	English
heyrt	heard
hézt	promised
hingat	here
hinir	others
hitta	find
hitti	found, met
hittust	found, met
hjá	beside, by
hjó	struck
hlaðna	loaded
hlaupa	running
hleypið	discharge
hleypir	released
hleypr	ran
hlífast	protect
hlítt	satisfactory
hljóp	ran
hlupu	ran
hlut	lot, part
hlutar	lot
hlutum	things
hnjóðhamar	hammer
höfðaskip	a-headed-ship
höfðaskipit	head-ship
höfði	head
höfðingja	chieftains
höfðu	had, had-they, they-had
höfuð	head
höfuðgjarnt	headstrong
höfuðsmenn	head-men
höfum	have
höggva	to-strike
höggvit	struck
holdi	flesh
Holtavatnsós	Holtavatnsos (place)
hönd	hand
höndum	handling
honum	he, him, his, to-him
horfðu	looked
horfir	looks, where
hríð	time
hrinda	repel
hringði	called
hringja	call
hríslu	clump
hríslunni	the-branch
hrísótt	shrubs
hugðu	thought
hugi	his-mind
hugr	mind
hún	she
hurðina	the-door
húsa	house
hvar	where
hvárirtveggja	either-side
hvárirtveggju	either-side
hvárrtveggi	each
hvárs	which
hvárt	each, whether
hváru	each
hvárum	each
hvasst	stormy
hvat	that, what
hverfa	turn
hverju	how
hverr	each, who
hversu	how-so
hvítabjörn	white-bear
Hvítserk	Hvitserk (name)
hygg	think

I, i

Old Norse	English
illa	angry, ill
illt	ill
inn	in, the
inni	in
innsiglum	seals
inu	the
it	the, then

Í, í

Old Norse	English
í	about, and, at, in, into, of, on, that, to
ís	ice
Ísa-Steingrímr	Isa-Steingrim (name)
ísinn	ice
íslandi	Iceland (place)

Word List (Old Norse to English)

Old Norse	English
íslands	Iceland (place)

J, j

Old Norse	English
jafnsnemma	equally-early
jafnt	equal
jarða	earthed
jarðhús	earth-house
játtuðu	agreed
jöfn	even
jöklinum	a-glacier
jöklum	glaciers
Jórsalafari	Jerusalem-Traveller (name)

K, k

Old Norse	English
kæmi	comes
Kálfsson	son-of-Kalf (name)
kalla	call, claim
kallaði	called
kallar	called
kambi	comb
kann	can
kastaði	cast
kaupmenn	the-merchants, the-trading-men, trading-men
kaupmennirnir	the-trading-men
kaupmönnum	the-trading-men, trading-men
kaupskip	merchant-ship
kaupskipin	merchant-ships
kaupskipit	merchant-ship
kaupum	a-deal
kemst	come
kennimanns	teaching
kennimenn	priests
kerling	old-woman
kerlingu	the-old-woman
Ketil	Ketil (name)
Ketill	Ketil (name)
Ketils	Ketil (name), Ketil's (name)
Kiðjabergs	Kidjaberg (place)
kilinum	the-keel
kippðu	pulled
kippim	jerk
kirkju	church, the-church
kirkjugarðsins	churchyard
kirkjumessu	church-mass
kirkjuna	the-church
kirkjuvegginn	church-wall
klerkr	cleric
knjám	knees
Koðránsson	son-of-Kodran (name)
Kolbein	Kolbein (name)
Kolbeini	Kolbein (name)
Kolbeinn	Kolbein (name)
Kolbeins	Kolbein (name)
kom	came
koma	come
komast	came, come
kominn	come, coming
komit	come
komst	came
kómu	came
kómust	came
konung	the-king
konungi	the-kind, the-king
konungr	the-king
konungs	the-king, the-king's
konungsbréfum	the-king's-brief
kostr	choice
Kráks	Krak (name)
kunni	known
kunnig	known
kvað	said
kvaðst	said
kváðu	said, saying
kváðust	said
kveðit	declared
kveðja	called
kveðst	said
kveld	night
kyrrlátir	still
kyrrt	still

L, l

Word List (Old Norse to English)

Old Norse	English
lá	lay
lagðist	laid
lagðr	laid
land	land
Landeyjum	the-Landeys (place)
landi	the-land
landit	the-land
landsins	the-lands
landsmenn	lands-men
landsmönnum	lands-men
Langanes	Langanes (place)
láta	lay-out
laun	reward
legðu	put
leggja	allow, have, lay
leggr	propose
legit	laid
leið	the-way
leit	looked
leita	seek
lengi	long
lengr	longer
lengra	longer
lét	had, laid, laid-out
létu	had
leyndust	innermost
leynivági	hidden-creek
leysti	released
lézt	had
lið	team
liði	company, team
liðit	passed
líðr	passed
liðskost	force
liðu	passed
liðveizlu	support
líftjóni	loss-of-life
lík	the-body
líka	alike, like
líkaði	liked
líkar	like, likes
líkast	likely
líkendi	alike
líkhringingina	the-funeral-procession
líkhringingu	funeral-procession
líkinu	the-body
líkligast	likely
líkum	bodies
lítil	little
lítillæti	humility
lítit	little
litlu	little
lítt	little
lízt	behold
lög	law, laws
lögðu	laid
lögum	law
Lundi	Lund (place)
lýkr	ends

M, m

Old Norse	English
maðr	a-man, man
mæla	badly
mælt	told
mælti	said, spoke
mæltu	said
mætti	might
mættir	might
makligast	most
mal	the-matter
mál	a-case, case, matter, matters, the-case, the-matter
málahlutr	matter-lot
máli	discuss, the-matter
málit	the-case
málsfyllingar	the-matter-fulfilling
málum	case, matter, the-matter
málum"	cases
málunum	the-matter
mánaðarmótit	month's-end
mann	a-man, man, the-man
manna	man's, men, of-men, peoples'
manndómsleysi	meanness
mannhættu	dangerous
manni	man
manninum	this-man

Word List (Old Norse to English)

Old Norse	English
mannjafnað	equal-man
mannshræ	dead-body, human-body
mannvænlegr	a-friendly
margt	many
mat	food
mátti	might
með	with
meðallagi	moderately
meðan	as-long-as, while
mega	may
megin	sides
megri	meagre
mein	disease, harm
meir	more
meira	more
meiri	more
menn	lessened, men, people
mér	I, me, mine, to-me
messu	mass
mest	most
mestr	the-most
metnir	important
metorð	esteem
miðju	the-middle
mik	me
mikil	great, much
mikill	great, much
mikils	much
mikinn	much
mikit	a-great, great, many, much
mikla	great, large, much
miklir	much
miklu	much
milli	between
mín	mine
minn	mine
minni	less, mine
minnka	decreased
mínum	mine, my
misst	lost
mitt	my
mjök	much, very
mönnum	men, the-men
morgininn	morning
mót	meet, meeting
móti	facing
mun	less, should, will, will-be, would
muna	remember
mundi	would
mundu	should, would, would-be
muni	shall, should, will, would
munni	mouth
munt	would
muntu	shall-you
munu	may, should, would
munum	shall
myndim	would

N, n

Old Norse	English
náðu	reached
næði	get
nær	as-far, close, nearer
næst	next
nætr	night, the-night
náir	getting
nátt	night
nauðsyn	necessary, needs
né	nor
neðan	below
nema	taking
nenna	bothered
nes	headland
niðr	down
Njálsson	son-of-Njal (name)
nökkur	some
nökkura	some
nökkurar	some
nökkurn	some
nökkurra	something
nökkuru	some
nökkurum	some
nökkut	some
Nóreg	Norway (place)
nóregi	Norway (place)

Word List (Old Norse to English)

Old Norse	English
Nóregs	Norway (place)
norrænir	Nordic (name)
norrænn	Nordic (name)
nótt	the-night
nú	not, now
nytjum	use

O, o

Old Norse	English
Odda	Odda (place)
of	of
ofan	above, over
ofsa	violence
ofsamenn	overbearing-men
oft	often
ok	also, and
orð	a-word, word, words
orða	words
orðinn	the-words
orðit	become, have-become
orðsending	word-sending
oss	to-us, us

Ó, ó

Old Norse	English
óbættr	uncompensated
óbyggðir	un-settled
óbyggðum	the-unsettled-land
óðir	angry
óforsjáll	impulsive
ófúss	reluctant
ójafnað	un-equal
ójafnaðr	unequal
ómegðarmaðr	poor-man
ór	from, out-from, out-of
órræði	solution
órræðit	solution
ósæmð	dishonourable
ósett	unsettled
óþekkðarsvip	dishonourable, ungraceful
óvirðing	un-worthy
óvíst	uncertain

Ö, ö

Old Norse	English
öðru	another, other
öðrum	other, others
öllu	all
öllum	all, ill
ört	swiftly
öx	axe
öxarhyrnunni	axe-horn
öxi	an-axe, axe
Özur	Ossur (name)
Özurar	of-Ossur (name), Ossur (name)
Özuri	Ossur (name)
Özurr	Ossur (name)

R, r

Old Norse	English
ráð	advice, advisable, decide
ráða	advice
ráðast	arrange, be-arranged
ráðist	advise
ráðligt	advisable
ráðum	advice
rak	drifted, drove
raunar	actually
réð	commanded
réðist	deal
réðst	ruled
refsa	punish
reið	rode
reiðisvipr	angry
reiðr	angry
reikaði	wandered
rétt	rights
réttara	more-correct
réttligast	correctness
reyndust	gave-him
rísi	giants
rjúfa	break-open
róg	slander
róstu	uproar

Word List (Old Norse to English)

Old Norse	English
rufu	broke-up, tore-up

S, s

Old Norse	English
sá	saw, so, that
sægarpr	sea-champion
sækja	seek, sought
sæmð	honour
sæmðar	honour
sæmðir	honour
Sæmundi	Saemund (name)
Sæmundur	Saemund (name)
sætt	settled
sættast	reconcile
sættir	reconciliation
sættirnar	reconciliation
sætu	reconcile
sagði	said, said
sagt	said, said, told
sakar	sake
sakir	sake
sáluhjápar	souls
sálum	souls
sama	same
saman	altogether, together
sami	same
samt	the-same, together
sanni	the-truth
sannligast	truthfully
sannyrði	true-words
sárir	wounded
sat	sat
satt	TRUE
sáttarfund	peace-meeting
sáttarfundinum	reconciliation-meeting
sáttargerð	settlement
sátu	sat
sauminn	the-seam
sé	are, being, him, is, they-are, this, to-be
segið	say
segir	said, say, says
segja	say
seinka	delay
sekðir	penalty
sem	as
senda	send
sendi	sent
sendiligstan	to-be-sent
sér	as, him, himself, them, themselves
sett	sat, set, settled
setti	set
settr	set
settust	sat
sex	six
síðan	then
síðar	later
síðast	last
sígast	sinking
sigldu	sailed
sigr	victory
Sigurði	Sigurd (name)
Sigurðr	Sigurd (name)
sik	him, himself
Símon	Simon (name)
Símonar	Simon (name)
símoni	Simon (name), Simon's (name)
sín	him, his, theirs
sína	his, their, themselves
sinn	his, theirs
sinna	his, theirs
sinni	his, they
síns	his
sínu	his, theirs
sínum	his, theirs
sitja	sit
sitt	his, this
sjá	saw, see
sjálfs	himself
sjálft	itself
sjást	looked
skal	shall
skála	cabin
skáladyrrnar	the-door
skálann	the-cabin, the-hut
skálanum	the-cabin
skammt	a-short-distance
skaplyndi	temper
skapraun	temperament

Word List (Old Norse to English)

Old Norse	English	Old Norse	English
skerast	cutting	Sokki	Sokki (name)
skilðu	parted, separated	Sólarfjöllum	Solarfjoll (place)
skilja	part	son	son
skip	ship	söng	sang
skipa	the-ships	sonr	son
skipi	ship, the-ship	sóttu	sought
skipinu	the-ship	spangabrynja	plate-mail
skipit	ship, the-ship	spillt	damaged
skips	ships, the-ships	spretta	sprang
skiptu	divided	spurði	learned
skipum	ships, the-ship	spurðist	heard-of
skipverjar	crew	spurðu	heard-of
Skjálgsbúða	Skjalgsbud (place)	spurðust	heard-of
skjótliga	shortly	spurt	learned
skjótt	away	spyrjast	known-about
skreið	fish	stað	stand
skulu	shall, would	staðar	stand
skyldi	should, should-be	staðarins	of-the-place, the-place
skyldir	should	staðit	stood
skyldu	should, would	stakk	thrust
skyli	shall	standa	stand
slær	struck	standist	to-stand
slæst	slipped	stefnur	plans
slátrgripa	carcasses	steig	stepped
sleit	tore-up	steinda	stone-one
slembidjákn	the-false-deacon	Steingrímr	Steingrim (name)
slík	such	Steingríms	Steingrim's (name)
slíka	such	steint	stone-carving
slíkan	such	Steinþórr	Steinthor (name)
slíks	such	stendr	standing
slíkt	such	sterkr	strong
slíku	such	stóð	standing, stood
slíkum	such	stofuna	sitting-room
slógu	strike	stokk	a-log
smáskipum	small-ships	stökki	blood-splattered
smjörs	of-butter	stól	seat
snaraðist	caught-up	stórfjörðu	large-fjords
snerist	turned	stórir	badly
snúast	return	stórskipum	large-ships
sofa	sleep	stórvirki	great-works
sofnaði	slept	studdist	stood
sögðu	said	stukku	went-away
sögu	saga	stutt	supported
Sokka	Sokki (name)	stýrimaðr	steersman
Sokkason	son-of-Sokki (name)	stýrimanns	steersman

43

Word List (Old Norse to English)

Old Norse	English
styrkðarmaðr	supporter
sú	so
suðr	south
sumarit	summer
sumars	summer
sumir	some
sumri	of-summer
sumur	summers
sunnan	to-the-south
svá	so
svara	answered
svarar	answered
svardaga	oath
sveit	company, the-company
sveitunga	men-company
sverði	to-the-sword
sveri	swear
sviptr	deprived
svívirðing	disgrace
svívirðliga	disgracefully
svörð	skins
syfjar	sleepy
sýndi	showed
sýndist	seemed
syngja	sing, sung
sýnir	showed
sýnist	seems
sýnt	shown
systursonr	sister's-son

T, t

Old Norse	English
taka	take, took
tala	spoke
talaði	told
tannvöru	walrus-tusks
tekinn	taken
tekit	taken
tekna	taken
teknir	taken
tíða	the-service
tíðamanni	worshippers
tíðenda	news
tíðendi	news, tidings
tíðendin	the-news
tíðendum	news
tigi	tens
tigir	tens
tignar	position
til	the, to, until
tilstilli	agency, guidance
tindinn	pin
tjáði	spoke, told, voiced
tjald	tent
tjalda	tent-up
tók	took
tóku	took
tólf	twelve
tóm	time
tómliga	time-like
torsóttligt	difficult
traust	trust
troða	tread
tvau	two
tveim	two
týnzt	lost

Þ, þ

Old Norse	English
þá	them, then, when
þakði	covered
þakkaði	thanked
þangat	from-then, from-there
þann	that, then
þannig	that-way
þar	here, that, then, there
þat	it, that, the, this, to
þau	then, those
þegar	instantly, straightaway, straight-away, them
þeim	of-them, theirs, them, they, to-them
þeir	they, was
þeira	of-them, theirs, them, they
þeirar	their
þennan	then
þér	to-you, you

Word List (Old Norse to English)

Old Norse	English
þess	this
þessa	this
þessi	these, this
þessir	these
þessu	this
þessum	these, this
þetta	it, that, this
þiggja	accepted
þik	you
þín	your
þína	yours
þing	assembly
þings	assembly, the-assembly
þjónustumenn	servants-of
þó	though
Þóarinn	Thorarin (name)
Þórarinn	Thorarin (name)
Þórðar	Thord (name)
Þórðarson	son-of-Thord (name)
Þórði	Thord's (name)
Þórðr	Thord (name)
Þorfinns	Thorfin (name)
Þorgils	Thorgils (name)
Þóris	Thori (name)
Þórisson	son-of-Thorri (name)
Þorljótsson	son-of-Thorljot (name)
þótt	though
þótti	thought
þóttumst	thought
þriðja	third, thirdly
þrír	three
þrjá	three
þú	you
þungligar	the-more-difficult
þungs	heavily
þungt	unhappy
þvá	washed
þverra	running-out
því	according, accordingly, as, because, because-of, that, then, therefore, they
þykkir	seems
þykkist	seems
þyrfti	needed

U, u

Old Norse	English
ullkamb	wool-comb
um	about, around
umdæmi	about-judgement
umdæmis	area
ummæli	about-matter
umræða	discussed
una	content
undan	away-from
undarligt	strange
undir	submit, under
uni	like
unna	win
unum	among
upp	up
uppgefnir	up-given
uppi	up
urðu	became

Ú, ú

Old Norse	English
úfar	misfortune
út	out
úti	outside
útlenda	foreign

V, v

Old Norse	English
vægja	make-peace
vænlig	hopeful
vænta	hoped
vænti	expect
væntu	expected
væri	be, should-be, should-they, to-be, was
vættir	weights
vaknaði	awoke
vald	power

Word List (Old Norse to English)

Old Norse	English
ván	expect, expected, hope
vanda	problem
vandi	custom
vanfærr	unable
vanizt	custom
vanmeginn	weak
vápnaðir	weaponed
var	was, were
vár	spring, us
varð	became, came
varða	happen
varist	weariness
várit	spring
várkunn	pity
varla	hardly
várn	our, ours
varnarmaðr	defender
varning	wares
várr	our, ours
várri	ours
váru	was, were
varúðgir	cautious
vaskir	brave
veðr	weather
vegna	slain
veiðiskap	hunting
veit	know, knowing
veita	grant
veitti	granted
veizlu	feast
veizlunni	the-feast
vel	well
veld	willed
veldr	brought-about, caused
vér	us, we, we-are
vera	be, being, to-be, would-be
verð	deserve
verða	be, become
verði	be
verðið	become
verðir	being
verðr	becomes
verit	been
verk	work
verum	we
vestan	western
Vestribyggð	Vestribyggd (place)
Vestribyggðar	Vestribyggd (place)
vetrinn	winter
við	by, to, with
víða	widely
viðbúnað	preparation
viðinn	the-trees
víg	killings, slaying
vígði	consecrated
Víghvats	Vighvats (name)
vígi	battle
vígit	killing
vígsgengi	in-battle
vil	will, wish
vildi	wanted, willed
vildu	willed
vilja	willed, wished-for
viljum	wish
villt	wildly
vini	friends
vinsæll	popular
virðim	worthiness
virðing	worthiness
virðingar	worthiness
virðr	respected
vís	aware
vissu	know
vist	resources
víst	certainly
vistaföng	resources
vistir	supplies
vistunum	provisions
vit	with
vitr	wise
vitrliga	wise-like
vitrum	wise
vitum	know-we
völlinn	the-field

Y, y

Old Norse	English
yðr	you

Word List (Old Norse to English)

Old Norse	English
yðru	your
yðvar	you, yours
yðvarn	with-you
yfir	over
yfirbóta	over-compensation
yrði	be, become, would

Ý, ý

ýldu	decay

Word List (Old Norse to English)

Word List (English to Old Norse)

Word List (English to Old Norse)

English	Old Norse

A, a

English	Old Norse
a	á, at, einn
a-bear	bjarndýri
ability	getu
a-bishop	byskup
about	á, í, um
about-judgement	umdæmi
about-matter	ummæli
above	ofan
a-case	mál
accepted	þiggja
according	því
accordingly	því
actually	raunar
a-deal	kaupum
advice	ráð, ráða, ráðum
advisable	ráð, ráðligt
advise	ráðist
a-falsehood	fals
a-farm	bæ
a-farmer	bóndi
a-friendly	mannvænlegr
after	áðr, eftir
afterwards	eftir
agency	tilstilli
a-glacier	jöklinum
a-great	mikit
agreed	játtuðu
a-Greenlander	grænlenzkr
a-headed-ship	höfðaskip
aided	duga
alike	líka, líkendi
all	alla, allan, allir, allir, allt, öllu, öllum
all-great	allmjök
allow	leggja
all-prepared	albúnir
all-well	allvel, allvel
a-log	stokk
alone	eigi, einn, einni
alone-going	einangr
also	ok
altogether	saman
a-man	maðr, mann
among	unum
an-axe	öxi
and	á, en, enda, er, í, ok
angry	illa, óðir, reiðisvipr, reiðr
another	annat, annat, öðru
answered	svara, svarar
anything-else	annat
archbishop	erkibyskups
are	er, eru, eruð, sé
area	umdæmis
are-they	eru
Arnald (name)	Arnald, Arnaldr
Arnbjarn (name)	Arnbjarnar
Arnbjarnar (name)	Arnbjarnar
Arnbjorn (name)	Arnbjörn
around	um
arrange	ráðast
as	á, er, sem, sér, því
as-far	nær
a-short-distance	skammt
asked	bað, báðu, bæði
asked-for	bauð
as-long-as	meðan
assembly	þing, þings
assistance	fulltingis, greiða
at	á, at, í
autumn	haustum
aware	vís
away	brott, brottu, skjótt
away-from	frá, undan
awoke	vaknaði
a-word	orð
a-wound	áverka
axe	öx, öxi
axe-horn	öxarhyrnunni

B, b

English	Old Norse
back	aftr, bak
badly	mæla, stórir

Word List (English to Old Norse)

English	Old Norse
battle	bardaga, vígi
be	er, gera, væri, vera, verða, verði, yrði
bear	bera, berast
bearing	byrrinn
be-arranged	ráðast
be-called	heita
became	gerðist, urðu, varð
because	því
because-of	því
become	orðit, verða, verðið, yrði
becomes	verðr
be-compensated	bæta
be-done	gera
been	gengit, verit
before	áðr, fyrir
before-done	fyrirgert
behold	lízt
being	sé, vera, verðir
below	neðan
beside	hjá
best	bezt
better	betr
between	milli
bid	bað, beiddi
bidding	bæn
bishop	byskup, byskups
bishop-less	byskupslaust
bishop's-appointment	byskupsvígslu
bishop's-seat	byskupsstóll, byskupsstólsins
Bjarn (name)	Bjarna
blood-splattered	stökki
boards	borð
boat-lose	bótalausir
bodies	líkum
boiling-cauldrons	heitukötlum
bones	bein, beinum
booth	búð
bore	bar
bore-up	borðit
borne	borit
both	báðir
bothered	nenna
Brand (name)	Brandr
Brattahlid (place)	Brattahlíð
brave	vaskir
breach-of-oath	eiðrofa
break-open	rjúfa
briefs	bréfum
bring	færa
broken	brotit
broke-up	rufu
brother	bróðir
brought	borin, borit, færði
brought-about	veldr
buck	bokki
burned	brenndu
but	eða, en, enn, er
by	at, hjá, við

C, c

English	Old Norse
cabin	skála
call	hringja, kalla
called	hringði, kallaði, kallar, kveðja
came	kom, komast, komst, kómu, kómust, varð
can	kann
captivity	fangs
carcasses	slátrgripa
carried	báru, borinn
carry	heimta
case	mál, málum
cases	málum"
cast	kastaði
caught-up	snaraðist
caused	veldr
cautious	varúðgir
certainly	víst
chest	brögð
chieftains	höfðingja
choice	kostr
church	kirkju
church-mass	kirkjumessu
church-wall	kirkjuvegginn
churchyard	kirkjugarðsins
circumstances	hag
claim	kalla

Word List (English to Old Norse)

English	Old Norse
clear-dreams	berdreyman
cleric	klerkr
close	nær
clump	hríslu
comb	kambi
come	kemst, koma, komast, kominn, komit
comes	kæmi
coming	kominn
commanded	réð
companions	félaga, félagar
company	liði, sveit
compensation	greiðslu
consecrated	vígði
content	una
coolly	fáliga
correctness	réttligast
court	dómi
covered	þakði
crags	hamarrifu
crew	skipverjar
custom	vandi, vanizt
cutting	skerast

D, d

English	Old Norse
damaged	spillt
dangerous	mannhættu
dead	dauða, dauðr
dead-body	mannshræ
deal	réðist
death	bana
death-blow	banahögg
death-wounds	banasár
decay	ýldu
decide	ráð
declared	kveðit
decreased	minnka
deemed	dæma
defender	varnarmaðr
delay	seinka
Denmark (place)	Danmarkar, Danmörk
deprived	sviptr
deserve	verð
desirable	agir

English	Old Norse
desire	fýsa
did	gerði, gerðu
died	andaðist, andaðist
difficult	erfitt, torsóttligt
discharge	hleypið
discuss	máli
discussed	umræða
disease	mein
disgrace	svívirðing
disgracefully	svívirðliga
dishonourable	ósæmð, óþekkðarsvip
divided	skiptu
do	gera
doing	gera
done	gera, gerðu, gert, gerzt
down	niðr
downhill	forbrekkis
dream	draum
dreamed	dreymði
drifted	rak
drove	rak
drowned	drukknaði
dwelling	bænum

E, e

English	Old Norse
each	hvárrtveggi, hvárt, hváru, hvárum, hverr
earthed	jarða
earth-house	jarðhús
Eastern-man	austmaðr
Eastern-men	austmanna, austmenn
Eid (place)	Eiði
Einar (name)	Einar, Einari, Einarr, Einars
Einar's	einars
Einar's (name)	Einars
Einarsfjord (place)	Einarsfjörð
either-side	hvárirtveggja, hvárirtveggju
empty	autt
ends	lýkr
equal	jafnt
equally-early	jafnsnemma

Word List (English to Old Norse)

English	Old Norse
equal-man	mannjafnað
equipment	búnaði, búnaðr
Eriksfjord (place)	Eiríksfjörð
errand	erendi, erendis
esteem	metorð
even	jöfn
events	atburði
execution	framkvæmð
expect	vænti, ván
expected	væntu, ván
Eyjafjolls (place)	Eyjafjöllum

F, f

English	Old Norse
facing	móti
fair	ferlig
fall	falla
fallen	fallinn
far	fjarri
farmer	bónda, bóndi
farmers	bændr
father-and-son	feðgar
feast	veizlu
fee-gifts	fégjöfum
feet	fótum
fee-trust	féván
fell	fell
fifteen	fimmtán
fight	berjast
find	hitta
fire-place	eldstóar
first	fyrst
firstly	fyrst
fish	skreið
fix	festa
fjord	fjörðinn
flesh	holdi
folk	fólk
follow	fylgði
followed	eftir, fylgði, fylgir
following	eftir, fylgðinni
following-men	fjölmenni
food	mat
for	fór, fyrir, fyrr
force	liðskost
foreign	útlenda
foremost	fyrir
foresight	forsjá
foster-brother	fóstbróðir
found	fundit, fundu, hitti, hittust
found-out	fréttu
friends	vini
from	af, af, frá, fram, frammi, ór
from-then	þangat
from-there	þangat
fulfil	fulltingja
funeral-procession	líkhringingu

G, g

English	Old Norse
gain	aflat
Gardar (place)	garða, Görðum
gave	gaf, gafst
gave-him	reyndust
get	fá, get, næði
getting	náir
giants	rísi
give	gefa, gefast
given	gefizt, gefnar
glaciers	jöklum
go	fari, farim, ganga
god's	guðs
going	færi, fara, farit, ganga, gengit, göngu
good	góð, góða, góðan, góðr, gott
good-bargain	hagkeypi
good-will	góðgirnd
got	fekk, fékk, fengu
go-to	færi
grant	veita
granted	veitti
grave	grafa
great	mikil, mikill, mikit, mikla
great-works	stórvirki
Greenland (place)	grænland, Grænlendinga, Grænlendingum

Word List (English to Old Norse)

English	Old Norse	English	Old Norse
Greenlanders (name)	grænlendinga, grænlendingar, grænlendingum	*Hermund (name)*	Hermundr
Greenlandic (name)	grænlenzk, grænlenzkum	*hidden-creek*	leynivági
		hiding	dyljast
grouped	flokk	*high-mass*	hámessu
guidance	tilstilli	*him*	hann, hans, honum, sé, sér, sik, sín
		himself	sér, sik, sjálfs
		his	hans, honum, sín, sína, sinn, sinna, sinni, síns, sínu, sínum, sitt

H, h

English	Old Norse	English	Old Norse
had	ætti, átt, áttu, hafa, hafði, hafi, haft, hefði, höfðu, lét, létu, lézt	*his-mind*	hugi
		hold	halda, haldi
		holding	haldit
had-they	höfðu	*Holtavatnsos (place)*	Holtavatnsós
Hall (name)	Hallr	*home*	heim
Hall's	halls	*homelands*	ættjarða
Hall's (name)	Halls	*honour*	sæmð, sæmðar, sæmðir
hammer	hnjóðhamar		
hand	hendi, hendr, hönd	*hope*	ván
handling	höndum	*hoped*	vænta
handy	hagr	*hopeful*	vænlig
happen	varða	*house*	húsa
Harald (name)	haraldi, haralds	*house-man*	heimamaðr
hardly	varla	*how*	hverju
harm	mein	*how-so*	hversu
harmed	harmaði	*human-body*	mannshræ
has	hafa, haft, hefir	*humility*	lítillæti
has-been	hafa	*hunting*	veiðiskap
have	áttu, eiga, hafa, hafið, hefi, hefir, höfum, leggja	*Hvitserk (name)*	Hvítserk

I, i

English	Old Norse	English	Old Norse
have-become	orðit		
he	hann, honum	*I*	ek, mér
head	höfði, höfuð	*ice*	ís, ísinn
headland	nes	*Iceland (place)*	íslandi, íslands
head-men	höfuðsmenn	*if*	ef
head-ship	höfðaskipit	*ill*	illa, illt, öllum
headstrong	höfuðgjarnt	*important*	metnir
hear	heyra	*impulsive*	óforsjáll
heard	heyrðu, heyrt	*in*	á, at, er, í, inn, inni
heard-of	spurðist, spurðu, spurðust	*in-battle*	vígsgengi
		innermost	leyndust
heavily	þungs	*instantly*	þegar
held	heldu, héldu	*intend*	ætla
help	fulltings		
here	hér, hingat, þar		

Word List (English to Old Norse)

English	Old Norse
intended	ætla, ætlaðir
intention	ætlan
in-the-grave	grafin
into	í
invited	bauð
is	er, sé
Isa-Steingrim (name)	Ísa-Steingrímr
is-named	heitir
it	at, er, þat, þetta
its	hans
itself	sjálft

J, j

English	Old Norse
jerk	kippim
Jerusalem-Traveller (name)	Jórsalafari
journey	ferð
judged	dæmði
judgement	dómr

K, k

English	Old Norse
Ketil (name)	Ketil, Ketill, Ketils
Ketil's (name)	Ketils
Kidjaberg (place)	Kiðjabergs
killed	bana
killing	dráp, drepa, vígit
killings	víg
kinsman	frænda, frændi, frændr
kinsmen	frændr
knees	knjám
know	veit, vissu
knowing	veit
known	kunni, kunnig
known-about	spyrjast
know-we	vitum
Kolbein (name)	Kolbein, Kolbeini, Kolbeinn, Kolbeins
Krak (name)	Kráks

L, l

English	Old Norse
laid	lagðist, lagðr, legit, lét, lögðu
laid-out	lét
land	land
lands-men	landsmenn, landsmönnum
Langanes (place)	Langanes
large	mikla
large-fjords	stórfjörðu
large-ships	stórskipum
last	síðast
later	eftir, síðar
law	lög, lögum
laws	lög
lay	lá, leggja
lay-out	láta
learned	fróði, spurði, spurt
less	minni, mun
lessened	menn
like	líka, líkar, uni
liked	líkaði
likely	líkast, líkligast
likes	líkar
little	lítil, lítit, litlu, lítt
lived	bjó
loaded	hlaðna
local-priest	heimilisprestr
long	lengi
longer	lengr, lengra
looked	horfðu, leit, sjást
looks	horfir
loss-of-life	líftjóni
lost	misst, týnzt
lot	hlut, hlutar
Lund (place)	Lundi

M, m

English	Old Norse
made	gerðir, gert
make	gera, gerir
make-peace	vægja
man	maðr, mann, manni
man's	manna
many	margt, mikit
many-people	fjölmenni

Word List (English to Old Norse)

English	Old Norse	English	Old Norse
mass	messu	night	kveld, nætr, nátt
matter	mál, málum	no	eigi, engi, engum
matter-lot	málahlutr	none	ekki
matters	mál	no-one	engi
may	mega, munu	nor	né
me	mér, mik	Nordic (name)	norrænir, norrænn
meagre	megri	Norway (place)	Nóreg, nóregi, Nóregs
meanness	manndómsleysi	not	eiga, eigi, ekki, nú
meet	fund, fundar, mót	now	nú
meeting	fund, fundar, mót		
men	manna, menn, mönnum		

O, o

English	Old Norse
men-company	sveitunga
merchant-ship	kaupskip, kaupskipit
merchant-ships	kaupskipin
met	hitti, hittust
might	mætti, mættir, mátti
mind	hugr
mine	mér, mín, minn, minni, mínum
misfortune	úfar
moderately	meðallagi
money	fjár
month's-end	mánaðarmótit
more	fleiri, meir, meira, meiri
more-correct	réttara
morning	morgininn
most	makligast, mest
mouth	munni
much	mikil, mikill, mikils, mikinn, mikit, mikla, miklir, miklu, mjök
my	mínum, mitt

English	Old Norse
oath	eið, eiðar, svardaga
Odda (place)	Odda
of	á, af, af, at, ef, í, of
of-butter	smjörs
off	af
offer	bjóðast
offering	boðit
of-men	manna
of-mind	æðimaðr
of-old	forn
of-Ossur (name)	Özurar
of-summer	sumri
often	oft
of-them	þeim, þeira
of-the-place	staðarins
old	gamall
old-woman	kerling
on	á, í
one	ein, eina, einn, einu, einum, enn
one-occasion	einhverju
opinion	fastmæli
opposite	gegnt
or	eða
Ossur (name)	Özur, Özurar, Özuri, Özurr
other	aðrir, annarra, annat, öðru, öðrum
other-either	annathvárt
others	hinir, öðrum
otherwise	annat
our	várn, várr
ours	várn, várr, várri

N, n

English	Old Norse
named	hét
nature	eðli
nearer	nær
necessary	nauðsyn
needed	þyrfti
needs	nauðsyn
news	tíðenda, tíðendi, tíðendum
next	næst

54

Word List (English to Old Norse)

English	Old Norse	English	Old Norse
out	á, út	promised	hézt
out-from	ór	property	eign, eigna
out-of	ór	propose	leggr
outside	úti	protect	hlífast
over	ofan, yfir	protected	hegna
overbearing-men	ofsamenn	provided	fremi
over-compensation	yfirbóta	provisions	fanga, feng, vistunum
own	eiga	pulled	kippðu
owned	átt	punish	refsa
owning	eignum	put	legðu

P, p

English	Old Norse
part	hlut, skilja
parted	skilðu
pass	gegna
passed	liðit, líðr, liðu
paying	greiðist
payment	gjalds
peace	fritt
peace-meeting	sáttarfund
penalty	sekðir
people	menn
peoples'	manna
pin	tindinn
pity	várkunn
plan	atgervi
plans	stefnur
plate-mail	spangabrynja
poor-man	ómegðarmaðr
popular	vinsæll
position	tignar
possible	auðit
power	vald
prayers	bæn, bænar
preparation	viðbúnað
preparations	búnað, búnaði
prepared	bjó, bjóst, búa, búinn, búit, búnir, býr
presented	borit, heimti
prevented	bægði
pride	dignuðu
priest	guði
priests	kennimenn
problem	vanda

R, r

English	Old Norse
ran	hleypr, hljóp, hlupu
rather	halda, heldr
reached	náðu
reconcile	sættast, sætu
reconciliation	sættir, sættirnar
reconciliation-meeting	sáttarfundinum
refusing	fyrirkveðast
released	hleypir, leysti
reluctant	ófúss
remaining	eftir
remember	muna
repel	hrinda
rescue	bjargar
rescuing	bjarga
residence	gilla
resources	fang, föngum, vist, vistaföng
respected	virðr
return	snúast
reward	laun
right	hægra
rights	rétt
river-mouth	árós
rocks	björg
rode	reið
ruled	réðst
running	hlaupa
running-out	þverra

S, s

Word List (English to Old Norse)

English	Old Norse	English	Old Norse
Saemund (name)	Sæmundi, Sæmundur	*should-they*	væri
saga	sögu	*shouting*	æpa
said	kvað, kvaðst, kváðu, kváðust, kveðst, mælti, mæltu, sagði, sagði, sagt, sagt, segir, sögðu	*showed*	sýndi, sýnir
		shown	sýnt
		shrubs	hrísótt
		sides	megin
		Sigurd (name)	Sigurði, Sigurðr
sailed	sigldu	*Simon (name)*	Símon, Símonar, símoni
sake	sakar, sakir		
same	sama, sami	*Simon's (name)*	Símoni
sang	söng	*sing*	syngja
sat	sat, sátu, sett, settust	*sinking*	sígast
satisfactory	hlítt	*sir*	herra
saw	sá, sjá	*sister's-son*	systursonr
say	segið, segir, segja	*sit*	sitja
saying	kváðu	*sitting-room*	stofuna
says	segir	*six*	sex
sea	haf	*skins*	svörð
sea-champion	sægarpr	*Skjalgsbud (place)*	Skjálgsbúða
sea-going-ship	hafskip	*slain*	vegna
seals	innsiglum	*slander*	róg
seat	stól	*slaying*	víg
see	sjá	*sleep*	sofa
seek	leita, sækja	*sleepy*	syfjar
seemed	sýndist	*slept*	sofnaði
seems	sýnist, þykkir, þykkist	*slipped*	slæst
self-will	einræði	*small-ships*	smáskipum
send	senda	*so*	sá, sú, svá
sent	sendi	*Sokki (name)*	Sokka, Sokki
separated	skilðu	*Solarfjoll (place)*	Sólarfjöllum
servants-of	þjónustumenn	*solution*	órræði, órræðit
set	sett, setti, settr	*some*	nökkur, nökkura, nökkurar, nökkurn, nökkuru, nökkurum, nökkut, sumir
settled	bjó, búit, sætt, sett		
settlement	sáttargerð		
shall	muni, munum, skal, skulu, skyli		
		something	nökkurra
shall-you	muntu	*son*	son, sonr
she	hún	*son-of-Kalf (name)*	Kálfsson
ship	skip, skipi, skipit	*son-of-Kodran (name)*	Koðránsson
ships	skips, skipum	*son-of-Njal (name)*	Njálsson
shortly	skjótliga	*son-of-Sokki (name)*	Sokkason
should	mun, mundu, muni, munu, skyldi, skyldir, skyldu	*son-of-Thord (name)*	Þórðarson
		son-of-Thorljot (name)	Þorljótsson
should-be	skyldi, væri	*son-of-Thorri (name)*	Þórisson
shoulders	herða	*sought*	sækja, sóttu

Word List (English to Old Norse)

English	Old Norse	*English*	Old Norse
souls	sáluhjápar, sálum	*taken*	tekinn, tekit, tekna, teknir
south	suðr	*taking*	nema
spoke	mælti, tala, tjáði	*teaching*	kennimanns
sprang	spretta	*team*	lið, liði
spring	vár, várit	*temper*	skaplyndi
stand	stað, staðar, standa	*temperament*	skapraun
standing	stendr, stóð	*tens*	tigi, tigir
steersman	stýrimaðr, stýrimanns	*tent*	tjald
Steingrim (name)	Steingrímr	*tent-up*	tjalda
Steingrim's (name)	Steingríms	*than*	en
Steinthor (name)	Steinþórr	*thanked*	þakkaði
stepped	steig	*that*	á, áðu, at, er, hvat, í, sá, þann, þar, þat, þetta, því
still	enn, kyrrlátir, kyrrt		
stone-carving	steint		
stone-one	steinda	*that-way*	þannig
stood	staðit, stóð, studdist	*the*	á, at, er, inn, inu, it, þat, til
stormy	hvasst		
straightaway	þegar	*the-after-boat*	eftirbátinn
straight-away	þegar	*the-animal*	dýrit
strange	undarligt	*the-archbishop*	erkibyskup
strengthened	efldr	*the-armour*	brynjunni
strike	slógu	*the-artefact-fee*	gripagjaldit
strong	sterkr	*the-assembly*	þings
struck	hjó, höggvit, slær	*the-bishop*	byskup, byskupi, byskups
submit	undir		
such	slík, slíka, slíkan, slíks, slíkt, slíku, slíkum	*the-bishop-elect*	byskupsefni
		the-bishop's	byskups
		the-bishop's-seat	byskupsstólinum, byskupsstólnum
suitable	henta		
summer	sumarit, sumars	*the-boat*	bátinn
summers	sumur	*the-boat-behind*	eftirbáti
sung	syngja	*the-body*	lík, líkinu
supplies	vistir	*the-branch*	hríslunni
support	liðveizlu	*the-cabin*	skálann, skálanum
supported	stutt	*the-case*	mál, málit
supporter	styrkðarmaðr	*the-church*	kirkju, kirkjuna
suppose	ætla	*the-company*	sveit
supposed	ætla, ætluðu	*the-court*	dómi, dóminum
swear	sveri	*the-crew*	hásetar
swiftly	ört	*the-day*	dag
		the-dead	daun
		the-door	hurðina, skáladyrrnar
		the-dream	drauminn
		the-dwelling	bænum
take	taka	*the-Easterner*	austmanns

T, t

Word List (English to Old Norse)

English	Old Norse
the-fairest	fagra
the-false-deacon	slembidjákn
the-feast	veizlunni
the-ferry	ferjuna
the-field	völlinn
the-fjord	fjörðu
the-funeral-procession	líkhringingina
the-Greenlander	grænlendings
the-Greenlanders	grænlendingar
the-Greenlanders'	grænlendinga
the-Hermunds (name)	Hermundr
the-hut	skálann
their	sína, þeirar
theirs	sín, sinn, sinna, sínu, sínum, þeim, þeira
the-judgement	dómrinn
the-keel	kilinum
the-kind	konungi
the-king	konung, konungi, konungr, konungs
the-king's	konungs
the-king's-brief	konungsbréfum
the-land	landi, landit
the-Landeys (place)	Landeyjum
the-lands	landsins
them	sér, þá, þegar, þeim, þeira
the-man	mann
the-matter	mal, mál, máli, málum, málunum
the-matter-fulfilling	málsfyllingar
the-men	mönnum
the-merchants	kaupmenn
the-middle	miðju
the-more-difficult	þungligar
the-most	mestr
themselves	sér, sína
then	er, it, síðan, þá, þann, þar, þau, þennan, því
the-news	tíðendin
the-night	nætr, nótt
the-old-woman	kerlingu
the-place	staðarins
there	þar
therefore	því
the-same	samt
these	þessi, þessir, þessum
the-seam	sauminn
the-service	tíða
the-settlement	byggðina
the-ship	skipi, skipinu, skipit, skipum
the-ships	skipa, skips
the-slope	brekku, brekkunni
the-storm	andviðri
the-table	borðit
the-tables	borð, borðum
the-trading-men	kaupmenn, kaupmennirnir, kaupmönnum
the-trees	viðinn
the-trunk	bolöx
the-truth	sanni
the-unsettled-land	óbyggðum
the-way	leið
the-words	orðinn
they	sinni, þeim, þeir, þeira, því
they-are	eru, sé
they-had	höfðu
things	hlutum
think	hygg
third	þriðja
thirdly	þriðja
this	sé, sitt, þat, þess, þessa, þessi, þessu, þessum, þetta
this-man	manninum
Thorarin (name)	Þóarinn, Þórarinn
Thord (name)	Þórðar, Þórðr
Thord's (name)	Þórði
Thorfin (name)	Þorfinns
Thorgils (name)	Þorgils
Thori (name)	Þóris
those	þau
though	þó, þótt
thought	hugðu, þótti, þóttumst
three	þrír, þrjá
throat	barkann
through	fyrir, gegnum
thrust	stakk
tidings	tíðendi

Word List (English to Old Norse)

English	Old Norse	English	Old Norse
time	hríð, tóm	under	undir
time-like	tómliga	unequal	ójafnaðr
to	á, at, fyrir, í, þat, til, við	un-equal	ójafnað
		ungraceful	óþekkðarsvip
to-be	sé, væri, vera	unhappy	þungt
to-be-sent	sendiligstan	unheard-of	endemi
to-catch	fangit	unsettled	ósett
to-do	gera, gerðu	un-settled	óbyggðir
together	saman, samt	until	til
to-give	gera	un-worthy	óvirðing
to-him	honum	up	upp, uppi
to-hold	halda	up-given	uppgefnir
told	mælt, sagt, talaði, tjáði	uproar	róstu
		upset	brugðit
to-me	mér	us	oss, vár, vér
took	taka, tók, tóku	use	nytjum
tore-up	rufu, sleit		
to-stand	standist		
to-strike	höggva		
to-them	þeim		

V, v

English	Old Norse
to-the-south	sunnan
to-the-sword	sverði
to-us	oss
to-you	þér
trading-men	kaupmenn, kaupmönnum
travel	færi, færim, fara, fórum
travelled	fór, fóru, fórum
tread	troða
treasure	gersemi, gripi, gripina
true	
true-words	sannyrði
trust	traust
truthfully	sannligast
turn	hverfa
turned	snerist
twelve	tólf
two	tvau, tveim

English	Old Norse
valid	gildr
very	mjök
Vestribyggd (place)	Vestribyggð, Vestribyggðar
victory	sigr
Vighvats (name)	Víghvats
violence	ofsa
voiced	tjáði

W, w

English	Old Norse
walked	gengit
walrus-tusks	tannvöru
wandered	reikaði
wanted	vildi
wares	varning
was	er, þeir, væri, var, váru
washed	þvá
was-named	hét
way	brott, burt
we	vér, verum
weak	fallinn, vanmeginn
wealth	fé, féit
wealth-finding	fjárfundinn

U, u

English	Old Norse
unable	vanfærr
uncertain	óvíst
uncompensated	óbættr

Word List (English to Old Norse)

English	Old Norse	English	Old Norse
weaponed	vápnaðir	would-be	mundu, vera
we-are	er, vér	would-get	fengi
weariness	varist	wounded	sárir
weather	veðr		
weights	vættir		
well	vel		
went	fara, fara, fekk, ferr, fór, fóru, ganga, gekk, gengr, gengu		

Y, y

English	Old Norse
you	þér, þik, þú, yðr, yðvar
your	þín, yðru
yours	þína, yðvar

English	Old Norse
went-away	stukku
were	eru, var, váru
western	vestan
what	er, hvat
when	er, þá
where	er, horfir, hvar
whether	hvárt
which	hvárs
while	en, meðan
white-bear	hvítabjörn
who	er, hverr
widely	víða
wildly	villt
will	mun, muni, vil
will-be	mun
willed	veld, vildi, vildu, vilja
willing	fúsari
win	unna
winter	vetrinn
wise	vitr, vitrum
wise-like	vitrliga
wish	vil, viljum
wished-for	vilja
with	er, með, við, vit
with-you	yðvarn
wool-comb	ullkamb
word	orð
words	orð, orða
word-sending	orðsending
work	verk
worshippers	tíðamanni
worthiness	virðim, virðing, virðingar
would	mun, mundi, mundu, muni, munt, munu, myndim, skulu, skyldu, yrði

The Tale of the Greenlanders (II) (The Tale of Einarr Sokkason) (*Old Icelandic*)

Old Icelandic	Literal	English
1	**1**	**1**
Sokki hét maður og var Þórisson.	Sokki was-named a-man and was Son-of-Thorri.	There was a man named Sokki, and he was the son of Thorri.
Hann bjó í Brattahlíð á Grænlandi.	He lived in Brattahlid in Greenland.	He lived in Brattahlid in Greenland.
Hann var mikils virður og vinsæll.	He was much respected and popular.	He was much respected and popular.
Einar hét son hans og var mannvænlegur maður.	Einar was-named son his and was a-friendly man.	His son was named Einar and he was a friendly man.
Þeir feðgar áttu mikið vald á Grænlandi og voru þeir þar mjög fyrir mönnum.	They father-and-son had great power in Greenland and were they there much foremost men.	The father and son had great power in Greenland and they were prominent men.
Einhverju sinni lét Sokki þings kveðja og tjáði það fyrir mönnum að hann vildi að landið væri eigi lengur biskupslaust og vildi að allir landsmenn legðu sína muni til að biskupsstóll væri efldur.	One-occasion they had Sokki assembly called and voiced that before the-men that he willed that the-land be no longer bishop-less and willed that all lands-men put themselves should to a bishop's-seat to-be strengthened.	On one occasion Sokki had an assembly called and announced before the men that he wished that the land should no longer be without a bishop, and he wished that all the men of the land should contribute towards a bishop's seat to be established.
Bændur játtuðu því allir.	Farmers agreed accordingly all.	Accordingly the farmers agreed to this.
Sokki bað Einar son sinn fara þessa ferð til Noregs, kvað hann vera sendilegastan mann þess erindis að fara.	Sokki bid Einar son his travel this journey to Norway, said he would-be to-be-sent man this errand to travel.	Sokki asked his son Einar to travel on a journey to Norway as the best man for this errand.
Hann kveðst fara mundu sem hann vildi.	He said travel would as he willed.	He said that he would travel as wished.
Einar hafði með sér tannvöru mikla og svörð að heimta sig fram við höfðingja.	Einar had with him walrus-tusks great and skins to carry himself from with chieftains.	Einar had great walrus tusks and skins with him to further his case with the chieftains.

The Tale of the Greenlanders (II) (The Tale of Einarr Sokkason) (Old Icelandic)

Old Icelandic	Literal	English
Þeir komu við Noreg.	They came to Norway.	They came to Norway.
Þá var Sigurður Jórsalafari konungur að Noregi.	Then was Sigurd Jerusalem-Traveller the-king of Norway.	Then Sigurd Jerusalem-farer was king of Norway.
Einar kom á fund konungs og heimti sig fram með fégjöfum og tjáði síðan mál sitt og erindi og beiddi konung þar til fulltings að hann næði slíku sem hann beiddi fyrir nauðsyn landsins.	Einar came to meeting the-king's and presented himself from with fee-gifts and spoke then matters his and errand and bid the-king there to help that he get such as he bid for needs the-lands.	Einar came to have a meeting with the king and presented himself well with wealthy gifts on account of his errand, and asked the king to help him get that which his lands needed.
Konungur lét þeim það víst betur henta.	The-king had them that certainly better suitable.	The king agreed that it would certainly be better suited.
Síðan kallaði konungur til sín þann mann er Arnaldur hét.	Then called the-king to him then a-man was Arnald named.	Then the king called to him a man who was named Arnald.
Hann var góður klerkur og vel til kennimanns fallinn.	He was good cleric and well to teaching fallen.	He was a good cleric and well fallen to teaching.
Konungur beiddi að hann réðist til þessa vanda fyrir guðs sakir og bænar hans "og mun eg senda þig til Danmerkur á fund Össurar erkibiskups í Lund með mínum bréfum og innsiglum".	The-king bid that he deal to this problem for god's sake and prayers his "and will I send you to Denmark to meet Ossur archbishop in Lund with my briefs and seals".	The king asked him to deal with this problem God's sake and his prayers, "And I will send you to Denmark to meet archbishop Ossur of Lund with my letters and seals".
Arnaldur kvaðst ófús til að ráðast, fyrst fyrir sjálfs síns sakir er hann væri lítt til fallinn og síðan að skilja við vini sína og frændur, í þriðja stað að eiga við torsóttlegt fólk.	Arnald said reluctant to that arrange, firstly for himself his sake as he was little to weak and then to part with friends his and kinsmen, and thirdly stand to not with difficult folk.	Arnald said that he was reluctant to arrange this, firstly for his sake because he was ill-fitted for it, and secondly to part with his friends and kinsmen, and thirdly he did not wish to have to talk to such difficult folk.
Konungur kvað hann því meira gott mundu eftir taka sem hann hefði meiri skapraun af mönnum.	The-king said he that more good would afterwards take as he had more temperament of men.	The king said that the more his difficulty at the hands of temperamental men, the greater his reward would be afterwards.

The Tale of the Greenlanders (II) (The Tale of Einarr Sokkason) (Old Icelandic)

Old Icelandic	Literal	English
Hann kveðst eigi nenna að skerast undan hans bæn "en ef þess verður auðið að eg taki biskupsvígslu þá vil eg að Einar sverji mér þess eið að halda og fulltingja rétt biskupsstólsins og eignum þeim er guði eru gefnar og hegna þeim er á ganga og sé varnarmaður fyrir öllum hlutum staðarins".	He said not bothered to cutting away-from his prayers "but if this becomes possible that I take bishop's-appointment then will I that Einar swear to-me this oath to hold and fulfil rights bishop's-seat and owning them the priest are given and protected they are to go and being defender for all things the-place".	He said that he did not want the bother of cutting away from his prayers "but if it becomes possible that I take the appointment of bishop, then I wish Einar to swear to me this oath, to hold and fulfil the rights of the bishop's seat, and all that is given to the priest, and to be the protector and defender of all things to do with the bishop's seat".
Konungur kvað hann það gera skyldu.	The-king said he that to-do should.	The king said that he should do this.
Einar kvaðst mundu undir það ganga.	Einar said would submit to go.	Einar said he would submit to going along with it.
Síðan fór biskupsefni á fund Össurar erkibiskups og sagði honum sitt erindi með konungsbréfum.	Then travelled the-bishop-elect to meet Ossur archbishop and said to-him this errand with the-king's-brief.	Then the bishop-elect went to meet archbishop Ossur and told him of his errand with the king's letters.
Erkibiskup tók honum vel og reyndust hugi við.	The-archbishop took him well and gave-him his-mind with.	The archbishop received him well and gave to him with his mind.
Og er biskup sá að þessi maður var vel til tignar fallinn vígði hann Arnald til biskups og leysti hann vel af hendi.	And when the-bishop saw that this man was well to position fallen consecrated he Arnald to bishop and released him well of hand.	And when the bishop saw that this man was well given to the position he consecrated Arnald to bishop and parted with him warmly.
Síðan kom Arnaldur biskup til konungs og tók hann við honum vel.	Then came Arnald bishop to the-king and took he with him well.	Then bishop Arnald went to the kind and he received him well.
Einar hafði haft með sér bjarndýri af Grænlandi og gaf það Sigurði konungi.	Einar had had with him a-bear from Greenland and gave it Sigurd the-king.	Einar had a bear with him from Greenland and gave it to Sigurd the king.
Fékk hann þar í mót sæmdir og metorð af konungi.	Got he then to meet honour and esteem from the-king.	He then got honour and esteem from the king.
Síðan fóru þeir á einu skipi, biskup og Einar.	Then travelled they on one ship, the-bishop and Einar.	Then they travelled on a ship, the bishop and Einar.

The Tale of the Greenlanders (II) (The Tale of Einarr Sokkason) (Old Icelandic)

Old Icelandic	Literal	English
Á öðru skipi bjóst Arnbjörn austmaður og norrænir menn með honum og vildu og fara út til Grænlands.	On another ship prepared Arnbjorn Eastern-man and Nordic men with him and willed also travel out to Greenland.	Prepared on another ship was Arnbjorn the Norwegian and other Norse men with him who wished to travel to Greenland.
Síðan létu þeir í haf og greiðast eigi byrinn mjög í hag þeim og komu þeir biskup og Einar í Holtavatnsós undir Eyjafjöllum á Íslandi.	Then had they to sea and paying not bearing much of circumstances theirs and came they bishop and Einar to Holtavatnsos under Eyjafjolls in Iceland.	Then they put to sea and the situation was not very favourable for them, and the bishop and Einar arrived in Holtavatnsós under the Eyjafjolls in Iceland.
Þá bjó Sæmundur hinn fróði í Odda.	Then lived Saemund the learned in Odda.	Then Saemund the learned lived in Odda.
Hann fór á fund biskups og bauð honum til sín um veturinn.	He went to meet the-bishop and invited him to his about winter.	He went to see the bishop and invited him to stay with him for the winter.
Biskup þakkaði honum og lést það þiggja mundu.	Bishop thanked him and had that accepted would.	The bishop thanked him and had accepted it.
Einar var undir Eyjafjöllum um veturinn.	Einar was under Eyjafjolls about winter.	Einar was under Eyjafjolls during the winter.
Það er sagt þá er biskup reið frá skipi og menn hans að þeir áðu á bæ nokkurum í Landeyjum og sátu úti.	It is said when that bishop rode from the-ship and men his that they that to a-farm some in The-Landeys and sat outside.	It is said that when the bishop and his men got off the ship, they went to a farm in the Landeys and sat outside.
Þá gekk út kerling ein og hafði ullkamb í hendi.	Then went out old-woman one and had wool-comb in hand.	Then an old woman walked out alone with a wool comb in her hand.
Hún gekk að einum manni og mælti:	She went to one man and said:	She walked up to one man and said:
"Muntu festa, bokki, tindinn í kambi mínum?"	"Shall-you fix, buck, pin in comb mine?"	"Will you fix the pin in my comb, buck?"
Hann tók við og kvaðst mundu að gera og tók hnjóðhamar úr mal einum og gerði að og líkaði kerlingu allvel,	He took with and said would to done and took hammer out-of the-matter one and did it and liked the-old-woman all-well,	He took it over and said that he would do it, and he took a hammer off the ground and did it, and the old woman liked this very well,
en það var biskup raunar.	and it was a-bishop actually.	and it was actually a bishop.

The Tale of the Greenlanders (II) (The Tale of Einarr Sokkason) (Old Icelandic)

Old Icelandic	Literal	English
Hann var hagur vel og er því frá þessu sagt að hann sýndi lítillæti sitt.	He was handy well and was therefore from this said that he showed humility his.	He was very handy and it is told from this of how he showed his humility.
Hann var í Odda um veturinn og fór með þeim Sæmundi allvel.	He was in Odda about winter and went with them Saemund all-well.	He was in Odda during the winter and got on very well with Saemund.
En til þeirra Arnbjarnar spurðist ekki.	But to them Arnbjarn heard-of not.	But they did not hear of Arnbjarn.
Ætluðu þeir biskup að hann mundi kominn til Grænlands.	Supposed they bishop that he would come to Greenland.	They thought the bishop would come to Greenland.
Um sumarið eftir fóru þeir biskup og Einar af Íslandi og komu við Grænland í Eiríksfjörð og tóku menn við þeim allvel.	About summer after went they the-bishop and Einar from Iceland and came to Greenland in Eriksfjord and took men with them all-well.	In the following summer, the bishop and Einar left Iceland and arrived at Greenland in Eriksfjord and were well received by the people.
Spurðu þeir þá enn ekki til Arnbjarnar og þótti það undarlegt og liðu svo nokkur sumur.	Heard-of they then but not to Arnbjarn and thought that strange and passed so some summers.	They still didn't hear about Arnbjarn and thought it was strange, and then a few summers passed.
Gerðist nú á umræða mikil að þeir muni týnst hafa.	Became now of discussed much that they would lost have.	There was now much discussion that they must have been lost.
Biskup setti stól sinn í Görðum og réðst þangað til.	Bishop set seat his in Gardar and ruled from-then to.	The bishop placed his chair in Gardar and ruled until then.
Var Einar honum þá mestur styrktarmaður og þeir feðgar.	Was Einar to-him then the-most supporter and they father-and-son.	Einar was his greatest supporter then, and they were father and son.
Þeir voru og mest metnir af öllum landsmönnum af biskupi.	They were and most important of all lands-men of the-bishop.	They were and the most valued of all the countrymen by the bishop.

2

Sigurður hét maður og var Njálsson, grænlenskur maður.	Sigurd was-named a-man and was Son-of-Njal, a-Greenlander man.	There was a man named Sigurd who was the son of Njal, a Greenlander man.
Hann fór oft á haustum til fangs í óbyggðir.	He travelled often out autumn to captivity in un-settled.	He often went in the fall to captivity in the wilderness.

The Tale of the Greenlanders (II) (The Tale of Einarr Sokkason) (Old Icelandic)

Old Icelandic	Literal	English
Hann var sægarpur mikill.	He was sea-champion much.	He was very much a champion of the sea.
Þeir voru fimmtán saman.	They were fifteen altogether.	There were fifteen of them together.
Þeir komu um sumarið að jöklinum Hvítserk og höfðu fundið nokkurar eldstóar manna og enn nokkurn veiðiskap.	They came about summer to a-glacier Hvitserk and had-they found some fire-place men and still some hunting.	They came in the summer to the glacier Hvitserk and had found several small groups of men and still some hunting.
Þá mælti Sigurður:	Then spoke Sigurd:	Then Sigurd said:
"Hvors eruð þér fúsari, að hverfa aftur eða fara lengra?	"Which are you willing, to turn back or travel longer?	"Which are you more willing to go back or go further?
Er nú eigi sumars mikið eftir en fang orðið lítið".	Is now not summer much remaining but resources have-become little".	There isn't much left of the summer now, but the catch has become short".
Hásetar kváðust fúsari aftur að hverfa og sögðu mannhættu mikla að fara um stórfjörðu undir jöklum.	The-crew said willing back to turn and said dangerous much to travel about large-fjords under glaciers.	The crew said they were more willing to turn back and said that it was very dangerous to go through a large fjord under glaciers.
Hann kvað það satt "en svo segir mér hugur um að eftir muni hið meira fangið ef því náir".	He said that true "but so says to-me mind about that later would then more to-catch if then getting".	He said it was true "but then my mind tells me that later the more will be caught if it is possible".
Þeir báðu hann ráða, kváðust lengi hans forsjá hlítt hafa og þó vel gefist.	They asked him advice, said long his foresight satisfactory had and though well given.	They asked him for advice, saying that they had been under his guardianship for a long time and that it had been successful.
Honum kveðst meira um að halda fram og svo var gert.	He said more about that to-hold from and so was done.	He said that there was more to claim, and so it was done.
Steinþór hét maður er á skipi þeirra var.	Steinthor was-named a-man was on ship theirs was.	A man on their ship was called Steinthor.
Hann tók til orða:	He took to words:	He spoke:
"Dreymdi mig í nótt Sigurður",	"Dreamed me about the-night Sigurd",	"I had a dream last night, Sigurd",

The Tale of the Greenlanders (II) (The Tale of Einarr Sokkason) (Old Icelandic)

Old Icelandic	Literal	English
sagði hann, "og mun eg segja þér drauminn	said he, "and will I say to-you the-dream	he said, "and I will tell you the dream
nú.	now.	Now
Er vér fórum á fjörðinn þennan hinn mikla þóttist eg kominn í milli bjarga nokkurra og æpa til bjargar mér".	When we travel to fjord then the much thought I coming in between rescuing something and shouting to rescue me".	when we went to this great fjord, I thought I came between something to be rescued from, and shouting for my rescue".
Sigurður kvað draum meðallagi góðan "og skyldir þú þar eigi björg undir fótum troða og hitta eigi í þann einangur að þú mættir eigi munni halda".	Sigurd said dream moderately good "and should you there not rocks under feet tread and find not in that alone-going that you might not mouth hold".	Sigurd said it was a moderately good dream "and you should not trample rocks under your feet there and you should not find yourself so alone that you could not keep your mouth shut".
Steinþór var heldur æðimaður í skaplyndi og óforsjáll.	Steinthor was rather of-mind in temper and impulsive.	Steinthor was rather a hot-tempered and impulsive person.
Og er þeir sækja inn á fjörðinn þá mælti Sigurður:	And when they sought in the fjord then spoke Sigurd:	And when they entered the fjord, Sigurd said:
"Hvort er sem mér sýnist að skip sé inn á fjörðinn?"	"Whether is as to-me seems that ship this in the fjord?"	"Does it seem to me that a ship is in the fjord?"
Þeir kváðu svo vera.	They said so being.	They said it was so.
Sigurður kvað það tíðindum mundu gegna.	Sigurd said that news would pass.	Sigurd said that this would bring great news.
Héldu nú síðan inn að og sáu að skipið var sett upp í einn árós og gert fyrir ofan.	Held now then in to and saw the ship was sat up in a river-mouth and made for above.	Now they went inward and saw that the ship was set up in one estuary and made covered.
Það var mikið hafskip.	It was a-great sea-going-ship.	It was a great sea-going ship.
Síðan gengu þeir á land og sáu skála og tjald skammt frá.	Then went they to land and saw cabin and tent a-short-distance from.	Then they went ashore and saw a cabin and a tent nearby.
Þá mælti Sigurður að þeir mundu tjalda fyrst "og er nú liðið á dag og vil eg að menn séu kyrrrlátir og varúðgir".	Then spoke Sigurd that they would tent-up first "and is now passed in the-day and wish I that men are still and cautious".	Then Sigurd said that they would camp first "and now it's late in the day and I want people to be quiet and careful".
Og svo gerðu þeir.	And so done was.	And so it was done.

The Tale of the Greenlanders (II) (The Tale of Einarr Sokkason) (Old Icelandic)

Old Icelandic	Literal	English
Og um morguninn ganga þeir og sjást um.	And about morning went they and looked about.	And in the morning they went and looked about.
Þeir sjá stokk einn hjá sér og stóð í bol öx og mannshræ hjá.	They saw a-log one beside them and stood in the-trunk an-axe and human-body beside.	They saw a log by them and an axe in the butt and a human carcass.
Sigurður kvað þann mann viðinn höggið hafa og hafa orðið vanmeginn af megri.	Sigurd said that the-man the-trees struck had and had become weak of meagre.	Sigurd said that the man had been striking trees and had become weak from hunger.
Síðan gengu þeir að skálanum og sáu þar annað mannshræ.	Then went they to the-cabin and saw there another dead-body.	Then they walked to the cabin and saw another corpse there.
Sigurður kvað þann gengið hafa meðan hann mátti "og munu þessir verið hafa þjónustumenn þeirra er í skálanum eru".	Sigurd said then walked had as-long-as he might "and would these been have servants-of they who about the-cabin were".	Sigurd said that he had walked for as long as he could "and these will be the servants of who are in the cabin".
Öx lá og hjá þessum.	Axe lay also beside these.	An axe lay beside these.
Þá mælti Sigurður:	Then spoke Sigurd:	Then Sigurd said:
"Það kalla eg ráð að rjúfa skálann og láta leggja út daun af líkum þeim er inni eru og ýldu er lengi mun legið hafa.	"It call I decide to break-open the-hut and lay-out have out the-dead of bodies they who in were and decay are long may laid have.	"This I call our plan, to break open the cabin and let the stench of the dead out, for the corpses will have been lying there for a long time.
Og varist menn fyrir að verða því að þess er eigi lítil von að mönnum verði að því mein og mjög er á mót eðli manna þótt líkindi séu á því að menn þessir muni oss ekki illt gera".	And weariness men for that be because that this is not little hope that men be that because-of disease and much is to meet nature man's though alike they-are that they the men these should to-us not ill be-done".	And men be wary of it, because there is nothing more certain than men will be harmed by it, and it is very against human wellbeing, and though there are similarities, these men will not harm us".
Steinþór kvað slíkt undarlegt að gera sér meira fyrir en þyrfti og gekk á hurðina en þeir rufu skálann.	Steinthor said such strange to do as more for than needed and went to the-door but they broke-up the-cabin.	Steinthor said that it was such a strange thing to do more than was necessary, and went to the door as they broke open the cabin.
Og er Steinþór gekk út þá leit Sigurður til hans og mælti:	And when Steinthor went out then looked Sigurd to him and said:	And when Steinthor came out Sigurd got a look at him and said:

The Tale of the Greenlanders (II) (The Tale of Einarr Sokkason) (Old Icelandic)

Old Icelandic	Literal	English
"Allmjög er manninum brugðið".	"All-great is this-man upset".	"This man is greatly upset".
Hann tók þegar að æpa og hlaupa en þeir eftir félagar hans.	He took straightaway to shouting and running but they followed companions his.	He started shouting and running away, but his companions followed him.
Hann hleypur síðan í hamarrifu nokkura þar er engi mátti að honum komast og þar fékk hann bana.	He ran then into crags some there where no-one might to him come and there got he death.	He ran into some crags and became stuck between them so that no-one could get to him, and there he died.
Sigurður kvað hann of berdreyman.	Sigurd said he of clear-dreams.	Sigurd said his dream was clearly true.
Síðan rufu þeir skálann og gerðu eftir því sem Sigurður mælti og varð þeim ekki mein að.	Then tore-up they the-cabin and did following according as Sigurd said and came to-them not harm by.	Then they tore up the cabin and followed accordingly as Sigurd had told them, and no harm came to them.
Þeir sáu þar í skálanum menn dauða og fé mikið.	They saw there in the-cabin men dead and wealth much.	They saw dead people and a lot of money in the cabin.
Þá mælti Sigurður:	Then said Sigurd:	Then Sigurd said:
"Það sýnist mér ráð að þér hleypið holdi af beinum þeirra í heitukötlum þeirra er þeir hafa átt og er svo hægra til kirkju að færa.	"That seems to-me advisable that you discharge flesh off bones theirs in boiling-cauldrons theirs that they had had and then so right to the-church to bring.	"It seems to me advisable that you get the flesh off their bones in their hot cauldrons that they have, and then move them to church.
Og er það líkast að Arnbjörn muni hér verið hafa því að skip þetta annað hið fagra er hér stendur á landi hefi eg heyrt að hann hafi átt".	And is that likely that Arnbjorn should here been has because that ship this other then the-fairest is here standing about the-land have I heard that he had had".	And it seems likely that Arnbjorn will have been here, because this ship is one of the most beautiful that is standing on this land, I have heard that he had".
Það var höfðaskip og steint og mikil gersemi.	It was a-headed-ship and stone-carving and much treasure.	It was a ship with a figurehead and stone-carving and great treasure.
Kaupskipið var brotið mjög neðan og kvaðst Sigurður ætla að það mundi að engum nytjum verða.	Merchant-ship was broken much below and said Sigurd suppose that it would to no use be.	The merchant ship was broken below, and Sigurd said that it would be of no use.

The Tale of the Greenlanders (II) (The Tale of Einarr Sokkason) (Old Icelandic)

Old Icelandic	Literal	English
Þeir taka úr sauminn en brenndu skipið og höfðu hlaðna ferjuna úr óbyggðum, eftirbátinn og höfðaskipið.	They took out-from the-seam and burned the-ship and had loaded the-ferry out-of the-unsettled-land, the-after-boat and head-ship.	They took out everything from the seams and burned the ship and had loaded to ferry out of the unsettled land, the second boat, and the head ship.
Þeir komu í byggðina og fundu biskup í Görðum og sagði Sigurður honum tíðindin og fjárfundinn.	They came to the-settlement and found bishop in Gardar and said Sigurd to-him the-news and wealth-finding.	They came to the settlement and found the bishop at Gardar, and Sigurd told him the news and of finding the wealth.
"Nú kann eg eigi annað að sjá",	"Now can I not anything-else to see",	"Now I can't see anything else",
sagði hann, "en það fé þeirra muni best komið er beinum þeirra fylgir og ef eg á nokkuru ráð þá vil eg að svo sé".	said he, "but that wealth theirs would best come that bones theirs followed and if I of some advice then wish I to so to-be".	he said, "but their money will be best served if their placed with their bones, and if I have any say, I want it to be so".
Biskup kvað hann vel hafa með farið og viturlega og það mæltu allir.	Bishop said he well had with going and wise-like and that said all.	The bishop said he had acted well and wisely, and everyone said so.
Mikið fé fylgdi líkum þeirra.	Much wealth followed bodies theirs.	A lot of money followed their corpses.
Biskup kvað gersemi mikla vera höfðaskipið.	Bishop said treasure much being head-ship.	The bishop said the great treasure was the head ship.
Sigurður kvað og það sannlegast að það færi til staðarins fyrir sálum þeirra.	Sigurd said and it truthfully that it going to the-place for souls theirs.	Sigurd said, and most truly, that it would go to the bishop's seat for the good of their souls.
Öðru fé skiptu þeir með sér er fundið höfðu að grænlenskum lögum.	Other wealth divided they with themselves as found had to Greenlandic law.	They shared the other money they had found according to Greenlandic law.
Og er þessi tíðindi komu til Noregs þá spurði það sá maður er Össur hét og var systurson Arnbjarnar.	And when these tidings came to Norway then learned that so man was Ossur named and was sister's-son Arnbjarnar.	And when these tidings came to Norway, the man whose name was Ossur, who was Arnbjorn's sister's son, learned about it.
...og	and...	...and
fleiri menn voru þeir á því skipi er sína frændur höfðu misst og væntu til greiðslu um féið.	more men were they in because the-ship was themselves kinsmen had lost and expected to compensation about wealth.	there were more men on the ship that had lost their cousins and were expecting payment for the money.

The Tale of the Greenlanders (II) (The Tale of Einarr Sokkason) (Old Icelandic)

Old Icelandic	Literal	English
Þeir komu í Eiríksfjörð og sóttu menn til fundar við þá og slógu kaupum.	They came to Eriksfjord and sought men to meet with then and strike a-deal.	They came to Eriksfjord and fetched people to meet them and make a deal.
Síðan tóku menn sér vistir.	Then took men themselves supplies.	Then people took supplies.
Össur stýrimaður fór í Garða til biskups og var þar um veturinn.	Ossur steersman went to Gardar to the-bishop and was there about winter.	Ossur the steersman went to Gardar to see the bishop and stayed there during the winter.
Í Vestribyggð var þá annað kaupskip.	In Vestribyggd was then another merchant-ship.	In the Western Settlement there was another merchant ship then.
Þar var Kolbeinn Þorljótsson, norrænn maður.	There was Kolbein Son-of-Thorljot, Nordic man.	There was Kolbein Son-of-Thorljot, a Nordic man.
Hinu þriðja skipi réð sá maður er Hermundur hét og var Koðránsson og Þorgils bróðir hans og höfðu mikla sveit manna.	The third ship commanded so man was Hermund named and was Son-of-Kodran and Thorgils brother his and had much company of-men.	The third ship was commanded by a man named Hermund, who was the son of Kodran, and his brother Thorgils, and they had a large force of men.

3 | 3 | 3

Old Icelandic	Literal	English
Um veturinn kom Össur að máli við biskup að hann ætti þangað févon eftir Arnbjörn frænda sinn og beiddi biskup þar gera greiða á bæði fyrir sína hönd og annarra manna.	About winter came Ossur to discuss with the-bishop that he had from-there fee-trust after Arnbjorn kinsman his and bid bishop there to-give assistance as asked for his hand and other men.	During the winter, Ossur discussed with the bishop that he had a trust there for his uncle Arnbjorn and asked the bishop there to give assistance both on his behalf and on other people's behalf.
Biskup kvaðst fé tekið hafa eftir grænlenskum lögum eftir slíka atburði, kvaðst þetta eigi gert hafa með einræði sitt, kvað það maklegast að það fé færi þeim til sáluhjápar er aflað höfðu og til þeirrar kirkju er bein þeirra voru að grafin, sagði það manndómsleysi að kalla nú til fjár þess.	The-bishop said wealth taken had after Greenlandic law after such events, said it not made had with self-will this, said that most that it wealth go-to them to souls who gain had and to their church where bones theirs were to in-the-grave, said that meanness to claim now to money this.	The bishop said that he had taken money according to Greenlandic laws after such events, he said that he had not done this with his decision-making, he said that it was most appropriate that the money should go to the souls they had earned and to the church where their bones were buried, he said it was mean to claim now to this money.

The Tale of the Greenlanders (II) (The Tale of Einarr Sokkason) (Old Icelandic)

Old Icelandic	Literal	English
Síðan vildi Össur eigi vera í Görðum með biskupi og fór til sveitunga sinna og héldu sig svo allir samt um veturinn.	Then willed Ossur not to-be at Gardar with the-bishop and went to men-company his and held him so all the-same about winter.	After that, Ossur did not want to stay in Gardar with the bishop and went to his companions, and they all stayed the winter anyway.
Um vorið bjó Össur mál til þings þeirra Grænlendinga og var það þing í Görðum.	About spring prepared Ossur a-case to the-assembly theirs Greenlanders and was it assembly in Gardar.	In the spring, Ossur prepared a case for the assembly of the Greenlanders, and that meeting was held in Gardar.
Kom þar biskup og Einar Sokkason og höfðu þeir fjölmenni mikið.	Came there bishop and Einar Son-of-Sokki and had they following-men many.	Bishop and Einar Sokkason came there and they had a lot of followers.
Össur kom þar og skipverjar hans.	Ossur came there and crew his.	Ossur and his crew arrived there.
Og er dómur var settur þá gekk Einar að dómi með fjölmenni og kveðst ætla að þeim mundi erfitt að eiga við útlenda menn í Noregi ef svo skyldi þar.	And when judgement was set then went Einar to the-court with many-people and said supposed to them would difficult to have with foreign men in Norway if so should there.	And when the sentence was passed, Einar went to the court with many people and said that they would find it difficult to deal with foreigners in Norway if it happened there.
"Viljum vér þau lög hafa er hér ganga",	"Wish we then law have that here going",	"We wish to have the law that goes here",
sagði Einar.	said Einar.	said Einar.
Og er dómurinn fór út náðu Austmenn eigi málum fram að koma og stukku frá.	And when the-judgement went out reached Eastern-men not case from to come and went-away from.	And when the judgement came out, the Eastern-men could not progress forward and went away.
Nú líkar Össuri illa, þykist hafa af óvirðing en fé ekki og varð það hans úrræði að hann fer til þar er skipið er það hið steinda og hjó úr tvö borð, sínu megin hvort upp frá kilinum.	Now likes Ossur ill, seems have of un-worthy but wealth not and became it his solution that he went to there where the-ship was that the stone-one and struck out-of two boards, theirs sides each up from the-keel.	Now Ossur did not like this and thought ill of it, because of the disrespect not the money, and so became his solution, that he went to where the ship was that had the stone and struck out two boards, one on each side, upwards from the keel.
Eftir það fór hann til Vestribyggðar og hitti þá Kolbein og Ketil Kálfsson og sagði þeim svo búið.	After that went he to Vestribyggd and met then Kolbein and Ketil Son-of-Kalf and said to-them so settled.	After that he went to Vestribyggd (The-Western-Settlement) and met Kolbein and Ketil Kalfsson and told them it was over.

The Tale of the Greenlanders (II) (The Tale of Einarr Sokkason) (Old Icelandic)

Old Icelandic	Literal	English
Kolbeinn kvað ósæmd til tekna enda sagði hann úrræðið eigi gott.	Kolbein said dishonourable to taken and said he solution not good.	Kolbein said that it was taken as dishonourable and that the solution was not good.
Ketill mælti:	Ketil said:	Ketil said:
"Fýsa vil eg þig að þú ráðist hingað til vor því að eg hefi spurt fastmæli biskups og Einars en þú munt vanfær að sitja fyrir tilstilli biskups en framkvæmd Einars og verum heldur allir saman".	"Desire will I you that you advise here until spring because that I have learned opinion the-bishop's and Einar's but you would unable to sit through guidance the-bishop's but execution Einar's and we rather all together".	"I want you to come here until spring, because I have learned the bishop's and Einar's opinion, and you will be unable to sit through the bishop's guidance, and Einar's actions and we should rather all stand together".
Hann kvað það og líklegast að það mundi af ráðast.	He said that and likely that it would of be-arranged.	He said that it was so, and it would likely be arranged.
Þar var í sveit með þeim kaupmönnum Ísa-Steingrímur.	There was in the-company with them trading-men Isa-Steingrim.	There was in the company of merchants with them a man named Isa-Steingrim.
Össur fór þá aftur til Kiðjabergs.	Ossur went then back to Kidjaberg.	Ossur then went back to Kidjaberg.
Þar hafði hann áður verið.	There had he before been.	He had been there before.

4

Biskup varð reiður mjög er hann spurði að spillt var skipinu og kallar til sín Einar Sokkason og mælti:	Bishop became angry much when he learned that damaged was the-ship and called to him Einar Son-of-Sokki and said:	The Bishop became very-much angry when he learned of the damage that was done to the ship, and called Einar Sokkason before him and said:
"Nú er til þess að taka er þú hést með svardaga er vér fórum af Noregi að refsa svívirðing staðarins og hans eigna við þá er það gerðu.	"Now it to this that take what you promised with oath was we travelled from Norway to punish disgrace of-the-place and its property with then is it to-do.	"Now it is for you to take action as you promised by oath when we travelled from Norway, to punish the disgrace to this place and its property and those who did it.
Nú kalla eg Össur hafa fyrirgert sér er hann hefir spillt eign vorri og sýnt oss í öllum hlutum óþekktarsvip.	Now call I Ossur have before-done himself as he has damaged property ours and shown us to ill things ungraceful.	Now I announce that Ossur's life is forfeit, as he has damaged our property and shown us the most disgraceful ill.

The Tale of the Greenlanders (II) (The Tale of Einarr Sokkason) (Old Icelandic)

Old Icelandic	Literal	English
Nú er ekki að dyljast við að mér líkar eigi svo búið og eg kalla þig eiðrofa ef kyrrt er".	Now is none to hiding with that to-me like not so settled and I call you breach-of-oath if still are".	Now there is no hiding that I do not like things as they so are, and I will call you in breach of oath if they still are".
Einar svarar:	Einar answered:	Einar answered:
"Eigi er þetta vel gert herra en mæla munu það sumir að nokkur vorkunn sé á við Össur, svo miklu sem hann er sviptur, þótt eigi sé vel í höndum haft þá er þeir sáu góða gripi er frændur þeirra höfðu átt og náðu eigi.	"Not is this well done sir but badly would that some that some pity is to with Ossur, so much as he is deprived, though not is well in handling has then is they saw good treasure that kinsmen theirs had owned and reached not.	"This is not a good thing to have done sir, but it would be bad for some may pity Ossur, for he has been deprived of so much, and it will not be handled well if they saw the good treasure that their kinsmen had owned and were unable to obtain it.
Og veit eg varla hverju eg skal hér um heita".	And knowing I hardly how I shall here about be-called".	And I hardly know how I shall call this.
Þeir skildu fálega og var reiðisvipur á biskupi.	They parted coolly and was angry of the-bishop.	They parted coolly, and the bishop looked angry.
Og þá er menn sóttu til kirkjumessu og til veislu á Langanes var biskup þar og Einar að veislunni.	And then when men sought to church-mass and to feast at Langanes was the-bishop there and Einar at the-feast.	And when people went to church mass and to a feast at Langanes, the bishop was there and Einar was at the feast.
Margt fólk var komið til tíða og söng biskup messu.	Many folk were come to the-service and sang the-bishop mass.	Many people had come and the bishop sang mass.
Þar var kominn Össur og stóð undir kirkju sunnan og við kirkjuvegginn og talaði sá maður við hann er Brandur hét og var Þórðarson, heimamaður biskups.	There was come Ossur and standing under the-church to-the-south and with church-wall and told so man with him was Brand named and was Son-of-Thord, house-man the-bishop's.	Ossur had arrived there and was standing under the church to the south and by the church wall, and talking to the man with him whose name was Brand Thorisson, the bishop's houseman.
Þessi maður bað Össur vægja til við biskup "og vænti eg",	This man bid Ossur make-peace to with the-bishop "and expect I",	This man asked Ossur to make peace with the bishop, "and I expect",
sagði hann, "að þá muni vel duga en nú agir við svo".	said he, "that then would well aided but not desirable with so".	he said, "that all will be well, but it is not desirable as it is".
Össur kvaðst ekki fá það af sér svo illa sem við hann var búið.	Ossur said not get that of him so ill as with he was settled.	Ossur said that he could not because of the ill with which it had been concluded.

The Tale of the Greenlanders (II) (The Tale of Einarr Sokkason) (Old Icelandic)

Old Icelandic	Literal	English
Og áttu þeir nú um þetta að tala.	And have they now about this to spoke.	And they now spoke about this.
Þá gengu þeir biskup frá kirkju og heim til húsa og var Einar þar í göngu.	Then went they the-bishop from the-church and home to house and was Einar there in going.	Then the bishop and the others went from the church to the house, and Einar went along.
Og er þeir komu fyrir skáladyrnar þá snerist Einar frá fylgdinni og gekk einn í brott til kirkjugarðsins og tók öxi úr hendi tíðamanni einum og gekk suður um kirkjuna.	And as they came before the-door then turned Einar from following and went alone to away to churchyard and took axe out-of hand worshippers one and went south around the-church.	And as they came to the door then Einar turned away from the followers and went away alone to the churchyard and took an axe out of the hand of one of the worshippers and went around to the south side of the church.
Össur stóð þar og studdist á öxi sína.	Ossur stood there and stood on axe his.	Ossur stood there leaning on his axe.
Einar hjó hann þegar banahögg og gekk inn eftir það og voru þá borð uppi.	Einar struck him straight-away death-blow and went in after that and were then the-tables up.	Einar struck him a death blow straight away and went inside by which time the tables were up.
Einar steig undir borðið gegnt biskupi og mælti ekki orð.	Einar stepped under the-table opposite the-bishop and spoke not a-word.	Einar took his seat at the table opposite the bishop and spoke not a word.
Síðan gekk hann Brandur Þórðarson í stofuna og fyrir biskup og mælti:	Then went he Brand Son-of-Thord in sitting-room and before bishop and said:	Then Brand Thordarson went into the sitting room before the bishop and said:
"Er nokkuð tíðinda sagt yður herra?"	"Is some news told you sir?"	"Has some news been told to you sir?"
Biskup kvaðst eigi spurt hafa "eða hvað segir þú?"	Bishop said not learned had "but what say you?"	The bishop said he had not heard "but what say you?"
Hann svarar:	He answered:	He answered:
"Sígast lét nú einn hér úti".	"Sinking laid now one here outside".	"Someone has dropped down laying dead here outside".
Biskup mælti:	Bishop spoke:	The bishop said:
"Hver veldur því eða hver er fyrir orðinn?"	"Who caused therefore or who is before the-words?"	"Who causes it or who is behind the word?"

The Tale of the Greenlanders (II) (The Tale of Einarr Sokkason) (Old Icelandic)

Old Icelandic	Literal	English
Brandur kvað þann nær er frá kunni að segja.	Brand said then as-far as from known to say.	Brand said someone as far away as him knew to say.
Biskup mælti:	Bishop said:	The bishop said:
"Veldur þú Einar líftjóni Össurar?"	"Brought-about you Einar loss-of-life Ossur?"	"Did you bring about Ossur's loss of life, Einar?"
Hann svarar:	He answered:	He answered:
"Því veld eg víst".	"Because willed I certainly".	"This I willed certainly".
Biskup mælti:	The-bishop said:	The bishop said:
"Eigi eru slík verk góð en þó er vorkunn á".	"Not are-they such work good but though is pity about".	"Such work is not good, but there is pity about it".
Brandur bað að þvo skyldi líkinu og syngja yfir.	Brand bid that washed should the-body and sung over.	Brand asked that the body should be washed and a service sung over.
Biskup kvað mundu gefa tóm til þess	Bishop said would give time to this	The bishop said that there would be time to give to this,
og sátu menn undir borðum og fóru að öllu tómlega og fékk biskup svo fremi menn til að syngja yfir líkinu en Einar bað þess og kvað það sama að gera það með sæmd.	and sat people under the-tables and went to all time-like and went bishop so provided men to that sing over the-body as Einar bid this and said that same that to-do that with honour.	and the people sat at the tables taking their time, and so it went that the bishop provided men to sing over the body as Einar had asked, saying that it should be done with some honour.
Biskuð kvaðst ætla að það mun réttara að grafa hann eigi að kirkju "en þó við bæn þína skal hann hér jarða að þessi kirkju að eigi er heimilisprestur".	The-bishop said supposed to that would more-correct to grave him not at church "but though with bidding yours shall he here earthed to this church that not with local-priest".	The bishop supposed that it would be more correct not to bury him at a church "but because of your asking, he shall be buried at this church that does not have a resident priest".
Og fékk hann eigi til fyrr kennimenn yfir að syngja en áður var um lík búið.	And got he not to for priests over to sing but after was about the-body prepared.	And he did not get priests to sing over him as his body was being prepared.
Þá mælti Einar:	Then said Einar:	Then Einar said:

The Tale of the Greenlanders (II) (The Tale of Einarr Sokkason) (Old Icelandic)

Old Icelandic	Literal	English
"Nú hefir orðið í stökki brang og ekki lítt af yðru tilstilli en hér eiga þó hlut í ofsamenn miklir og get eg að stórir úfar rísi á með oss".	"Now has-been become in blood-splattered chest and not little of your agency but here not though part in overbearing-men much and get I that badly misfortune giants of with us".	"Now there has become bloodshed, in no small amount by your doing, and here are very powerful men, and I can tell that a great misfortune will be with us".
Biskup kvaðst vænta að menn munu þessum ofsa af sér hrinda en unna sæmdar fyrir mál þetta og umdæmis ef eigi væri með ofsa að gengið.	The-bishop said hoped that people would this violence of themselves repel but win honour for matter this and area if not was with violence of going.	The bishop said that he hoped that the people who would bring this violence would be repelled, and that they would win honour in this matter as long as there was no violence.

5

Old Icelandic	Literal	English
Tíðindi þessi spurðust og fréttu það kaupmenn.	News this heard-of and found-out the trading-men.	News of this was heard of, and it was found out among the merchants.
Þá mælti Ketill Kálfsson:	Then said Ketil Son-of-Kalf:	Then Ketil Kalfsson said:
"Ekki fór fjarri getu minni að honum mundi höfuðgjarnt verða".	"Not for far ability mine that he would headstrong be".	"It is not outside of my ability if he would be headstrong".
Maður hét Símon, frændi Össurar, mikill maður og sterkur.	Man was-named Simon, kinsman Ossur, great man and strong.	There was a man named Simon, a kinsman of Ossur, a great and strong man.
Ketill kvað vera mega ef Símon fylgdi atgervi sinni "að hann mun muna dráp Össurar frænda síns".	Ketil said to-be may of Simon follow plan his "that he would remember killing Of-Ossur kinsman his".	Ketil said that if Simon followed his plan "that he would remember the killing of his kinsman Ossur".
Símon kvaðst þar eigi mundu ferleg orð um hafa.	Simon said that not would-be fair words about had.	Simon said that there would be no good words to be had about it.
Ketill lét búa skip þeirra og sendi menn á fund Kolbeins stýrimanns og sagði honum tíðindin "og segið honum svo að eg skal fara með máli á hendur Einari því mér eru kunnig grænlensk lög og er eg búinn til við þá.	Ketil had prepared ship theirs and sent men to meet Kolbein steersman and said to-him the-news "and say to-him so that I shall travel with the-matter in hand Einar because to-me they-are known Greenlandic laws and that I prepared to with them.	Ketil had prepared their ship and sent men to meet Kolbein the steersman and tell him the news "and say to him that I will prosecute Einar for the matter in hand, because the Greenlandic laws are known to me, and I am prepared to deal with them.

The Tale of the Greenlanders (II) (The Tale of Einarr Sokkason) (Old Icelandic)

Old Icelandic	Literal	English
Höfum vér og mikinn liðskost ef að oss kemst".	Have we-are and much force of to us come".	We have a great advantage of company if it comes to us".
Símon kvaðst vilja Ketils ráðum fram fara.	Simon said wished-for Ketil's advice from going.	Simon said that he wished for Ketil's advice going forward.
Síðan fór hann og hitti Kolbein, sagði honum vígið og þar með orðsending Ketils og þeir skyldu snúast til liðveislu við þá úr Vestribyggð og sækja til þings þeirra Grænlendinga.	Then went he and found Kolbein, said to-him killing and there with word-sending Ketil's and they should return to support with then out-of Vestribyggd and seek to assembly theirs Greenland.	Then he went and found Kolbein, and told him of the killing, and that they should return to support them at Vestribyggd and attend the Greenland assembly.
Kolbeinn kvaðst koma mundu að vissu ef hann mætti og kvaðst vilja að Grænlendingum yrði það eigi hagkeypi að drepa menn þeirra.	Kolbein said come would to know if he might and said willed to Greenland become that not good-bargain that killing men theirs.	Kolbein said that they would certainly come if he did and said that he wanted the Greenlanders to not have to kill their men.
Ketill tók þegar mál af Símoni og fór með nokkura sveit manna en sagði að þeir kaupmenn skyldu halda skjótt eftir "og hafið varning með yður".	Ketil took them the-matter of Simon and went with some company men but said that they trading-men should rather away afterwards "and have wares with you".	Ketil immediately took the matter with Simon and went with a few men, but said that the merchants should leave quickly "and take your goods with you".
Kolbeinn fór þegar er honum komu þessi orð, bað og félaga sína fara til þings og kveðst þá hafa svo mikla sveit að óvíst væri að Grænlendingar sætu yfir hlut þeirra.	Kolbein went straightaway when he came these words, asked and companions his went to the-assembly and said then had so much company that uncertain was that Greenlanders reconcile over lot theirs.	Kolbein left as soon as these words came to him, and asked his companions to go to the assembly and declared that they had such a large force that it was uncertain that the Greenlanders would be able to handle their lot.
Nú hittust þeir Kolbeinn og Ketill og báru ráð sín saman.	Now found they Kolbein and Ketil and carried advice theirs together.	Now they met Kolbein and Ketil and discussed their advice.
Hvortveggji þeirra var gildur maður.	Each of-them was valid man.	Each of them was a valid man.
Nú fóru þeir og bægði þeim veður og komast þó fram og höfðu mikla sveit manna en þó minni en þeir hugðu.	Now travelled they and prevented them weather and came though from and they-had large company of-men but though less than they thought.	Now they travelled and the weather prevented them but they came through it, and they had a large company of men but less than they thought.

The Tale of the Greenlanders (II) (The Tale of Einarr Sokkason) (Old Icelandic)

Old Icelandic	Literal	English
Nú komu menn til þings.	Now came men to the-assembly.	Now the men came to the assembly.
Sokki var þar kominn Þórisson.	Sokki was there coming Son-of-Thorri.	Sokki Thorisson came there too.
Hann var vitur maður og var þá gamall og mjög tekinn til að gera um mál manna.	He was wise man and was then old and very taken to that doing about matters peoples'.	He was a wise man and was very old by then, and was often taken to dealing with peoples' matters.
Hann gengur á fund þeirra Kolbeins og Ketils og kvaðst vilja leita um sættir.	He went to meet them Kolbein and Ketil and said willed seek about reconciliation.	He went to meet Kolbein and Ketil and said that he wished to seek reconciliation.
"Vil eg bjóðast til",	"Will I offer to",	"I wish to offer",
segir hann, "að gera í milli yðvar.	said he, "to make in between you.	he said, "to make this between you.
Og þótt mér sé meiri vandi á við Einar son minn þá skal það þó um gera er mér og öðrum vitrum mönnum líst nær sanni".	And though I him more custom to with Einar son mine then shall it though about be-done that I and others wise men behold nearer the-truth".	And even though I have a bigger custom with Einar my son, it will still be about what I and other wise men think is closer to the truth".
Ketill kvaðst ætla að þeir mundu málum fram halda til málsfyllingar en fyrirkveðast eigi að taka sættir "en þó er ört að gengið við oss en höfum ekki vanist því hér til að minnka vorn hlut".	Ketil said intended that they would the-matter from hold until the-matter-fulfilling but refusing not to take reconciliation "but though we-are swiftly to going with us but have not custom as here to of decreased our lot".	Ketil said that they intended to take the matter to its conclusion, and refused to rule out a reconciliation "and though we are being treated swiftly, we are not accustomed to reducing our share".
Sokki kveðst ætla að þeir munu eigi jafnt að vígi standa og kvað óvíst að þeir fengju meiri sæmd þó hann dæmdi eigi.	Sokki said supposed that they would not equal to battle stand and said uncertain that they would-get more honour though he judged not.	Sokki said he supposed that they won't be equal if it came to a battle, and said it was uncertain that they would get any more honour though he would not judge the matter.
Kaupmenn gengu að dómi og hafði Ketill mál frammi á hönd Einari.	The-merchants went to court and had Ketil the-case from in hand Einar.	The merchants went to court and Ketil had the case in hand from Einar.
Það mælti Einar:	This said Einar:	Then Einar said:
"Það mun víða spyrjast ef þeir bera oss hér málum"	"It will-be widely known-about if they bear us here cases"	"It will be widely known about if they bear this case here"

The Tale of the Greenlanders (II) (The Tale of Einarr Sokkason) (Old Icelandic)

Old Icelandic	Literal	English
og gekk að dóminum og hleypir upp og fengu þeir eigi haldið.	and went to the-court and released up and got they not holding.	and went into the court and broke it up and they did not get their proceedings.
Þá mælti Sokki:	Then said Sokki:	Then Sokki said:
"Kostur skal enn þess er eg bauð, að sættast og geri eg um málið".	"Choice shall one this that I asked-for, to reconcile and make I about the-case".	"The choice shall be one that I asked for to reconcile, and I shall make the case".
Ketill kvaðst ætla að það mundi nú ekki verða "er þú leggur til yfirbóta það er þó er hinn sami ójafnaður Einars um þetta mál"	Ketil said intended that it would now not be "but you propose to over-compensation it that though is the same unequal Einar about that case"	Ketil said that he supposed that it would now not be "but to propose more compensation would be just as unequal to Einar in the case"
og skildu að því.	and separated to accordingly.	and they separated accordingly.
En því komu kaupmenn eigi úr Vestribyggð til þings að þá var andviðri er þeir voru búnir með tveim skipum.	But then came the-merchants alone from Vestribyggd to the-assembly that then were the-storm that they were prepared with two ships.	But then came the merchants from Vestribyggd to the assembly that were in the storm and prepared with two ships.
En að miðju sumri skyldi sætt gera á Eiði.	But in the-middle of-summer should settled be in Eid.	But in the middle of summer a settlement should be made at Eid.
Þá komu þeir kaupmenn vestan og lögðu að við nes nokkuð og hittust þeir þá allir saman og áttu stefnur.	Then came they the-trading-men western and laid at with headland some and met they then all together and had plans.	Then the merchants came from the west and laid at a certain headland, and they all met up and made their plans.
Þá mælti Kolbeinn að eigi skyldi svo nær hafa gengið um sættirnar ef þeir hefðu allir samt verið "en það þykir mér nú ráð að vér förum allir til þessa fundar með slíkum föngum sem til eru".	Then said Kolbein that not should so close have been about reconciliation if they had all together been "but it seems to-me now advisable that we go all to this meeting with such resources as to they-are".	Then Kolbein said that it should not have been so close to a reconciliation if they had all been together "but it seems to me now advisable that we all go to this meeting with such resources as they are".
Og svo var að þeir fóru og leyndust í leynivogi einum skammt frá biskupsstólnum.	And so was it they went and innermost in hidden-creek one a-short-distance from the-bishop's-seat.	And so it was that they went to the innermost of a certain hidden creek a short distance from the bishop's seat.

The Tale of the Greenlanders (II) (The Tale of Einarr Sokkason) (Old Icelandic)

Old Icelandic	Literal	English
Það bar saman að biskupsstólinum, að hringdi til hámessu og það að Einar Sokkason kom.	It bore together that the-bishop's-seat, that called to high-mass and it that Einar Son-of-Sokki came.	And so it came together that the bishop's seat called a high mass, and Einar Sokkason arrived.
Og er kaupmennirnir heyrðu þetta þá sögðu þeir að mikla skyldi gera virðing til Einars að hringja skal í mót honum og kváðu slík mikil endemi og urðu illa við.	And when the-trading-men heard that then said they that great should be-done worthiness to Einar to call shall in meeting him and saying such great unheard-of and became angry with.	And when the merchants heard that they said that it was paying a great honour to Einar to meet him in such a way, saying that it was a great unheard of, and they became angry with.
Kolbeinn mælti:	Kolbein said:	Kolbein said:
"Verðið eigi illa við þetta því að svo mætti að berast að þetta yrði að líkhringingu áður kveld kæmi".	"Become not ill with this because that so might that bear that this would to funeral-procession before night comes".	"Do not become ill with this, because it might come to be that this will be a funeral procession before night comes".
Nú komu þeir Einar og settust niður í brekku einni.	Now came they Einar and sat down in the-slope alone.	Now came Einar and his men and sat down alone.
Sokki lét fram gripi til virðingar og þá er til gjalds voru ætlaðir.	Sokki laid-out from treasure to worthiness and then when the payment was intended.	Sokki laid out treasures of value that were intended for payment.
Ketill mælti:	Ketil said:	Ketil said:
"Það vil eg að við Hermundur Koðránsson virðum gripina".	"That will I that with Hermund Son-of-Kodran worthiness treasure".	"I wish for Hermund Kodransson and I to value these treasures".
Sokki kvað svo vera skyldu.	Sokki said so being would.	Sokki said that it would be so.
Símon frændi Össurar sýndi á sér óþekktarsvip og reikaði hjá meðan gripagjaldið var sett.	Simon kinsman Of-Ossur showed of himself dishonourable and wandered by while the-artefact-fee was set.	Simon, a kinsman of Ossur, showed himself to be dishonourable and wandered by while the artefacts were being set.
Síðan var fram borin spangabrynja ein forn.	Then was from brought plate-mail one of-old.	Then an ancient plate mal was brought out.
Símon mælti þá:	Simon said then:	Then Simon said:
"Svívirðlega er slíkt boðið fyrir slíkan mann sem Össur var"	"Disgracefully is such offering for such man as Ossur was"	"Such an offering is disgraceful for such a man as Ossur was"

The Tale of the Greenlanders (II) (The Tale of Einarr Sokkason) (Old Icelandic)

Old Icelandic	Literal	English
og kastaði brynjunni á völlinn á burt og gekk upp að þeim er þeir sátu í brekkunni.	and cast the-armour on the-field and way and went up to them as they sat on the-slope.	and he threw the armour away on the field and went up to them as they sat on the slope.
Og er það sáu þeir Grænlendingar þá spretta þeir upp og horfðu forbrekkis og í móti honum Símoni.	And when that saw they Greenlanders then sprang they up and looked downhill and in facing him Simon.	And when the Greenlanders saw that, they sprang up and looked downhill at Simon and faced towards him.
Og því næst gekk Kolbeinn upp hjá þeim er þeir horfðu allir frá og slæst á bak þeim og fór einn frá sínum mönnum.	And then next went Kolbein up beside them when they looked all away-from and slipped in back of-them and went alone from his men.	And then Kolbein went up beside them whey they all looked away and slipped behind them alone from his men.
Og var það jafnsnemma að hann komst á bak Einari og hjó með öxi milli herða honum og Einars öx kom í höfuð Símoni og fengu báðir banasár.	And was it equally-early that he came to back Einar and struck with an-axe between shoulders his and Einar's axe came in head Simon's and got both death-wounds.	And it was just as soon that he got behind Einar and cut him with an axe between his shoulders, and Einar's axe hit Simon in the head and both received mortal wounds.
Einar mælti er hann féll:	Einar said when he fell:	Einar said when he fell:
"Slíks var að von".	"Such was it expected".	"It was so as I expected".
Síðan hljóp Þórður fóstbróðir Einars að Kolbeini og vildi höggva hann en Kolbeinn snaraðist við honum og stakk fram öxarhyrnunni og kom í barkann Þórði og hafði hann þegar bana.	Then ran Thord foster-brother Einar's to Kolbein and wanted to-strike him but Kolbein caught-up with him and thrust from axe-horn and came in throat Thord's and had he instantly killed.	Then Thord, Einar's foster brother, ran to Kolbein and wanted to cut him down, but Kolbein caught up with him and stuck out the axe horn and hit Thord in the throat, killing him instantly.
Síðan slær í bardaga með þeim.	Then struck to battle with them.	Then a battle was struck between them.
Biskup sat hjá Einari og andaðist hann í knjám honum.	Bishop sat beside Einar and died he in knees his.	The bishop sat beside Einar and he died in his lap.
Steingrímur hét maður er það mælti að þeir skyldu gera svo vel að berjast eigi og gekk á milli með nokkura menn en hvorirtveggju voru svo óðir að Steingrímur var lagður sverði í gegnum í þessi hríð.	Steingrim was-named a-man who this said that they should do so well to fight not and went in between with some men but either-side were so angry that Steingrim was laid to-the-sword in through in this time.	There was a man named Steingrim who said that they would do well not to fight and went in between some of the men, but either side was so angry that Steingrim was laid to the sword through him in this time.

The Tale of the Greenlanders (II) (The Tale of Einarr Sokkason) (Old Icelandic)

Old Icelandic	Literal	English
Einar andaðist uppi á brekkunni við búð Grænlendinga.	Einar died up on the-slope by booth The-Greenlanders'.	Einar died up on the slope by the Greenlanders' booth.
Og nú urðu menn sárir mjög og komust þeir Kolbeinn til skips með þrjá sína menn vegna og fóru síðan yfir Einarsfjörð til Skjálgsbúða.	And now became men wounded much and came they Kolbein to ships with three their men slain and went then over Einarsfjord to Skjalgsbud.	And now men became much wounded and Kolbein and his men came to their ships with three men killed and went over to Einarsfjord to Skjalgsbud.
Þar voru kaupskipin og voru þá mjög í búnaði.	There were merchant-ships and were then much in preparations.	The merchant ships were there and they were very much prepared.
Kolbeinn kvað í hafa gerst nokkura róstu "og vil eg ætla að Grænlendingar uni nú eigi betur við en áður".	Kolbein said that had done some uproar "and will I suppose that Greenlanders like now not better with than before".	Kolbein said that there had been some uproar "and I would like to say that the Greenlanders are now no better pleased than before".
Ketill mælti:	Ketil said:	Ketil said:
"Sannyrði gafst þér Kolbeinn",	"True-words gave to-you Kolbein",	"You gave true words Kolbein",
sagði hann, "að vér mundum heyra líkhringinguna áður vér færum í burt og ætla eg að hann Einar sé dauður borinn til kirkju".	said he, "that we would hear the-funeral-procession before we travel to away and suppose I that he Einar is dead carried to the-church".	he said, "that we would hear the funeral procession before we travel away and I suppose that Einar who is dead will be carried to the church".
Kolbeinn kvaðst heldur þannig hafa að stutt.	Kolbein said rather that-way had it supported.	Kolbein said that it was rather that way, that he had supported it.
Ketill mælti:	Ketil said:	Ketil said:
"Þess er von að Grænlendingar muni sækja á vorn fund og kalla eg ráð að menn haldi á búnaði sínum eftir föngum og séu allir á skipum um nætur".	"This is expect that The-Greenlanders will seek to ours meet and call I advice that men hold of equipment theirs after resources and are all to ships about night".	"It is expected that the Greenlanders will seek to meet us, and I advise that the men take hold of their equipment and resources and all stay on the ships overnight".
Og svo gerðu þeir.	And so did they.	And so they did.
Sokki harmaði mjög þessi tíðindi og bað menn fulltingis að veita sér vígsgengi.	Sokki harmed much this news and asked men assistance to grant him in-battle.	Sokki was much harmed by this news and asked the men to grant him assistance in battle.

The Tale of the Greenlanders (II) (The Tale of Einarr Sokkason) (Old Icelandic)

Old Icelandic	Literal	English
6	**6**	**6**
Hallur hét maður.	Hall was-named man.	There was a man named Hall.
Hann bjó að Sólarfjöllum, vitur maður og góður bóndi.	He lived at Solarfjoll, wise man and good farmer.	He lived at Solarfjoll, he was a wise man and a good farmer.
Hann var í liði með Sokka og kom síðast með sínu liði.	He was in company with Sokki and came last with his team.	He was in company with Sokki and was the last to come to his team.
Hann mælti til Sokka:	He said to Sokki:	He said to Sokki:
"Ekki vænleg líst mér þín ætlan að leggja smáskipum að stórskipum við slíkan viðbúnað sem eg hygg að þeir munu hafa.	"Not hopeful behold I your intention to lay small-ships to large-ships with such preparation as I think that they shall have.	"I am not hopeful of your intention to lay small ships against large ships with such preparations as I think they will have.
En eg veit eigi hversu traust lið er þú hefir en allir vaskir menn munu vel gefast en hinir munu hlífast meir, og verða höfuðsmenn fyrir það uppgefnir og horfir þá enn þunglegar vor málahlutur en áður.	But I know not how-so trust team is you have but all brave men should well give but others should protect more, and become head-men for that up-given and where then but the-more-difficult our matter-lot than before.	But I don't know how strong a team you have, but all the good men will give well, but the others will be more careful, and the leaders will be exhausted because of it, and then our affairs will be even more difficult than before.
Nú sýnist mér ráð ef menn skulu að leggja að eiðar fari fram að hver maður skuli annaðhvort hér falla eða hafa sigur".	Now seems to-me advisable if men shall to allow that oath go from to each man shall other-either here fall or have victory".	Now it seems to me that if men are to make an oath, each man shall either fall here or be victorious".
En við þessu orð Halls dignuðu menn mjög.	But with this word Hall's pride lessened much.	But at this word of Hall's, peoples' pride lessened much.
Sokki mælti:	Sokki said:	Sokki said:
"Eigi munum vér þó skilja við þetta, að ósett sé málunum".	"Not shall we though part with this, that unsettled is the-matter".	"However, we will not part with this, that things are not settled".
Hallur kvaðst mundu leita um sættir milli þeirra og kallaði á kaupmenn og mælti:	Hall said should seek about reconciliation between them and called the trading-men and spoke:	Hall said that they should seek reconciliation between them and called the merchants and spoke:

The Tale of the Greenlanders (II) (The Tale of Einarr Sokkason) (Old Icelandic)

Old Icelandic	Literal	English
"Hvort skal mér fritt að ganga á fund yðvarn?"	"Whether shall I peace to go to meet with-you?"	"Should I be at peace to go to a meeting with you?"
Þeir Kolbeinn og Ketill svara að honum skyldi fritt.	They Kolbein and Ketil answered that to-him should-be peace.	Kolbein and his men answered that he should be at peace.
Síðan hitti hann þá og lét nauðsyn að málum væri sett eftir slík stórvirki.	Then met he then and had necessary to matter should-be settled after such great-works.	Then he met them and made it necessary that matters should be settled after such great deeds.
Þeir kváðust nú búnir við hvoru sem aðrir vildu, kváðu af þeim landsmönnum allan þennan ójafnað staðið hafa "en nú er þú sýnir svo mikla góðgirnd þá unum vér því að þú gerir í milli vor".	They said now prepared with each as other willed, saying of them lands-men all then un-equal stood have "but now are you showed so much good-will then among us therefore that you make to between us".	They said they were ready to do whatever others wanted, they said of those countrymen who have been through this uneven situation "but now you are showing so much kindness, we hope that you do among us".
Hann kvaðst eftir því gera mundu og dæma er honum sýndist réttlegast hversu sem hvorum líkaði.	He said after therefore be-done should and deemed that to-him seemed correctness how-so as each liked.	He said that he would do what he thought was the right thing to do, however everyone liked it.
Síðan var þetta fyrir Sokka borið.	Then was that for Sokki borne.	Then this was put before Sokki.
Hann kveðst og mundu una umdæmi Halls.	He said and would content about-judgement Hall's.	He said that he would be content with Hall's judgement about it.
Kaupmenn skyldu um nætur að búnaði sínum vera og kváðu Sokka ekki annað líka en þeir yrðu í burtu sem fyrst "en ef þeir seinka búnað sinn og gera mér skapraun í því þá er vís von að þeir skulu bótalausir ef þeir verða teknir".	The-trading-men should about the-night to equipment theirs be and said Sokki not other like but they be to away as first "but if they delay preparations theirs and make to-me temperament in because then be aware hope that they shall boat-lose if they become taken".	The merchants had to make their preparations through the night and Sokki said that there was no other way except that they were to be away as soon as possible "but if they delay in their preparations and make to my temperament, then they shall lose their boat if they become taken".
Nú skildu þeir að því og var á sáttarfund kveðið.	Now separated they that accordingly and were in peace-meeting declared.	Now they separated accordingly and a reconciliation meeting was declared.
Ketill mælti:	Ketil said:	Ketil said:

The Tale of the Greenlanders (II) (The Tale of Einarr Sokkason) (Old Icelandic)

Old Icelandic	Literal	English
"Ekki horfir skjótlega búnaður vor en vistföng þverra heldur og er það mitt ráð að leita eftir vistunum og veit eg hvar sá maður býr er mikinn mat á og kalla eg ráð að sækja eftir".	"Not looks shortly equipment ours but resources running-out rather and is it my advice to seek after provisions and know I where so man prepared is much food to and call I advice to seek after".	"It does not look like our equipment will be prepared shortly, and resources are running out, and it is my advice to seek provisions, and I know where there is a man who has much food, and I advise we seek him out".
Þeir kváðust þess albúnir.	They said this all-prepared.	They said they were all ready.
Síðan hlupu þeir upp eina nátt frá skipum, þrír tigir manna saman, allir vopnaðir, og komu að bænum og var þar autt allt.	Then ran they up one night from the-ship, three tens of-men together, all weaponed, and came to dwelling and were there empty all.	They hurried up one night from the ship, and thirty men together, all armed, came to the dwelling but it was all empty.
Þórarinn hét bóndi sá er þar bjó.	Thorarin was-named a-farmer that was there settled.	Thorarin was the name of the farmer that was settled there.
Ketill mælti:	Ketil said:	Ketil said:
"Eigi hefir mitt ráð vel gefist"	"Not has my advice well given"	"My advice has not given well"
og fara síðan í burt frá bænum og ofan á leið til skipa og var þar hrísótt er þeir fóru.	and went then to away from the-dwelling and over to the-way to the-ships and were there shrubs where they went.	and then went away from the dwelling and over to the ships, and there were shrubs along where they went.
Þá mælti Ketill:	Then said Ketil:	Then Ketil said:
"Syfjar mig",	"Sleepy me",	"I feel sleepy",
sagði hann, "og verð eg að sofa".	said he, "and deserve I to sleep".	he said, "and I deserve to sleep".
Þeir kváðu það ekki mjög ráðlegt	They said that not much advisable	They said that it was not advisable,
en þó lagðist hann niður og sofnaði en þeir sátu yfir.	but though laid he down and slept while they sat over.	but he laid down and slept while they sat and watched over.
Litlu síðar vaknaði hann og mælti:	Little later awoke he and said:	A little later he awoke and said:
"Mart hefir fyrir mig borið.	"Many have before me brought.	"Much has brought before me.

The Tale of the Greenlanders (II) (The Tale of Einarr Sokkason) (Old Icelandic)

Old Icelandic	Literal	English
Hvað mun varða þótt vér kippum upp hríslu þessi er hér er undir höfði mér?"	What should happen though we jerk up clump this that here is under head mine?"	What would happen if we jerked up this clump that is here under my head?"
Þeir kipptu upp hríslunni og var þar undir jarðhús mikið.	They pulled up the-branch and was there under earth-house great.	They pulled up the branches and under it was a great cave.
Ketill mælti:	Ketil said:	Ketil said:
"Vitum fyrst hvað hér er fanga".	"Know-we first what here is provisions".	"We should know first what provisions are here".
Þeir fundu þar sex tigi sláturgripa og tólf vættir smjörs, skreið mikla.	They found there six tens carcasses and twelve weights of-butter, fish much.	They found sixty carcasses, twelve weights of butter, and a lot of fish.
"Vel er það",	"Well is that",	"That is good",
sagði Ketill, "að eg hefi eigi villt upp borið fyrir yður".	said Ketil, "that I have not wildly up presented for you".	said Ketil, "that I have not wildly brought up for you".
Nú fara þeir til skips með feng sinn.	Now went they to the-ships with provisions theirs.	Now they went to the ships with their provisions.
Nú líður að sáttarfundinum og komu hvorirtveggju til þess fundar, kaupmenn og landsmenn.	Now passed to reconciliation-meeting and came either-side to this meeting, trading-men and lands-men.	Now it passed to the reconciliation meeting, and both sides came to the meeting, the merchants and the landsmen.
Þá mælti Hallur:	Then said Hall:	Then Hall said:
"Sú er sáttargerð mín yðvar í milli að eg vil að á standist víg Össurar og Einars en fyrir manna minna mun koma sektir Austmanna, að þeir skulu hér ekki eiga vist né væri.	"So is settlement mine yours in between that I will to a to-stand slaying Ossur and Einar but for men less would come penalty Eastern-men, that they shall here not own resources nor should-they.	"This is my settlement among you, that I wish for the killing of Ossur to stand for that of Einar, but for the loss of men, the Norwegians shall not be here nor shall they own resources here.
Þau víg skulu og jöfn vera, Steingríms bónda og Símonar, Kráks austmanns og Þorfinns Grænlendings, Víghvats austmanns og Bjarnar Grænlendings, Þóris og Þórðar.	Those killings shall and even be, Steingrim's farmer and Simon, Krak the-Easterner and Thorfin The-Greenlander, Vighvats the-Easterner and Bjarn The-Greenlander, Thori and Thord.	Those killings shall be even, Steingrim the farmer and Simon, Krak the Easterner and Thorfin the Greenlander, Vighvats the Easterner and Bjarn the Greenlander, Thori and Thord.

The Tale of the Greenlanders (II) (The Tale of Einarr Sokkason) (Old Icelandic)

Old Icelandic	Literal	English
Nú er einn óbættur vor maður er Þóarinn heitir, ómegðarmaður.	Now that one uncompensated our man that Thorarin is-named, poor-man.	Now one of our men is uncompensated, named Thorarin, a poor man.
Hann skal fé bæta".	He shall wealth be-compensated".	He shall be compensated with wealth".
Sokki hvað sér þungt gerðir líka og svo öðrum Grænlendingum er þannig fór um mannjafnað.	Sokki that himself unhappy made alike and so other Greenlanders that that-way went about equal-man.	Sokki said that he was unhappy with how it was done that Greenlanders and the other men were equally paired in that way.
Hallur kvaðst ætla að þar muni þó staðar nema hans ummæli	Hall said intend that there should though stand taking his about-matter	Hall said he intended that it should though stand as he took the matter,
og við það skildu þeir.	and with that separated they.	and with that they separated.
Síðan rak ís að og þakti alla fjörðu og hugðu Grænlendingar þá gott til ef þeir mættu taka þá og þeir færu eigi svo burt sem mælt var.	Then drifted ice to and covered all the-fjord and thought The-Greenlanders then good to of they might take then and they travel alone so away as told were.	Then ice drifted in and covered the whole fjord, and the Greenlanders thought it would be good if they could take them and they didn't go away as they were told.
En við það sjálft að mánaðarmótið kom þá rak í burt allan ísinn og gaf kaupmönnum burt af Grænlandi og skildu við það.	But with that itself to month's-end came then drove to way all ice and gave the-trading-men away of Greenland and separated with it.	But as soon as the end of the month came, all the ice was swept away and the merchants left Greenland and parted with it.
Þeir komu við Noreg.	They came to Norway.	They came to Norway.
Kolbeinn hafði haft einn hvítabjörn af Grænlandi og fór með dýrið á fund Haralds konungs gilla og gaf honum og tjáði fyrir konungi hversu þungs hlutar Grænlendingar voru af verðir og færði þá mjög í róg.	Kolbein had had one white-bear of Greenland and went with the-animal to meet Harald the-king residence and gave him and told for the-kind how-so heavily lot The-Greenlanders were of being and brought them much to slander.	Kolbein had had one white bear from Greenland and took the animal to King Harald's meeting and gave it to him and expressed to the king how much of a burden the Greenlanders were becoming and brought them into great slander.
En konungur spurði annað síðar og þótti honum Kolbeinn hafa fals fyrir sig borðið og komu engi laun fyrir dýrið.	But the-king learned otherwise later and thought he Kolbein had a-falsehood for him bore-up and came no reward for the-animal.	But the king learned otherwise later and it seemed to him that Kolbein had borne up a falsehood for him and there was no reward for the animal.

The Tale of the Greenlanders (II) (The Tale of Einarr Sokkason) (Old Icelandic)

Old Icelandic	Literal	English
Síðan hljóp Kolbeinn í flokk með Sigurði slembidjákn og gekk inn að Haraldi konungi gilla og veitti honum áverka.	Then ran Kolbein to grouped with Sigurd the-false-deacon and went in to Harald the-king residence and granted to-him a-wound.	Then Kolbein hurried to group with Sigurd the false deacon, and went into King Harald's residence and gave him a wound.
Og síðan er þeir fóru fyrir Danmörk og sigldu mjög en Kolbeinn var á eftirbáti en veður hvasst þá sleit frá bátinn og drukknaði Kolbeinn.	And then when they travelled to Denmark and sailed much but Kolbein was in the-boat-behind but weather stormy then tore-up from the-boat and drowned Kolbein.	And then when they travelled to Denmark their sail was carried much, but Kolbein was in the boat behind in stormy weather which then tore up the boat behind and Kolbein drowned.
En þeir Hermundur komu til Íslands til ættjarða sinna.	But they The-Hermunds came to Iceland to homelands theirs.	But Hermund and the others came to Iceland, their homeland.
Og lýkur þar þessi sögu.	And ends here this saga.	And here ends this saga.

Word List (Old Icelandic to English)

Word List (Old Icelandic to English)

Old Icelandic	English

A, a

að	a, at, by, in, it, of, that, the, to
aðrir	other
af	from, from, of, of, off
aflað	gain
aftur	back
agir	desirable
albúnir	all-prepared
alla	all
allan	all
allir	all, all
allmjög	all-great
allt	all
allvel	all-well, all-well
andaðist	died, died
andviðri	the-storm
annað	another, another, anything-else, other, other, otherwise
annaðhvort	other-either
annarra	other
Arnald	Arnald (name)
Arnaldur	Arnald (name)
Arnbjarnar	Arnbjarn (name), Arnbjarn (name), Arnbjarnar (name)
Arnbjörn	Arnbjorn (name), Arnbjorn (name)
atburði	events
atgervi	plan
auðið	possible
austmaður	Eastern-man
austmanna	Eastern-men
austmanns	the-Easterner, the-Easterner
austmenn	Eastern-men
autt	empty

Á, á

á	a, about, and, as, at, in, of, on, out, that, the, to
áðu	that
áður	after, before
árós	river-mouth
átt	had, had, owned
áttu	had, have
áverka	a-wound

Æ, æ

æðimaður	of-mind
æpa	shouting
ætla	intend, intended, suppose, supposed
ætlaðir	intended
ætlan	intention
ætluðu	supposed
ætti	had
ættjarða	homelands

B, b

bað	asked, bid
báðir	both
báðu	asked
bæ	a-farm
bæði	asked
bægði	prevented
bæn	bidding, prayers
bænar	prayers
bændur	farmers
bænum	dwelling, the-dwelling
bæta	be-compensated
bak	back
bana	death, killed
banahögg	death-blow
banasár	death-wounds
bar	bore
bardaga	battle
barkann	throat

90

Word List (Old Icelandic to English)

Old Icelandic	English	Old Icelandic	English
báru	carried	*bótalausir*	boat-lose
bátinn	the-boat	*Brandur*	Brand (name)
bauð	asked-for, invited	*brang*	chest
beiddi	bid	*Brattahlíð*	Brattahlid (place)
bein	bones	*bréfum*	briefs
beinum	bones	*brekku*	the-slope
bera	bear	*brekkunni*	the-slope
berast	bear	*brenndu*	burned
berdreyman	clear-dreams	*bróðir*	brother
berjast	fight	*brotið*	broken
best	best	*brott*	away
betur	better	*brugðið*	upset
biskuð	the-bishop	*brynjunni*	the-armour
biskup	a-bishop, bishop, the-bishop	*búa*	prepared
		búð	booth
biskupi	the-bishop	*búið*	prepared, settled
biskups	bishop, the-bishop, the-bishop's	*búinn*	prepared
		búnað	preparations
biskupsefni	the-bishop-elect	*búnaði*	equipment, preparations
biskupslaust	bishop-less		
biskupsstólinum	the-bishop's-seat	*búnaður*	equipment
biskupsstóll	bishop's-seat	*búnir*	prepared
biskupsstólnum	the-bishop's-seat	*burt*	away, way
biskupsstólsins	bishop's-seat	*burtu*	away
biskupsvígslu	bishop's-appointment	*byggðina*	the-settlement
bjarga	rescuing	*býr*	prepared
bjargar	rescue	*byrinn*	bearing
Bjarnar	Bjarn (name)		
bjarndýri	a-bear		
bjó	lived, prepared, settled		

D, d

Old Icelandic	English
bjóðast	offer
björg	rocks
bjóst	prepared
boðið	offering
bokki	buck
bol	the-trunk
bónda	farmer
bóndi	a-farmer, farmer
borð	boards, the-tables
borðið	bore-up, the-table
borðum	the-tables
borið	borne, brought, presented
borin	brought
borinn	carried

Old Icelandic	English
dæma	deemed
dæmdi	judged
dag	the-day
Danmerkur	Denmark (place)
Danmörk	Denmark (place)
dauða	dead
dauður	dead
daun	the-dead
dignuðu	pride
dómi	court, the-court
dóminum	the-court
dómur	judgement
dómurinn	the-judgement
dráp	killing
draum	dream

Word List (Old Icelandic to English)

Old Icelandic	English
drauminn	the-dream
drepa	killing
dreymdi	dreamed
drukknaði	drowned
duga	aided
dyljast	hiding
dýrið	the-animal

E, e

eða	but, or
eðli	nature
ef	if, of
efldur	strengthened
eftir	after, afterwards, followed, following, later, remaining
eftirbáti	the-boat-behind
eftirbátinn	the-after-boat
eg	I
eið	oath
eiðar	oath
Eiði	Eid (place)
eiðrofa	breach-of-oath
eiga	have, not, own
eigi	alone, no, not
eign	property
eigna	property
eignum	owning
ein	one
eina	one
einangur	alone-going
Einar	Einar (name)
Einari	Einar (name)
Einars	Einar (name), Einar's, Einar's (name)
Einarsfjörð	Einarsfjord (place)
einhverju	one-occasion
einn	a, alone, one
einni	alone
einræði	self-will
einu	one
einum	one
Eiríksfjörð	Eriksfjord (place)
ekki	none, not

Old Icelandic	English
eldstóar	fire-place
en	and, as, but, than, while
enda	and
endemi	unheard-of
engi	no, no-one
engum	no
enn	but, one, still
er	are, as, be, but, is, it, that, the, then, was, we-are, what, when, where, who, with
erfitt	difficult
erindi	errand
erindis	errand
erkibiskup	the-archbishop
erkibiskups	archbishop
eru	are, are-they, they-are, were
eruð	are
Eyjafjöllum	Eyjafjolls (place)

F, f

fá	get
færa	bring
færði	brought
færi	going, go-to
færu	travel
færum	travel
fagra	the-fairest
fálega	coolly
falla	fall
fallinn	fallen, weak
fals	a-falsehood
fang	resources
fanga	provisions
fangið	to-catch
fangs	captivity
fara	going, travel, went, went
fari	go
farið	going
fastmæli	opinion
fé	wealth
feðgar	father-and-son

92

Word List (Old Icelandic to English)

Old Icelandic	English
fégjöfum	fee-gifts
féið	wealth
fékk	got, went
félaga	companions
félagar	companions
féll	fell
feng	provisions
fengju	would-get
fengu	got
fer	went
ferð	journey
ferjuna	the-ferry
ferleg	fair
festa	fix
févon	fee-trust
fimmtán	fifteen
fjár	money
fjárfundinn	wealth-finding
fjarri	far
fjölmenni	following-men, many-people
fjörðinn	fjord
fjörðu	the-fjord
fleiri	more
flokk	grouped
fólk	folk
föngum	resources
fór	for, travelled, went
forbrekkis	downhill
forn	of-old
forsjá	foresight
fóru	travelled, went
fórum	travel, travelled
förum	go
fóstbróðir	foster-brother
fótum	feet
frá	away-from, from
frænda	kinsman
frændi	kinsman
frændur	kinsmen
fram	from
framkvæmd	execution
frammi	from
fremi	provided
fréttu	found-out
fritt	peace
fróði	learned
fulltingis	assistance
fulltingja	fulfil
fulltings	help
fund	meet, meeting
fundar	meet, meeting
fundið	found
fundu	found
fúsari	willing
fylgdi	follow, followed
fylgdinni	following
fylgir	followed
fyrir	before, for, foremost, through, to
fyrirgert	before-done
fyrirkveðast	refusing
fyrr	for
fyrst	first, firstly
fýsa	desire

G, g

Old Icelandic	English
gaf	gave
gafst	gave
gamall	old
ganga	go, going, went
garða	Gardar (place)
gefa	give
gefast	give
gefist	given
gefnar	given
gegna	pass
gegnt	opposite
gegnum	through
gekk	went
gengið	been, going, walked
gengu	went
gengur	went
gera	be, be-done, do, doing, done, make, to-do, to-give
gerði	did
gerðir	made
gerðist	became
gerðu	did, done, to-do

Word List (Old Icelandic to English)

Old Icelandic	English
geri	make
gerir	make
gersemi	treasure
gerst	done
gert	done, made
get	get
getu	ability
gildur	valid
gilla	residence
gjalds	payment
góð	good
góða	good
góðan	good
góðgirnd	good-will
góður	good
göngu	going
Görðum	Gardar (place)
gott	good
grænland	Greenland (place)
Grænlendinga	Greenland (place), Greenlanders (name), the-Greenlanders'
grænlendingar	Greenlanders (name), the-Greenlanders
grænlendings	the-Greenlander
Grænlendingum	Greenland (place), Greenlanders (name)
grænlensk	Greenlandic (name)
grænlenskum	Greenlandic (name)
grænlenskur	a-Greenlander
grafa	grave
grafin	in-the-grave
greiða	assistance
greiðast	paying
greiðslu	compensation
gripagjaldið	the-artefact-fee
gripi	treasure
gripina	treasure
guði	priest
guðs	god's

H, h

Old Icelandic	English
hægra	right
haf	sea
hafa	had, has, have
hafði	had
hafi	had
hafið	have
hafskip	sea-going-ship
haft	had, has
hag	circumstances
hagkeypi	good-bargain
hagur	handy
halda	hold, rather, to-hold
haldi	hold
haldið	holding
halls	Hall's, Hall's (name)
Hallur	Hall (name)
hamarrifu	crags
hámessu	high-mass
hann	he, him
hans	him, his, its
haraldi	Harald (name)
haralds	Harald (name)
harmaði	harmed
hásetar	the-crew
haustum	autumn
hefði	had
hefðu	had
hefi	have
hefir	has, has-been, have
hegna	protected
heim	home
heimamaður	house-man
heimilisprestur	local-priest
heimta	carry
heimti	presented
heita	be-called
heitir	is-named
heitukötlum	boiling-cauldrons
héldu	held
heldur	rather
hendi	hand
hendur	hand
henta	suitable
hér	here
herða	shoulders
Hermundur	Hermund (name), the-Hermunds (name)
herra	sir

Word List (Old Icelandic to English)

Old Icelandic	English
hést	promised
hét	named, was-named
heyra	hear
heyrðu	heard
heyrt	heard
hið	the, then
hingað	here
hinir	others
hinn	the
hinu	the
hitta	find
hitti	found, met
hittust	found, met
hjá	beside, by
hjó	struck
hlaðna	loaded
hlaupa	running
hleypið	discharge
hleypir	released
hleypur	ran
hlífast	protect
hlítt	satisfactory
hljóp	ran
hlupu	ran
hlut	lot, part
hlutar	lot
hlutum	things
hnjóðhamar	hammer
höfðaskip	a-headed-ship
höfðaskipið	head-ship
höfði	head
höfðingja	chieftains
höfðu	had, had-they, they-had
höfuð	head
höfuðgjarnt	headstrong
höfuðsmenn	head-men
höfum	have
hoggið	struck
höggva	to-strike
holdi	flesh
Holtavatnsós	Holtavatnsos (place)
hönd	hand
höndum	handling
honum	he, him, his, to-him
horfðu	looked
horfir	looks, where
hríð	time
hrinda	repel
hringdi	called
hringja	call
hríslu	clump
hríslunni	the-branch
hrísótt	shrubs
hugðu	thought
hugi	his-mind
hugur	mind
hún	she
hurðina	the-door
húsa	house
hvað	that, what
hvar	where
hvasst	stormy
hver	each, who
hverfa	turn
hverju	how
hversu	how-so
hvítabjörn	white-bear
Hvítserk	Hvitserk (name)
hvorirtveggju	either-side
hvors	which
hvort	each, whether
hvortveggji	each
hvoru	each
hvorum	each
hygg	think

I, i

Old Icelandic	English
illa	angry, ill
illt	ill
inn	in
inni	in
innsiglum	seals

Í, í

Old Icelandic	English
í	about, and, at, in, into, of, on, that, to
ís	ice

Word List (Old Icelandic to English)

Old Icelandic	English
Ísa-Steingrímur	Isa-Steingrim (name)
ísinn	ice
Íslandi	Iceland (place)
Íslands	Iceland (place)

J, j

Old Icelandic	English
jafnsnemma	equally-early
jafnt	equal
jarða	earthed
jarðhús	earth-house
játtuðu	agreed
jöfn	even
jöklinum	a-glacier
jöklum	glaciers
Jórsalafari	Jerusalem-Traveller (name)

K, k

Old Icelandic	English
kæmi	comes
Kálfsson	son-of-Kalf (name)
kalla	call, claim
kallaði	called
kallar	called
kambi	comb
kann	can
kastaði	cast
kaupmenn	the-merchants, the-trading-men, trading-men
kaupmennirnir	the-trading-men
kaupmönnum	the-trading-men, trading-men
kaupskip	merchant-ship
kaupskipið	merchant-ship
kaupskipin	merchant-ships
kaupum	a-deal
kemst	come
kennimanns	teaching
kennimenn	priests
kerling	old-woman
kerlingu	the-old-woman
Ketil	Ketil (name)
Ketill	Ketil (name)
Ketils	Ketil (name), Ketil's (name)
Kiðjabergs	Kidjaberg (place)
kilinum	the-keel
kipptu	pulled
kippum	jerk
kirkju	church, the-church
kirkjugarðsins	churchyard
kirkjumessu	church-mass
kirkjuna	the-church
kirkjuvegginn	church-wall
klerkur	cleric
knjám	knees
Koðránsson	son-of-Kodran (name)
Kolbein	Kolbein (name)
Kolbeini	Kolbein (name)
Kolbeinn	Kolbein (name)
Kolbeins	Kolbein (name)
kom	came
koma	come
komast	came, come
komið	come
kominn	come, coming
komst	came
komu	came
komust	came
konung	the-king
konungi	the-kind, the-king
konungs	the-king, the-king's
konungsbréfum	the-king's-brief
konungur	the-king
kostur	choice
Kráks	Krak (name)
kunni	known
kunnig	known
kvað	said
kvaðst	said
kváðu	said, saying
kváðust	said
kveðið	declared
kveðja	called
kveðst	said
kveld	night
kyrrrlátir	still
kyrrt	still

Word List (Old Icelandic to English)

Old Icelandic	English

L, l

Old Icelandic	English
lá	lay
lagðist	laid
lagður	laid
land	land
Landeyjum	the-Landeys (place)
landi	the-land
landið	the-land
landsins	the-lands
landsmenn	lands-men
landsmönnum	lands-men
Langanes	Langanes (place)
láta	lay-out
laun	reward
legðu	put
leggja	allow, have, lay
leggur	propose
legið	laid
leið	the-way
leit	looked
leita	seek
lengi	long
lengra	longer
lengur	longer
lést	had
lét	had, laid, laid-out
létu	had
leyndust	innermost
leynivogi	hidden-creek
leysti	released
lið	team
liði	company, team
liðið	passed
liðskost	force
liðu	passed
líður	passed
liðveislu	support
líftjóni	loss-of-life
lík	the-body
líka	alike, like
líkaði	liked
líkar	like, likes
líkast	likely
líkhringingu	funeral-procession
líkhringinguna	the-funeral-procession
líkindi	alike
líkinu	the-body
líklegast	likely
líkum	bodies
líst	behold
lítið	little
lítil	little
lítillæti	humility
litlu	little
lítt	little
lög	law, laws
lögðu	laid
lögum	law
Lund	Lund (place)
lýkur	ends

M, m

Old Icelandic	English
maður	a-man, man
mæla	badly
mælt	told
mælti	said, spoke
mæltu	said
mætti	might
mættir	might
mættu	might
maklegast	most
mal	the-matter
mál	a-case, case, matter, matters, the-case, the-matter
málahlutur	matter-lot
máli	discuss, the-matter
málið	the-case
málsfyllingar	the-matter-fulfilling
málum	case, cases, matter, the-matter
málunum	the-matter
mánaðarmótið	month's-end
mann	a-man, man, the-man
manna	man's, men, of-men, peoples'

Word List (Old Icelandic to English)

Old Icelandic	English	Old Icelandic	English
manndómsleysi	meanness	minnka	decreased
mannhættu	dangerous	mínum	mine, my
manni	man	misst	lost
manninum	this-man	mitt	my
mannjafnað	equal-man	mjög	much, very
mannshræ	dead-body, human-body	mönnum	men, the-men
		morguninn	morning
mannvænlegur	a-friendly	mót	meet, meeting
margt	many	móti	facing
mart	many	mun	may, should, will, will-be, would
mat	food		
mátti	might	muna	remember
með	with	mundi	would
meðallagi	moderately	mundu	should, would, would-be
meðan	as-long-as, while		
mega	may	mundum	would
megin	sides	muni	should, will, would
megri	meagre	munni	mouth
mein	disease, harm	munt	would
meir	more	muntu	shall-you
meira	more	munu	shall, should, would
meiri	more	munum	shall
menn	lessened, men, people		

N, n

Old Icelandic	English
mér	I, me, mine, to-me
messu	mass
mest	most	náðu	reached
mestur	the-most	næði	get
metnir	important	nær	as-far, close, nearer
metorð	esteem	næst	next
miðju	the-middle	nætur	night, the-night
mig	me	náir	getting
mikið	a-great, great, many, much	nátt	night
		nauðsyn	necessary, needs
mikil	great, much	né	nor
mikill	great, much	neðan	below
mikils	much	nema	taking
mikinn	much	nenna	bothered
mikla	great, large, much	nes	headland
miklir	much	niður	down
miklu	much	Njálsson	son-of-Njal (name)
milli	between	nokkuð	some
mín	mine	nokkur	some
minn	mine	nokkura	some
minna	less	nokkurar	some
minni	less, mine	nokkurn	some

Word List (Old Icelandic to English)

Old Icelandic	English
nokkurra	something
nokkuru	some
nokkurum	some
Noreg	Norway (place)
noregi	Norway (place)
Noregs	Norway (place)
norrænir	Nordic (name)
norrænn	Nordic (name)
nótt	the-night
nú	not, now
nytjum	use

O, o

Old Icelandic	English
Odda	Odda (place)
of	of
ofan	above, over
ofsa	violence
ofsamenn	overbearing-men
oft	often
og	also, and
orð	a-word, word, words
orða	words
orðið	become, have-become
orðinn	the-words
orðsending	word-sending
oss	to-us, us

Ó, ó

Old Icelandic	English
óbættur	uncompensated
óbyggðir	un-settled
óbyggðum	the-unsettled-land
óðir	angry
óforsjáll	impulsive
ófús	reluctant
ójafnað	un-equal
ójafnaður	unequal
ómegðarmaður	poor-man
ósæmd	dishonourable
ósett	unsettled
óþekktarsvip	dishonourable, ungraceful

Old Icelandic	English
óvirðing	un-worthy
óvíst	uncertain

Ö, ö

Old Icelandic	English
öðru	another, other
öðrum	other, others
öllu	all
öllum	all, ill
ört	swiftly
Össur	Ossur (name)
Össurar	of-Ossur (name), Ossur (name)
Össuri	Ossur (name)
öx	an-axe, axe
öxarhyrnunni	axe-horn
öxi	an-axe, axe

R, r

Old Icelandic	English
ráð	advice, advisable, decide
ráða	advice
ráðast	arrange, be-arranged
ráðist	advise
ráðlegt	advisable
ráðum	advice
rak	drifted, drove
raunar	actually
réð	commanded
réðist	deal
réðst	ruled
refsa	punish
reið	rode
reiðisvipur	angry
reiður	angry
reikaði	wandered
rétt	rights
réttara	more-correct
réttlegast	correctness
reyndust	gave-him
rísi	giants
rjúfa	break-open
róg	slander

Word List (Old Icelandic to English)

Old Icelandic	English
róstu	uproar
rufu	broke-up, tore-up

S, s

Old Icelandic	English
sá	saw, so, that
sægarpur	sea-champion
sækja	seek, sought
sæmd	honour
sæmdar	honour
sæmdir	honour
Sæmundi	Saemund (name)
Sæmundur	Saemund (name)
sætt	settled
sættast	reconcile
sættir	reconciliation
sættirnar	reconciliation
sætu	reconcile
sagði	said, said
sagt	said, said, told
sakir	sake
sáluhjápar	souls
sálum	souls
sama	same
saman	altogether, together
sami	same
samt	the-same, together
sanni	the-truth
sannlegast	truthfully
sannyrði	true-words
sárir	wounded
sat	sat
satt	TRUE
sáttarfund	peace-meeting
sáttarfundinum	reconciliation-meeting
sáttargerð	settlement
sátu	sat, sat
sáu	saw, saw
sauminn	the-seam
sé	being, him, is, this, to-be
segið	say
segir	said, say, says
segja	say
seinka	delay
sektir	penalty
sem	as
senda	send
sendi	sent
sendilegastan	to-be-sent
sér	as, him, himself, them, themselves
sett	sat, set, settled
setti	set
settur	set
settust	sat
séu	are, they-are
sex	six
síðan	then
síðar	later
síðast	last
sig	him, himself
sígast	sinking
sigldu	sailed
sigur	victory
Sigurði	Sigurd (name)
Sigurður	Sigurd (name)
Símon	Simon (name)
Símonar	Simon (name)
símoni	Simon (name), Simon's (name)
sín	him, his, theirs
sína	his, their, themselves
sinn	his, theirs
sinna	his, theirs
sinni	his, they
síns	his
sínu	his, theirs
sínum	his, theirs
sitja	sit
sitt	his, this
sjá	saw, see
sjálfs	himself
sjálft	itself
sjást	looked
skal	shall
skála	cabin
skáladyrnar	the-door
skálann	the-cabin, the-hut
skálanum	the-cabin
skammt	a-short-distance

Word List (Old Icelandic to English)

Old Icelandic	English
skaplyndi	temper
skapraun	temperament
skerast	cutting
skildu	parted, separated
skilja	part
skip	ship
skipa	the-ships
skipi	ship, the-ship
skipið	ship, the-ship
skipinu	the-ship
skips	ships, the-ships
skiptu	divided
skipum	ships, the-ship
skipverjar	crew
Skjálgsbúða	Skjalgsbud (place)
skjótlega	shortly
skjótt	away
skreið	fish
skuli	shall
skulu	shall
skyldi	should, should-be
skyldir	should
skyldu	should, would
slær	struck
slæst	slipped
sláturgripa	carcasses
sleit	tore-up
slembidjákn	the-false-deacon
slík	such
slíka	such
slíkan	such
slíks	such
slíkt	such
slíku	such
slíkum	such
slógu	strike
smáskipum	small-ships
smjörs	of-butter
snaraðist	caught-up
snerist	turned
snúast	return
sofa	sleep
sofnaði	slept
sögðu	said
sögu	saga
Sokka	Sokki (name)
Sokkason	son-of-Sokki (name)
Sokki	Sokki (name)
Sólarfjöllum	Solarfjoll (place)
son	son
söng	sang
sóttu	sought
spangabrynja	plate-mail
spillt	damaged
spretta	sprang
spurði	learned
spurðist	heard-of
spurðu	heard-of
spurðust	heard-of
spurt	learned
spyrjast	known-about
stað	stand
staðar	stand
staðarins	of-the-place, the-place
staðið	stood
stakk	thrust
standa	stand
standist	to-stand
stefnur	plans
steig	stepped
steinda	stone-one
Steingríms	Steingrim's (name)
Steingrímur	Steingrim (name)
steint	stone-carving
Steinþór	Steinthor (name)
stendur	standing
sterkur	strong
stóð	standing, stood
stofuna	sitting-room
stokk	a-log
stökki	blood-splattered
stól	seat
stórfjörðu	large-fjords
stórir	badly
stórskipum	large-ships
stórvirki	great-works
studdist	stood
stukku	went-away
stutt	supported
stýrimaður	steersman

Word List (Old Icelandic to English)

Old Icelandic	English
stýrimanns	steersman
styrktarmaður	supporter
sú	so
suður	south
sumarið	summer
sumars	summer
sumir	some
sumri	of-summer
sumur	summers
sunnan	to-the-south
svara	answered
svarar	answered
svardaga	oath
sveit	company, the-company
sveitunga	men-company
sverði	to-the-sword
sverji	swear
sviptur	deprived
svívirðing	disgrace
svívirðlega	disgracefully
svo	so
svörð	skins
syfjar	sleepy
sýndi	showed
sýndist	seemed
syngja	sing, sung
sýnir	showed
sýnist	seems
sýnt	shown
systurson	sister's-son

T, t

Old Icelandic	English
taka	take, took
taki	take
tala	spoke
talaði	told
tannvöru	walrus-tusks
tekið	taken
tekinn	taken
tekna	taken
teknir	taken
tíða	the-service
tíðamanni	worshippers
tíðinda	news
tíðindi	news, tidings
tíðindin	the-news
tíðindum	news
tigi	tens
tigir	tens
tignar	position
til	the, to, until
tilstilli	agency, guidance
tindinn	pin
tjáði	spoke, told, voiced
tjald	tent
tjalda	tent-up
tók	took
tóku	took
tólf	twelve
tóm	time
tómlega	time-like
torsóttlegt	difficult
traust	trust
troða	tread
tveim	two
tvö	two
týnst	lost

Þ, þ

Old Icelandic	English
þá	them, then, when
það	it, that, the, this, to
þakkaði	thanked
þakti	covered
þangað	from-then, from-there
þann	that, then
þannig	that-way
þar	here, that, then, there
þau	then, those
þegar	instantly, straightaway, straight-away, them
þeim	of-them, theirs, them, they, to-them
þeir	they, was
þeirra	of-them, theirs, them, they
þeirrar	their

Word List (Old Icelandic to English)

Old Icelandic	English
þennan	then
þér	to-you, you
þess	this
þessa	this
þessi	these, this
þessir	these
þessu	this
þessum	these, this
þetta	it, that, this
þig	you
þiggja	accepted
þín	your
þína	yours
þing	assembly
þings	assembly, the-assembly
þjónustumenn	servants-of
þó	though
Þóarinn	Thorarin (name)
Þórarinn	Thorarin (name)
Þórðar	Thord (name)
Þórðarson	son-of-Thord (name)
Þórði	Thord's (name)
Þórður	Thord (name)
Þorfinns	Thorfin (name)
Þorgils	Thorgils (name)
Þóris	Thori (name)
Þórisson	son-of-Thorri (name)
Þorljótsson	son-of-Thorljot (name)
þótt	though
þótti	thought
þóttist	thought
þriðja	third, thirdly
þrír	three
þrjá	three
þú	you
þunglegar	the-more-difficult
þungs	heavily
þungt	unhappy
þverra	running-out
því	according, accordingly, as, because, because-of, that, then, therefore, they
þvo	washed
þykir	seems
þykist	seems
þyrfti	needed

U, u

Old Icelandic	English
ullkamb	wool-comb
um	about, around
umdæmi	about-judgement
umdæmis	area
ummæli	about-matter
umræða	discussed
una	content
undan	away-from
undarlegt	strange
undir	submit, under
uni	like
unna	win
unum	among
upp	up
uppgefnir	up-given
uppi	up
urðu	became

Ú, ú

Old Icelandic	English
úfar	misfortune
úr	from, out-from, out-of
úrræði	solution
úrræðið	solution
út	out
úti	outside
útlenda	foreign

V, v

Old Icelandic	English
vægja	make-peace
vænleg	hopeful
vænta	hoped
vænti	expect
væntu	expected

Word List (Old Icelandic to English)

Old Icelandic	English
væri	be, should-be, should-they, to-be, was
vættir	weights
vaknaði	awoke
vald	power
vanda	problem
vandi	custom
vanfær	unable
vanist	custom
vanmeginn	weak
var	was, were
varð	became, came
varða	happen
varist	weariness
varla	hardly
varnarmaður	defender
varning	wares
varúðgir	cautious
vaskir	brave
veður	weather
vegna	slain
veiðiskap	hunting
veislu	feast
veislunni	the-feast
veit	know, knowing
veita	grant
veitti	granted
vel	well
veld	willed
veldur	brought-about, caused
vér	us, we, we-are
vera	be, being, to-be, would-be
verð	deserve
verða	be, become
verði	be
verðið	become
verðir	being
verður	becomes
verið	been
verk	work
verum	we
vestan	western
Vestribyggð	Vestribyggd (place)
Vestribyggðar	Vestribyggd (place)
veturinn	winter
við	by, to, with
víða	widely
viðbúnað	preparation
viðinn	the-trees
víg	killings, slaying
vígði	consecrated
Víghvats	Vighvats (name)
vígi	battle
vígið	killing
vígsgengi	in-battle
vil	will, wish
vildi	wanted, willed
vildu	willed
vilja	willed, wished-for
viljum	wish
villt	wildly
vini	friends
vinsæll	popular
virðing	worthiness
virðingar	worthiness
virðum	worthiness
virður	respected
vís	aware
vissu	know
vist	resources
víst	certainly
vistföng	resources
vistir	supplies
vistunum	provisions
vitrum	wise
vitum	know-we
vitur	wise
viturlega	wise-like
völlinn	the-field
von	expect, expected, hope
vopnaðir	weaponed
vor	our, ours, spring, us
vorið	spring
vorkunn	pity
vorn	our, ours
vorri	ours
voru	was, were

Word List (Old Icelandic to English)

Old Icelandic	English

Y, y

yðru	your
yður	you
yðvar	you, yours
yðvarn	with-you
yfir	over
yfirbóta	over-compensation
yrði	become, would
yrðu	be

Ý, ý

ýldu	decay

Word List (English to Old Icelandic)

Word List (English to Old Icelandic)

English	Old Icelandic	English	Old Icelandic
		agreed	játtuðu
		a-glacier	jöklinum
A, a		a-deal	kaupum
		allow	leggja
a	á, á, á	alike	líka, líka
about	á, á, á	a-man	maður, maður
and	á, á, á, á, að	a-case	mál
as	á, á, á, að, að, að	a-friendly	mannvænlegur
at	á, á, að	as-long-as	meðan
after	áður, áður	a-great	mikið
all-prepared	albúnir	as-far	nær
all	alla, allan, allir, allir, allmjög, allt, allvel	above	ofan
		also	og
all-great	allmjög	a-word	orð
all-well	allvel, allvel	an-axe	öx, öx
another	annað, annað, annað	axe	öx, öxarhyrnunni
anything-else	annað	axe-horn	öxarhyrnunni
Arnald (name)	Arnald, Arnaldur	advice	ráð, ráð, ráð
Arnbjarn (name)	Arnbjarnar, Arnbjarnar	advisable	ráð, ráð
Arnbjarnar (name)	Arnbjarnar	arrange	ráðast
Arnbjorn (name)	Arnbjörn, Arnbjörn	advise	ráðist
a-wound	áverka	actually	raunar
asked	bað, bað, báðir	altogether	saman
a-farm	bæ	a-short-distance	skammt
asked-for	bauð	a-log	stokk
a-bishop	biskup	answered	svara, svarar
a-bear	bjarndýri	accepted	þiggja
a-farmer	bóndi	assembly	þing, þings
away	brott, búð, búnaði, búnaður	according	því
		accordingly	því
aided	duga	agency	tilstilli
afterwards	eftir	around	um
alone	eigi, einangur, Einar	about-judgement	umdæmi
alone-going	einangur	area	umdæmis
are	er, er, er, er	about-matter	ummæli
archbishop	erkibiskups	among	unum
are-they	eru	awoke	vaknaði
a-falsehood	fals	aware	vís
away-from	frá, frá		
assistance	fulltingis, fulltingja	**B, b**	
ability	getu		
a-Greenlander	grænlenskur	by	að, að, að
autumn	haustum	before	áður, ætla
a-headed-ship	höfðaskip		
angry	illa, illa, illt, inn		

Word List (English to Old Icelandic)

English	*Old Icelandic*	*English*	*Old Icelandic*
back	aftur, agir	between	milli
bid	bað, báðir	below	neðan
both	báðir	bothered	nenna
bidding	bæn	become	orðið, orðið, ósæmd, óþekktarsvip
be-compensated	bæta		
bore	bar	be-arranged	ráðast
battle	bardaga, báru	break-open	rjúfa
bones	bein, beinum	broke-up	rufu
bear	bera, berast	being	sé, sé, sé
best	best	blood-splattered	stökki
better	betur	because	því
bishop	biskup, biskups	because-of	því
bishop-less	biskupslaust	brave	vaskir
bishop's-seat	biskupsstóll, biskupsstólsins	brought-about	veldur
		becomes	verður
bishop's-appointment	biskupsvígslu		
Bjarn (name)	Bjarnar	# C, c	
buck	bokki		
boards	borð	carried	báru, bauð
bore-up	borðið	clear-dreams	berdreyman
borne	borið	chest	brang
brought	borið, borin, borinn	court	dómi
boat-lose	bótalausir	coolly	fálega
Brand (name)	Brandur	captivity	fangs
Brattahlid (place)	Brattahlíð	companions	félaga, félagar
briefs	bréfum	compensation	greiðslu
burned	brenndu	circumstances	hag
brother	bróðir	crags	hamarrifu
broken	brotið	carry	heimta
booth	búð	chieftains	höfðingja
bearing	byrinn	called	hringdi, hringja, hríslu, hugi
but	eða, ef, eftir, eftir		
breach-of-oath	eiðrofa	call	hringja, hríslu
be	er, er, er, er, erfitt, erindi, erindis	clump	hríslu
		comes	kæmi
bring	færa	claim	kalla
before-done	fyrirgert	comb	kambi
been	gengið, gengið	can	kann
be-done	gera	cast	kastaði
became	gerðist, gerðu, gerðu	come	kemst, Ketil, Ketill, Ketils, Ketils
be-called	heita		
boiling-cauldrons	heitukötlum	church	kirkju
beside	hjá	churchyard	kirkjugarðsins
bodies	líkum	church-mass	kirkjumessu
behold	líst	church-wall	kirkjuvegginn
badly	mæla, mætti		

107

Word List (English to Old Icelandic)

English	Old Icelandic	English	Old Icelandic
cleric	klerkur	discharge	hleypið
came	kom, koma, komast, komast, komið, kominn	declared	kveðið
		discuss	máli
coming	kominn	dangerous	mannhættu
choice	kostur	dead-body	mannshræ
company	liði, liðskost	disease	mein
case	mál, mál	decreased	minnka
cases	málum	down	niður
close	nær	dishonourable	ósæmd, óþekktarsvip
commanded	réð	decide	ráð
correctness	réttlegast	drifted	rak
cabin	skála	drove	rak
cutting	skerast	deal	réðist
crew	skipverjar	delay	seinka
carcasses	sláturgripa	divided	skiptu
caught-up	snaraðist	damaged	spillt
covered	þakti	deprived	sviptur
content	una	disgrace	svívirðing
custom	vandi, vanist	disgracefully	svívirðlega
cautious	varúðgir	discussed	umræða
caused	veldur	defender	varnarmaður
consecrated	vígði	deserve	verð
certainly	víst	decay	ýldu

D, d

E, e

English	Old Icelandic	English	Old Icelandic
desirable	agir	events	atburði
died	andaðist, andaðist	Eastern-man	austmaður
dwelling	bænum	Eastern-men	austmanna, austmenn
death	bana	empty	autt
death-blow	banahögg	equipment	búnaði, búnaður
death-wounds	banasár	Eid (place)	Eiði
deemed	dæma	Einar (name)	Einar, Einari, Einars
Denmark (place)	Danmerkur, Danmörk	Einar's	einars
dead	dauða, dauður	Einar's (name)	Einars
dream	draum	Einarsfjord (place)	Einarsfjörð
dreamed	dreymdi	Eriksfjord (place)	Eiríksfjörð
drowned	drukknaði	errand	erindi, erindis
difficult	erfitt, erindi	Eyjafjolls (place)	Eyjafjöllum
downhill	forbrekkis	execution	framkvæmd
desire	fýsa	each	hver, hverju, hversu, Hvítserk, hvorirtveggju
do	gera		
doing	gera	either-side	hvorirtveggju
done	gera, gera, gerði, gerðir	equally-early	jafnsnemma
did	gerði, gerðir	equal	jafnt

Word List (English to Old Icelandic)

English	Old Icelandic
earthed	jarða
earth-house	jarðhús
even	jöfn
ends	lýkur
equal-man	mannjafnað
esteem	metorð
expect	vænti, væntu
expected	væntu, væri

F, f

English	Old Icelandic
from	af, af, aflað, aftur, agir, albúnir
farmers	bændur
fight	berjast
farmer	bónda, bóndi
followed	eftir, eftir, eftir
following	eftir, eftir
fire-place	eldstóar
fall	falla
fallen	fallinn
father-and-son	feðgar
fee-gifts	fégjöfum
fell	féll
fair	ferleg
fix	festa
fee-trust	févon
fifteen	fimmtán
far	fjarri
following-men	fjölmenni
fjord	fjörðinn
folk	fólk
for	fór, forbrekkis, forsjá
foresight	forsjá
foster-brother	fóstbróðir
feet	fótum
found-out	fréttu
fulfil	fulltingja
found	fundið, fundu, fylgdi, fylgdi
follow	fylgdi
foremost	fyrir
first	fyrst
firstly	fyrst
find	hitta
flesh	holdi
force	liðskost
funeral-procession	líkhringingu
food	mat
facing	móti
fish	skreið
from-then	þangað
from-there	þangað
foreign	útlenda
feast	veislu
friends	vini

G, g

English	Old Icelandic
gain	aflað
get	fá, færa, færði
going	færi, færi, fálega, falla, fallinn, fals
go-to	færi
go	fari, farið, feðgar
got	fékk, félaga
grouped	flokk
gave	gaf, gafst
Gardar (place)	garða, gefa
give	gefa, gefast
given	gefist, gefnar
good	góð, góða, góðan, góðgirnd, góður
good-will	góðgirnd
Greenland (place)	grænland, Grænlendinga, grænlendinga
Greenlanders (name)	grænlendinga, grænlendingar, Grænlendingum
Greenlandic (name)	grænlensk, grænlenskum
grave	grafa
god's	guðs
good-bargain	hagkeypi
glaciers	jöklum
great	mikið, mikið, mikið, mikil
getting	náir
gave-him	reyndust
giants	rísi
great-works	stórvirki

Word List (English to Old Icelandic)

English	Old Icelandic	English	Old Icelandic
guidance	tilstilli	had-they	höfðu
grant	veita	headstrong	höfuðgjarnt
granted	veitti	head-men	höfuðsmenn
		Holtavatnsos (place)	Holtavatnsós

H, h

English	Old Icelandic	English	Old Icelandic
		handling	höndum
		his-mind	hugi
had	ætti, ættjarða, af, af, aflað, aftur, agir, albúnir, alla, allan, allir, allir, allmjög, allt	house	húsa
		how	hverju
		how-so	hversu
		Hvitserk (name)	Hvítserk
homelands	ættjarða	hidden-creek	leynivogi
have	áttu, austmaður, austmanna, austmenn, autt, áverka, bað, bað	humility	lítillæti
		human-body	mannshræ
		harm	mein
hiding	dyljast	headland	nes
help	fulltings	have-become	orðið
has	hafa, hafa, hafði	honour	sæmd, sæmdar, sæmdir
handy	hagur		
hold	halda, haldi	himself	sér, séu, síðar
holding	haldið	heard-of	spurðist, spurðu, spurðust
Hall's	halls		
Hall's (name)	Halls	heavily	þungs
Hall (name)	Hallur	hopeful	vænleg
high-mass	hámessu	hoped	vænta
he	hann, hann	happen	varða
him	hann, hans, hans, hans, haraldi, haralds, harmaði	hardly	varla
		hunting	veiðiskap
		hope	von
his	hans, hans, haraldi, haralds, harmaði, haustum, hefði, hefðu, hefi, hefir, hefir		

I, i

English	Old Icelandic	English	Old Icelandic
Harald (name)	haraldi, haralds	in	á, að, að, að, að
harmed	harmaði	it	að, áður, áður, ætla
has-been	hefir	intend	ætla
home	heim	intended	ætla, ætlaðir
house-man	heimamaður	intention	ætlan
held	héldu	invited	bauð
hand	hendi, hendur, hér	if	ef
here	hér, Hermundur, heyra	I	eg, Eiði
Hermund (name)	Hermundur	is	er, er
hear	heyra	in-the-grave	grafin
heard	heyrðu, heyrt	its	hans
hammer	hnjóðhamar	is-named	heitir
head-ship	höfðaskipið	into	í
head	höfði, höfðingja	ill	illa, illt, inn

110

Word List (English to Old Icelandic)

English	Old Icelandic
ice	ís, Ísa-Steingrímur
Isa-Steingrim (name)	Ísa-Steingrímur
Iceland (place)	Íslandi, Íslands
innermost	leyndust
important	metnir
impulsive	óforsjáll
itself	sjálft
instantly	þegar
in-battle	vígsgengi

J, j

English	Old Icelandic
judged	dæmdi
judgement	dómur
journey	ferð
Jerusalem-Traveller (name)	Jórsalafari
jerk	kippum

K, k

English	Old Icelandic
killed	bana
killing	dráp, draum, drepa
kinsman	frænda, frændi
kinsmen	frændur
Ketil (name)	Ketil, Ketill, Ketils
Ketil's (name)	Ketils
Kidjaberg (place)	Kiðjabergs
knees	knjám
Kolbein (name)	Kolbein, Kolbeini, Kolbeinn, Kolbeins
Krak (name)	Kráks
known	kunni, kunnig
known-about	spyrjast
know	veit, veit
knowing	veit
killings	víg
know-we	vitum

L, l

English	Old Icelandic
lived	bjó
later	eftir, eg
learned	fróði, fulltingis, fulltingja
local-priest	heimilisprestur
loaded	hlaðna
lot	hlut, hlutar
looked	horfðu, horfir, hringdi
looks	horfir
lay	lá, lagðist
laid	lagðist, lagður, land, landsmenn, landsmönnum
land	land
lands-men	landsmenn, landsmönnum
Langanes (place)	Langanes
lay-out	láta
long	lengi
longer	lengra, lengur
laid-out	lét
loss-of-life	líftjóni
like	líka, líkaði, líkar
liked	líkaði
likes	líkar
likely	líkast, líkhringingu
little	lítið, lítil, lítillæti, litlu
law	lög, lög
laws	lög
Lund (place)	Lund
lessened	menn
large	mikla
less	minna, minni
lost	misst, mitt
last	síðast
large-fjords	stórfjörðu
large-ships	stórskipum

M, m

English	Old Icelandic
money	fjár
many-people	fjölmenni
more	fleiri, flokk, fólk, fór
meet	fund, fund, fundar
meeting	fund, fundar, fundar
make	gera, gerði, gerðir
made	gerðir, gerðist
met	hitti, hittust

Word List (English to Old Icelandic)

English	Old Icelandic	English	Old Icelandic
mind	hugur	necessary	nauðsyn
merchant-ship	kaupskip, kaupskipið	needs	nauðsyn
merchant-ships	kaupskipin	nor	né
man	maður, mæla, mætti	Norway (place)	Noreg, noregi, Noregs
might	mætti, mættir, mættu, maklegast	Nordic (name)	norrænir, norrænn
most	maklegast, mál	now	nú
matter	mál, mál	needed	þyrfti
matters	mál	news	tíðinda, tíðindi, tíðindi
matter-lot	málahlutur		
month's-end	mánaðarmótið		
man's	manna		
men	manna, manndómsleysi, mannhættu		

O, o

English	Old Icelandic
of	á, á, á, á, á, á, að
on	á, á
out	á, á
other	aðrir, áðu, æðimaður, æpa, ætla, ætla
of-mind	æðimaður
off	af
otherwise	annað
other-either	annaðhvort
owned	átt
offer	bjóðast
offering	boðið
or	eða
oath	eið, eiðar, eiga
own	eiga
owning	eignum
one	ein, eina, einhverju, einn, einræði, einu
one-occasion	einhverju
opinion	fastmæli
of-old	forn
old	gamall
opposite	gegnt
others	hinir, hinn
old-woman	kerling
of-men	manna
Odda (place)	Odda
over	ofan, ofsa
overbearing-men	ofsamenn
often	oft
Ossur (name)	Össur, Össurar, Össurar
of-Ossur (name)	Össurar
of-butter	smjörs

English	Old Icelandic
meanness	manndómsleysi
many	margt, mart, mat
moderately	meðallagi
may	mega, megri
meagre	megri
me	mér, mér
mine	mér, messu, mest, metnir, metorð
mass	messu
much	mikið, mikil, mikil, mikill, mikill, mikils, mikinn, mikla, mikla
my	mínum, misst
morning	morguninn
mouth	munni
more-correct	réttara
men-company	sveitunga
misfortune	úfar
make-peace	vægja

N, n

English	Old Icelandic
nature	eðli
not	eiga, eiga, eigi, eigi
no	eigi, eigi, eign
none	ekki
no-one	engi
named	hét
night	kveld, kyrrrlátir, kyrrt
nearer	nær
next	næst

Word List (English to Old Icelandic)

English	Old Icelandic	English	Old Icelandic
of-the-place	staðarins	plate-mail	spangabrynja
of-summer	sumri	plans	stefnur
of-them	þeim, þeim	position	tignar
out-from	úr	pin	tindinn
out-of	úr	power	vald
outside	úti	problem	vanda
our	vor, vor	preparation	viðbúnað
ours	vor, vor, vor	popular	vinsæll
over-compensation	yfirbóta	pity	vorkunn

P, p

R, r

English	Old Icelandic	English	Old Icelandic
plan	atgervi	river-mouth	árós
possible	auðið	rescuing	bjarga
prevented	bægði	rescue	bjargar
prayers	bæn, bænar	rocks	björg
prepared	bjó, bjó, bjóðast, björg, bjóst, boðið, bol	remaining	eftir
		resources	fang, fanga, fangið, fara
presented	borið, brekku	refusing	fyrirkveðast
preparations	búnað, búnaði	residence	gilla
pride	dignuðu	right	hægra
property	eign, eigna	rather	halda, halda
provisions	fanga, fangið, fara	running	hlaupa
provided	fremi	released	hleypir, hleypur
peace	fritt	ran	hleypur, hlífast, hlítt
pass	gegna	repel	hrinda
payment	gjalds	reward	laun
paying	greiðast	remember	muna
priest	guði	reached	náðu
protected	hegna	reluctant	ófús
promised	hést	ruled	réðst
protect	hlífast	rode	reið
part	hlut, hlutum	rights	rétt
priests	kennimenn	reconcile	sættast, sættir
pulled	kipptu	reconciliation	sættir, sættirnar
put	legðu	reconciliation-meeting	sáttarfundinum
propose	leggur	return	snúast
passed	liðið, liðu, líður	running-out	þverra
peoples'	manna	respected	virður
people	menn		
poor-man	ómegðarmaður		
punish	refsa	## S, s	
peace-meeting	sáttarfund		
penalty	sektir	shouting	æpa
parted	skildu	suppose	ætla

Word List (English to Old Icelandic)

English	*Old Icelandic*	*English*	*Old Icelandic*
supposed	ætla, ætluðu	*souls*	sáluhjápar, sálum
settled	bjó, bjóðast, björg, bjóst	*same*	sama, saman
strengthened	efldur	*sat*	sat, satt, sáttarfund, sáttarfundinum, sáttargerð
self-will	einræði		
still	enn, er, er		
sea	haf	*settlement*	sáttargerð
sea-going-ship	hafskip	*say*	segið, segir, segir
suitable	henta	*says*	segir
shoulders	herða	*send*	senda
sir	herra	*sent*	sendi
struck	hjó, hlaupa, hleypir	*set*	sett, sett, setti
satisfactory	hlítt	*six*	sex
shrubs	hrísótt	*sinking*	sígast
she	hún	*sailed*	sigldu
stormy	hvasst	*Sigurd (name)*	Sigurði, Sigurður
seals	innsiglum	*Simon (name)*	Símon, Símonar, símoni
son-of-Kalf (name)	Kálfsson	*Simon's (name)*	Símoni
son-of-Kodran (name)	Koðránsson	*sit*	sitja
said	kvað, kvaðst, kváðu, kváðu, kváðust, kveðst, kveld, kyrrrlátir, kyrrt, Landeyjum, landi, landið, landsins	*see*	sjá
		separated	skildu
		ship	skip, skipa, skipi
		ships	skips, skips
		Skjalgsbud (place)	Skjálgsbúða
saying	kváðu	*shortly*	skjótlega
seek	leita, leysti	*should-be*	skyldi, skyldir
support	liðveislu	*slipped*	slæst
spoke	mælti, mæltu, mal	*such*	slík, slíka, slíkan, slíks, slíkt, slíku, slíkum
sides	megin		
should	mun, mun, mun, mun, muna, mundi, mundu	*strike*	slógu
		small-ships	smáskipum
shall-you	muntu	*sleep*	sofa
shall	munu, munu, munu, munum, náðu	*slept*	sofnaði
		saga	sögu
son-of-Njal (name)	Njálsson	*Sokki (name)*	Sokka, Sokkason
some	nokkuð, nokkur, nokkura, nokkurar, nokkurn, nokkurra, nokkuru, nokkurum	*son-of-Sokki (name)*	Sokkason
		Solarfjoll (place)	Sólarfjöllum
		son	son
something	nokkurra	*sang*	söng
swiftly	ört	*sprang*	spretta
slander	róg	*stand*	stað, staðar, staðarins
saw	sá, sá, sá, sægarpur	*stood*	staðið, stakk, standa
so	sá, sá, sægarpur	*stepped*	steig
sea-champion	sægarpur	*stone-one*	steinda
sought	sækja, Sæmundi	*Steingrim's (name)*	Steingríms
Saemund (name)	Sæmundi, Sæmundur	*Steingrim (name)*	Steingrímur
sake	sakir	*stone-carving*	steint

Word List (English to Old Icelandic)

English	Old Icelandic	English	Old Icelandic
Steinthor (name)	Steinþór	the-storm	andviðri
standing	stendur, sterkur	the-Easterner	austmanns, austmanns
strong	sterkur	the-dwelling	bænum
sitting-room	stofuna	throat	barkann
seat	stól	the-boat	bátinn
supported	stutt	the-bishop	biskuð, biskup, biskupi, biskups
steersman	stýrimaður, stýrimanns		
supporter	styrktarmaður	the-bishop's	biskups
south	suður	the-bishop-elect	biskupsefni
summer	sumarið, sumars	the-bishop's-seat	biskupsstólinum, biskupsstólnum
summers	sumur		
swear	sverji	the-trunk	bol
skins	svörð	the-tables	borð, borðið
sleepy	syfjar	the-table	borðið
showed	sýndi, sýndist	the-slope	brekku, brekkunni
seemed	sýndist	the-armour	brynjunni
sing	syngja	the-settlement	byggðina
sung	syngja	the-day	dag
seems	sýnist, sýnt, systurson	the-dead	daun
shown	sýnt	the-court	dómi, dóminum
sister's-son	systurson	the-judgement	dómurinn
straightaway	þegar	the-dream	drauminn
straight-away	þegar	the-animal	dýrið
servants-of	þjónustumenn	the-boat-behind	eftirbáti
son-of-Thord (name)	Þórðarson	the-after-boat	eftirbátinn
son-of-Thorri (name)	Þórisson	than	en
son-of-Thorljot (name)	Þorljótsson	then	er, er, er, er, er, er, er, erkibiskup
strange	undarlegt		
submit	undir	the-archbishop	erkibiskup
solution	úrræði, úrræðið	they-are	eru, eru
should-they	væri	travel	færu, færum, fagra, fallinn
slain	vegna		
slaying	víg	the-fairest	fagra
supplies	vistir	to-catch	fangið
spring	vor, vor	the-ferry	ferjuna
		the-fjord	fjörðu
		travelled	fór, fór, forn
		through	fyrir, fyrir

T, t

		to-do	gera, gera
		to-give	gera
that	á, á, á, að, að, að, að, aðrir, áðu, æðimaður, æpa, ætla	treasure	gersemi, gildur, gilla
		the-Greenlanders'	grænlendinga
		the-Greenlanders	grænlendingar
the	á, á, að, að, að, að, aðrir, áðu	the-Greenlander	grænlendings
		the-artefact-fee	gripagjaldið
to	á, að, að, að, að, aðrir, áðu	to-hold	halda

Word List (English to Old Icelandic)

English	Old Icelandic	English	Old Icelandic
the-crew	hásetar	taking	nema
the-Hermunds (name)	Hermundur	the-unsettled-land	óbyggðum
things	hlutum	the-words	orðinn
they-had	höfðu	to-us	oss
to-strike	höggva	tore-up	rufu, sá
to-him	honum	together	saman, sami
time	hríð, hrinda	the-same	samt
the-branch	hríslunni	the-truth	sanni
thought	hugðu, hún, hurðina	truthfully	sannlegast
the-door	hurðina, hvað	true-words	sannyrði
turn	hverfa	true	
think	hygg	the-seam	sauminn
the-merchants	kaupmenn	this	sé, sé, segið, segir, segir, segir, segja, sektir, senda
the-trading-men	kaupmenn, kaupmenn, kaupmennirnir		
trading-men	kaupmenn, kaupmennirnir	to-be	sé, segið, segir
		to-be-sent	sendilegastan
teaching	kennimanns	them	sér, sér, sett, sett, sett
the-old-woman	kerlingu	themselves	sér, sett
the-keel	kilinum	theirs	sín, sína, sína, sinn, sinna, sinni, sínu
the-church	kirkju, kirkjuna		
the-king	konung, konungi, konungi, konungs	their	sína, sína
the-kind	konungi	they	sinni, sínu, sínum, sitja, sitt
the-king's	konungs	the-cabin	skálann, skálann
the-king's-brief	konungsbréfum	the-hut	skálann
the-Landeys (place)	Landeyjum	temper	skaplyndi
the-land	landi, landið	temperament	skapraun
the-lands	landsins	the-ships	skipa, skipi
the-way	leið	the-ship	skipi, skipið, skipið, skipinu
team	lið, liði		
the-body	lík, líkhringinguna	the-false-deacon	slembidjákn
the-funeral-procession	líkhringinguna	turned	snerist
told	mælt, mælti, mælti, mæltu	the-place	staðarins
		thrust	stakk
the-matter	mal, mál, mál, máli, málið	to-stand	standist
		to-the-south	sunnan
the-case	mál, mál	the-company	sveit
the-matter-fulfilling	málsfyllingar	to-the-sword	sverði
the-man	mann	take	taka, taka
this-man	manninum	took	taka, taki, tala
to-me	mér	taken	tekið, tekinn, tekna, teknir
the-most	mestur		
the-middle	miðju	thanked	þakkaði
the-men	mönnum	that-way	þannig
the-night	nætur, nátt	there	þar

Word List (English to Old Icelandic)

English	Old Icelandic
those	þau
to-them	þeim
to-you	þér
these	þessi, þessi, þessir
the-assembly	þings
though	þó, Þóarinn
Thorarin (name)	Þóarinn, Þórarinn
Thord (name)	Þórðar, Þórðarson
Thord's (name)	Þórði
Thorfin (name)	Þorfinns
Thorgils (name)	Þorgils
Thori (name)	Þóris
third	þriðja
thirdly	þriðja
three	þrír, þrjá
the-more-difficult	þunglegar
therefore	því
the-service	tíða
tidings	tíðindi
the-news	tíðindin
tens	tigi, tigir
tent	tjald
tent-up	tjalda
twelve	tólf
time-like	tómlega
trust	traust
tread	troða
two	tveim, tvö
the-feast	veislunni
the-trees	viðinn
the-field	völlinn

U, u

English	Old Icelandic
upset	brugðið
unheard-of	endemi
use	nytjum
uncompensated	óbættur
un-settled	óbyggðir
un-equal	ójafnað
unequal	ójafnaður
unsettled	ósett
us	oss, Össur, Össurar
ungraceful	óþekktarsvip
un-worthy	óvirðing

English	Old Icelandic
uncertain	óvíst
uproar	róstu
unhappy	þungt
until	til
under	undir
up	upp, uppgefnir
up-given	uppgefnir
unable	vanfær

V, v

valid	gildur
very	mjög
violence	ofsa
victory	sigur
voiced	tjáði
Vestribyggd (place)	Vestribyggð, Vestribyggðar
Vighvats (name)	Víghvats

W, w

way	burt
while	en, endemi
was	er, er, er, er, er
we-are	er, er
what	er, er
when	er, er
where	er, er, er
who	er, er
with	er, erkibiskup, eru
were	eru, færu, færum
weak	fallinn, fang
went	fara, fara, fastmæli, fé, féið, fékk, feng, fengju, fer, ferjuna
wealth	fé, féið
would-get	fengju
wealth-finding	fjárfundinn
willing	fúsari
walked	gengið
was-named	hét
white-bear	hvítabjörn
which	hvors

Word List (English to Old Icelandic)

English	*Old Icelandic*	*English*	*Old Icelandic*
whether	hvort	yours	þína, þings
will	mun, mun, mun		
will-be	mun		
would	mun, muna, mundi, mundu, mundu, mundu, mundum, muni, muni		
would-be	mundu, mundum		
word	orð		
words	orð, orða		
word-sending	orðsending		
wandered	reikaði		
wounded	sárir		
went-away	stukku		
walrus-tusks	tannvöru		
washed	þvo		
worshippers	tíðamanni		
wool-comb	ullkamb		
win	unna		
weights	vættir		
weariness	varist		
wares	varning		
weather	veður		
well	vel		
willed	veld, vér, vér, vér		
we	vér, vér		
work	verk		
western	vestan		
winter	veturinn		
widely	víða		
wish	vil, vildi		
wanted	vildi		
wished-for	vilja		
wildly	villt		
worthiness	virðing, virðingar, virðum		
wise	vitrum, vitur		
wise-like	viturlega		
weaponed	vopnaðir		
with-you	yðvarn		

Y, y

you	þér, þess, þessa, þessi, þessi
your	þín, þína

A Word Comparison of Old Norse and Old Icelandic Words

A Word Comparison of Old Norse and Old Icelandic Words

Old Norse	Old Icelandic	English	Old Norse	Old Icelandic	English
áðr	áður	after	brugðit	brugðið	upset
áðr	áður	before	búit	búið	prepared
æðimaðr	æðimaður	of-mind	búit	búið	settled
aflat	aflað	gain	búnaðr	búnaður	equipment
aftr	aftur	back	byrrinn	byrinn	bearing
allmjök	allmjög	all-great	byskup	biskuð	the-bishop
annat	annað	another	byskup	biskup	a-bishop
annat	annað	anything-else	byskup	biskup	bishop
annat	annað	other	byskup	biskup	the-bishop
annat	annað	otherwise	byskupi	biskupi	the-bishop
annathvárt	annaðhvort	other-either	byskups	biskups	bishop
Arnaldr	Arnaldur	Arnald (name)	byskups	biskups	the-bishop
at	að	a	byskups	biskups	the-bishop's
at	að	at	byskupsefni	biskupsefni	the-bishop-elect
at	að	by	byskupslaust	biskupslaust	bishop-less
at	að	in	byskupsstólinum	biskupsstólinum	the-bishop's-seat
at	að	it	byskupsstóll	biskupsstóll	bishop's-seat
at	að	of	byskupsstólnum	biskupsstólnum	the-bishop's-seat
at	að	that	byskupsstólsins	biskupsstólsins	bishop's-seat
at	að	the	byskupsvígslu	biskupsvígslu	bishop's-appointment
at	að	to	dæmði	dæmdi	judged
auðit	auðið	possible	Danmarkar	Danmerkur	Denmark (place)
austmaðr	austmaður	Eastern-man	dauðr	dauður	dead
bændr	bændur	farmers	dómr	dómur	judgement
betr	betur	better	dómrinn	dómurinn	the-judgement
bezt	best	best	dreymði	dreymdi	dreamed
Bjarna	Bjarnar	Bjarn (name)	dýrit	dýrið	the-animal
boðit	boðið	offering	efldr	efldur	strengthened
bolöx	bol	the-trunk	einangr	einangur	alone-going
borðit	borðið	bore-up	Einarr	Einar	Einar (name)
borðit	borðið	the-table	ek	eg	I
borit	borið	borne	ekki	eigi	not
borit	borið	brought	er	á	in
borit	borið	presented	er	en	as
Brandr	Brandur	Brand (name)	er	og	and
brögð	brang	chest	erendi	erindi	errand
brotit	brotið	broken			
brott	burt	away			
brott	burt	way			
brottu	burtu	away			

A Word Comparison of Old Norse and Old Icelandic Words

Old Norse	Old Icelandic	English	Old Norse	Old Icelandic	English
erendis	erindis	errand	haldit	haldið	holding
erkibyskup	erkibiskup	the-archbishop	Hallr	Hallur	Hall (name)
			hefði	hefðu	had
erkibyskups	erkibiskups	archbishop	heimamaðr	heimamaður	house-man
færi	færu	travel	heimilisprestr	heimilisprestur	local-priest
færim	færum	travel			
fáliga	fálega	coolly	heldr	heldur	rather
fangit	fangið	to-catch	heldu	héldu	held
farim	förum	go	hendr	hendur	hand
farit	farið	going	Hermundr	Hermundur	Hermund (name)
féit	féið	wealth			
fekk	fékk	got	Hermundr	Hermundur	the-Hermunds (name)
fekk	fékk	went			
fell	féll	fell	hézt	hést	promised
fengi	fengju	would-get	hingat	hingað	here
ferlig	ferleg	fair	hleypr	hleypur	ran
ferr	fer	went	höfðaskipit	höfðaskipið	head-ship
féván	févon	fee-trust	höggvit	hoggið	struck
frændr	frændur	kinsmen	hringði	hringdi	called
framkvæmð	framkvæmd	execution	hugr	hugur	mind
fundit	fundið	found	hvárirtveggja	hvorirtveggju	either-side
fylgði	fylgdi	follow	hvárirtveggju	hvorirtveggju	either-side
fylgði	fylgdi	followed	hvárrtveggi	hvortveggji	each
fylgðinni	fylgdinni	following	hvárs	hvors	which
gefizt	gefist	given	hvárt	hvort	each
gengit	gengið	been	hvárt	hvort	whether
gengit	gengið	going	hváru	hvoru	each
gengit	gengið	walked	hvárum	hvorum	each
gengr	gengur	went	hvat	hvað	that
gera	geri	make	hvat	hvað	what
gerzt	gerst	done	hverr	hver	each
gildr	gildur	valid	hverr	hver	who
góðr	góður	good	inn	hinn	the
grænlenzk	grænlensk	Greenlandic (name)	inu	hinu	the
grænlenzkr	grænlenskur	a-Greenlander	Ísa-Steingrímr	Ísa-Steingrímur	Isa-Steingrim (name)
grænlenzkum	grænlenskum	Greenlandic (name)	it	hið	the
			it	hið	then
greiðist	greiðast	paying	kaupskipit	kaupskipið	merchant-ship
gripagjaldit	gripagjaldið	the-artefact-fee	kippðu	kipptu	pulled
hafa	hefir	has-been	kippim	kippum	jerk
hagr	hagur	handy	klerkr	klerkur	cleric

A Word Comparison of Old Norse and Old Icelandic Words

Old Norse	*Old Icelandic*	English
komit	komið	come
kómu	komu	came
kómust	komust	came
konungr	konungur	the-king
kostr	kostur	choice
kveðit	kveðið	declared
kveðst	kvaðst	said
kyrrlátir	kyrrrlátir	still
lagðr	lagður	laid
landit	landið	the-land
leggr	leggur	propose
legit	legið	laid
lengr	lengur	longer
leynivági	leynivogi	hidden-creek
lézt	lést	had
liðit	liðið	passed
líðr	líður	passed
liðveizlu	liðveislu	support
líkendi	líkindi	alike
líkhringingina	líkhringinguna	the-funeral-procession
líkligast	líklegast	likely
lítit	lítið	little
lízt	líst	behold
Lundi	Lund	Lund (place)
lýkr	lýkur	ends
maðr	maður	a-man
maðr	maður	man
mætti	mættu	might
makligast	maklegast	most
málahlutr	málahlutur	matter-lot
málit	málið	the-case
málum"	málum	cases
mánaðarmótit	mánaðarmótið	month's-end
mannvænlegr	mannvænlegur	a-friendly
margt	mart	many
mestr	mestur	the-most
mik	mig	me
mikit	mikið	a-great
mikit	mikið	great
mikit	mikið	many
mikit	mikið	much

Old Norse	*Old Icelandic*	English
mjök	mjög	much
mjök	mjög	very
morgininn	morguninn	morning
mun	minna	less
mundi	mundu	would
muni	munu	shall
munu	mun	may
myndim	mundum	would
nætr	nætur	night
nætr	nætur	the-night
niðr	niður	down
nökkur	nokkur	some
nökkura	nokkura	some
nökkurar	nokkurar	some
nökkurn	nokkurn	some
nökkurra	nokkurra	something
nökkuru	nokkuru	some
nökkurum	nokkurum	some
nökkut	nokkuð	some
Nóreg	Noreg	Norway (place)
nóregi	noregi	Norway (place)
Nóregs	Noregs	Norway (place)
óbættr	óbættur	uncompensated
ófúss	ófús	reluctant
ójafnaðr	ójafnaður	unequal
ok	og	also
ok	og	and
ómegðarmaðr	ómegðarmaður	poor-man
ór	úr	from
ór	úr	out-from
ór	úr	out-of
orðit	orðið	become
orðit	orðið	have-become
órræði	úrræði	solution
órræðit	úrræðið	solution
ósæmð	ósæmd	dishonourable
óþekkðarsvip	óþekktarsvip	dishonourable
óþekkðarsvip	óþekktarsvip	ungraceful

A Word Comparison of Old Norse and Old Icelandic Words

Old Norse	Old Icelandic	English
Özur	Össur	Ossur (name)
Özurar	Össurar	of-Ossur (name)
Özurar	Össurar	Ossur (name)
Özuri	Össuri	Ossur (name)
Özurr	Össur	Ossur (name)
ráðligt	ráðlegt	advisable
reiðisvipr	reiðisvipur	angry
reiðr	reiður	angry
réttligast	réttlegast	correctness
sá	sáu	saw
sægarpr	sægarpur	sea-champion
sæmð	sæmd	honour
sæmðar	sæmdar	honour
sæmðir	sæmdir	honour
sakar	sakir	sake
sannligast	sannlegast	truthfully
sé	séu	are
sé	séu	they-are
sekðir	sektir	penalty
sendiligstan	sendilegastan	to-be-sent
settr	settur	set
sigr	sigur	victory
Sigurðr	Sigurður	Sigurd (name)
sik	sig	him
sik	sig	himself
skáladyrrnar	skáladyrnar	the-door
skilðu	skildu	parted
skilðu	skildu	separated
skipit	skipið	ship
skipit	skipið	the-ship
skjótliga	skjótlega	shortly
skulu	mun	would
skyldi	skyldu	should
skyli	skuli	shall
slátrgripa	sláturgripa	carcasses
sonr	son	son
staðit	staðið	stood
Steingrímr	Steingrímur	Steingrim (name)
Steinþórr	Steinþór	Steinthor (name)
stendr	stendur	standing
sterkr	sterkur	strong
stýrimaðr	stýrimaður	steersman
styrkðarmaðr	styrktarmaður	supporter
suðr	suður	south
sumarit	sumarið	summer
svá	svo	so
sveri	sverji	swear
sviptr	sviptur	deprived
svívirðliga	svívirðlega	disgracefully
systursonr	systurson	sister's-son
taka	taki	take
tekit	tekið	taken
þakði	þakti	covered
þangat	þangað	from-then
þangat	þangað	from-there
þat	það	it
þat	það	that
þat	það	the
þat	það	this
þat	það	to
þeira	þeirra	of-them
þeira	þeirra	theirs
þeira	þeirra	them
þeira	þeirra	they
þeirar	þeirrar	their
þessi	þessu	this
þik	þig	you
Þórðr	Þórður	Thord (name)
þóttumst	þóttist	thought
þungligar	þunglegar	the-more-difficult
þvá	þvo	washed
þykkir	þykir	seems
þykkist	þykist	seems
tíðenda	tíðinda	news
tíðendi	tíðindi	news
tíðendi	tíðindi	tidings
tíðendin	tíðindin	the-news
tíðendum	tíðindum	news
tómliga	tómlega	time-like
torsóttligt	torsóttlegt	difficult
tvau	tvö	two

A Word Comparison of Old Norse and Old Icelandic Words

Old Norse	Old Icelandic	English
týnzt	*týnst*	lost
undarligt	*undarlegt*	strange
vænlig	*vænleg*	hopeful
ván	*von*	expect
ván	*von*	expected
ván	*von*	hope
vanfærr	*vanfær*	unable
vanizt	*vanist*	custom
vápnaðir	*vopnaðir*	weaponed
vár	*vor*	spring
vár	*vor*	us
várit	*vorið*	spring
várkunn	*vorkunn*	pity
várn	*vorn*	our
várn	*vorn*	ours
varnarmaðr	*varnarmaður*	defender
várr	*vor*	our
várr	*vor*	ours
várri	*vorri*	ours
váru	*voru*	was
váru	*voru*	were
veðr	*veður*	weather
veizlu	*veislu*	feast
veizlunni	*veislunni*	the-feast
veldr	*veldur*	brought-about
veldr	*veldur*	caused
verðr	*verður*	becomes
verit	*verið*	been
vetrinn	*veturinn*	winter
vígit	*vígið*	killing
vildi	*vildu*	willed
virðim	*virðum*	worthiness
virðr	*virður*	respected
vistaföng	*vistföng*	resources
vit	*við*	with
vitr	*vitur*	wise
vitrliga	*viturlega*	wise-like
yðr	*yður*	you
yrði	*yrðu*	be

The Tale of Hreiðarr the Fool (*Old Norse*)

Old Norse	Literal	English
1	**1**	**1**
Þórðr hét maðr.	Thord was-named a-man.	There was a man named Thord.
Hann var Þorgrímsson, Hreiðarssonar, þess er Glúmr vá.	He was Son-of-Thorgrim, Son-of-Hreidar, this whom Glum killed.	He was the son of Thorgrim, the son of Hreidar who killed Glum.
Þórðr var lítill maðr vexti ok vænn.	Thord was a-little man grown and handsome.	He was a small man in size and handsome.
Hann átti sér bróður, er Hreiðarr hét.	He had himself a-brother, who Hreidar was-named.	He had a brother, who was named Hreidar.
Hann var ljótr maðr ok varla sjálfbjargi fyrir vits sökum.	He was ugly man and scarcely self-supported for wits sake.	He was an ugly man and he could scarcely take care of himself.
Hann var manna frávastr ok vel at afli búinn ok hógværr í skapi, ok var hann heima jafnan.	He was a-man swift and well to strength prepared and humble in character, and was he at-home always.	He was a fast man and very strong, and humble in character, and he was always at home.
En Þórðr var í förum ok var hirðmaðr Magnúss konungs ok mazt vel.	But Thord was in travelling and was court-man Magnus the-king and most well.	But Thord was a travelling man, and a court man of King Magnus who thought most well of him.
Ok eitt sinn, er Þórðr bjó skip sitt í Eyjafirði, þá kom Hreiðarr þar, bróðir hans.	And once his, was Thord prepared ship his in Eyjafjord, then came Hreidar there, brother his.	And one day when Thord was preparing his ship in Eyjafjord, then came Hreidar his brother.
Ok er Þórðr sá hann, spurði hann, hví hann væri þar kominn.	And when Thord saw him, asked he, why he was there coming.	And when Thord saw him, he asked why he had come there.
Hreiðarr segir:	Hreidar said:	Hreidar said:
"Eigi nema erendit væri".	"Nothing except errand was".	"I would not have come unless I had business".
"Hvat villtu þá?"	"What will-you then?"	"What do you want then?"
segir Þórðr.	said Thord.	said Thord.

The Tale of Hreiðarr the Fool (Old Norse)

Old Norse	Literal	English
"Ek Vil fara útan",	"I Wish travel out",	"I wish to travel abroad",
segir Hreiðarr.	said Hreidar.	said Hreidar.
Þórðr mælti:	Thord spoke:	Thord spoke:
"Ekki þykkir mér þér fallin förin".	"Not think I you fallen for-travelling".	"I don't think you are destined for travelling".
Vil ek heldr þat til leggja við þik, at þú hafir föðurarf okkarn, ok er þat hálfu meira fé en þat, er ek hefi í förum".	Wish I rather that to let from you, that you have inheritance ours, and is that half more money than that, which I have in trading-voyages".	"I wish rather than to let you go, for you to have our inheritance, and that is more than half the money which I have in trading voyages".
Hreiðarr svarar:	Hreidar answered:	Hreidar answered:
"Þá er lítit vit mitt",	"Then would little know me",	"Then I would know little",
segir hann, "ef ek tek þenna fjárskakka til þess at gefa mik svá upp sjálfan ok láta þína umsjá, ok mun þá hverr maðr draga af mér fé okkart, alls ek kann engi forræði, þau er nýt eru.	said he, "if I took that uneven-share to this to gave I so up myself and left your guidance, and would then every man draw of me money ours, all I know no self-control, then where used they-are.	he said, "if I took that uneven share, then gave myself up and left your guidance, and then every man would cheat money out of us, and I know no self-control where they are used.
Ok era þér þá betra hlut í at eiga, ef ek ber á mönnum eða gerik aðra óvísu þeim, er um fé mitt sitja at lokka af mér, en eftir þat sé ek barðr eða meiddr fyrir mínar tilgerðir, enda er þat sannast í, at þér mun torsótt at halda mér eftir, er ek vil fara".	And are you then better share in that own, if I bear to people or do other unknown them, is about money mine sit that lure off me, but after that so is beat or hurt for mine to-do, and is that true in, that you should difficulty that rather to-me after, that I will travel".	And it is better for you to own a share, if I bear to people or do otherwise unknown things to them, those who attend in luring money away from me, but after that I will be beaten or hurt for my deeds, for that is true, that you will have a hard time keeping me, when I want to go".
"Vera kann þat",	"Be can that",	"That may be",
segir Þórðr, "en get ekki þá um ferð þína fyrir öðrum mönnum".	said Thord, "but mention not then about travel yours before other people".	said Thord, "but don't mention your travel in front of other people".
Því hét hann.	Therefore promised he.	Therefore he promised.

The Tale of Hreiðarr the Fool (Old Norse)

Old Norse	Literal	English
Ok þegar er þeir eru skilðir, þá segir Hreiðarr hverjum, er heyra vill, at hann ætlar útan at fara með bróður sínum.	And as-soon-as that they were parted, then told Hreidar everyone, that heard would, that he intended out to travel with brother his.	And as soon as they had parted, Hreidar told everyone that would hear him, that he intended to travel abroad with his brother.
Ok firna allir Þórð um, ef hann flytr útan afglapa.	And criticised all Thord about, if he transport out fool.	And everyone criticised Thord, if he travel abroad with such a fool.

2

Ok er þeir eru búnir, sigla þeir í haf ok Verða vel reiðfara, koma við Björgyn, ok þegar spyrr Þórðr eftir konungi, ok var honum sagt, at Magnús konungr var í bænum ok hafði skömmu áðr komit ok vildi eigi láta kæja sik samdægris, þóttist þurfa hvíldar, er hann var nýkominn.	And when they were prepared, sailed they to sea and Became well voyage, came to Bergen, and there asked Thord after the-king, and was he told, that Magnus the-king was in residence and had recently returned come and willed not be-allowed disturbed him same-day, thought needed rest, when he was newly-come.	And when they were ready, they sailed to sea and began their voyage well, they came to Bergen, and there Thord asked for the king, and he was told that King Magnus was in residence and had recently returned home and did not wish to be disturbed that day, because he needed rest after newly coming home.
Brátt litu menn Hreiðar, at hann var afbragð annarra manna.	Soon noticed people Hreidar, that he was stood-out other men.	Soon people noticed Hreidar, that he stood out from other men.
Hann var mikill ok ljótr, ómállatr við þá, er hann hitti.	He was tall and ugly, chatty with then, who he met.	He was tall and ugly, and chatty with whoever he met.
Ok snemma um morgininn, áðr menn Væri vaknaðir, stendr Hreiðarr upp ok kallar:	And early about morning, before people Were woken, stood Hreidar up and called:	And early in the morning, before people were awake, Hreidar stood up and called:
"Vaki þú, bróðir.	"Wake you, brother.	"Wake up, brother.
Fátt veit sá, er sefr.	Little knows so, who sleeps.	He who sleeps knows little.
Ek veit tíðendi, ok heyrðak áðan læti kynlig".	I know news, and heard earlier noise strange".	I have some news, and earlier I heard a strange noise.
"Hverju var líkast?"	"What was like?"	"What was it like?"
spyrr Þórðr.	asked Thord.	asked Thord.
"Sem yfir kykvendum",	"Like about some-beast",	"Like some beast",

The Tale of Hreiðarr the Fool (Old Norse)

Old Norse	Literal	English
segir Hreiðarr, "ok þaut við mjök, en aldri veit ek, hvat látum var".	said Hreidar, "and shrill as much, but never knew i, what have was".	said Hreidar, "and as shrill as one, but I never knew what it was".
"Lát eigi svá undarliga",	"Have not so strange",	"That is not so strange",
segir Þórðr.	said Thord.	said Thord.
"Þat mun verit hafa hornblástr".	"It must been have trumpet-blast".	"It must have been a blast from a trumpet".
"Hvat skal þat tákna?"	"What shall it betoken?"	"What does that mean?"
spyrr Hreiðarr.	asked Hreidar.	asked Hreidar.
Þórðr svarar:	Thord answered:	Thord answered:
"Blásit er jafnan til móts eða til skipdráttar".	"Trumpet-blast is always to meetings or to ship-launching".	"A trumpet blast always means a meeting being summoned or for the launching of ships".
"Hvat táknar mótit?"	"What taken meetings?"	"What are these meetings taken for?"
spyrr Hreiðarr.	asked Hreidar.	asked Hreidar.
"Þar eru dæmð vandamál jafnan",	"They are to-deem disputes equally",	"They are to judge disputes equally",
segir Þórðr, "ok slíkt talat, sem konungr þykkist þurfa, at fyrir alþýðu sé upp borit".	said Thord, "and such told, as the-king seems needed, that before the-people so up bear".	said Thord, "and for things to be told, such as the king sees fit, to bear to the people".
"Hvárt mun konungr nú á mótinu?"	"Whether shall the-king now at meeting?"	"Will the king be there now at the meeting?"
spyrr Hreiðarr.	asked Hreidar.	asked Hreidar.
"Þat ætla ek víst",	"That suppose I certainly",	"I suppose so, certainly",
svarar Þórðr.	answered Thord.	answered Thord.
"Þangat verð ek þá at fara",	"From-here worth I then to go",	"Then it is worth me going there",

The Tale of Hreiðarr the Fool (Old Norse)

Old Norse	Literal	English
segir Hreiðarr, "því at ek vilda þar koma fyrst, er ek sæja sem flesta menn í senn".	said Hreidar, "because that I wish there to-come first, that I see as most people to together".	said Hreidar, "because I wish to go there first, to see as many people together at once".
"Þá skýtr í tvau horn með okkr",	"Then throws to two corners with us",	"Then that throws into two corners with us",
segir Þórðr.	said Thord.	said Thord.
"Mér þætti því betr er þú kæmir þar síðr, er fjölmennt væri, ok vil ek hvergi fara".	"To-me seems therefore better that you come there less, when crowded will-be, and wish I nowhere to-go".	"It seems better to me therefore that you go there less, when it will be crowded, and I don't wish to go there myself".
"Ekki tjáir slíkt at mæla",	"Not express such to discuss",	"It does not do to say such a thing",
segir Hreiðarr, "fara skulum vit báðir.	said Hreidar, "travel shall we both.	said Hreidar, "we shall travel both.
Muna þér betra þykkja, at ek fara einn, en ekki fær þú mik lattan þessarar farar".	Should you better to-think, that I travel alone, and not can you me dissuade this-kind-of journey".	I think you had better realise, that I am going alone, and you can not dissuade me from making this journey".
Hleypr Hreiðarr á brott.	Ran Hreidar to away.	Then Hreidar ran away,
En Þórðr sér nú, at fara mun verða, ok ferr hann eftir, er Hreiðarr ferr hart undan, ok er mjök langt milli þeira.	When Thord saw now, that going should be, also went he after, as Hreidar went hard away, and was much long between them.	But now Thord saw that this would happen, he also went after him, as Hreidar went hard away, and there was a long way between them.
Ok er Hreiðarr sér, at Þórðr fór seint, þá mælti hann:	And when Hreidar saw, that Thord went slowly, then spoke he:	And when Hreidar saw, that Thord was going slowly, then he spoke:
"Þat er þó satt, at illt er lítill at vera, þá er aflit nær ekki.	"It is though true, that bad is small to be, then that strength near is-not.	"It is true that it is bad to be small, because then strength is not near.
En þó mætti vera fráleikrinn, en lítit ætla ek þik af honum hafa hlotit,	But though may be swiftness, but little suppose I you of it have bound-to,	But though one can still be swift, but I suppose you have little of that,
ok væria þér verri vænleikr minni, ok kæmist þú með öðrum mönnum".	and be to-you worse handsome less, and come you as other men".	and you should be less handsome, and quicker as other men are".

128

The Tale of Hreiðarr the Fool (Old Norse)

Old Norse	Literal	English
Þórðr svaraði:	Thord answered:	Thord answered:
"Eigi veit ek mér verr fara óknáleik minn en þér afl þitt".	"Not know I me worse to-be prowess mine than you strength yours".	"I do not know if it is worse to have my weakness than your strength".
"Handkrækjumst þá, bróðir",	"Hands-hook-us then, brother",	"Let us hook hands then, brother",
segir Hreiðarr,	said Hreidar,	said Hreidar,
ok nú gera þeir svá, fara um hríð, ok er svá, at Þórði tekr at dofna höndin, ok lætr hann laust, þykkir eigi verða vinveitt, at þeir haldist á, við álpun Hreiðars.	and now did they so, went about awhile, and was seen, that Thord took that numb hand, and had he let-go, felt not was friendly, that they rather that, against rough Hreidar.	and so they did, and after a while, and Thord's hand became so numb, that he had to let go, and he felt it was not friendly, because Hreidar was too rough.
Hreiðarr ferr nú undan svá við fót ok nemr stað síðan á hæð nökkurri ok er allstarsýnn, sér þaðan fjölmennit, þangat sem mótit var.	Hreidar went now away-from so with foot and took place afterwards to height some and was fixed-upon, saw from-there many-people, there as meeting were.	Hreidar now went away and ran, and so it happened afterwards, that he came to a hill and stopped there, he looked from there and saw many people, that were at a meeting.
Ok er Þórðr kemr eftir, mælti hann:	And as Thord came after, spoke he:	And as Thord came afterwards, he spoke:
"Förum nú báðir saman, bróðir".	"Going now both together, brother".	"Let's go both together now, brother".
Ok Hreiðarr gerir svá.	And Hreidar did so.	And Hreidar did so.

3

Ok er þeir koma á þingit, kenna margir menn Þórð ok fagna honum vel, ok verðr konungr áheyrsli.	And when they came to assembly, knew many people Thord and welcomed him well, and became the-king to-hear.	And when they came to the assembly, many people knew Thord and welcomed him well, and the king came to hear of him.
Ok þegar gengr Þórðr fyrir konung ok kveðr hann vel, ok tekr konungr blíðlíga kveðju hans.	And soon went Thord before the-king and greeted he well, and took the-king joyfully greeting his.	And soon Thord went before the king and greeted him well, and the king received his greeting joyfully.

The Tale of Hreiðarr the Fool (Old Norse)

Old Norse	Literal	English
Þegar skilði með þeim bræðrum, er þeir kómu til þingsins, ok verðr Hreiðarr skauttogaðr mjök ok færðr í reikuð.	When parted with them brothers, that they came to their-assembly, and became Hreidar roughly much and brought to roughly-handled.	When the brothers parted when they came to the assembly, Hreidar was treated roughly and pushed about.
Hann er málugr ok hlær mjök, ok þykkir mönnum ekki at minna gaman at eiga við hann, ok verðr honum nú förin ógreið.	He was talkative and laughed much, and thought people not that less fun that had with him, and became he now travelling un-passable.	He was talkative and laughed a lot, and people thought it no less fun to tease him, and he now became blocked in the crowd.
Konungr spyrr Þórð tíðenda, ok síðan spyrr hann, hvat þeira manna væri í för með honum, er hann vildi, at til hirðvistar færi með honum.	The-king asked Thord news, and then asked he, what they people were by travelling with him, that he wished, that to court-visit bring with him.	The king asked Thord for news, and then he asked, and what people were travelling with him, and whether he wished to join him at court.
"Þar er bróðir minn í för",	"There has brother mine so travelled",	"My brother has also travelled here",
segir Þórðr.	said Thord.	said Thord.
"Sá maðr mun vel vera",	"Such man should well be",	"Such a man should be well",
segir konungr, "ef þér er líkr".	said the-king, "if you is like".	said the king, "if he is like you".
Þórðr segir:	Thord said:	Thord said:
"Ekki er hann mér glíkr".	"Not is he me like".	"He is not like me".
Konungr mælti:	The-king spoke:	The king spoke:
"Þó má enn vel vera, eða hvat er ólíkast með ykkr?"	"Though may but well be, but how is unlike with you?"	"That may be, but now is he not like you?"
Þórðr mælti:	Thord spoke:	Thord spoke:
"Hann er mikill maðr vexti.	"He is great man grown.	"He is very large.
Hann er ljótr ok heldr ósýknligr, srterkr at afli ok lundhægr maðr".	He is ugly and behold un-innocent-looking, strong in strength and even-spirit man".	He is ugly, and he appears devious looking, and he is greatly strong, but even spirited".
Konungr mælti:	The-king spoke:	The king spoke:

The Tale of Hreiðarr the Fool (Old Norse)

Old Norse	Literal	English
"Þó má honum vel vera farit at mörgu".	"Though may he well be going that many-ways".	"He may be well in other ways".
Þórðr segir:	Thord said:	Thord said:
"Ekki var hann kallaðr vizkumaðr á unga aldri".	"Not was he called wise-man in young age".	"He was not called a wise man in his youth".
"At því fer ek meir",	"That then go I further",	"Then I go further",
segir konungr, "sem nú er, eða hvárt má hann sjálfr annast sik?"	said the-king, "as now to, but how may he himself take-care-of such?"	said the king, "to how he is now, and how he takes care of himself?"
"Ekki dála er þat",	"Not bad is that",	"Not bad",
segir Þórðr.	said Thord.	said Thord.
Konungr mælti:	The-king spoke:	The king spoke:
"Hví fluttir þú hann útan?"	"Why brought you him out?"	"Why did you bring him out?"
"Herra",	"Lord",	"Lord",
segir Þórðr, "hann á allt hálft við mik, en hefir engar nytjar fjárins ok engi afskipti sér veitt um peninga, beiðzt þessa eins hlutar, at fara útan með mér, ok þótti mér ósannligt, at eigi réði hann einum hlut, þars hann lætr mik mörgum ráða.	said Thord, "he has altogether half with me, but has no use of-wealth and none dealings so given about money, best this one's share, that travel out with me, and thought me untrue, that not decide he alone share, there he leaves much many advice.	said Thord, "he has half of everything with me, but he has no use of wealth and no interest in money, the only thing he has asked me is to travel abroad with me, and I thought it would be unfair to decide to leave him alone, when he lets me decide so much.
Þótti mér ok glíkligt, at hann mundi gæfu af yðr hljóta, ef hann kæmi á yðvarn fund".	Thought me and favourable, that he would be-gifted of your luck, if he came to you meet".	I thought it would be favourable and good luck if he came to meet you".
"Sjá vilda ek hann",	"So willed I him",	"So I wish to meet him",
segir konungr.	said the-king.	said the king.
"Svá skal ok",	"So shall and",	"So shall it be",
segir Þórðr, "en brottu er hann nú rjáðr nökkur".	said Thord, "but steep is he now worried somewhat".	said Thord, "but he is now somewhat worried".
Konungr sendi nú eftir honum.	The-king sent now after him.	The king now sent for him.

The Tale of Hreiðarr the Fool (Old Norse)

Old Norse	Literal	English
Ok er Hreiðarr heyrði sagt, at konungr vildi hitta hann, þá gengr hann uppstert mjök ok nær á hvat, sem fyrir var, ok var hann því óvanr, at konungr hefði beiðzt fundar hans.	And when Hreidar heard said, that the-king wished meet him, then walked he upright much and near to what, as before was, and was he then unaccustomed, to the-king having asked to-meet him.	And when Hreidar heard it said, that the king wished to meet him, then he walked very upright and near to what was before him, and he was then unaccustomed to the king having asked to meet him.
Hann var á þá leið búinn, at hann var í ökulbrókum ok hafði feld grán yfir sér.	He was that then way dressed, that he was in ankle-breeches and had cloak grey over himself.	He was dressed in such a way, that he was wearing ankle-breeches and a grey cloak over him.
Ok er hann kemr fyrir konung, þá fellr hann á kné fyrir konung ok kveðr hann Vel.	And when he came before the-king, then fell he on knees before the-king and greeted him Well.	And when he came before the king, he then fell on his knees before the king and greeted him well.
Konungr svaraði honum hlæjandi ok mælti:	The-king answered him laughing and spoke:	The king laughed and said:
"Ef þú átt við mik erendi, þá mæl þú skjótt slíkt, er þú vill.	"If you have with me business, then say you swiftly such, as you will.	"If you have business with me, then say as swiftly as you will.
Aðrir eigu enn nauðsyn at tala við mik síðan".	Others have but need to talk with me after".	There are others who need to talk with me afterwards".
Hreiðarr segir:	Hreidar said:	Hreidar said:
"Mitt erendi þykkir mér skyldast.	"My business think to-me obliged.	"I think my business is more urgent.
Ek vilda sjá þik, konungr".	I wished to-see you, king".	I wished to see you, king".
"Þykkir þér nú vel þá",	"Think you now well then",	"Do you think it well now",
segir konungr, "er þú sér mik?"	said the-king, "that you saw me?"	said the king, "that you saw me?"
"Vel víst",	"Well certainly",	"Well certainly",
segir Hreiðarr, "en eigi þykkjumst ek enn til gerla sjá þik".	said Hreidar, "but not think I that to completely saw you".	said Hreidar, "but I don't think that I have seen you completely".
"Hvernig skulum vit nú þá?"	"Which shall we now then?"	"What shall we do now then?"

The Tale of Hreiðarr the Fool (Old Norse)

Old Norse	Literal	English
segir konungr.	said the-king.	said the king.
"Vildir þú, at ek stæða upp?"	"Would you, that I stand up?"	"Would you like me to stand up?"
Hreiðarr svarar:	Hreidar answered:	Hreidar answered:
"Þat vilda ek",	"That wish i",	"That I would wish",
segir hann.	said he.	he said.
Konungr mælti, er hann var upp staðinn:	The-king spoke, then he was up standing:	The king spoke, when he stood up:
"Nú muntu þykkjast gerla sjá mik mega?"	"Now should-you consider completely seen me may?"	"Now have you seen me completely?"
"Eigi enn til gerla",	"Not then to completely",	"Not completely",
segir Hreiðarr, "ok er nú þó nær hófi".	said Hreidar, "and are now though near measure".	said Hreidar, "but it is now closer".
"Villtu þá",	"Wish-you then",	"Do you wish then",
segir konungr, "at ek leggja af mér skikkjuna?"	said the-king, "that I take off my cloak?"	said the king, "that I take off my cloak?"
"Þat vilda ek víst,	"That wish I certainly",	"That I certainly wish",
segir Hreiðarr.	said Hreidar.	said Hreidar.
Konungr mælti:	The-king spoke:	The king spoke:
"Vit skulum þar þó nökkut innast til áðr um þat málit.	"We should there though some do to before about that discuss.	"We should then discuss the matter before doing it.
Þér eruð hugkvæmir margir, Íslendingar, ok Veit ek eigi, nema þú virðir þetta til ginningar.	You are very-smart many, Icelander, and Know I not, except you worth this to mocking.	You Icelanders are very smart, and I do not know, if this is mockery.
Nú vil ek þat undan skilja".	Now wish I that away-from understand".	Now I wish to be away from that, you understand".
Hreiðarr segir:	Hreidar said:	Hreidar said:

133

The Tale of Hreiðarr the Fool (Old Norse)

Old Norse	Literal	English
"Engi er til þess færr, konungr, at ginna þik eða ljúga at þér".	"None that to this capable, king, of mocking you or lie to you".	"I am not capable of this, king, of mocking you or lying to you".
Konungr leggr nú af sér skikkjuna ok mælti:	The-king laid now off his cloak and spoke:	The king now took off his cloak and poke:
"Hyggðu nú at mér svá vandliga sem þik tíðir".	"Think now that me so closely as you wish".	"Think now that you may see me as closely as you wish".
"Svá skal vera",	"So shall be",	"So it shall be",
segir Hreiðarr.	said Hreidar.	said Hreidar.
Hann gengr í hring um konunginn ok mælti oft it sama fyrir munni sér:	He walked in a-ring around the-king and spoke frequently to himself before mouth his:	He walked in a ring around the king and spoke frequently to himself and mumbling:
"Allvel, allvel",	"All-well, all-well",	"Splendid, splendid",
segir hann.	said he.	he said.
Konungr mælti:	The-king spoke:	The king spoke:
"Hefir þú nú sét mik sem þú villt?"	"Have you now seen me as you wish?"	"Have you now seen me as you wish?"
"At vísu",	"That certainly",	"Certainly"
segir hann.	said he.	he said.
Konungr spurði:	The-king asked:	The king asked:
"Hversu lízt þér nú á mik þá?"	"How-so appears to-you now of me then?"	"How do I appear to you now then?"
Hreiðarr svarar:	Hreidar answered:	Hreidar answered:
"Ekki hefir Þórðr, bróðir minn, ofsögum frá þér sagt, þat er vel er".	"Not had Thord, brother mine, off-said from you said, that is well be".	"My brother Thord did not exaggerate when he said of your well being".
Konungr mælti:	The-king spoke:	The king spoke:
"Máttu nökkut at finna um þat, er þú sér nú, ok þat, er eigi sé í alþýðu viti?"	"May-you something to find about that, which you see now, and that, is not seen by all-the-people knowing?"	"Can you find something that you see now, that has not been seen by other people?"

The Tale of Hreiðarr the Fool (Old Norse)

Old Norse	Literal	English
"Ekki vil ek at finna",	"Not wish I to find",	"I do not wish to find",
segir hann, "ok ekki má ek þegar, því at þannig myndi hverr sik kjósa sem þú ert, þó at sjálfr mætti ráða".	said he, "and not may I from-there, accordingly that thus would each themselves choose as you are, though that self may advise".	he said, "and I can not find, because thus would everyone choose to be as you are, if they could".
"Mikinn tekr þú af",	"Great take you of",	"You are taking off",
segir konungr.	said the-king.	said the king.
Hreiðarr svarar:	Hreidar answered:	Hreidar answered:
"Háttung er öðrum á þá",	"Risk are others for then",	"It is a risk for others then",
segir hann, "at lofgjarnliga sé við mælt, ef þú átt þetta eigi at sönnu, sem mér lízt á þik ok ek sagða áðan".	said he, "that praise-will you of speaking, if you that this not that true, as to-me appears of you and I said earlier".	he said, "for those who praise you, if it is not true, how you appear to me as I said earlier".
Konungr mælti:	The-king spoke:	The king spoke:
"Finn til nökkut, þó at smátt sé".	"Find to something, though that small is".	"Find something, though it is small".
"Þat helzt þá, herra",	"Is rather then, lord",	"It is then rather",
segir hann, "at auga þitt annat er litlu því ofar en annat".	said he, "that eye the other is a-little before above the other".	he said, "that one eye is a little above the other".
"Þat hefir einn maðr fyrr fundit",	"That has one man before found",	"Only one man has noticed that before",
segir konungr, "en sá er Haraldr konungr, frændi minn.	said the-king, "and that was Harald the-king, kinsman mine.	said the king, "and that was King Harald, my kinsman.
Nú skal jafnmæli með okkr",	Now shall equal-speak with you",	Now I shall equally say of you",
segir konungr.	said the-king.	said the king.
"Skaltu nú standa upp ok leggja af þér skikkju, ok vil ek sjá þik".	"Shall-you now stand up and allow off your cloak, and will I see you".	"Stand up and take off your cloak, and I will see you".

The Tale of Hreiðarr the Fool (Old Norse)

Old Norse	Literal	English
Hreiðarr fleygir af sér feldinum ok hefir saurgar krummur, - maðrinn hentr mjök ok ljótr - en þvegnar heldr latliga.	Hreidar threw off his cloak and had dirty hands, a-man suited much and ugly but to-wash rather negligently.	Hreidar threw off his cloak, and he had large dirty hands, suited to such an ugly man, and washed negligently.
Konungr hyggr at honum vandliga.	The-king looked at him closely.	The king looked at him closely.
Ok þá mælir Hreiðarr:	And then spoke Hreidar:	And then Hreidar spoke:
"Herra",	"Lord",	"Lord",
segir hann, "hvat þykkist þú nú mega at mér finna?"	said he, "what think you now may that me find?"	he said, "what do you think you may find?"
Konungr segir:	The-king said:	The king said:
"Þat ætla ek, at eigi fæðist ljótari maðr upp en þú ert".	"That suppose i, that not born uglier man up than you are".	"That I suppose that there is not a man born uglier than you".
"Slíkt verðr mælt",	"Such becomes spoken",	"This is what is said",
segir Hreiðarr.	said Hreidar.	said Hreidar.
"Er nökkut þá",	"But some then",	"But are there some",
segir hann, "at til fríðenda sé um mik, at því sem þú leggr ætlan á?"	said he, "that to good-things see about me, that therefore which you have suppose of?"	he said, "good things to see about me, that you might suppose?"
Konungr mælti:	The-king spoke:	The king spoke:
"Þat sagði Þórðr, bróðir þinn, af þú værir lundhægr maðr".	"That said Thord, brother yours, of you be tempered-even man".	"That your brother Thord said you are an even-tempered man".
"Þat er satt ok",	"That is true also",	"That is also true",
sagði Hreiðarr, "ok þykkir mér þat illt, er svá er".	said Hreidar, "and think me that ill, is so to-be".	said Hreidar, "and I think that it is bad to be".
"Þú munt reiðast þó",	"Though shall-you anger though",	"Though one day you will become angry",
sagði konungr.	said the-king.	said the king.
"Mæl heill, herra",	"Say whole, lord",	"Speak well, lord",

136

The Tale of Hreiðarr the Fool (Old Norse)

Old Norse	Literal	English
segir Hreiðarr, "eða hvé langt mun til þess?"	said Hreidar, "but how long could until this?"	said Hreidar, "but how long could it be until this happens?"
"Eigi veit ek þat gerla",	"Not know I that completely",	"That I do not know completely",
segir konungr, "helzt á þessum vetri, at því er ek get til".	said the-king, "rather of this winter, that since that I guess to".	said the king, "rather some time this winter, if my guess is right".
Hreiðarr mælti:	Hreidar spoke:	Hreidar spoke:
"Seg heill sögu".	"Tell a-complete story".	"Tell a complete story".
Konungr mælti:	The-king spoke:	The king spoke:
"Ertu nökkut hagr?"	"Are-you of-any benefit?"	"Are you any good at anything?"
Hreiðarr segir:	Hreidar said:	Hreidar said:
"Aldrigi hefi ek reynt, má ek því eigi vita".	"Never have I tried, may I therefore not know".	"I have never tried, and therefore I do not know".
"Til þess þætti þó ekki ólíkligt",	"To this seems though not unlikely",	"It does not seem unlikely"
segir konungr.	said the-king.	said the king.
"Seg heill sögu",	"Tell the-whole story",	"Tell the whole story",
kvað Hreiðarr.	said Hreidar.	said Hreidar.
"Svá mun vera jafnt þegar, er þú segir þat.	"So should be equally then, as you say it.	"So shall it be, just as you say.
En vetrvistar þættumst ek þurfa".	And winter-provisions we-have I need".	And I need winter provisions".
Konungr sagði:	The-king said:	The king said:
"Heimil er mín umsjá.	"Home being mine about.	"My home is so about.
En betr þykkir mér þér þar vistin felld vera, er heldr er fátt manna".	But better think I you then stay shed be, where rather are few people".	But I think it better if you stay in the shed, where there are few people".

137

The Tale of Hreiðarr the Fool (Old Norse)

Old Norse	Literal	English
Hreiðarr svaraði:	Hreidar answered:	Hreidar answered:
"Svá er þat ok",	"So is it and",	"So it may be",
segir hann.	said he.	he said.
"En eigi mun svá mannfátt vera, at eigi komi þat þó upp, er mælt verðr, allra helzt þat, er hlægi þykkir í, en ek maðr ekki orðvarr, ok jafnan berr mér margt á góma.	"But not would so people-few be, that not come that though up, in spoken become, all rather that, is ridicule thought in, that I people not discreet, and equally carry I many about gums.	"But there would not be so few people, that none came up though, and in speaking something that is a joke, people think I am not discreet, and many people carry this about in their mouths.
Nú kann vera, at þeir reiði orð mín fyrir aðra menn ok spotti mik ok drepi þat at ferligu, er ek hefi at gamni eða mælik.	Now can be, that their anger words mine before other people and small me and kill that to monstrous, what I have been amuse or speak.	Now it may be that they angered my words before other people, and mocked me, and kill me for what I have been amused to speak.
Nú sýnist mér hitt vitrligra at vera heldr hjá þeim, er um mik hyggr, sem Þórðr er, bróðir minn, þótt þar sé heldr fjölmenni, en hinnig, þótt menn sé fáir ok sé þar engi til umbóta".	Now seems I find wisely to be rather by them, that about me think, as Thord is, brother mine, thought then be rather followers-many, that there, though people as few and as there no-one to put-right".	Now it seems to me the wiser thing to be beside those, who about me consider, such as Thord, my brother, though there are more people there than otherwise and there is no one to put things right".
Konungr mælti:	The-king spoke:	The king spoke:
"Ráð þú þá, ok farið báðir bræðr til hirðarinnar, ef ykkr líkar þat betr".	"Decide you then, and go both brothers to court, if you like that better".	"You decide then, and you and your brother can both come to court if you would like that better".
Þegar hljóp Hreiðarr á brott, er hann heyrði þessi orð konungs", ok segir hverjum manni, er á vill hlýða, at hans för hefir allgóð orðit á konungs fund, segir ok einkum Þórði, bróður sínum, at konungr hefir leyft honum at fara til hirðvistar.	Straightaway ran Hreidar to away, that he heard these words the-king's, and told each of-the-people, that from well listened, that his going had all-good words from the-king visit, said and especially Thord, brother his, that the-king had given-leave him to travel to court.	Then Hreidar ran away when he heard the king's words, and told every person who listened, how it had gone with all the good words from his visit to the king, and said especially to his brother Thord, that the king had given them leave to travel to court.
Þá mælti Þórðr:	Then spoke Thord:	Then Thord spoke:

The Tale of Hreiðarr the Fool (Old Norse)

Old Norse	Literal	English
"Bú þik þá sæmiliga at klæðum eða vápnum, því at þ-at eitt samir, ok skortir okkr ekki til þess, ok skipast margir menn vel við góðan búning, enda er vandara at búa sik í konungs herbergi en annars staðar, ok verðr síðr at hlægi gerr af hirðmönnum".	"Prepare you then well-enough with clothes and weapons, because that it one in-common, and shortage ours not to this, and changed many people well with good clothing, and is important to dress such as the-king's room than any-other place, and become less the ridicule made of court-men".	"Prepare yourself well with clothes and weapons, because there is one thing in common, and we have no shortage in this, and many people are changed by good clothing, and it is important to dress well in the king's room more than any other place, and it will avoid ridicule from the court-men".
Hreiðarr svarar:	Hreidar answered:	Hreidar answered:
"Eigi getr þú allnær, at ek muna skrúðklæðin á mik láta koma".	"Not get you all-near, that I should costly-clothing of me allow coming".	"You will not get anywhere near me coming along wearing fancy clothing".
Þórðr mælti:	Thord spoke:	Thord spoke:
"Skerum vaðmál þá til".	"Cut homespun-cloth then to".	"Then you will wear cut home-spun cloth".
Hreiðarr svarar:	Hreidar answered:	Hreidar answered:
"Nær er þat",	"Near is that",	"That would be better",
segir hann.	said he.	he said.
Svá er nú gert við ráð Þórðar, ok lætr Hreiðarr eftir leiðast.	So that now did with advice Thord's, and had Hreidar afterwards carried-out.	So now it was done with Thord's advice, and then Hreidar had carried it out.
Hefir hann nú vaðmálsklæði ok fágar sik ok þykkir nú þegar allr annarr maðr, sýnist nú maðr ljótr ok greitt vaskligr.	Had he now wadding-clothes and cleaned himself and seemed now already all another man, seemed now a-man ugly and ready-to-serve valiant.	Now he had wadding-clothes and cleaned himself, and he already seemed like a different man, he was still ugly, but now valiant looking.
Svá er þó mót á manninum, er þeir Þórðr eru með hirðinni, at Hreiðarr verðr í fyrstu fyrir miklum ágang af hirðmönnum, ok breyttu þeir marga vega orðum við hann ok fundu, at hann var ómállatr.	So was though against about the-people, that they Thord were with court-men, that Hreidar became the first before much aggression of court-men, and varied they many ways words with him and found, that he was talkative.	So it was though, in meeting the people, that with Thord and with the court-men, that Hreidar became singled out for much aggression from the court-me, and there were many ways in which they had words with him, and he was talkative.

The Tale of Hreiðarr the Fool (Old Norse)

Old Norse	Literal	English
Kom við sem mátti, ok hendu þeir mikit gaman at því at eiga við hann, ok var hann jafnan hlæjandi við því, er þeir mæltu, ok lagði hvern þeira fyrir, svá var hann leikmikill, bæði um mælgina ok allra helzt - -	Came with how it-may, and handed they much fun that because that had with he, and was he equally laughing with such, that they spoke, and had each they before, so was he playful, both about talking and all rather	It became how it may, that they had much fun with him, and he was laughing equally as much with them, with what they said, and with each of them he was playful, both in talking and rather in all things.
En fyrir því, at hann var rammi at afli ok er þeir finna, at hann gefst ekki at grandi, þá þvarr þat allt af þeim hirðmönnum - - [nú með] hirðinni.	When for then, that he was frame that strength and when they found, that he gave not to injury, then decreased that all of them court-men [now with] court.	Then when they realised how strong his frame was, and when they found that he did not give in to injury, then the mocking of him decreased with all the court-men.

4

Í þetta mund váru þeir báðir konungar yfir landi, Magnús konungr ok Haraldr konungr.	In that time were they both kings over the-land, Magnus the-king and Harald the-king.	At that time there were two kings ruling over the land, King Magnus, and King Harald.
En þá höfðu sakar gerzt - - hirðmaðr Magnúss konungs hafði vegit hirðmann Haralds konungs, ok var lagðr til sáttarfundr, at konungar skyldi [sjálfir finnast] ok skipa málinu.	But then had conviction made court-man Magnus's the-king had slain court-man Harald's the-king, and was laid to peace-meeting, that kings should [themselves meet-up] and exchange the-matter.	But then trouble came when one of Magnus's court-men had slain one of Harald's court-men, and they had a peace meeting, so that the kings themselves could meet up and discuss the matter.
Ok er Hreiðarr heyrir þetta, at Magnús konungr skal fara til móts við Harald konung, þá ferr hann á fund Magnúss konungs ok mælti:	And when Hreidar heard this, that Magnus the-king shall travel to meet with Harald the-king, then went he to find Magnus the-king and spoke:	And when Hreidar heard this, that King Magnus would travel to meet with King Harald, then he went to find King Magnus and spoke:
"Sá hlutr er",	"So share i",	"So I share",
segir hann, "er ek vilda þik biðja".	said he, "that I Wish you to-ask".	he said, "something that I wish to ask you".
"Hverr er sá?"	"What is so?"	"What is it?"
sagði konungr.	said the-king.	said the king.
Hreiðarr mælti:	Hreidar spoke:	Hreidar spoke:
"At fara til sáttarfundar.	"To travel to peace-meeting.	"To travel to the peace meeting.

The Tale of Hreiðarr the Fool (Old Norse)

Old Norse	Literal	English
Em ek ekki víðförull, en mér er mikil forvitni á at sjá tvá konunga senn í einum stað".	Am I not widely-travelled, but I am much curious about to see two kings they in one place".	I am not widely travelled, but I am very curious to see two kings in one place".
Konungr svarar:	The-king answered:	The king answered:
"Satt segir þú, at þú ert ekki víðförull.	"True say you, that you are not widely-travelled.	"It is true to say that you are not widely travelled.
En þeygi mun ek leyfa þér þessa förna, því at ekki er þér fellt at ganga í greipr mönnum Haralds konungs.	But yet-not could I allow you this sacrificing, for that not are you falling to go in grasp people Harald's the-king.	But I could not allow this, to sacrifice you, if you fall into the grasp of King Harald.
Ok beri svá til, at þér verði at því ólið eða öðrum ok, em ek um þat hræddr, at þá sæki þik heim reiðin, er þú langar til, en mér þætti bezt, at við bærist".	And bear so to, that you became that for unaccompanied or others and, am I about that worried, that then conviction you home uproar, that you long to, then me seems best, that with bearing".	And so it carries, that if you become separated from the others, I am worried that, then you might be involved in trouble, and then you would become angry, and so it seems best to me, with that in mind".
Hreiðarr svarar:	Hreidar answered:	Hreidar answered:
"Nú mæltir þú gott orð.	"Now speak you good words.	"Now you speak good words.
Þá skal at vísu fara, ef ek veit þess vánir, at ek reiðumst".	Then shall to certainly travel, if I know this custom, that I become-angry".	Then I am more certain to travel, if I know that I am accustomed to becoming angry".
Konungr segir:	The-king said:	The king said:
"Muntu fara, ef ek leyfi eigi?"	"Shall-you travel, if I leave not?"	"Will you travel, if I do not give leave for it?"
Hreiðarr svarar:	Hreidar answered:	Hreidar answered:
"Eigi þá síðr".	"None then less".	"None the less".
"Ætlar þú, at þér muni þvílíkt við mik at eiga sem við Þórð, bróður þinn, því at þar hefir þú jafnan þitt mál?"	"Suppose you, that you would therefore-like with me that have as with Thord, brother yours, because that there have you always your way?"	"Do you suppose, that you would therefore liken me to that which you have with your brother Thord, because you always have your way?"

The Tale of Hreiðarr the Fool (Old Norse)

Old Norse	Literal	English
Hreiðarr segir:	Hreidar said:	Hreidar said:
"Því öllu betra mun mér við yðr at eiga sem þú ert vitrari en hann".	"Because all better would me with you than have as you are wiser than he".	"It would be better with you than with him as you are wiser than he is".
Konungr sér nú, at hann mun fara, þó at hann banni eða hann fari eigi í hans föruneyti, ok þykkir eigi þat bezt, ef hann kemr annars staðar til föruneytis, ok þykkir þá í reiðingum vera, hversu honum eirir, ef hann vælir einn um, ok leyfir honum nú heldr at fara með sér, ok er Hreiðari fenginn hestr til reiðar.	The-king saw now, that he would travel, though that he banned either he travelled not in his companionship, and thought not that best, if he came another's place to company, and thought then in uproar being, how-so he own, if he wilful one about, and leave him now rather that travel with him, and was Hreidar given a-horse to ride.	The king saw now that he would travel, even though he had banned him, he would travel outside of his companionship, and he thought it not best if he came into another place's company and there was an uproar, how he would be if he was wilful about something, and had him rather travelling with him, and Hreidar was given a horse to ride.
Ok þegar er þeir váru á ferð komnir, þá reið hann mjök ok ætlaði sér varla hóf um, ok þraut hestinn undir honum.	And as-soon as they were to travel coming, then rode he much and intended himself hardly in-moderation about, and faltered the-horse under him.	And as soon as they were coming to travel, then he rode hard, and hardly in moderation about, and the horse faltered under him.
Ok er konungr verðr þess varr, mælti hann:	And when the-king became this aware, spoke he:	And when the king became aware of this, he spoke:
"Nú gefr vel til.	"Now give well to.	"Now it is well.
Fylgið nú Hreiðari heim, ok fari hann eigi".	Follow now Hreidar home, and travel he not".	Hreidar is to be followed home and he is not to travel".
Hann segir:	He said:	"He said:
"Eigi heftir þetta ferðina mína, þótt hestrinn sé þrotinn.	"Not have this travelling mine, thought horse's being ended.	"Not having this my journey, though the horse has given out".
Kemr mér til lítils fráleikrinn, ef ek fæ eigi fylgt yðr".	Came me to little game, if I give not follow you".	I would not be a good sportsman, if I could not keep up with you".
Fara þeir nú, ok lögðu margir fram hjá honum hesta sína ok þótti gaman at reyna fráleik hans, svá gropasamliga sem hann sjálfr tók á.	Travelled they now, and had many from beside him horse his and thought fun to test from-game his, so grouped-together as he himself took of.	Travelled they now and many brought their horses beside his and thought it fun to test his sport. And so grouped together as he took them on.

The Tale of Hreiðarr the Fool (Old Norse)

Old Norse	Literal	English
En svá gafst, at hann þreytti hvern hest, er frammi var lagðr, ok lézt eigi verðr at koma til fundarins, ef hann gæti eigi fylgt þeim.	But so gave, that he tired each horse, that from was had, and let not were to come to the-meeting, if he got not follow them.	But it so happened that he tired each horse, that was laid before him, and he was not to come to the meeting if he could not follow pace with them.
Ok fyrir þetta sátu nú margir af sínum hestum.	And ahead that sat now many of his horses.	And for this many of their horses now sat.

5

Old Norse	Literal	English
Ok er þeir koma þar, er konungar skulu finnast, þá mælti Magnús konungr við Hreiðar:	And when they came there, that the-kings shall meet, then spoke Magnus the-king with Hreiðar:	And when they came to where the kings were to meet, then King Magnus said to Hreidar:
"Ver þú mér nú fylgjusamr ok ver á aðra hönd mér ok skilst ekki frá mér.	"Be you me now follow-same and be on other hand mine and separate not from me.	"Be obedient to me now and me on my other side and do not part with me"
En miðlungi segir mér hugr um, hversu ferr, þá er menn Haralds konungs koma ok sjá þik".	But poorly say me think about, how-so goes, then when men Harald's the-king come and see you".	But I think that it will go badly, when King Harald's men come and see you".
Hreiðarr kvað svá vera skyldu sem konungr mælti, "ok þykkir mér því betr er ek geng yðr nær".	Hreidar spoke so be should as the-king spoke, "and think me then better that I go you near".	Hreidar said that it should be as the king said, "and then I think it better that I go nearer to you".
Nú finnast konungar, ok ganga þeir á tal ok ræða mál sín.	Now met the-kings, and went they to talk and discuss matters theirs.	Now the kings met, and they talked and discussed their matters.
En menn Haralds konungs gátu líta, hvar Hreiðarr gekk, ok höfðu heyrt getit hans, ok þótti þeim um it vænsta.	When men Harald's the-king got company, where Hreidar went, and had heard told he, and thought they about that good.	But King Harold's men could see where Hreidar went, and they had heard his name, and they thought it good.
Ok er konungar töluðu, þá gengr Hreiðarr í flokk Haralds manna, ok höfðu þeir hann til skógar, er skammt var þaðan, skauttoguðu hann mjök ok hrundu honum stundum.	And as the-kings talked, then went Hreidar in group Harald's men, and had they he to woods, which short-distance was from-there, pull-cloak, handle-roughly he much and teased him awhile.	And when the kings were talking, Hreidar went into the company of Harold's men, and they took him to a forest, which was not far from there, they rough-handled him a lot, and sometimes knocked him down.

The Tale of Hreiðarr the Fool (Old Norse)

Old Norse	Literal	English
En þar lék á ýmsu.	But then played about variously.	But they played at him in various ways.
Stundum fauk hann fyrir sem vindli, en stundum var hann fastr fyrir sem veggr, ok hrutu þeir frá honum.	Sometimes drifted he before as wind, then sometimes was he secure before as a-wall, and fell they away-from him.	Sometimes he drifted before them like the wind, and sometimes he was as secure as a wall, and they fell away from him.
Nú dregst þó svá leikrinn, at þeir gera honum nökkut harðleikit, létu ganga honum öxarsköft ok skálpana, ok námu naddar af sverðskónum í höfði honum, ok skeindist hann af, ok svá lét hann sem honum þætti it mesta gaman at ok hló við jafnan.	Now drawn though so the-game, that they did him some hardness, had going him axe-handles and scabbards, and took studded of sword-studded at head him, and scratched he of, and so had he as him seemed the most game that and laughed with equally.	And as the game drew on, they became hard and were going at him with axe handles and scabbards, and a studded sword scabbard hit him on the head, and scratched him, and he appeared to enjoy the game and laughed equally with them.
Ok er svá hafði fram farit um hríð, þá tók leikrinn ekki at batna af þeira hendi.	And was so had from going about awhile, then took the-game not to better of them hand.	And when this had been going on for a while, the game did not begin to get any better from them.
Þá mælti Hreiðarr:	Then spoke Hreidar:	Then Hreidar spoke:
"Nú höfum vér átt góðan leik um stund, ok er nú ráð at hætta, því at nú tekr mér at leiðast.	"Now have we had good sport about awhile, and am-i now decide that conclude, therefore that now take me to hand.	"How we have had good sport for a while, and I have now decided that it shall conclude, therefore take my hand.
Förum nú til konungs yðvars, ok vil ek sjá hann".	Go now to king yours, and will I see him".	Let's go now to your king, and I will see him.
"Þat skal verða aldri",	"That shall be never",	"That shall never be",
sögðu þeir, "svá fjandligr sem þú ert, at þú skulir sjá konung várn, ok skulum vér færa þik til heljar".	said they, "so fiendish as you are, that you should see the-king ours, and shall we bring you to death".	they said, "so fiendish as you are, that you should see our king, and we shall bring you to death".

The Tale of Hreiðarr the Fool (Old Norse)

Old Norse	Literal	English
Honum finnst þá fátt um ok þykkist sjá, at þat mun fram fara, ok er nú þar komit, at honum rennr í skap, ok reiðist hann, ferr höndum þann mann, er mest sótti at honum ok verst lék við hann, ok vegr á loft ok færði niðr at höfðinu, svá at heilinn var úti, ok er sá dauðr.	He found then little about and thought seemed, that it would from go, and that now there came, that he run of mood, and angered he, went seized then man, the most took with him and worse played with he, and proceeded to lift and brought down on head, so that brain was out, and was so dead.	He found that he did not like this at all, and where it seemed it would go, and then it happened, that his mood changed, and he became very angry, he seized the man who had taunted him the worst, and proceeded to lift him up and bring him down on his head, so that his brains came out, and he was dead.
Nú þykkir þeim hann trautt mennskr maðr at afli, ok stukku þeir nú í víginu, fara ok segja Haraldi konungi, at drepinn var hirðmaðr hans.	Now thought they he scarcely human man that strength, and leapt they now from the-slaying, went and told Harald the-king, that killed was court-man his.	Now they thought that he was scarcely human with that strength, and they leapt away from the slaying and told King Harald, that one of his court-men had been killed.
Konungr svarar:	The-king answered:	The king answered:
"Drepið þann þá, er þat hefir unnit".	"Kill he then, who this has done".	"Kill him then, the one who has done this".
"Eigi er þat enn hægra",	"Not is that then easy",	"That is not easy",
segja þeir.	said they.	they said.
"Hann er nú í brottu".	"He is now to away".	"He has now gone away".
Þat er nú frá Hreiðari at segja, at hann hittir Magnús konung.	That is now from Hreidar to say, that he found Magnus the-king.	It is now said of Hreidar that he met King Magnus.
Konungr mælti:	The-king spoke:	The king spoke:
"Veiztu nú, hvernig þat er at reiðast?"	"Know-you now, how that is that anger?"	"Now do you know how your anger is?"
"Já",	"Yes",	"Yes",
segir hann, "nú veit ek".	said he, "now know i".	he said, "now I know".
"Hvernig þótti þér?"	"How thought you?"	"What did you think of it?"
segir konungr.	said the-king.	said the king?
"Hitt fann ek, at þér var forvitni á".	"It found i, that you were curious to".	"I found it that you were curious about it".

The Tale of Hreiðarr the Fool (Old Norse)

Old Norse	Literal	English
Hreiðarr svarar:	Hreidar answered:	Hreidar answered:
"Illt þótti mér.	"Badly thought i.	"I thought it bad.
Þess var ek fúsastr at drepa þá alla".	This was I wished to kill then all".	This was my wish, to then kill them all".
Konungr mælti:	The-king spoke:	The king spoke:
"Þat kom mér jafnt í hug",	"That came to-me equally in thought",	"The same thing came to my thoughts",
segir konungr, "at þú myndir illa reiðr verða.	said the-king, "that you would badly angry become.	said the king, "that you would become bad when angry.
Nú vil ek senda þik á Upplönd til Eyvindar, lends manns míns, at hann haldi þik fyrir Haraldi konungi.	Now will I send you to Uplands to Eyvind, land man mine, that he hold you from Harald the-king.	Now I will send you to Uplands to Eyvind, a land man of mine, so that he protects you from King Harald.
Því at ek treystumst eigi, at þín verði gætt, ef þú ert með hirðinni, því at vér finnumst, en Haraldr frændi er brögðóttr, ok er vant við at sjá.	Because that I we-trust not, that you become taken-care-of, if you are with court-men, because that we find, that Harald's kinsmen are tricky, and are difficult with to see.	I do not trust that you will be taken care of if you are with the court-men, because we find Harald's kinsmen are tricky, and difficult to see.
Kom þá aftr til mín, er ek sendi eftir þér".	Come then back to me, when I send after you".	Then come back to me, when I send for you".
Nú ferr Hreiðarr í brott, unz hann kemr á Upplönd, ok tekr Eyvindr við honum eftir orðsending konungs.	Now went Hreidar to away, until he came to Uplands, and took Eyvind with him after message the-king's.	Now Hreidar went away, until he came to Uplands, and Eyvind received him as per the king's message.
Konungar höfðu sáttir orðit á þat mál, er áðr var milli þeira, ok var því sætt.	The-kings had agreed words of the matter, that before was between them, and was therefore settled.	The kings had agreed words about the matter, which was between them, and it was therefore settled.
En hér verða þeir eigi á sáttir.	But here became they not about agreed.	But here they became not in agreement.

The Tale of Hreiðarr the Fool (Old Norse)

Old Norse	Literal	English
Þykkir Magnúsi þessir menn hafa sjálfir fyrirgert sér ok valdit öllum sökum ok þykkir hirðmaðr fallit hafa óheilagr.	Thought Magnus these men had themselves fore-done him and wielded all blame and thought court-man fallen had unholy.	Magnus thought that these men had forgiven themselves and wielded all the blame, and thought that the court-man had fallen unholy.
En Haraldr konungr beiðir bóta fyrir hirðmann ísinn, ok skilðust nú með engri sætt.	Then Harald the-king asked compensation for court-man his, and separated now with no settlement.	But King Harald begged compensation for his court-man, and now they parted with no settlement.

6

Old Norse	Literal	English
Eigi liðu langar stundir, áðr Haraldr konungr spyrr, hvar Hreiðarr er niðr kominn, gerir síðan ferð sína ok kemr á Upplönd til Eyvindar, hefir með sér sex tigu manna.	Not passed long while, before Harald the-king learned, where Hreidar then down came, made afterwards travelled he and came to Uplands to Eyvind, had with him six tens men.	Not a long while had passed, before King Harald learned where Hreidar had come down to, and went afterwards to travel and come to Uplands to Eyvind, having with him sixty men.
Hann kemr þar um morgin snemma ok ætlaði at koma á óvart.	He came there about morning early and intended to come to un-warned.	He came there early in the morning and intended to come without warning.
En þat var þó eigi, því at Eyvindr þóttist vita fyrir, at hann myndi koma, ok var hann á engri stundu vanbúinn við.	But that was though not, therefore that Eyvind thought knowing before, that he would come, and was he that no time unprepared against.	But that was not to be, because Eyvind had thought before that he knew that he would come, and at no time was he unprepared against this.
Hafði hann stefnt liði at sér af launungu, ok var þat í skógum þeim, er nálægir váru bænum.	Had he located company that he of secretly, and was that in the-woods they, were near-lying were dwelling.	He had located a company secretly, and they were in the woods, lying near the dwelling.
Skyldi Eyvindr gefa þeim mark, ef Haraldr konungr kæmi, ok þættist hann liðs þurfa.	Should Eyvind give them sign, if Harald the-king came, and thought he company needed.	And Eyvind was to give them a sign, if King Harald came, and if he thought he needed company.
Þat er sagt, einhverju sinni, áðr Haraldr konungr kæmi, at Hreiðarr beiddist, at Eyvindr skyldi fá honum silfr ok nökkut gull.	It was said, once this, after Harald the-king came, that Hreidar asked, that Eyvind should get him silver and some gold.	It was said that once King Harald had arrived, Hreidar asked Eyvind to get him silver and some gold.
"Ertu hagr?"	"Are-you handy?"	"Are you handy?"

The Tale of Hreiðarr the Fool (Old Norse)

Old Norse	Literal	English
segir hann..	said he.	he said.
Hreiðarr svarar:	Hreidar answered:	Hreidar answered:
"Þat sagði Magnús konungr mér.	"That said Magnus the-king to-me.	"King Magnus said that to me.
En eigi má ek annat til vita, því at ek hefi aldri við leitat.	But not may I other to know, because that I have never with sought.	But I must know nothing else, for I have never sought.
En því myndi hann þat segja, at hann myndi vita, ok því trúi ek, er hann sagði".	But because should he that say, that he would know, and therefore trust i, what he said".	But because he said that, he should know, and therefore I trust what he said".
Eyvindr mælti:	Eyvind spoke:	Eyvind spoke:
"Þú ert undarligr maðr",	"You are a-strange man",	"You are a strange man",
segir hann.	said he.	he said.
"Nú mun ek fá þér efnin.	"Now should I give you materials.	"Now should I get you the materials.
Skaltu fá mér silfrit, ef ónýtt verðr smíðat, en njót sjálfr elligar".	Shall-you get me silver, if ruined becomes made, then enjoy yourself otherwise".	You shall get silver from me, but if the construction becomes ruined, give it back to me, if not, enjoy yourself".
Hreiðarr er byrgðr í einu húsi, ok er hann þar at smíðinni.	Hreidar then closed in a house, and was he there to smith.	Hreidar was then kept in a house, and he began there his smithery.
Ok áðr en gert verði þat, er Hreiðarr smíðaði, þá kemr Haraldr konungr, ok er nú sem ek gat áðr, at Eyvindr er at engu óbúinn, ok gerir hann konungi veizlu góða.	And before then made was that, which Hreidar making, then came Harald the-king, and was now as I got before, that Eyvind was that none unprepared, and made he the-king feast good.	And before Hreidar finished what he was making, then came King Harald, and it was now as said before, that Eyvind was not unprepared, and he made the king a good feast.
Ok nú er þeir sitja í drykkju, þá fréttir konungr eftir, ef Hreiðarr sé þar, - ok muntu hafa vináttu af mér í móti, ef þú selr oss manninn".	And now were they sitting to drinking, then news the-king afterwards, of Hreidar seeing there, and shall-you have friendship of me in meeting, if you sell us the-man".	And now when they were sitting drinking, then the King heard that Hreidar had been seen there, "and you shall have my friendship meeting if you sell us the man".
Eyvindr svarar:	Eyvind answered:	Eyvind answered:

The Tale of Hreiðarr the Fool (Old Norse)

Old Norse	Literal	English
"Eigi er hann hér nú".	"Not is he here now".	"He is not here now".
"Ek veit", *segir konungr, "at hann er, ok þarftu eigi dylja".*	"I know", said the-king, "that he is, and need-you not disguise".	"I know", said the king, "that he is, and you need not disguise it".
Eyvindr mælti:	Eyvind spoke:	Eyvind spoke:
"Enn þótt þat sé, þá geri ek eigi þann mun ykkar Magnúss konungs, at ek selja þann mann í hendr þér, er hann vill skýla láta", - gekk út síðan ór stofunni.	"But though that he, then do I not then would you Magnus the-king, that I sell then that-man in hand you, then he will protect be", went out afterwards out-of the-room.	"Even though he is, then I would not then betray King Magnus by selling that man to you and handing over the man he wishes to be protected", and with that he went out of the room.
Ok er hann kemr út, þá brýzt Hreiðarr á hurðina ok kallar, at hann vill á brott.	And when he came out, then hammering Hreidar to the-door and called, that he wished to away.	And when he came out, then Hreidar began hammering on the door and calling that he wished to get out.
"Þegi þú", *segir Eyvindr.*	"Silent you", said Eyvind.	"Be quiet" said Eyvind.
"Haraldr konungr er hér kominn ok vill drepa þik".	"Harald the-king is here come and wishes to-kill you".	"King Harald has come here and he wishes to kill you".
Hreiðarr brýzt út eigi at síðr ok lézt hitta vildu konung.	Hreidar hammering out not the less and let meet wiled the-king.	Hreidar hammered on the door no less, and wished to meet the king.
Eyvindr sér þá, at hann mun brjóta upp hurðina, gengr til ok lýkr upp ok mælir:	Eyvind himself then, that he would break up the-door, going to and concluded up and spoke:	Eyvind saw then that he was going to break open the door, and went and unlocked it and said:
"Gramir munu taka þik", *segir hann, "er þú gengr til banans".*	"Anger shall take you", said he, "then you go to death".	"Anger shall take you", he said, "then you go to your death".

149

The Tale of Hreiðarr the Fool (Old Norse)

Old Norse	Literal	English
Hreiðarr gengr inn í stofuna ok fyrir konung ok kveðr hann ok mælti:	Hreidar went in to the-room and before the-king and spoke he and said:	Hreidar went into the room and before the king and spoke to him and said:
"Herra, tak af mér reiðina, því at ek em þér vel felldr fyrir margs sakar at gera þat, er þú vill gera láta, þó at eigi sé allrífligt, í mannraunum eða því, er við berr, ok mun ek þess ólatr, er þú vill mik til hafa sendan.	"Lord, take off me anger, because that I am to-you well situated for many reasons to do that, which you wish done have, though that not is all-abundant, in human-trials or otherwise, is with carrying, and should I this not-forget, when you wish me to have sent.	"Lord, do not be angry with me, because I am pleased to do that which you wish to have done, even though it may not seem rich in human trials or so carried with, and I will not forget it, when you will have me sent for.
Hér er nú gripr, er ek vil gefa þér", - setr á borðit fyrir hann, en þat var svín, gert af silfri ok gyllt.	Here is now treasure, that I wish to-give you", set on table before him, then that was a-pig, made of silver and gold.	Here is now a treasure, that I wish to give you", he set it on the table before him, and it was a pig made of silver and gold.
Þá mælti konungr, er hann leit á svínit:	Then spoke the-king, that he looked at the-pig:	Then the king spoke when he looked at the-pig:
"Þú ert hagr, svá at trautt hefi ek sét jafnvel smíðat með því móti, sem er".	"You are skilled, so that scarcely have I seen equally-well smithery with this of, such as".	"You are so skilled, that scarcely have I seen such craftsmanship as this".
Nú ferr þat með manna höndum.	Now passed that among the-men handed.	Now it passed among people's hands.
Segir konungr, at hann mun taka sættir af honum, - "ok er gott at senda þik til stórvirkja.	Said the-king, that he would take settle of him, "and was god that sending you to great-work.	The king said that he would he would take settlement with him, "and it would be good to send you on great work.
Þú ert maðr sterkr ok ófælinn, at því er ek hygg".	You are a-man strong and without-fear, that therefore am I minded".	You are a strong man and without fear, and therefore I am minded".
Nú kemr svínit aftr fyrir konung.	Now came the-pig before in-front-of the-king.	Now came the pig back to the king.
Tekr hann þá upp ok hyggr at smíðinni enn vandligar ok sér þá, at spenar eru á ok þat var gyltr, fleygir þegar í brott ok sér, at til háðs var gert, ok mælti:	Took he then up and considered that the-work then carefully and saw then, that suckling was then and that was young-sow, threw then to away and he, that to mockery was done, and spoke:	He then picked it up and looked at the work then carefully, and then he saw that the pig was a suckling and a young-sow, then he threw it away, because he believed that it insulted him, and he spoke:

The Tale of Hreiðarr the Fool (Old Norse)

Old Norse	Literal	English
"Hafi þik allan tröll.	"Have you all monstrous.	"Have you all, the devil.
Standi menn upp ok drepi hann".	Stand men up and kill him".	Stand up men and kill him".
En Hreiðarr tekr svínit ok gengr út ok ferr þegar á brott þaðan, korn á fund Magnúss konungs ok segir honum, hvat í hefir gerzt.	Then Hreidar took the-pig and went away and travelled straightaway to away from-there, came to meet Magnus the-king and told him, what so had done.	Then Hreidar took the pig, went away and travelled straightaway from there to meet King Magnus and told him how it had gone.
En í öðru lagi standa menn upp ok út eftir honum ok ætla at drepa hann.	Then with others lead standing men up and out after him and intended to kill him.	Then the others stood up and went out after him intending to kill him.
Ok er þeir koma út, þá er Eyvindr þar fyrir ok hefir fjölmenni mikit, svá at ekki máttu þeir eftir Hreiðari halda, ok skilja þeir Eyvindr ok Haraldr konungr við svá búit, ok líkar konungi illa.	And when they came out, then was Eyvind there before and had followers many, so that not may they after Hreidar held, and parted they Eyvind and Harald the-king with so settled, and liked the-king badly.	And when they came outside, then Eyvind was there with many followers, so they could not go after Hreidar. Then Eyvind and King Harald parted, and the king was far from pleased.
Ok er þeir hittast., Magnús konungr ok Hreiðarr, fréttir konungr eftir, hvernig farit hefir.	And when they met, Magnus the-king and Hreidar, news the-king after, how fared had.	And when they met, King Magnus and Hreidar, the king asked for news of how it had gone.
En Hreiðarr segir frá it sanna ok sýndi konungi svínit.	Then Hreidar told from the truth and showed the-king the-pig.	Then Hreidar told the truth about what happened and showed the king the pig.
Magnús konungr mælti, þá er hann hugði at svíninu:	Magnus the-king spoke, then that he thought that the-pig:	King Magnus then spoke and said that he thought that the pig was:
"Geysihagliga er þetta smíðat.	"Exceedingly-skilful was that crafted.	"Exceedingly skilfully crafted.
En hefnt hefir Haraldr konungr, frændi várr, mjök minni háðungar en í þessu er, ok eigi ertu alláræðislítill ok þó með öllu hugkvæmr".	But revenge had Harald the-king, kinsman ours, much less insult than in this has, and not are-you very-timid and though with all ingenuity".	But King Harald, our kinsman, had revenge for much less of an insult than this, and you are not at all timid and though you are full of ingenuity".

The Tale of Hreiðarr the Fool (Old Norse)

Old Norse	Literal	English
7	**7**	**7**
Hreiðarr var nú þar nökkura stund með Magnúsi konungi.	Hreidar was now there some time with Magnus the-king.	Hreidar was now there some time with Magnus the-king.
Ok eitthvert sinn kemr hann at máli við konung ok mælti:	And one occasion came he to speak with the-king and spoke:	And on one occasion he came to speak with the king and said:
"Þat vilda ek, konungr, at þú veittir mér þat, er ek mun biðja þik".	"It wish i, king, that you grant me that, which I may ask you".	"It is my wish, king, that you grant me that which I ask you".
"Hvat er þat?"	"What is that?"	"What is that?"
spyrr konungr.	asked the-king.	asked the-king.
"Þat, herra",	"That, lord",	"That, lord",
segir Hreiðarr, "at þér hlýddið kvæði, er ek hefi ort um yðr".	said Hreidar, "that you listen-to poem, that I have worded about you".	said Hreidar, "that you listen-to poem, that I have worded about you".
"Hví skal eigi þat?"	"Why should not that?"	"Why should not that?"
segir konungr.	said the-king.	said the-king.
Nú kveðr Hreiðarr kvæðit, ok er þat allundarligt, fyrst kynligast, en því betra er síðar er.	Now recited Hreidar the-poem, and was it all-wonderful, first strangely, then since better then afterwards was.	Now Hreidar recited the poem, and it was all wonderful, strange at first, but then it got better after that.
Ok er lokit er kvæði, mælti konungr:	And when ended was the-poem, spoke the-king:	And when the poem had ended, the king spoke:
"Þetta kvæði sýnist mér undarligt ok þó gott at nestlokum.	"That poem seems to-me wonderful and though good as the-end.	"That poem seems to be to be wonderful, particularly good at the end.
En kvæðit mun vera með þeim hætti sem ævi þín.	Then poem should be with the way as life yours.	Then the poem should be the same way as your life.
Hon hefir fyrst verit með kynligu móti ok einrænligu, en hon mun þó vera því betr er meir líðr á.	It has first been with strange meeting and eccentric, but it shall though become therefore better the more passes so.	First it has been strange and eccentric, but it shall become better the more passes.

The Tale of Hreiðarr the Fool (Old Norse)

Old Norse	Literal	English
Hér eftir skal ek ok velja kvæðislaunin.	Here after shall I and will poem-reward.	Here after I shall give you a poem's reward.
Hér er hólmr einn fyrir Nóregi, sá er ek vil þér gefa.	Here is small-island one along Norway, so that I will you give.	Here is a small island along Norway, so I will give it to you.
Hann er með góðum grösum, ok er þat gott land, þó at eigi sé mikit".	It is with good grass, and is that good land, though is not so large".	It is good with grass, and good land, though it is not so large".
Hreiðarr mælti:	Hreidar spoke:	Hreidar spoke:
"Þar skal ek samtengja með Nóreg ok Ísland".	"There shall I unite with Norway and Iceland".	"There shall I unite with Norway and Iceland".
Konungr mælti:	The-king spoke:	The king spoke:
"Eigi veit ek, hversu þat ferr.	"One-thing know i, how-so that goes.	"I know one thing about how it goes.
Hitt veit ek, at margir menn munu búnir at kaupa at þér hólminn ok gefa þér fé fyrir.	This know i, that many people shall offer to buy of you the-island and give you fee for.	This I know, that many people shall offer to buy the island from you and give you wealth for.
En ráðligra ætla ek vera, at ek leysa til mín, at eigi verði at bitbeini þér eða þeim, er kaupa vilja.	But advisable suppose I be, that I redeem to me, that not becomes a bite-bone to-you or they, who buy wish-to.	But. I advise you to sell the island to me, so that it does not become a bone of contention to you, or those who wish to buy it.
Er nú ok ekki vel felld vist þín vilgis lengi hér í Nóregi, því at ek þykkjumst sjá, hvern Haraldr konungr vill þinn hlut, ef hann á at ráða, sem hann mun ráða, ef þú ert lengi í Nóregi".	Then now also I well end hospitality yours very long here in Norway, because that I think so, who Harald the-king will your matter, if he has the decision, as he shall decide, if you are long in Norway".	Then I will also end your very long stay here in Norway, because I think that King Harald will do to you, if he gets the chance, and he shall do what he wants if you stay here much longer".
Nú gaf Magnús konungr honum silfr fyrir hólminn ok vill nú eigi þar hætta honum, ok fór Hreiðarr út til Íslands ok bjó norðr í Svarfaðardal, [þar sem síðan heitir á Hreiðarsstöðum], ok gerist mikill maðr fyrir sér.	Now gave Magnus the-king him silver for the-island and wished now not there endanger him, and travelled Hreidar out to Iceland and settled north in Svarfardal, [there which afterwards is-named by Hreidar's-Place], and became a-great man before himself.	Now King Magnus gave him silver for the island and wished that he now not endanger himself, and Hreidar travelled to Iceland and settled north in Svarfardal, which was afterwards named Hreidar's Place, and he became a great man before himself.

The Tale of Hreiðarr the Fool (Old Norse)

Old Norse	Literal	English
Ok ferr hans ráð mjök eftir getu Magnúss konungs, at þess betr er er meir líðr fram hans ævi, ok hefir hann gert sér at mestum hluta þau kynjalæti, er hann sló á sik inn fyrra hlut ævinnar.	And went his advised much after could Magnus the-king, that this better was that more passed from his life, and had he done himself the most share then eccentricities, that he struck to himself the last-years share of-life.	And his life went much as King Magnus had advised, that his life would get better the more it passed, for he had made up for the greater share of eccentricities that he inflicted on himself in the first part of his life.
Bjó hann til elli í Svarfaðardal, ok eru margir menn frá honum komnir.	Lived he to old-age in Svarfardal, and are many people from him coming.	He lived to old age in Svarfardale and many people are descended from him.
Ok lýkr hér þessi ræðu.	And concluded here this speech.	And here this speech is concluded.

Word List (Old Norse to English)

Word List (Old Norse to English)

Old Norse	English

A, a

aðra	other
aðrir	others
af	of, of, off
afbragð	stood-out
afglapa	fool
afl	strength
afli	strength
aflit	strength
afskipti	dealings
aftr	back, before
aldri	age, never, never
aldrigi	never
alla	all
allan	all
alláræðislítill	very-timid
allgóð	all-good
allir	all
allnær	all-near
allr	all
allra	all
allrífligt	all-abundant
alls	all
allstarsýnn	fixed-upon
allt	all, altogether
allundarligt	all-wonderful
allvel	all-well, all-well
alþýðu	all-the-people, the-people
annarr	another
annarra	other
annars	another's, any-other
annast	take-care-of
annat	other, other
at	a, as, at, been, in, is, of, of, on, than, that, that, the, the, to, to, with, with
auga	eye

Á, á

á	about, at, by, for, from, has, in, of, on, so, that, then, to
áðan	earlier
áðr	after, before, returned
ágang	aggression
áheyrsli	to-hear
álpun	rough
átt	had, have, that
átti	had

Æ, æ

ætla	intended, suppose
ætlaði	intended
ætlan	suppose
ætlar	intended, suppose
ævi	life
ævinnar	of-life

B, b

báðir	both
bæði	both
bænum	dwelling, residence
bærist	bearing
banans	death
banni	banned
barðr	beat
batna	better
beiddist	asked
beiðir	asked
beiðzt	asked, best
ber	bear
beri	bear
berr	carry, carrying
betr	better
betra	better
bezt	best
biðja	ask, to-ask
bitbeini	bite-bone

Word List (Old Norse to English)

Old Norse	English
bjó	lived, prepared, settled
Björgyn	Bergen
blásit	trumpet-blast
blíðlíga	joyfully
borðit	table
borit	bear
bóta	compensation
bræðr	brothers
bræðrum	brothers
brátt	soon
breyttu	varied
brjóta	break
bróðir	brother
bróður	a-brother, brother
brögðóttr	tricky
brott	away
brottu	away, steep
brýzt	hammering
bú	prepare
búa	dress
búinn	dressed, prepared
búit	settled
búning	clothing
búnir	offer, prepared
byrgðr	closed

D, d

Old Norse	English
dæmð	to-deem
dála	bad
dauðr	dead
dofna	numb
draga	draw
dregst	drawn
drepa	kill, to-kill
drepi	kill
drepið	kill
drepinn	killed
drykkju	drinking
dylja	disguise

E, e

Old Norse	English
eða	and, but, either, or
ef	if, of
efnin	materials
eftir	after, afterwards
eiga	had, have, own
eigi	none, not, nothing, one-thing
eigu	have
einhverju	once
einkum	especially
einn	alone, one
einrænligu	eccentric
eins	one's
einu	a
einum	alone, one
eirir	own
eitt	once, one
eitthvert	one
ek	i, is
ekki	i, is-not, not
elli	old-age
elligar	otherwise
em	am
en	and, but, than, that, the, then, when
enda	and
engar	no
engi	no, none, no-one
engri	no
engu	none
enn	but, that, then
er	am, am-i, are, as, be, being, but, has, i, in, is, that, the, then, to, to-be, was, were, what, when, where, which, who, whom, would
era	are
erendi	business
erendit	errand
ert	are
ertu	are-you
eru	are, they-are, was, were
eruð	are
Eyjafirði	Eyjafjord

Word List (Old Norse to English)

Old Norse	English
Eyvindar	Eyvind
Eyvindr	Eyvind

F, f

Old Norse	English
fá	get, give
fæ	give
fæðist	born
fær	can
færa	bring
færði	brought
færðr	brought
færi	bring
færr	capable
fágar	cleaned
fagna	welcomed
fáir	few
fallin	fallen
fallit	fallen
fann	found
fara	go, going, to-be, to-go, travel, travelled, went
farar	journey
fari	travel, travelled
farið	go
farit	fared, going
fastr	secure
fátt	few, little
fauk	drifted
fé	fee, money
feld	cloak
feldinum	cloak
felld	end, shed
felldr	situated
fellr	fell
fellt	falling
fenginn	given
fer	go
ferð	travel, travelled
ferðina	travelling
ferligu	monstrous
ferr	goes, passed, travelled, went
finn	find

Old Norse	English
finna	find, found
finnast	meet, meet-up, met
finnst	found
finnumst	find
firna	criticised
fjandligr	fiendish
fjárins	of-wealth
fjárskakka	uneven-share
fjölmenni	followers, followers-many
fjölmennit	many-people
fjölmennt	crowded
flesta	most
fleygir	threw
flokk	group
fluttir	brought
flytr	transport
föðurarf	inheritance
fór	travelled, went
för	going, travelled, travelling
förin	for-travelling, travelling
förna	sacrificing
forræði	self-control
förum	go, going, trading-voyages, travelling
föruneyti	companionship
föruneytis	company
forvitni	curious
fót	foot
frá	away-from, from
frændi	kinsman, kinsmen
fráleik	from-game
fráleikrinn	game, swiftness
fram	from
frammi	from
frávastr	swift
fréttir	news
fríðenda	good-things
fund	find, meet, visit
fundar	to-meet
fundarins	the-meeting
fundit	found
fundu	found
fúsastr	wished

Word List (Old Norse to English)

Old Norse	English
fylgið	follow
fylgjusamr	follow-same
fylgt	follow
fyrir	ahead, along, before, for, from, in-front-of
fyrirgert	fore-done
fyrr	before
fyrra	last-years
fyrst	first
fyrstu	first

G, g

Old Norse	English
gæfu	be-gifted
gæti	got
gætt	taken-care-of
gaf	gave
gafst	gave
gaman	fun, game
gamni	amuse
ganga	go, going, went
gat	got
gátu	got
gefa	gave, give, to-give
gefr	give
gefst	gave
gekk	went
geng	go
gengr	go, going, walked, went
gera	did, do, done
geri	do
gerik	do
gerir	did, made
gerist	became
gerla	completely
gerr	made
gert	did, done, made
gerzt	done, made
get	guess, mention
getit	told
getr	get
getu	could
geysihagliga	exceedingly-skilful
ginna	mocking
ginningar	mocking
glíkligt	favourable
glíkr	like
Glúmr	Glum
góða	good
góðan	good
góðum	good
góma	gums
gott	god, good
gramir	anger
grán	grey
grandi	injury
greipr	grasp
greitt	ready-to-serve
gripr	treasure
gropasamliga	grouped-together
grösum	grass
gull	gold
gyllt	gold
gyltr	young-sow

H, h

Old Norse	English
háðs	mockery
háðungar	insult
hæð	height
hægra	easy
hætta	conclude, endanger
hætti	way
haf	sea
hafa	had, have
hafði	had
hafi	have
hafir	have
hagr	benefit, handy, skilled
halda	held, rather
haldi	hold
haldist	rather
hálft	half
hálfu	half
handkrækjumst	hands-hook-us
hann	he, him, it
hans	he, him, his
Harald	Harald
Haraldi	Harald

Word List (Old Norse to English)

Old Norse	English
Haraldr	Harald, Harald's
Haralds	Harald's
harðleikit	hardness
hart	hard
háttung	risk
hefði	having
hefi	have
hefir	had, has, have
hefnt	revenge
heftir	have
heilinn	brain
heill	a-complete, the-whole, whole
heim	home
heima	at-home
heimil	home
heitir	is-named
heldr	behold, rather
heljar	death
helzt	rather
hendi	hand
hendr	hand
hendu	handed
hentr	suited
hér	here
herbergi	room
herra	lord
hest	horse
hesta	horse
hestinn	the-horse
hestr	a-horse
hestrinn	horse's
hestum	horses
hét	promised, was-named
heyra	heard
heyrðak	heard
heyrði	heard
heyrir	heard
heyrt	heard
hinnig	there
hirðarinnar	court
hirðinni	court, court-men
hirðmaðr	court-man
hirðmann	court-man
hirðmönnum	court-men
hirðvistar	court, court-visit

Old Norse	English
hitt	find, it, this
hitta	meet
hittast	met
hitti	met
hittir	found
hjá	beside, by
hlægi	ridicule
hlæjandi	laughing
hlær	laughed
hleypr	ran
hljóp	ran
hljóta	luck
hló	laughed
hlotit	bound-to
hlut	matter, share
hluta	share
hlutar	share
hlutr	share
hlýða	listened
hlýddið	listen-to
hóf	in-moderation
höfði	head
höfðinu	head
höfðu	had
hófi	measure
höfum	have
hógværr	humble
hólminn	the-island
hólmr	small-island
hon	it
hönd	hand
höndin	hand
höndum	handed, seized
honum	he, him, it
horn	corners
hornblástr	trumpet-blast
hræddr	worried
Hreiðar	Hreidar
Hreiðari	Hreidar
Hreiðarr	Hreidar
Hreiðars	Hreidar
Hreiðarssonar	Son-of-Hreidar
Hreiðarsstöðum	Hreidar's-Place
hríð	awhile
hring	a-ring

Word List (Old Norse to English)

Old Norse	English
hrundu	teased
hrutu	fell
hug	thought
hugði	thought
hugkvæmir	very-smart
hugkvæmr	ingenuity
hugr	think
hurðina	the-door
húsi	house
hvar	where
hvárt	how, whether
hvat	how, what
hvé	how
hvergi	nowhere
hverju	what
hverjum	each, everyone
hvern	each, who
hvernig	how, which
hverr	each, every, what
hversu	how-so
hví	why
hvíldar	rest
hygg	minded
hyggðu	think
hyggr	considered, looked, think

I, i

Old Norse	English
illa	badly
illt	bad, badly, ill
inn	in, the
innast	do
it	that, the, to

Í, í

Old Norse	English
í	as, at, by, from, in, of, so, the, to, with
ísinn	his
Ísland	Iceland
Íslands	Iceland
íslendingar	icelander

J, j

Old Norse	English
já	yes
jafnan	always, equally
jafnmæli	equal-speak
jafnt	equally
jafnvel	equally-well

K, k

Old Norse	English
kæja	disturbed
kæmi	came
kæmir	come
kæmist	come
kallaðr	called
kallar	called
kann	can, know
kaupa	buy
kemr	came
kenna	knew
kjósa	choose
klæðum	clothes
kné	knees
kom	came, come
koma	came, come, coming, to-come
komi	come
kominn	came, come, coming
komit	came, come
komnir	coming
kómu	came
konung	the-king
konunga	kings
konungar	kings, the-kings
konungi	the-king
konunginn	the-king
konungr	king, the-king
konungs	king, the-king, the-king's
korn	came
krummur	hands
kvað	said, spoke
kvæði	poem, the-poem
kvæðislaunin	poem-reward

Word List (Old Norse to English)

Old Norse	English
kvæðit	poem, the-poem
kveðju	greeting
kveðr	greeted, recited, spoke
kykvendum	some-beast
kynjalæti	eccentricities
kynlig	strange
kynligast	strangely
kynligu	strange

L, l

Old Norse	English
læti	noise
lætr	had, leaves
lagði	had
lagðr	had, laid
lagi	lead
land	land
landi	the-land
langar	long
langt	long
lát	have
láta	allow, be, be-allowed, have, left
latliga	negligently
lattan	dissuade
látum	have
launungu	secretly
laust	let-go
leggja	allow, let, take
leggr	have, laid
leið	way
leiðast	carried-out, hand
leik	sport
leikmikill	playful
leikrinn	the-game
leit	looked
leitat	sought
lék	played
lends	land
lengi	long
lét	had
létu	had
leyfa	allow
leyfi	leave
leyfir	leave
leyft	given-leave
leysa	redeem
lézt	let
liði	company
líðr	passed, passes
liðs	company
liðu	passed
líkar	like, liked
líkast	like
líkr	like
líta	company
lítill	a-little, small
lítils	little
lítit	little
litlu	a-little
litu	noticed
lízt	appears
ljótari	uglier
ljótr	ugly
ljúga	lie
lofgjarnliga	praise-will
loft	lift
lögðu	had
lokit	ended
lokka	lure
lundhægr	even-spirit, tempered-even
lýkr	concluded

M, m

Old Norse	English
má	may
maðr	a-man, man, people
maðrinn	a-man
mæl	say
mæla	discuss
mælgina	talking
mælik	speak
mælir	spoke
mælt	speaking, spoken
mælti	said, spoke
mæltir	speak
mæltu	spoke
mætti	may

Word List (Old Norse to English)

Old Norse	English
Magnús	Magnus
Magnúsi	Magnus
Magnúss	Magnus, Magnus's
mál	matter, matters, way
máli	speak
málinu	the-matter
málit	discuss
málugr	talkative
mann	man, that-man
manna	a-man, men, people, the-men
mannfátt	people-few
manni	of-the-people
manninn	the-man
manninum	the-people
mannraunum	human-trials
manns	man
marga	many
margir	many
margs	many
margt	many
mark	sign
mátti	it-may
máttu	may, may-you
mazt	most
með	among, as, with
mega	may
meiddr	hurt
meir	further, more
meira	more
menn	men, people
mennskr	human
mér	i, me, mine, my, to-me
mest	most
mesta	most
mestum	most
miðlungi	poorly
mik	i, me, much
mikil	much
mikill	a-great, great, tall
mikinn	great
mikit	large, many, much
miklum	much
milli	between
mín	me, mine
mína	mine
mínar	mine
minn	mine
minna	less
minni	less
míns	mine
mitt	me, mine, my
mjök	much
mönnum	men, people
morgin	morning
morgininn	morning
mörgu	many-ways
mörgum	many
mót	against
móti	meeting, of
mótinu	meeting
mótit	meeting, meetings
móts	meet, meetings
mun	could, may, must, shall, should, would
muna	should
mund	time
mundi	would
muni	would
munni	mouth
munt	shall-you
muntu	shall-you, should-you
munu	shall
myndi	should, would
myndir	would

N, n

Old Norse	English
naddar	studded
nær	near
nálægir	near-lying
námu	took
nauðsyn	need
nema	except
nemr	took
nestlokum	the-end
niðr	down
njót	enjoy
nökkur	somewhat
nökkura	some

Word List (Old Norse to English)

Old Norse	English
nökkurri	some
nökkut	of-any, some, something
norðr	north
Nóreg	Norway
Nóregi	Norway
nú	now
nýkominn	newly-come
nýt	used
nytjar	use

O, o

Old Norse	English
ofar	above
ofsögum	off-said
oft	frequently
ok	also, and
okkarn	ours
okkart	ours
okkr	ours, us, you
orð	words
orðit	words
orðsending	message
orðum	words
orðvarr	discreet
ort	worded
oss	us

Ó, ó

Old Norse	English
óbúinn	unprepared
ófælinn	without-fear
ógreið	un-passable
óheilagr	unholy
óknáleik	prowess
ólatr	not-forget
ólið	unaccompanied
ólíkast	unlike
ólíkligt	unlikely
ómállatr	chatty, talkative
ónýtt	ruined
ór	out-of
ósannligt	untrue
ósýknligr	un-innocent-looking

Old Norse	English
óvanr	un-accustomed
óvart	un-warned
óvísu	unknown

Ö, ö

Old Norse	English
öðru	others
öðrum	other, others
ökulbrókum	ankle-breeches
öllu	all
öllum	all
öxarsköft	axe-handles

P, p

Old Norse	English
penninga	money

R, r

Old Norse	English
ráð	advice, advised, decide
ráða	advice, advise, decide, decision
ráðligra	advisable
ræða	discuss
ræðu	speech
rammi	frame
réði	decide
reið	rode
reiðar	ride
reiðast	anger
reiðfara	voyage
reiði	anger
reiðin	uproar
reiðina	anger
reiðingum	uproar
reiðist	angered
reiðr	angry
reiðumst	become-angry
reikuð	roughly-handled
rennr	run
reyna	test
reynt	tried

Word List (Old Norse to English)

Old Norse	English
rjáðr	worried

S, s

Old Norse	English
sá	saw, so, such, that
sæja	see
sæki	conviction
sæmiliga	well-enough
sætt	settled, settlement
sættir	settle
sagða	said
sagði	said
sagt	said, told
sakar	conviction, reasons
sama	himself
saman	together
samdægris	same-day
samir	in-common
samtengja	unite
sanna	truth
sannast	true
satt	true
sáttarfundar	peace-meeting
sáttarfundr	peace-meeting
sáttir	agreed
sátu	sat
saurgar	dirty
sé	as, be, being, he, is, see, seeing, seen, so, you
sefr	sleeps
seg	tell
segir	said, say, told
segja	said, say, told
seint	slowly
selja	sell
selr	sell
sem	as, how, like, such, which
senda	send, sending
sendan	sent
sendi	send, sent
senn	they, together
sér	he, him, himself, his, saw, see, so
sét	seen
setr	set
sex	six
síðan	after, afterwards, then
síðar	afterwards
síðr	less
sigla	sailed
sik	him, himself, such, themselves
silfr	silver
silfri	silver
silfrit	silver
sín	theirs
sína	he, his
sinn	his, occasion
sinni	this
sínum	his
sitja	sit, sitting
sitt	his
sjá	saw, see, seemed, seen, so, to-see
sjálfan	myself
sjálfbjargi	self-supported
sjálfir	themselves
sjálfr	himself, self, yourself
skal	shall, should
skálpana	scabbards
skaltu	shall-you
skammt	short-distance
skap	mood
skapi	character
skauttogaðr	roughly
skauttoguðu	pull-cloak, handle-roughly
skeindist	scratched
skerum	cut
skikkju	cloak
skikkjuna	cloak
skilði	parted
skilðir	parted
skilðust	separated
skilja	parted, understand
skilst	separate
skip	ship
skipa	exchange
skipast	changed

164

Word List (Old Norse to English)

Old Norse	English
skipdráttar	ship-launching
skjótt	swiftly
skógar	woods
skógum	the-woods
skömmu	recently
skortir	shortage
skrúðklæðin	costly-clothing
skulir	should
skulu	shall
skulum	shall, should
skýla	protect
skyldast	obliged
skyldi	should
skyldu	should
skýtr	throws
slíkt	such
sló	struck
smátt	small
smíðaði	making
smíðat	crafted, made, smithery
smíðinni	smith, the-work
snemma	early
sögðu	said
sögu	story
sökum	blame, sake
sönnu	true
sótti	took
spenar	suckling
spotti	small
spurði	asked
spyrr	asked, learned
srterkr	strong
stað	place
staðar	place
staðinn	standing
stæða	stand
standa	stand, standing
standi	stand
stefnt	located
stendr	stood
sterkr	strong
stofuna	the-room
stofunni	the-room
stórvirkja	great-work
stukku	leapt

Old Norse	English
stund	awhile, time
stundir	while
stundu	time
stundum	awhile, sometimes
svá	seen, so
svaraði	answered
svarar	answered
Svarfaðardal	Svarfardal
sverðskónum	sword-studded
svín	a-pig
svíninu	the-pig
svínit	the-pig
sýndi	showed
sýnist	seemed, seems

T, t

Old Norse	English
tak	take
taka	take
tákna	betoken
táknar	taken
tal	talk
tala	talk
talat	told
tek	took
tekr	take, took
tíðenda	news
tíðendi	news
tíðir	wish
tigu	tens
til	to, until
tilgerðir	to-do
tjáir	express
tók	took
töluðu	talked
torsótt	difficulty
trautt	scarcely
treystumst	we-trust
tröll	monstrous
trúi	trust
tvá	two
tvau	two

Þ, þ

Word List (Old Norse to English)

Old Norse	English
þá	then
þaðan	from-there
þætti	seemed, seems
þættist	thought
þættumst	we-have
þangat	from-here, there
þann	he, then, then
þannig	thus
þar	then, there, they
þarftu	need-you
þars	there
þat	is, it, that, the, this
þ-at	it
þau	then
þaut	shrill
þegar	already, as-soon, as-soon-as, from-there, soon, straightaway, then, there, when
þegi	silent
þeim	the, them, they
þeir	their, they
þeira	them, they
þenna	that
þér	to-you, you, your
þess	this
þessa	this
þessarar	this-kind-of
þessi	these, this
þessir	these
þessu	this
þessum	this
þetta	that, this
þeygi	yet-not
þik	you
þín	you, yours
þína	your, yours
þingit	assembly
þingsins	their-assembly
þinn	your, yours
þitt	the, your, yours
þó	though
Þórð	Thord
Þórðar	Thord's
Þórðr	Thord
Þorgrímsson	Son-of-Thorgrim
þótt	though, thought
þótti	thought
þóttist	thought
þraut	faltered
þreytti	tired
þrotinn	ended
þú	though, you
þurfa	need, needed
þvarr	decreased
þvegnar	to-wash
því	accordingly, because, before, for, otherwise, since, such, then, therefore, this
þvílíkt	therefore-like
þykkir	felt, seemed, think, thought
þykkist	seems, think, thought
þykkja	to-think
þykkjast	consider
þykkjumst	think

U, u

Old Norse	English
um	about, around
umbóta	put-right
umsjá	about, guidance
undan	away, away-from
undarliga	strange
undarligr	a-strange
undarligt	wonderful
undir	under
unga	young
unnit	done
unz	until
upp	up
upplönd	uplands
uppstert	upright

Ú, ú

Old Norse	English
út	away, out
útan	out

Word List (Old Norse to English)

Old Norse	English
úti	out

V, v

Old Norse	English
vá	killed
vaðmál	homespun-cloth
vaðmálsklæði	wadding-clothes
vælir	wilful
vænleikr	handsome
vænn	handsome
vænsta	good
væri	was, were, will-be
væria	be
værir	be
vaki	wake
vaknaðir	woken
valdit	wielded
vanbúinn	unprepared
vandamál	disputes
vandara	important
vandliga	closely
vandligar	carefully
vánir	custom
vant	difficult
vápnum	weapons
var	was, were
varla	hardly, scarcely
várn	ours
varr	aware
várr	ours
váru	were
vaskligr	valiant
vega	ways
veggr	a-wall
vegit	slain
vegr	proceeded
veit	knew, know, knows
veitt	given
veittir	grant
veizlu	feast
veiztu	know-you
vel	well
velja	will
ver	be
vér	we
vera	be, become, being
verð	worth
verða	be, became, become, was
verði	became, become, becomes, was
verðr	became, become, becomes, were
verit	been
verr	worse
verri	worse
verst	worse
vetri	winter
vetrvistar	winter-provisions
vexti	grown
við	against, as, from, of, to, with
víðförull	widely-travelled
víginu	the-slaying
vil	will, wish
vilda	willed, wish, wished
vildi	willed, wished
vildir	would
vildu	wiled
vilgis	very
vilja	wish-to
vill	well, will, wish, wished, wishes, would
villt	wish
villtu	will-you, wish-you
vináttu	friendship
vindli	wind
vinveitt	friendly
virðir	worth
vist	hospitality
víst	certainly
vistin	stay
vísu	certainly
vit	know, we
vita	know, knowing
viti	knowing
vitrari	wiser
vitrligra	wisely
vits	wits
vizkumaðr	wise-man

Word List (Old Norse to English)

Old Norse English

Y, y

yðr	you, your
yðvarn	you
yðvars	yours
yfir	about, over
ykkar	you
ykkr	you

Ý, ý

ýmsu	variously

Word List (English to Old Norse)

Word List (English to Old Norse)

English	Old Norse
A, a	
about	*á, á, á, á*
at	*á, á, á*
after	*áðr, áðr, ætla*
aggression	*ágang*
age	*aldri*
all	*alla, allan, allgóð, allir, allnær, allr, allra, allrífligt, alls*
all-good	*allgóð*
all-near	*allnær*
all-abundant	*allrífligt*
altogether	*allt*
all-wonderful	*allundarligt*
all-well	*allvel, allvel*
all-the-people	*alþýðu*
another	*annarr*
another's	*annars*
any-other	*annars*
a	*at, at*
as	*at, at, at, at, at, átt, átt*
asked	*beiddist, beiðir, beiðzt, beiðzt, ber*
ask	*biðja*
a-brother	*bróður*
away	*brott, brottu, brýzt, búa*
and	*eða, eða, eða, ef*
afterwards	*eftir, eiga, eiga*
alone	*einn, einrænligu*
am	*em, en*
am-i	*er*
are	*er, er, er, er, er*
are-you	*ertu*
away-from	*frá, frá*
ahead	*fyrir*
along	*fyrir*
amuse	*gamni*
anger	*gramir, grán, grandi, greipr*
a-complete	*heill*
at-home	*heima*
a-horse	*hestr*
awhile	*hríð, hring, hrutu*
a-ring	*hring*
always	*jafnan*
allow	*láta, láta, láta*
a-little	*lítill, lítils*
appears	*lízt*
a-man	*maðr, maðr, maðrinn*
among	*með*
a-great	*mikill*
against	*mót, móti*
above	*ofar*
also	*ok*
ankle-breeches	*ökulbrókum*
axe-handles	*öxarsköft*
advice	*ráð, ráð*
advised	*ráð*
advise	*ráða*
advisable	*ráðligra*
angered	*reiðist*
angry	*reiðr*
agreed	*sáttir*
answered	*svaraði, svarar*
a-pig	*svín*
already	*þegar*
as-soon	*þegar*
as-soon-as	*þegar*
assembly	*þingit*
accordingly	*því*
around	*um*
a-strange	*undarligr*
aware	*varr*
a-wall	*veggr*
B, b	
by	*á, á, á*
before	*áðr, ætla, ætlaði, ætlar, ævi*
back	*aftr*
been	*at, at*
both	*báðir, bæði*
bearing	*bærist*
banned	*banni*

Word List (English to Old Norse)

English	*Old Norse*	English	*Old Norse*
beat	*barðr*	capable	*færr*
better	*batna, beiddist, beiðir*	cleaned	*fágar*
best	*beiðzt, ber*	cloak	*feld, feldinum, felld, fellr*
bear	*ber, beri, berr*		
bite-bone	*bitbeini*	criticised	*firna*
Bergen	*Björgyn*	crowded	*fjölmennt*
brothers	*bræðr, bræðrum*	companionship	*föruneyti*
break	*brjóta*	company	*föruneytis, forvitni, fót, frá*
brother	*bróðir, bróður*		
bad	*dála, dauðr*	curious	*forvitni*
but	*eða, eða, ef, efnin*	completely	*gerla*
be	*er, er, er, er, er, er, er, era*	could	*getu, geysihagliga*
		conclude	*hætta*
being	*er, er, er*	court	*hirðarinnar, hirðinni, hirðinni*
business	*erendi*		
born	*fæðist*	court-men	*hirðinni, hirðmaðr*
bring	*færa, færði*	court-man	*hirðmaðr, hirðmann*
brought	*færði, færðr, færi*	court-visit	*hirðvistar*
be-gifted	*gæfu*	corners	*horn*
became	*gerist, gerla, gerr, gert*	considered	*hyggr*
benefit	*hagr*	came	*kæmi, kæmir, kæmist, kallaðr, kallar, kann, kann, kaupa*
brain	*heilinn*		
behold	*heldr*		
beside	*hjá*	come	*kæmir, kæmist, kallaðr, kallar, kann, kann, kaupa*
bound-to	*hlotit*		
badly	*illa, illt*		
buy	*kaupa*	called	*kallaðr, kallar*
be-allowed	*láta*	choose	*kjósa*
between	*milli*	clothes	*klæðum*
become-angry	*reiðumst*	coming	*koma, komi, kominn*
blame	*sökum*	carried-out	*leiðast*
betoken	*tákna*	concluded	*lýkr*
because	*því*	chatty	*ómállatr*
become	*vera, vera, verða, verða*	conviction	*sæki, sakar*
		character	*skapi*
becomes	*verði, verðr*	cut	*skerum*
		changed	*skipast*
		costly-clothing	*skrúðklæðin*

C, c

		crafted	*smíðat*
		consider	*þykkjast*
		closely	*vandliga*
carry	*berr*	carefully	*vandligar*
carrying	*berr*	custom	*vánir*
compensation	*bóta*	certainly	*víst, vísu*
clothing	*búning*		
closed	*byrgðr*		
can	*fær, færa*		

D, d

Word List (English to Old Norse)

English	Old Norse
dealings	afskipti
dwelling	bænum
death	banans, banni
dress	búa
dressed	búinn
dead	dauðr
draw	draga
drawn	dregst
drinking	drykkju
disguise	dylja
drifted	fauk
did	gera, gera, gera
do	gera, gera, geri, gerik
done	gera, geri, gerik, gerir
disturbed	kæja
dissuade	lattan
discuss	mæla, mætti, Magnús
down	niðr
discreet	orðvarr
decide	ráð, ráða, ráða
decision	ráða
dirty	saurgar
decreased	þvarr
difficulty	torsótt
disputes	vandamál
difficult	vant

E, e

English	Old Norse
earlier	áðan
eye	auga
either	eða
especially	einkum
eccentric	einrænligu
errand	erendit
Eyjafjord	Eyjafirði
Eyvind	Eyvindar, Eyvindr
end	felld
exceedingly-skilful	geysihagliga
easy	hægra
endanger	hætta
each	hverjum, hverjum, hvern
everyone	hverjum
every	hverr
equally	jafnan, jafnmæli
equal-speak	jafnmæli
equally-well	jafnvel
eccentricities	kynjalæti
ended	lokit, lokka
even-spirit	lundhægr
except	nema
enjoy	njót
exchange	skipa
early	snemma
express	tjáir

F, f

English	Old Norse
for	á, á, á
from	á, á, á, áðan, áðr, áðr, ætla
fool	afglapa
fixed-upon	allstarsýnn
few	fáir, fallin
fallen	fallin, fallit
found	fann, fara, fara, farar, farið, farit
fared	farit
fee	fé
fell	fellr, fellt
falling	fellt
find	finn, finna, finna, finnast, finnast
fiendish	fjandligr
followers	fjölmenni
followers-many	fjölmenni
for-travelling	förin
foot	fót
from-game	fráleik
follow	fylgið, fylgjusamr
follow-same	fylgjusamr
fore-done	fyrirgert
first	fyrst, fyrstu
fun	gaman
favourable	glíkligt
further	meir
frequently	oft
frame	rammi

Word List (English to Old Norse)

English	Old Norse	English	Old Norse
from-there	þaðan, þangat	has	á, á, áðan
from-here	þangat	had	átt, átt, átti, auga, báðir, bæði, bænum, bærist, banans, banni, barðr, batna, beiddist
faltered	þraut		
felt	þykkir		
feast	veizlu		
friendship	vináttu		
friendly	vinveitt		
		have	átt, átti, auga, báðir, bæði, bænum, bærist, banans, banni, barðr, batna, beiddist, beiðir, beiðzt

G, g

English	Old Norse	English	Old Norse
get	fá, fá	hammering	brýzt
give	fá, fæ, fæðist, fær	height	hæð
go	fara, fara, farar, farið, farit, farit, fátt	handy	hagr
		held	halda
going	fara, farar, farið, farit, farit, fátt	hold	haldi
		half	hálft, hálfu
given	fenginn, fer	hands-hook-us	handkrækjumst
goes	ferr	he	hann, hann, hann, hans, hans, hans, Harald
group	flokk		
game	fráleikrinn, fram		
good-things	fríðenda	him	hann, hann, hans, hans, hans
got	gæti, gaf, gafst		
gave	gaf, gafst, gaman, gaman	his	hans, Harald, Haraldi, Haraldr, Haraldr, Haralds, harðleikit
guess	get		
Glum	Glúmr	Harald	Harald, Haraldi, Haraldr
good	góða, góðan, góðum, góma, gott		
		Harald's	Haraldr, Haralds
gums	góma	hardness	harðleikit
god	gott	hard	hart
grey	grán	having	hefði
grasp	greipr	home	heim, heima
grouped-together	gropasamliga	hand	hendi, hendr, hendu, hér, herra
grass	grösum		
gold	gull, gyllt	handed	hendu, hér
greeting	kveðju	here	hér
greeted	kveðr	horse	hest, hesta
given-leave	leyft	horse's	hestrinn
great	mikill, mikinn	horses	hestum
great-work	stórvirkja	heard	heyra, heyrðak, heyrði, heyrir, heyrt
guidance	umsjá		
grant	veittir	head	höfði, höfðinu
grown	vexti	humble	hógværr
		Hreidar	Hreiðar, Hreiðari, Hreiðarr, Hreiðars

H, h

English	Old Norse
Hreidar's-Place	Hreiðarsstöðum

172

Word List (English to Old Norse)

English	*Old Norse*	English	*Old Norse*
house	*húsi*		
how	*hvárt, hvat, hvé, hverjum, hverjum*	**K, k**	
how-so	*hversu*		
hands	*krummur*	kill	*drepa, drepi, drepið*
human-trials	*mannraunum*	killed	*drepinn, drykkju*
hurt	*meiddr*	kinsman	*frændi*
human	*mennskr*	kinsmen	*frændi*
himself	*sama, samir, sáttir, saurgar*	know	*kann, kaupa, kemr, kenna*
homespun-cloth	*vaðmál*	knew	*kenna, kjósa*
handsome	*vænleikr, vænn*	knees	*kné*
hardly	*varla*	kings	*konunga, konungar*
hospitality	*vist*	king	*konungr, konungs*
		knows	*veit*
		know-you	*veiztu*
		knowing	*vita, viti*

I, i

L, l

English	*Old Norse*
in	*á, áðan, áðr, áðr, ætla*
intended	*ætla, ætlaði, ætlar*
is	*at, átt, átt, átti, auga*
if	*ef*
i	*ek, ek, ekki, ekki, em*
is-not	*ekki*
inheritance	*föðurarf*
in-front-of	*fyrir*
injury	*grandi*
insult	*háðungar*
it	*hann, hans, hans, hans, Harald, Haraldi*
is-named	*heitir*
in-moderation	*hóf*
ingenuity	*hugkvæmr*
ill	*illt*
Iceland	*Ísland, Íslands*
icelander	*íslendingar*
it-may	*mátti*
in-common	*samir*
important	*vandara*

English	*Old Norse*
life	*ævi*
lived	*bjó*
little	*fátt, fauk, fé*
last-years	*fyrra*
like	*glíkr, Glúmr, góða, góðan, góðum*
lord	*herra*
laughing	*hlæjandi*
laughed	*hlær, hljóta*
luck	*hljóta*
listened	*hlýða*
listen-to	*hlýddið*
looked	*hyggr, í*
leaves	*lætr*
laid	*lagðr, lagi*
lead	*lagi*
land	*land, langar*
long	*langar, langt, lát*
left	*láta*
let-go	*laust*
let	*leggja, leggr*
leave	*leyfi, leyfir*
liked	*líkar*
lie	*ljúga*
lift	*loft*

J, j

English	*Old Norse*
joyfully	*blíðlíga*
journey	*farar*

Word List (English to Old Norse)

English	*Old Norse*	English	*Old Norse*
lure	*lokka*	much	*mik, mikil, mikill, mikill, mikinn*
large	*mikit*	morning	*morgin, morgininn*
less	*minna, minni, míns*	many-ways	*mörgu*
learned	*spyrr*	meeting	*móti, mótinu, mótit*
located	*stefnt*	meetings	*mótit, móts*
leapt	*stukku*	must	*mun*
		mouth	*munni*
		message	*orðsending*
		myself	*sjálfan*
		mood	*skap*
		making	*smíðaði*

M, m

English	*Old Norse*
materials	*efnin*
money	*fé, feld*
monstrous	*ferligu, ferr*
meet	*finnast, finnast, finnast, finnst*
meet-up	*finnast*
met	*finnast, finnst, finnumst*
many-people	*fjölmennit*
most	*flesta, flokk, fluttir, föðurarf, för*
made	*gerir, gerist, gerla, gerr, gert*
mention	*get*
mocking	*ginna, ginningar*
mockery	*háðs*
matter	*hlut, hlýða*
measure	*hófi*
minded	*hygg*
may	*má, maðr, maðr, maðrinn, mæla*
man	*maðr, maðrinn, mæla*
Magnus	*Magnús, Magnúsi, Magnúss*
Magnus's	*Magnúss*
matters	*mál*
men	*manna, mannraunum, manns*
many	*marga, margir, margs, margt, mátti, máttu*
may-you	*máttu*
more	*meir, meira*
me	*mér, mér, mér, mest*
mine	*mér, mér, mest, mesta, mestum, mik, mik*
my	*mér, mest*

N, n

English	*Old Norse*
never	*aldri, aldri, aldrigi*
numb	*dofna*
none	*eigi, eigi, eigi*
not	*eigi, eigi*
nothing	*eigi*
no	*engar, engi, engi*
no-one	*engi*
news	*fréttir, fund, fundar*
nowhere	*hvergi*
noise	*læti*
negligently	*latliga*
noticed	*litu*
near	*nær*
near-lying	*nálægir*
need	*nauðsyn, nemr*
north	*norðr*
Norway	*Nóreg, Nóregi*
now	*nú*
newly-come	*nýkominn*
not-forget	*ólatr*
need-you	*þarftu*
needed	*þurfa*

O, o

English	*Old Norse*
of	*á, á, á, á, á, á, áðr, aðra, aðrir*
on	*á, á*

Word List (English to Old Norse)

English	*Old Norse*	English	*Old Norse*
other	*aðra, aðrir, ætla, ætlan, ætlar*	pull-cloak, handle-roughly	*skauttoguðu*
others	*aðrir, ætla, ætlan*	parted	*skilði, skilðir, skilðust*
of-life	*ævinnar*	protect	*skýla*
off	*af*	place	*stað, staðar*
offer	*búnir*	put-right	*umbóta*
or	*eða*	proceeded	*vegr*
own	*eiga, eigi*		
one-thing	*eigi*		
once	*einhverju, einn*		
one	*einn, eins, einum, eirir*		

R, r

English	*Old Norse*
one's	*eins*
old-age	*elli*
otherwise	*elligar, en*
of-wealth	*fjárins*
of-the-people	*manni*
of-any	*nökkut*
off-said	*ofsögum*
ours	*okkarn, okkart, okkr, okkr, okkr*
out-of	*ór*
occasion	*sinn*
obliged	*skyldast*
out	*út, útan, úti*
over	*yfir*

returned	*áðr*
rough	*álpun*
residence	*bænum*
ready-to-serve	*greitt*
rather	*halda, haldist, háttung, hefnt*
risk	*háttung*
revenge	*hefnt*
room	*herbergi*
ridicule	*hlægi*
ran	*hleypr, hljóp*
rest	*hvíldar*
recited	*kveðr*
redeem	*leysa*
ruined	*ónýtt*
rode	*reið*
ride	*reiðar*
roughly-handled	*reikuð*
run	*rennr*
reasons	*sakar*
roughly	*skauttogaðr*
recently	*skömmu*

P, p

prepared	*bjó, bjó, blásit*
prepare	*bú*
passed	*ferr, ferr, ferr*
promised	*hét*
poem	*kvæði, kvæði*
poem-reward	*kvæðislaunin*
playful	*leikmikill*
played	*lék*
passes	*líðr*
praise-will	*lofgjarnliga*
people	*maðr, mæl, mælgina, mælik*
people-few	*mannfátt*
poorly	*miðlungi*
prowess	*óknáleik*
peace-meeting	*sáttarfundar, sáttarfundr*

S, s

so	*á, á, á, á, áðr, aðra, aðrir*
suppose	*ætla, ætlan, ætlar*
stood-out	*afbragð*
strength	*afl, afli, aflit*
settled	*bjó, blásit, borðit*
soon	*brátt, breyttu*
steep	*brottu*
secure	*fastr*

Word List (English to Old Norse)

English	*Old Norse*	English	*Old Norse*
shed	*felld*	such	*sá, sá, sæja, sæmiliga, sætt*
situated	*felldr*	see	*sæja, sæmiliga, sætt, sætt*
sacrificing	*förna*	settlement	*sætt*
self-control	*forræði*	settle	*sættir*
swiftness	*fráleikrinn*	same-day	*samdægris*
swift	*frávastr*	sat	*sátu*
sea	*haf*	seeing	*sé*
skilled	*hagr*	seen	*sé, sé, sé, sefr*
suited	*hentr*	sleeps	*sefr*
share	*hlut, hluta, hlutar, hlutr*	slowly	*seint*
small-island	*hólmr*	sell	*selja, selr*
seized	*höndum*	send	*senda, senda*
Son-of-Hreidar	*Hreiðarssonar*	sending	*senda*
said	*kvað, kvað, kvæði, kvæði, kvæðislaunin, kvæðit, kvæðit, kveðr*	sent	*sendan, sendi*
		set	*setr*
spoke	*kvað, kvæði, kvæði, kvæðislaunin, kvæðit*	six	*sex*
		sailed	*sigla*
some-beast	*kykvendum*	silver	*silfr, silfri, silfrit*
strange	*kynlig, kynligast, kynligu*	sit	*sitja*
		sitting	*sitja*
strangely	*kynligast*	seemed	*sjá, sjá, sjá, sjá*
secretly	*launungu*	self-supported	*sjálfbjargi*
sport	*leik*	self	*sjálfr*
sought	*leitat*	scabbards	*skálpana*
small	*lítill, litu, ljótari*	short-distance	*skammt*
say	*mæl, mælgina, mælik*	scratched	*skeindist*
speak	*mælik, mælir, mælt*	separated	*skilðust*
speaking	*mælt*	separate	*skilst*
spoken	*mælt*	ship	*skip*
sign	*mark*	ship-launching	*skipdráttar*
shall	*mun, mun, mun, muna, mund*	swiftly	*skjótt*
		shortage	*skortir*
should	*mun, mun, muna, mund, mundi, muni, munt, muntu*	struck	*sló*
		smithery	*smíðat*
		smith	*smíðinni*
shall-you	*munt, muntu, muntu*	story	*sögu*
should-you	*muntu*	sake	*sökum*
studded	*naddar*	suckling	*spenar*
somewhat	*nökkur*	strong	*srterkr, stað*
some	*nökkura, nökkurri, nökkut*	standing	*staðinn, stæða*
		stand	*stæða, standa, standa*
something	*nökkut*		
speech	*ræðu*		
saw	*sá, sá, sá*	stood	*stendr*
		sometimes	*stundum*

176

Word List (English to Old Norse)

English	Old Norse	English	Old Norse
Svarfardal	*Svarfaðardal*	to-meet	*fundar*
sword-studded	*sverðskónum*	the-meeting	*fundarins*
showed	*sýndi*	taken-care-of	*gætt*
seems	*sýnist, tak, taka*	to-give	*gefa*
shrill	*þaut*	told	*getit, greitt, gripr, gyltr, hætti*
straightaway	*þegar*		
silent	*þegi*	treasure	*gripr*
Son-of-Thorgrim	*Þorgrímsson*	the-whole	*heill*
since	*því*	the-horse	*hestinn*
scarcely	*trautt, treystumst*	there	*hinnig, hitt, hlægi, hleypr, hljóp*
slain	*vegit*		
stay	*vistin*	this	*hitt, hlægi, hleypr, hljóp, hlut, hluta, hlutar, hlutr, hólminn, hólmr*

T, t

English	Old Norse	English	Old Norse
		the-island	*hólminn*
		teased	*hrundu*
that	*á, á, á, áðr, aðra, aðrir, ætla, ætlan, ætlar, ævinnar, af, af*	thought	*hug, hugði, hugkvæmir, hugr, hurðina, hvar, hvárt, hvat*
then	*á, á, áðr, aðra, aðrir, ætla, ætlan, ætlar, ævinnar, af, af, af*	think	*hugr, hurðina, hvar, hvárt, hvat, hvergi*
to	*á, áðr, aðra, aðrir, ætla, ætlan, ætlar, ævinnar*	the-door	*hurðina*
		to-come	*koma*
to-hear	*áheyrsli*	the-king	*konung, konungar, konungi, konunginn, konungr*
the-people	*alþýðu, annarra*		
take-care-of	*annast*	the-kings	*konungar*
than	*at, at*	the-king's	*konungs*
the	*at, at, at, at, at, at, átt, bænum, biðja, bjó*	the-poem	*kvæði, kvæðislaunin*
		the-land	*landi*
to-ask	*biðja*	take	*leggja, leið, leik, leikmikill*
trumpet-blast	*blásit, borðit*		
table	*borðit*	the-game	*leikrinn*
tricky	*brögðóttr*	tempered-even	*lundhægr*
to-deem	*dæmð*	talking	*mælgina*
to-kill	*drepa*	the-matter	*málinu*
to-be	*er, er*	talkative	*málugr, mann*
they-are	*eru*	that-man	*mann*
to-go	*fara*	the-men	*manna*
travel	*fara, fara, fara*	the-man	*manninn*
travelled	*fara, fara, fari, fari, fastr, felld*	to-me	*mér*
		tall	*mikill*
travelling	*ferðina, ferr, ferr, ferr*	time	*mund, mundi, muni*
threw	*fleygir*	took	*námu, nauðsyn, nemr, nestlokum, nökkur, nökkura*
transport	*flytr*		
trading-voyages	*förum*		

Word List (English to Old Norse)

English	Old Norse	English	Old Norse
the-end	nestlokum	uglier	ljótari
test	reyna	ugly	ljótr
tried	reynt	used	nýt
together	saman, samdægris	use	nytjar
truth	sanna	unprepared	óbúinn, öðru
true	sannast, satt, sáttarfundar	un-passable	ógreið
tell	seg	unholy	óheilagr
they	senn, senn, sér, sér, sér	us	okkr, okkr
		unaccompanied	ólið
themselves	sik, silfr	unlike	ólíkast
theirs	sín	unlikely	ólíkligt
to-see	sjá	untrue	ósannligt
the-woods	skógum	un-innocent-looking	ósýknligr
throws	skýtr	un-accustomed	óvanr
the-work	smíðinni	un-warned	óvart
the-room	stofuna, stofunni	unknown	óvísu
the-pig	svíninu, svínit	uproar	reiðin, reiðingum
taken	táknar	unite	samtengja
talk	tal, tala	understand	skilja
thus	þannig	until	til, tilgerðir
them	þeim, þeim	under	undir
their	þeir	up	upp
to-you	þér	uplands	upplönd
this-kind-of	þessarar	upright	uppstert
these	þessi, þessi		
their-assembly	þingsins		
though	þó, Þórð, Þórðar	**V, v**	
Thord	Þórð, Þórðar		
Thord's	Þórðar	very-timid	alláræðislítill
tired	þreytti	varied	breyttu
to-wash	þvegnar	visit	fund
therefore	því	very-smart	hugkvæmir
therefore-like	þvílíkt	voyage	reiðfara
to-think	þykkja	valiant	vaskligr
tens	tigu	very	vilgis
to-do	tilgerðir	variously	ýmsu
talked	töluðu		
trust	trúi		
two	tvá, tvau		
the-slaying	víginu	**W, w**	
U, u		with	at, at, átt, bænum, biðja
uneven-share	fjárskakka	when	en, engar, engi

Word List (English to Old Norse)

English	Old Norse	English	Old Norse
was	er, er, er, er, er, er	winter	vetri
were	er, er, er, er, er, er	winter-provisions	vetrvistar
what	er, er, er, er	widely-travelled	víðförull
where	er, er	willed	vilda, vilda
which	er, er, er	wiled	vildu
who	er, er	wish-to	vilja
whom	er	wishes	vill
would	er, eru, eru, eru, fagna, fara, fara, fara	will-you	villtu
		wish-you	villtu
welcomed	fagna	wind	vindli
went	fara, fari, fari, fastr, felld, felldr	wiser	vitrari
		wisely	vitrligra
wished	fúsastr, gætt, ganga, gefa	wits	vits
		wise-man	vizkumaðr
walked	gengr		
way	hætti, haf, hagr		
whole	heill		
was-named	hét		
worried	hræddr, Hreiðarssonar		

Y, y

English	Old Norse
young-sow	gyltr
yes	já
you	okkr, óknáleik, ólatr, ólið, ólíkast, ólíkligt, ómállatr, ónýtt, ór, orð
yourself	sjálfr
your	þér, þess, þessa, þessarar, þessi
yet-not	þeygi
yours	þín, þína, þína, þingsins, þinn
young	unga

English	Old Norse
whether	hvárt
why	hví
without-fear	ófælinn
words	orð, orðit, orðum
worded	ort
well-enough	sæmiliga
woods	skógar
while	stundir
we-have	þættumst
wish	tíðir, tigu, til, til, tilgerðir
we-trust	treystumst
wonderful	undarligt
wadding-clothes	vaðmálsklæði
wilful	vælir
will-be	væri
wake	vaki
woken	vaknaðir
wielded	valdit
weapons	vápnum
ways	vega
well	vel, velja
will	velja, vér, verð
we	vér, verð
worth	verð, verða
worse	verr, verri, verst

The Tale of Hreiðarr the Fool (*Old Icelandic*)

Old Icelandic	Literal	English
1	**1**	**1**
Þórður hét maður.	Thord was-named a-man.	There was a man named Thord.
Hann var Þorgrímsson, Hreiðarssonar, þess er Glúmur vó.	He was Son-of-Thorgrim, Son-of-Hreidar, this whom Glum killed.	He was the son of Thorgrim, the son of Hreidar who killed Glum.
Þórður var lítill maður vexti og vænn.	Thord was a-little man grown and handsome.	He was a small man in size and handsome.
Hann átti sér bróður er Hreiðar hét.	He had himself a-brother who Hreidar was-named.	He had a brother, who was named Hreidar.
Hann var ljótur maður og varla sjálfbjargi fyrir vits sökum.	He was ugly man and scarcely self-supported for wits sake.	He was an ugly man and he could scarcely take care of himself.
Hann var manna frávastur og vel að afli búinn og hógvær í skapi og var hann heima jafnan.	He was a-man swift and well to strength prepared and humble in character and was he at-home always.	He was a fast man and very strong, and humble in character, and he was always at home.
En Þórður var í förum og var hirðmaður Magnúss konungs og mast vel.	But Thord was in travelling and was court-man Magnus the-king and most well.	But Thord was a travelling man, and a court man of King Magnus who thought most well of him.
Og eitt sinni er Þórður bjó skip sitt í Eyjafirði þá kom Hreiðar þar bróðir hans.	And once his was Thord prepared ship his in Eyjafjord then came Hreidar there brother his.	And one day when Thord was preparing his ship in Eyjafjord, then came Hreidar his brother.
Og er Þórður sá hann spurði hann hví hann væri þar kominn.	And when Thord saw him asked he why he was there coming.	And when Thord saw him, he asked why he had come there.
Hreiðar segir:	Hreidar said:	Hreidar said:
"Eigi nema erindið væri".	"Nothing except errand was".	"I would not have come unless I had business".
"Hvað viltu þá?"	"What will-you then?"	"What do you want then?"
segir Þórður.	said Thord.	said Thord.

The Tale of Hreiðarr the Fool (Old Icelandic)

Old Icelandic	Literal	English
"Eg vil fara utan",	"I wish travel out",	"I wish to travel abroad",
segir Hreiðar.	said Hreidar.	said Hreidar.
Þórður mælti:	Thord spoke:	Thord spoke:
"Ekki þykir mér þér fallin förin.	"Not think I you fallen for-travelling.	"I don't think you are destined for travelling".
Vil eg heldur það til leggja við þig að þú hafir föðurarf okkarn og er það hálfu meira fé en það er eg hefi í förum".	Wish I rather that to let from you that you have inheritance ours and is that half more money than that which I have in trading-voyages".	"I wish rather than to let you go, for you to have our inheritance, and that is more than half the money which I have in trading voyages".
Hreiðar svarar:	Hreidar answered:	Hreidar answered:
"Þá er lítið vit mitt",	"Then would little know me",	"Then I would know little",
segir hann, "ef eg tek þenna fjárskakka til þess að gefa mig svo upp sjálfan og láta þína umsjá og mun þá hver maður draga af mér fé okkað alls eg kann engi forræði þau er nýt eru.	said he, "if I took that uneven-share to this to gave I so up myself and left your guidance and would then every man draw of me money ours all I know no self-control then where used they-are.	he said, "if I took that uneven share, then gave myself up and left your guidance, and then every man would cheat money out of us, and I know no self-control where they are used.
Og era þér þá betra hlut í að eiga ef eg ber á mönnum eða geri eg aðra óvísu þeim er um fé mitt sitja að lokka af mér en eftir það sé eg barður eða meiddur fyrir mínar tilgerðir enda er það sannast í að þér mun torsótt að halda mér eftir er eg vil fara".	And are you then better share in that own if I bear to people or do I other unknown them is about money mine sit that lure off me but after that so is beat or hurt for mine to-do and is that true in that you should difficulty that rather to-me after that I will travel".	And it is better for you to own a share, if I bear to people or do otherwise unknown things to them, those who attend in luring money away from me, but after that I will be beaten or hurt for my deeds, for that is true, that you will have a hard time keeping me, when I want to go".
"Vera kann það",	"Be can that",	"That may be",
segir Þórður, "en get ekki þá um ferð þína fyrir öðrum mönnum".	said Thord, "but mention not then about travel yours before other people".	said Thord, "but don't mention your travel in front of other people".
Því hét hann.	Therefore promised he.	Therefore he promised.

The Tale of Hreiðarr the Fool (Old Icelandic)

Old Icelandic	Literal	English
Og þegar er þeir bræður eru skildir þá segir Hreiðar hverjum er heyra vill að hann ætlar utan að fara með bróður sínum.	And as-soon-as that they brother were parted then told Hreidar everyone that heard would that he intended out to travel with brother his.	And as soon as they had parted, Hreidar told everyone that would hear him, that he intended to travel abroad with his brother.
Og firna allir Þórð um ef hann flytur utan afglapa.	And criticised all Thord about if he transport out fool.	And everyone criticised Thord, if he travel abroad with such a fool.

2

Old Icelandic	Literal	English
Og er þeir eru búnir sigla þeir í haf og verða vel reiðfara, koma við Björgyn og þegar spyr Þórður eftir konungi og var honum sagt að Magnús konungur var í bænum og hafði skömmu áður komið og vildi eigi láta kæja sig samdægris, þóttist þurfa hvíldar er hann var nýkominn.	And when they were prepared sailed they to sea and became well voyage, came to Bergen and there asked Thord after the-king and was he told that Magnus the-king was in residence and had recently returned come and willed not be-allowed disturbed him same-day, thought needed rest when he was newly-come.	And when they were ready, they sailed to sea and began their voyage well, they came to Bergen, and there Thord asked for the king, and he was told that King Magnus was in residence and had recently returned home and did not wish to be disturbed that day, because he needed rest after newly coming home.
Brátt litu menn Hreiðar að hann var afbragð annarra manna.	Soon noticed people Hreidar that he was stood-out other men.	Soon people noticed Hreidar, that he stood out from other men.
Hann var mikill og ljótur, ómállatur við þá er hann hitti.	He was tall and ugly, chatty with then who he met.	He was tall and ugly, and chatty with whoever he met.
Og snemma um morguninn áður menn væru vaknaðir stendur Hreiðar upp og kallar:	And early about morning before people were woken stood Hreidar up and called:	And early in the morning, before people were awake, Hreidar stood up and called:
"Vaki þú bróðir.	"Wake you brother.	"Wake up, brother.
Fátt veit sá er sefur.	Little knows so who sleeps.	He who sleeps knows little.
Eg veit tíðindi og heyrði eg áðan læti kynleg".	I know news and heard I earlier noise strange".	I have some news, and earlier I heard a strange noise.
"Hverju var líkast?"	"What was like?"	"What was it like?"
spyr Þórður.	asked Thord.	asked Thord.
"Sem yfir kykvendum",	"Like about some-beast",	"Like some beast",

The Tale of Hreiðarr the Fool (Old Icelandic)

Old Icelandic	Literal	English
segir Hreiðar, "og þaut við mjög en aldrei veit eg hvað látum var".	said Hreidar, "and shrill as much but never knew I what have was".	said Hreidar, "and as shrill as one, but I never knew what it was".
"Lát eigi svo undarlega",	"Have not so strange",	"That is not so strange",
segir Þórður.	said Thord.	said Thord.
"Það mun verið hafa hornblástur".	"It must been have trumpet-blast".	"It must have been a blast from a trumpet".
"Hvað skal það tákna?"	"What shall it betoken?"	"What does that mean?"
spyr Hreiðar.	asked Hreidar.	asked Hreidar.
Þórður svarar:	Thord answered:	Thord answered:
"Blásið er jafnan til móts eða til skipdráttar".	"Trumpet-blast is always to meetings or to ship-launching".	"A trumpet blast always means a meeting being summoned or for the launching of ships".
"Hvað táknar mótið?"	"What taken meetings?"	"What are these meetings taken for?"
spyr Hreiðar.	asked Hreidar.	asked Hreidar.
"Þar eru dæmd vandamál jafnan",	"They are to-deem disputes equally",	"They are to judge disputes equally",
segir Þórður, "og slíkt talað sem konungur þykist þurfa að fyrir alþýðu sé upp borið".	said Thord, "and such told as the-king seems needed that before the-people so up bear".	said Thord, "and for things to be told, such as the king sees fit, to bear to the people".
"Hvort mun konungur nú á mótinu?"	"Whether shall the-king now at meeting?"	"Will the king be there now at the meeting?"
spyr Hreiðar.	asked Hreidar.	asked Hreidar.
"Það ætla eg víst",	"That suppose I certainly",	"I suppose so, certainly",
svarar Þórður.	answered Thord.	answered Thord.
"Þangað verð eg þá að fara",	"From-here worth I then to go",	"Then it is worth me going there",

The Tale of Hreiðarr the Fool (Old Icelandic)

Old Icelandic	Literal	English
segir Hreiðar, "því að eg vildi þar koma fyrst er eg sæi sem flesta menn í senn".	said Hreidar, "because that I wish there to-come first that I see as most people to together".	said Hreidar, "because I wish to go there first, to see as many people together at once".
"Þá skýtur í tvö horn með okkur",	"Then throws to two corners with us",	"Then that throws into two corners with us",
segir Þórður.	said Thord.	said Thord.
"Mér þætti því betur er þú kæmir þar síður er fjölmennt væri og vil eg hvergi fara".	"To-me seems therefore better that you come there less when crowded will-be and wish I nowhere to-go".	"It seems better to me therefore that you go there less, when it will be crowded, and I don't wish to go there myself".
"Ekki tjáir slíkt að mæla",	"Not express such to discuss",	"It does not do to say such a thing",
segir Hreiðar, "fara skulum við báðir.	said Hreidar, "travel shall we both.	said Hreidar, "we shall travel both.
Muna þér betra þykja að eg fari einn en ekki færð þú mig lattan þessarar farar".	Should you better to-think that I travel alone and not can you me dissuade this-kind-of journey".	I think you had better realise, that I am going alone, and you can not dissuade me from making this journey".
Hleypur Hreiðar á brott.	Ran Hreidar to away.	Then Hreidar ran away,
En Þórður sér nú að fara mun verða og fer hann eftir er Hreiðar fer hart undan og er mjög langt milli þeirra.	When Thord saw now that going should be also went he after as Hreidar went hard away and was much long between them.	But now Thord saw that this would happen, he also went after him, as Hreidar went hard away, and there was a long way between them.
Og er Hreiðar sér að Þórður fór seint þá mælti hann:	And when Hreidar saw that Thord went slowly then spoke he:	And when Hreidar saw, that Thord was going slowly, then he spoke:
"Það er þó satt, að illt er lítill að vera þá er aflið nær ekki.	"It is though true, that bad is small to be then that strength near is-not.	"It is true that it is bad to be small, because then strength is not near.
En þó mætti vera fráleikurinn en lítið ætla eg þig af honum hafa hlotið.	But though may be swiftness but little suppose I you of it have bound-to.	But though one can still be swift, but I suppose you have little of that,
Og væria þér verri vænleikur minni og kæmist þú með öðrum mönnum".	And be to-you worse handsome less and come you as other men".	and you should be less handsome, and quicker as other men are".

The Tale of Hreiðarr the Fool (Old Icelandic)

Old Icelandic	Literal	English
Þórður svaraði:	Thord answered:	Thord answered:
"Eigi veit eg mér verr fara óknáleik minn en þér afl þitt".	"Not know I me worse to-be prowess mine than you strength yours".	"I do not know if it is worse to have my weakness than your strength".
"Handkrækjumst þá bróðir",	"Hands-hook-us then brother",	"Let us hook hands then, brother",
segir Hreiðar.	said Hreidar.	said Hreidar,
Og nú gera þeir svo, fara um hríð og er svo að Þórði tekur að dofna höndin og lætur hann laust, þykir eigi verða vinveitt að þeir haldist á við álpun Hreiðars.	And now did they so, went about awhile and was seen that Thord took that numb hand and had he let-go, felt not was friendly that they rather that against rough Hreidar.	and so they did, and after a while, and Thord's hand became so numb, that he had to let go, and he felt it was not friendly, because Hreidar was too rough.
Hreiðar fer nú undan svo við fót og nemur stað síðan á hæð nakkvarri og er allstarsýnn, sér þaðan fjölmennið þangað sem mótið var.	Hreidar went now away-from so with foot and took place afterwards to height some and was fixed-upon, saw from-there many-people there as meeting were.	Hreidar now went away and ran, and so it happened afterwards, that he came to a hill and stopped there, he looked from there and saw many people, that were at a meeting.
Og er Þórður kemur eftir mælti hann:	And as Thord came after spoke he:	And as Thord came afterwards, he spoke:
"Förum nú báðir saman bróðir".	"Going now both together brother".	"Let's go both together now, brother".
Og Hreiðar gerir svo.	And Hreidar did so.	And Hreidar did so.

3

Og er þeir koma á þingið kenna margir menn Þórð og fagna honum vel og verður konungur áheyrsli.	And when they came to assembly knew many people Thord and welcomed him well and became the-king to-hear.	And when they came to the assembly, many people knew Thord and welcomed him well, and the king came to hear of him.
Og þegar gengur Þórður fyrir konung og kveður hann vel og tekur konungur blíðlega kveðju hans.	And soon went Thord before the-king and greeted he well and took the-king joyfully greeting his.	And soon Thord went before the king and greeted him well, and the king received his greeting joyfully.

The Tale of Hreiðarr the Fool (Old Icelandic)

Old Icelandic	Literal	English
Þegar skildi með þeim bræðrum er þeir komu til þingsins og verður Hreiðar skauttogaður mjög og færður í reikuð.	When parted with them brothers that they came to their-assembly and became Hreidar roughly much and brought to roughly-handled.	When the brothers parted when they came to the assembly, Hreidar was treated roughly and pushed about.
Hann er málugur og hlær mjög og þykir mönnum ekki að minna gaman að eiga við hann og verður honum nú förin ógreið.	He was talkative and laughed much and thought people not that less fun that had with him and became he now travelling un-passable.	He was talkative and laughed a lot, and people thought it no less fun to tease him, and he now became blocked in the crowd.
Konungur spyr Þórð tíðinda og síðan spyr hann hvað þeirra manna væri í för með honum er hann vildi að til hirðvistar færi með honum".	The-king asked Thord news and then asked he what they people were by travelling with him that he wished that to court-visit bring with him".	The king asked Thord for news, and then he asked, and what people were travelling with him, and whether he wished to join him at court.
"Þar er bróðir minn í för,	"There has brother mine so travelled,	"My brother has also travelled here",
segir Þórður.	said Thord.	said Thord.
"Sá maður mun vel vera",	"Such man should well be",	"Such a man should be well",
segir konungur, "ef þér er líkur".	said the-king, "if you is like".	said the king, "if he is like you".
Þórður segir:	Thord said:	Thord said:
"Ekki er hann mér líkur".	"Not is he me like".	"He is not like me".
Konungur mælti:	The-king spoke:	The king spoke:
"Þó má enn vel vera eða hvað er ólíkast með ykkur?"	"Though may but well be but how is unlike with you?"	"That may be, but now is he not like you?"
Þórður mælti:	Thord spoke:	Thord spoke:
"Hann er mikill maður vexti.	"He is great man grown.	"He is very large.
Hann er ljótur og heldur ósýknlegur, sterkur að afli og lundhægur maður".	He is ugly and behold un-innocent-looking, strong in strength and even-spirit man".	He is ugly, and he appears devious looking, and he is greatly strong, but even spirited".
Konungur mælti:	The-king spoke:	The king spoke:

The Tale of Hreiðarr the Fool (Old Icelandic)

Old Icelandic	Literal	English
"Þó má honum vel vera farið að mörgu".	"Though may he well be going that many-ways".	"He may be well in other ways".
Þórður segir:	Thord said:	Thord said:
"Ekki, ekki var hann kallaður viskumaður á unga aldri".	"Not not was he called wise-man in young age".	"He was not called a wise man in his youth".
"Að því fer eg meir",	"That then go I further",	"Then I go further",
segir konungur, "sem nú er eða hvort má hann sjálfur annast sig?"	said the-king, "as now to but how may he himself take-care-of such?"	said the king, "to how he is now, and how he takes care of himself?"
"Ekki dála er það",	"Not bad is that",	"Not bad",
segir Þórður.	said Thord.	said Thord.
Konungur mælti:	The-king spoke:	The king spoke:
"Hví fluttir þú hann utan?"	"Why brought you him out?"	"Why did you bring him out?"
"Herra",	"Lord",	"Lord",
segir Þórður, "hann á allt hálft við mig en hefir öngar nytjar fjárins og engi afskipti sér veitt um peninga, beiðst þessa eins hlutar að fara utan með mér og þótti mér ósannlegt að eigi réði hann einum hlut þars hann lætur mig mörgum ráða.	said Thord, "he has altogether half with me but has no use of-wealth and none dealings so given about money, best this one's share that travel out with me and thought me untrue that not decide he alone share there he leaves much many advice.	said Thord, "he has half of everything with me, but he has no use of wealth and no interest in money, the only thing he has asked me is to travel abroad with me, and I thought it would be unfair to decide to leave him alone, when he lets me decide so much.
Þótti mér og líklegt að hann mundi gæfu af yður hljóta ef hann kæmi á yðarn fund".	Thought me and favourable that he would be-gifted of your luck if he came to you meet".	I thought it would be favourable and good luck if he came to meet you".
"Sjá vildi eg hann",	"So willed I him",	"So I wish to meet him",
segir konungur.	said the-king.	said the king.
"Svo skal og",	"So shall and",	"So shall it be",
segir Þórður, "en brottu er hann nú rjáður nokkur".	said Thord, "but steep is he now worried somewhat".	said Thord, "but he is now somewhat worried".
Konungur sendi nú eftir honum.	The-king sent now after him.	The king now sent for him.

The Tale of Hreiðarr the Fool (Old Icelandic)

Old Icelandic	Literal	English
Og er Hreiðar heyrði sagt að konungur vildi hitta hann þá gengur hann uppstert mjög og nær á hvað sem fyrir var og var hann því óvanur að konungur hefði beiðst fundar hans.	And when Hreidar heard said that the-king wished meet him then walked he upright much and near to what as before was and was he then unaccustomed to the-king having asked to-meet him.	And when Hreidar heard it said, that the king wished to meet him, then he walked very upright and near to what was before him, and he was then unaccustomed to the king having asked to meet him.
Hann var á þá leið búinn að hann var í hökulbrókum og hafði feld grán yfir sér.	He was that then way dressed that he was in ankle-breeches and had cloak grey over himself.	He was dressed in such a way, that he was wearing ankle-breeches and a grey cloak over him.
Og er hann kemur fyrir konung þá fellur hann á kné fyrir konung og kveður hann vel.	And when he came before the-king then fell he on knees before the-king and greeted him well.	And when he came before the king, he then fell on his knees before the king and greeted him well.
Konungur svaraði honum hlæjandi og mælti:	The-king answered him laughing and spoke:	The king laughed and said:
"Ef þú átt við mig erindi þá mæl þú skjótt slíkt er þú vilt.	"If you have with me business then say you swiftly such as you will.	"If you have business with me, then say as swiftly as you will.
Aðrir eiga enn nauðsyn að tala við mig síðan".	Others have but need to talk with me after".	There are others who need to talk with me afterwards".
Hreiðar segir:	Hreidar said:	Hreidar said:
"Mitt erindi þykir mér skyldast.	"My business think to-me obliged.	"I think my business is more urgent.
Eg vildi sjá þig konungur".	I wished to-see you king".	I wished to see you, king".
"Þykir þér nú vel þá",	"Think you now well then",	"Do you think it well now",
segir konungur, "er þú sérð mig?"	said the-king, "that you saw me?"	said the king, "that you saw me?"
"Vel víst",	"Well certainly",	"Well certainly",
segir Hreiðar, "en eigi þykist eg enn til gjörla sjá þig".	said Hreidar, "but not think I that to completely saw you".	said Hreidar, "but I don't think that I have seen you completely".
"Hvernug skulum við nú þá?"	"Which shall we now then?"	"What shall we do now then?"

The Tale of Hreiðarr the Fool (Old Icelandic)

Old Icelandic	Literal	English
segir konungur,	said the-king,	said the king.
"vildir þú að eg stæði upp?"	"would you that I stand up?"	"Would you like me to stand up?"
Hreiðar svarar:	Hreidar answered:	Hreidar answered:
"Það vildi eg",	"That wish i",	"That I would wish",
segir hann.	said he.	he said.
Konungur mælti er hann var upp staðinn:	The-king spoke then he was up standing:	The king spoke, when he stood up:
"Nú munt þú þykjast gjörla sjá mig mega?"	"Now should-you you consider completely seen me may?"	"Now have you seen me completely?"
"Eigi enn til gjörla",	"Not then to completely",	"Not completely",
segir Hreiðar, "og er nú þó nær hófi".	said Hreidar, "and are now though near measure".	said Hreidar, "but it is now closer".
"Viltu þá",	"Wish-you then",	"Do you wish then",
segir konungur, "að eg leggi af mér skikkjuna?"	said the-king, "that I take off my cloak?"	said the king, "that I take off my cloak?"
"Það vildi eg víst",	"That wish I certainly",	"That I certainly wish",
segir Hreiðar.	said Hreidar.	said Hreidar.
Konungur mælti:	The-king spoke:	The king spoke:
"Við skulum þar þó nokkuð innast til áður um það málið.	"We should there though some do to before about that discuss.	"We should then discuss the matter before doing it.
Þér eruð hugkvæmir margir Íslendingar og veit eg eigi nema þú virðir þetta til ginningar.	You are very-smart many Icelander and know I not except you worth this to mocking.	You Icelanders are very smart, and I do not know, if this is mockery.
Nú vil eg það undan skilja".	Now wish I that away-from understand".	Now I wish to be away from that, you understand".
Hreiðar segir:	Hreidar said:	Hreidar said:

The Tale of Hreiðarr the Fool (Old Icelandic)

Old Icelandic	Literal	English
"Engi er til þess fær konungur að ginna þig eða ljúga að þér".	"None that to this capable king of mocking you or lie to you".	"I am not capable of this, king, of mocking you or lying to you".
Konungur leggur nú af sér skikkjuna og mælti:	The-king laid now off his cloak and spoke:	The king now took off his cloak and poke:
"Hyggðu nú að mér svo vandlega sem þig tíðir".	"Think now that me so closely as you wish".	"Think now that you may see me as closely as you wish".
"Svo skal vera",	"So shall be",	"So it shall be",
segir Hreiðar.	said Hreidar.	said Hreidar.
Hann gengur í hring um konunginn og mælti oft hið sama fyrir munni sér:	He walked in a-ring around the-king and spoke frequently to himself before mouth his:	He walked in a ring around the king and spoke frequently to himself and mumbling:
"Allvel, allvel",	"All-well all-well",	"Splendid, splendid",
segir hann.	said he.	he said.
Konungur mælti:	The-king spoke:	The king spoke:
"Hefir þú nú séð mig sem þú vilt?"	"Have you now seen me as you wish?"	"Have you now seen me as you wish?"
"Að vísu",	"That certainly",	"Certainly"
segir hann.	said he.	he said.
Konungur spurði:	The-king asked:	The king asked:
"Hversu líst þér nú á mig þá?"	"How-so appears to-you now of me then?"	"How do I appear to you now then?"
Hreiðar svarar:	Hreidar answered:	Hreidar answered:
"Ekki hefir Þórður bróðir minn ofsögum frá þér sagt það er vel er".	"Not had Thord brother mine off-said from you said that is well be".	"My brother Thord did not exaggerate when he said of your well being".
Konungur mælti:	The-king spoke:	The king spoke:
"Máttu nokkuð að finna um það er þú sérð nú og það er eigi sé í alþýðu viti?"	"May-you something to find about that which you see now and that is not seen by all-the-people knowing?"	"Can you find something that you see now, that has not been seen by other people?"

The Tale of Hreiðarr the Fool (Old Icelandic)

Old Icelandic	Literal	English
"Ekki vil eg að finna",	"Not wish I to find",	"I do not wish to find",
segir hann, "og ekki má eg þegar því að þannug mundi hver sig kjósa sem þú ert þó að sjálfur mætti ráða".	said he, "and not may I from-there accordingly that thus would each themselves choose as you are though that self may advise".	he said, "and I can not find, because thus would everyone choose to be as you are, if they could".
"Mikinn tekur þú af",	"Great take you of",	"You are taking off",
segir konungur.	said the-king.	said the king.
Hreiðar svarar:	Hreidar answered:	Hreidar answered:
"Háttung er öðrum á þá",	"Risk are others for then",	"It is a risk for others then",
segir hann, "að lofgjarnlega sé við mælt ef þú átt þetta eigi að sönnu sem mér líst á þig og eg sagði áðan".	said he, "that praise-will you of speaking if you that this not that true as to-me appears of you and I said earlier".	he said, "for those who praise you, if it is not true, how you appear to me as I said earlier".
Konungur mælti:	The-king spoke:	The king spoke:
"Finn til nokkuð þó að smátt sé".	"Find to something though that small is".	"Find something, though it is small".
"Það helst þá herra",	"Is rather then lord",	"It is then rather",
segir hann, "að auga þitt annað er litlu því ofar en annað".	said he, "that eye the other is a-little before above the other".	he said, "that one eye is a little above the other".
"Það hefir einn maður fyrr fundið",	"That has one man before found",	"Only one man has noticed that before",
segir konungur, "en sá er Haraldur konungur frændi minn.	said the-king, "and that was Harald the-king kinsman mine.	said the king, "and that was King Harald, my kinsman.
Nú skal jafnmæli með okkur",	Now shall equal-speak with you",	Now I shall equally say of you",
segir konungur.	said the-king.	said the king.
"Skaltu nú standa upp og leggja af þér skikkju og vil eg sjá þig".	"Shall-you now stand up and allow off your cloak and will I see you".	"Stand up and take off your cloak, and I will see you".

The Tale of Hreiðarr the Fool (Old Icelandic)

Old Icelandic	Literal	English
Hreiðar fleygir af sér feldinum og hefir saurgar krummur, - maðurinn hentur mjög og ljótur, - en þvegnar heldur latlega.	Hreidar threw off his cloak and had dirty hands, a-man suited much and ugly, but to-wash rather negligently.	Hreidar threw off his cloak, and he had large dirty hands, suited to such an ugly man, and washed negligently.
Konungur hyggur að honum vandlega.	The-king looked at him closely.	The king looked at him closely.
Og þá mælir Hreiðar:	And then spoke Hreidar:	And then Hreidar spoke:
"Herra",	"Lord",	"Lord",
segir hann, "hvað þykist þú nú mega að mér finna?"	said he, "what think you now may that me find?"	he said, "what do you think you may find?"
Konungur segir:	The-king said:	The king said:
"Það ætla eg að eigi fæðist ljótari maður upp en þú ert".	"That suppose I that not born uglier man up than you are".	"That I suppose that there is not a man born uglier than you".
"Slíkt verður mælt",	"Such becomes spoken",	"This is what is said",
segir Hreiðar.	said Hreidar.	said Hreidar.
"Er nokkuð þá",	"But some then",	"But are there some",
segir hann, "að til fríðinda sé um mig að því sem þú leggur ætlun á?"	said he, "that to good-things see about me that therefore which you have suppose of?"	he said, "good things to see about me, that you might suppose?"
Konungur mælti:	The-king spoke:	The king spoke:
"Það sagði Þórður bróðir þinn að þú værir lundhægur maður".	"That said Thord brother yours of you be tempered-even man".	"That your brother Thord said you are an even-tempered man".
"Það er satt og",	"That is true also",	"That is also true",
sagði Hreiðar, "og þykir mér það illt er svo er".	said Hreidar, "and think me that ill is so to-be".	said Hreidar, "and I think that it is bad to be".
"Þú munt reiðast þó",	"Though shall-you anger though",	"Though one day you will become angry",
sagði konungur.	said the-king.	said the king.
"Mæl heill herra",	"Say whole lord",	"Speak well, lord",

The Tale of Hreiðarr the Fool (Old Icelandic)

Old Icelandic	Literal	English
segir Hreiðar, "eða hve langt mun til þess?"	said Hreidar, "but how long could until this?"	said Hreidar, "but how long could it be until this happens?"
"Eigi veit eg það gjörla",	"Not know I that completely",	"That I do not know completely",
segir konungur, "helst á þessum vetri að því er eg get til".	said the-king, "rather of this winter that since that I guess to".	said the king, "rather some time this winter, if my guess is right".
Hreiðar mælti:	Hreidar spoke:	Hreidar spoke:
"Seg heill sögu".	"Tell a-complete story".	"Tell a complete story".
Konungur mælti:	The-king spoke:	The king spoke:
"Ertu nokkuð hagur?"	"Are-you of-any benefit?"	"Are you any good at anything?"
Hreiðar segir:	Hreidar said:	Hreidar said:
"Aldregi hefi eg reynt, má eg því eigi vita".	"Never have I tried, may I therefore not know".	"I have never tried, and therefore I do not know".
"Til þess þætti þó ekki ólíklegt",	"To this seems though not unlikely",	"It does not seem unlikely"
segir konungur.	said the-king.	said the king.
"Seg heill sögu",	"Tell the-whole story",	"Tell the whole story",
kvað Hreiðar.	said Hreidar.	said Hreidar.
"Svo mun vera jafnt þegar er þú segir það.	"So should be equally then as you say it.	"So shall it be, just as you say.
En veturvistar þættist eg þurfa".	And winter-provisions we-have I need".	And I need winter provisions".
Konungur sagði:	The-king said:	The king said:
"Heimil er mín umsjá.	"Home being mine about.	"My home is so about.
En betur þykir mér þér þar vistin felld vera er heldur er fátt manna".	But better think I you then stay shed be where rather are few people".	But I think it better if you stay in the shed, where there are few people".

The Tale of Hreiðarr the Fool (Old Icelandic)

Old Icelandic	Literal	English
Hreiðar svaraði:	Hreidar answered:	Hreidar answered:
"Svo er það og",	"So is it and",	"So it may be",
segir hann.	said he.	he said.
"En eigi mun svo mannfátt vera að eigi komi það þó upp er mælt verður, allra helst það er hlægi þykir í, en eg maður ekki orðvar og jafnan ber mér mart á góma.	"But not would so people-few be that not come that though up in spoken become, all rather that is ridicule thought in, that I people not discreet and equally carry I many about gums.	"But there would not be so few people, that none came up though, and in speaking something that is a joke, people think I am not discreet, and many people carry this about in their mouths.
Nú kann vera að þeir reiði orð mín fyrir aðra menn og spotti mig og drepi það að ferlegu er eg hefi að gamni eða mæli eg.	Now can be that their anger words mine before other people and small me and kill that to monstrous what I have been amuse or speak i.	Now it may be that they angered my words before other people, and mocked me, and kill me for what I have been amused to speak.
Nú sýnist mér hitt viturlegra að vera heldur hjá þeim er um mig hyggur sem Þórður er bróðir minn þótt þar sé heldur fjölmenni en hinnug þótt menn séu fáir og sé þar engi til umbóta".	Now seems I find wisely to be rather by them that about me think as Thord is brother mine thought then be rather followers-many that there though people as few and as there no-one to put-right".	Now it seems to me the wiser thing to be beside those, who about me consider, such as Thord, my brother, though there are more people there than otherwise and there is no one to put things right".
Konungur mælti:	The-king spoke:	The king spoke:
"Ráð þú þá og farið báðir bræður til hirðarinnar ef ykkur líkar það betur".	"Decide you then and go both brothers to court if you like that better".	"You decide then, and you and your brother can both come to court if you would like that better".
Þegar hljóp Hreiðar á brott er hann heyrði þessi orð konungs og segir hverjum manni er á vill hlýða að hans för hefir allgóð orðið á konungs fund, segir og einkum Þórði bróður sínum að konungur hefir leyft honum að fara til hirðvistar.	Straightaway ran Hreidar to away that he heard these words the-king's and told each of-the-people that from well listened that his going had all-good words from the-king visit, said and especially Thord brother his that the-king had given-leave him to travel to court.	Then Hreidar ran away when he heard the king's words, and told every person who listened, how it had gone with all the good words from his visit to the king, and said especially to his brother Thord, that the king had given them leave to travel to court.
Þá mælti Þórður:	Then spoke Thord:	Then Thord spoke:

The Tale of Hreiðarr the Fool (Old Icelandic)

Old Icelandic	Literal	English
"Bú þig þá sæmilega að klæðum eða vopnum því að það eitt samir og skortir okkur ekki til þess og skipast margir menn vel við góðan búning enda er vandara að búa sig í konungs herbergi en annarstaðar og verður síður athlægi ger af hirðmönnum".	"Prepare you then well-enough with clothes and weapons because that it one in-common and shortage ours not to this and changed many people well with good clothing and is important to dress such as the-king's room than any-other-place and become less the made of court-men".	"Prepare yourself well with clothes and weapons, because there is one thing in common, and we have no shortage in this, and many people are changed by good clothing, and it is important to dress well in the king's room more than any other place, and it will avoid ridicule from the court-men".
Hreiðar svarar:	Hreidar answered:	Hreidar answered:
"Eigi getur þú allnær að eg muni skrúðklæðin á mig láta koma".	"Not get you all-near that I should costly-clothing of me allow coming".	"You will not get anywhere near me coming along wearing fancy clothing".
Þórður mælti:	Thord spoke:	Thord spoke:
"Skerum vaðmál þá til".	"Cut homespun-cloth then to".	"Then you will wear cut homespun cloth".
Hreiðar svarar:	Hreidar answered:	Hreidar answered:
"Nær er það",	"Near is that",	"That would be better",
segir hann.	said he.	he said.
Svo er nú gert við ráð Þórðar og lætur Hreiðar eftir leiðast.	So that now did with advice Thord's and had Hreidar afterwards carried-out.	So now it was done with Thord's advice, and then Hreidar had carried it out.
Hefir hann nú vaðmálsklæði og fágar sig og þykir nú þegar allur annar maður, sýnist nú maður ljótur og greitt vasklegur.	Had he now wadding-clothes and cleaned himself and seemed now already all another man, seemed now a-man ugly and ready-to-serve valiant.	Now he had wadding-clothes and cleaned himself, and he already seemed like a different man, he was still ugly, but now valiant looking.
Svo er þó mót á manninum er þeir Þórður eru með hirðinni að Hreiðar verður í fyrstu fyrir miklum ágang af hirðmönnum og breyttu þeir marga vega orðum við hann og fundu að hann var ómállatur.	So was though against about the-people that they Thord were with court-men that Hreidar became the first before much aggression of court-men and varied they many ways words with him and found that he was talkative.	So it was though, in meeting the people, that with Thord and with the court-men, that Hreidar became singled out for much aggression from the court-me, and there were many ways in which they had words with him, and he was talkative.

The Tale of Hreiðarr the Fool (Old Icelandic)

Old Icelandic	Literal	English
Kom við sem mátti og hentu þeir mikið gaman að því að eiga við hann og var hann jafnan hlæjandi við því er þeir mæltu og lagði hvern þeirra fyrir, svo var hann leikmikill, bæði um mælgina og allra helst - -	Came with how it-may and handed they much fun that because that had with he and was he equally laughing with such that they spoke and had each they before, so was he playful, both about talking and all rather	It became how it may, that they had much fun with him, and he was laughing equally as much with them, with what they said, and with each of them he was playful, both in talking and rather in all things.
En fyrir því að hann var rammur að afli og er þeir finna að hann gefst ekki að grandi þá þvarr það allt af þeim hirðmönnum - - nú með hirðinni.	When for then that he was frame that strength and when they found that he gave not to injury then decreased that all of them court-men now with court	Then when they realised how strong his frame was, and when they found that he did not give in to injury, then the mocking of him decreased with all the court-men.

4

Í þetta mund voru þeir báðir konungar yfir landi, Magnús konungur og Haraldur konungur,	In that time were they both kings over the-land, Magnus the-king and Harald the-king,	At that time there were two kings ruling over the land, King Magnus, and King Harald.
en þá höfðu sakar gerst - - hirðmaður Magnúss konungs hafði vegið hirðmann Haralds konungs og var lagður til sáttarfundur að konungar skyldu sjálfir finnast og skipa málinu.	but then had conviction made court-man Magnus's the-king had slain court-man Harald's the-king and was laid to peace-meeting that kings should themselves meet-up and exchange the-matter	But then trouble came when one of Magnus's court-men had slain one of Harald's court-men, and they had a peace meeting, so that the kings themselves could meet up and discuss the matter.
Og er Hreiðar heyrir þetta að Magnús konungur skal fara til móts við Harald konung þá fer hann á fund Magnúss konungs og mælti:	And when Hreidar heard this that Magnus the-king shall travel to meet with Harald the-king then went he to find Magnus the-king and spoke:	And when Hreidar heard this, that King Magnus would travel to meet with King Harald, then he went to find King Magnus and spoke:
"Sá hlutur er",	"So share i",	"So I share",
segir hann, "er eg vildi þig biðja".	said he, "that I wish you to-ask".	he said, "something that I wish to ask you".
"Hver er sá?"	"What is so?"	"What is it?"
sagði konungur.	said the-king	said the king.
Hreiðar mælti:	Hreidar spoke:	Hreidar spoke:

The Tale of Hreiðarr the Fool (Old Icelandic)

Old Icelandic	Literal	English
"Að fara til sáttarfundar.	"To travel to peace-meeting	"To travel to the peace meeting.
Em eg ekki víðförull en mér er mikil forvitni á að sjá tvo konunga senn í einum stað".	Am I not widely-travelled but I am much curious about to see two kings they in one place".	I am not widely travelled, but I am very curious to see two kings in one place".
Konungur svarar:	The-king answered:	The king answered:
"Satt segir þú að þú ert ekki víðförull	"True say you that you are not widely-travelled	"It is true to say that you are not widely travelled.
en þeygi mun eg leyfa þér þessa förina því að ekki er þér fellt að ganga í greipur mönnum Haralds konungs.	but yet-not could I allow you this sacrificing for that not are you falling to go in grasp people Harald's the-king	But I could not allow this, to sacrifice you, if you fall into the grasp of King Harald.
Og beri svo til að þér verði að því ólið eða öðrum og em eg um það hræddur að þá sæki þig heim reiðin er þú langar til en mér þætti best að við bærist".	And bear so to that you became that for unaccompanied or others and am I about that worried that then conviction you home uproar that you long to then me seems best that with bearing".	And so it carries, that if you become separated from the others, I am worried that, then you might be involved in trouble, and then you would become angry, and so it seems best to me, with that in mind".
Hreiðar svarar:	Hreidar answered:	Hreidar answered:
"Nú mæltir þú gott orð.	"Now speak you good words	"Now you speak good words.
Þá skal að vísu fara ef eg veit þess vonir að eg reiðist".	Then shall to certainly travel if I know this custom that I become-angry".	Then I am more certain to travel, if I know that I am accustomed to becoming angry".
Konungur segir:	The-king said:	The king said:
"Muntu fara ef eg leyfi eigi?"	"Shall-you travel if I leave not?"	"Will you travel, if I do not give leave for it?"
Hreiðar svarar:	Hreidar answered:	Hreidar answered:
"Eigi þá síður".	"None then less".	"None the less".
"Ætlar þú að þér muni þvílíkt við mig að eiga sem við Þórð bróður þinn því að þar hefir þú jafnan þitt mál?"	"Suppose you that you would therefore-like with me that have as with Thord brother yours because that there have you always your way?"	"Do you suppose, that you would therefore liken me to that which you have with your brother Thord, because you always have your way?"

The Tale of Hreiðarr the Fool (Old Icelandic)

Old Icelandic	Literal	English
Hreiðar segir:	Hreidar said:	Hreidar said:
"Því öllu betra mun mér við yður að eiga sem þú ert vitrari en hann".	"Because all better would me with you than have as you are wiser than he".	"It would be better with you than with him as you are wiser than he is".
Konungur sér nú að hann mun fara þó að hann banni eða hann fari eigi í hans föruneyti og þykir eigi það best ef hann kemur annarstaðar til föruneytis og þykir þá í reiðingum vera hversu honum eirir ef hann vélir einn um og leyfir honum nú heldur að fara með sér og er Hreiðari fenginn hestur til reiðar.	The-king saw now that he would travel though that he banned either he travelled not in his companionship and thought not that best if he came any-other-place to company and thought then in uproar being how-so he own if he wilful one about and leave him now rather that travel with him and was Hreidar given a-horse to ride	The king saw now that he would travel, even though he had banned him, he would travel outside of his companionship, and he thought it not best if he came into another place's company and there was an uproar, how he would be if he was wilful about something, and had him rather travelling with him, and Hreidar was given a horse to ride.
Og þegar er þeir voru á ferð komnir þá reið hann mjög og ætlaði sér varla hóf um og braut hestinn undir honum.	And as-soon as they were to travel coming then rode he much and intended himself hardly in-moderation about and faltered the-horse under him	And as soon as they were coming to travel, then he rode hard, and hardly in moderation about, and the horse faltered under him.
Og er konungur verður þess var mælti hann:	And when the-king became this aware spoke he:	And when the king became aware of this, he spoke:
"Nú gefur vel til.	"Now give well to	"Now it is well.
Fylgið nú Hreiðari heim og fari hann eigi".	Follow now Hreidar home and travel he not".	Hreidar is to be followed home and he is not to travel".
Hann segir:	He said:	"He said:
"Eigi heftir þetta ferðina mína þótt hesturinn sé þrotinn.	"Not have this travelling mine thought horse's being ended	"Not having this my journey, though the horse has given out".
Kemur mér til lítils fráleikurinn ef eg fæ eigi fylgt yður".	Came me to little game if I give not follow you".	I would not be a good sportsman, if I could not keep up with you".
Fara þeir nú og lögðu margir fram hjá honum hesta sína og þótti gaman að reyna fráleik hans svo gropasamlega sem hann sjálfur tók á.	Travelled they now and had many from beside him horse his and thought fun to test from-game his so grouped-together as he himself took of	Travelled they now and many brought their horses beside his and thought it fun to test his sport. And so grouped together as he took them on.

The Tale of Hreiðarr the Fool (Old Icelandic)

Old Icelandic	Literal	English
En svo gafst að hann þreytti hvern hest er frammi var lagður og lést eigi verður að koma til fundarins ef hann gæti eigi fylgt þeim.	But so gave that he tired each horse that from was had and let not were to come to the-meeting if he got not follow them	But it so happened that he tired each horse, that was laid before him, and he was not to come to the meeting if he could not follow pace with them.
Og fyrir þetta sátu nú margir af sínum hestum.	And ahead that sat now many of his horses	And for this many of their horses now sat.

5

Old Icelandic	Literal	English
Og er þeir koma þar er konungar skulu finnast þá mælti Magnús konungur við Hreiðar:	And when they came there that the-kings shall meet then spoke Magnus the-king with Hreidar:	And when they came to where the kings were to meet, then King Magnus said to Hreidar:
"Ver þú mér nú fylgjusamur og ver á aðra hönd mér og skilst ekki frá mér.	"Be you me now follow-same and be on other hand mine and separate not from me	"Be obedient to me now and me on my other side and do not part with me"
En miðlung segir mér hugur um hversu fer þá er menn Haralds konungs koma og sjá þig".	But poorly say me think about how-so goes then when men Harald's the-king come and see you".	But I think that it will go badly, when King Harald's men come and see you".
Hreiðar kvað svo vera skyldu sem konungur mælti "og þykir mér því betur er eg geng yður nær".	Hreidar spoke so be should as the-king spoke "and think me then better that I go you near".	Hreidar said that it should be as the king said, "and then I think it better that I go nearer to you".
Nú finnast konungar og ganga þeir á tal og ræða mál sín.	Now met the-kings and went they to talk and discuss matters theirs	Now the kings met, and they talked and discussed their matters.
En menn Haralds konungs gátu líta hvar Hreiðar gekk og höfðu heyrt getið hans og þótti þeim um hið vænsta.	When men Harald's the-king got company where Hreidar went and had heard told he and thought they about that good	But King Harold's men could see where Hreidar went, and they had heard his name, and they thought it good.
Og er konungar töluðu þá gengur Hreiðar í flokk Haralds manna og höfðu þeir hann til skógar er skammt var þaðan, skauttoguðu hann mjög og hrundu honum stundum.	And as the-kings talked then went Hreidar in group Harald's men and had they he to woods which short-distance was from-there, pull-cloak, handle-roughly he much and teased him awhile	And when the kings were talking, Hreidar went into the company of Harold's men, and they took him to a forest, which was not far from there, they rough-handled him a lot, and sometimes knocked him down.
En þar lék á ýmsu.	But then played about variously	But they played at him in various ways.

The Tale of Hreiðarr the Fool (Old Icelandic)

Old Icelandic	Literal	English
Stundum fauk hann fyrir sem vindli en stundum var hann fastur fyrir sem veggur og hrutu þeir frá honum.	Sometimes drifted he before as wind then sometimes was he secure before as a-wall and fell they away-from him	Sometimes he drifted before them like the wind, and sometimes he was as secure as a wall, and they fell away from him.
Nú dregst þó svo leikurinn að þeir gera honum nakkvað harðleikið, létu ganga honum öxarsköft og skálpana og námu naddar af sverðskónum í höfði honum og skeindist hann af og svo lét hann sem honum þætti hið mesta gaman að og hló við jafnan.	Now drawn though so the-game that they did him some hardness, had going him axe-handles and scabbards and took studded of sword-studded at head him and scratched he of and so had he as him seemed the most game that and laughed with equally	And as the game drew on, they became hard and were going at him with axe handles and scabbards, and a studded sword scabbard hit him on the head, and scratched him, and he appeared to enjoy the game and laughed equally with them.
Og er svo hafði fram farið um hríð þá tók leikurinn ekki að batna af þeirra hendi.	And was so had from going about awhile then took the-game not to better of them hand	And when this had been going on for a while, the game did not begin to get any better from them.
Þá mælti Hreiðar:	Then spoke Hreidar:	Then Hreidar spoke:
"Nú höfum vér átt góðan leik um stund og er nú ráð að hætta því að nú tekur mér að leiðast.	"Now have we had good sport about awhile and am-i now decide that conclude therefore that now take me to hand	"How we have had good sport for a while, and I have now decided that it shall conclude, therefore take my hand.
Förum nú til konungs yðvars og vil eg sjá hann".	Go now to king yours and will I see him".	Let's go now to your king, and I will see him.
"Það skal verða aldrei",	"That shall be never",	"That shall never be",
sögðu þeir, "svo fjandlegur sem þú ert, að þú skulir sjá konung vorn og skulum vér færa þig til heljar".	said they, "so fiendish as you are, that you should see the-king ours and shall we bring you to death".	they said, "so fiendish as you are, that you should see our king, and we shall bring you to death".
Honum finnst þá fátt um og þykist sjá að það mun fram fara og er nú þar komið að honum rennur í skap og reiðist hann, fer höndum þann mann er mest sótti að honum og verst lék við hann og vegur á loft og færði niður að höfðinu svo að heilinn var úti og er sá dauður.	He found then little about and thought seemed that it would from go and that now there came that he run of mood and angered he, went seized then man the most took with him and worse played with he and proceeded to lift and brought down on head so that brain was out and was so dead	He found that he did not like this at all, and where it seemed it would go, and then it happened, that his mood changed, and he became very angry, he seized the man who had taunted him the worst, and proceeded to lift him up and bring him down on his head, so that his brains came out, and he was dead.

The Tale of Hreiðarr the Fool (Old Icelandic)

Old Icelandic	Literal	English
Nú þykir þeim hann trautt mennskur maður að afli og stukku þeir nú í víginu, fara og segja Haraldi konungi að drepinn var hirðmaður hans.	Now thought they he scarcely human man that strength and leapt they now from the-slaying, went and told Harald the-king that killed was court-man his	Now they thought that he was scarcely human with that strength, and they leapt away from the slaying and told King Harald, that one of his courtmen had been killed.
Konungur svarar:	The-king answered:	The king answered:
"Drepið þann þá er það hefir unnið".	"Kill he then who this has done".	"Kill him then, the one who has done this".
"Eigi er það enn hægra",	"Not is that then easy",	"That is not easy",
segja þeir,	said they,	they said.
"hann er nú í brottu".	"he is now to away".	"He has now gone away".
Það er nú frá Hreiðari að segja að hann hittir Magnús konung.	That is now from Hreidar to say that he found Magnus the-king	It is now said of Hreidar that he met King Magnus.
Konungur mælti:	The-king spoke:	The king spoke:
"Veistu nú hvernug það er að reiðast?"	"Know-you now how that is that anger?"	"Now do you know how your anger is?"
"Já",	"Yes",	"Yes",
segir hann, "nú veit eg".	said he, "now know i".	he said, "now I know".
"Hvernug þótti þér?"	"How thought you?"	"What did you think of it?"
segir konungur,	said the-king,	said the king?
"hitt fann eg að þér var forvitni á".	"it found I that you were curious to".	"I found it that you were curious about it".
Hreiðar svarar:	Hreidar answered:	Hreidar answered:
"Illt þótti mér",	"Badly thought i",	"I thought it bad",
segir hann,	said he,	he said,
"þess var eg fúsastur að drepa þá alla".	"this was I wished to kill then all".	"This was my wish, to then kill them all".
Konungur mælti:	The-king spoke:	The king spoke:

The Tale of Hreiðarr the Fool (Old Icelandic)

Old Icelandic	Literal	English
"Það kom mér jafnt í hug",	"That came to-me equally in thought",	"The same thing came to my thoughts",
segir konungur, "að þú mundir illa reiður verða.	said the-king, "that you would badly angry become	said the king, "that you would become bad when angry.
Nú vil eg senda þig á Upplönd til Eyvindar, lends manns míns, að hann haldi þig fyrir Haraldi konungi	Now will I send you to Uplands to Eyvind, land man mine, that he hold you from Harald the-king	Now I will send you to Uplands to Eyvind, a land man of mine, so that he protects you from King Harald.
því að eg treystist eigi að þín verði gætt ef þú ert með hirðinni, því að vér finnumst, en Haraldur frændi er brögðóttur og er vant við að sjá.	because that I we-trust not that you become taken-care-of if you are with court-men, because that we find, that Harald's kinsmen are tricky and are difficult with to see	I do not trust that you will be taken care of if you are with the court-men, because we find Harald's kinsmen are tricky, and difficult to see.
Kom þá aftur til mín er eg sendi eftir þér".	Come then back to me when I send after you".	Then come back to me, when I send for you".
Nú fer Hreiðar í brott uns hann kemur á Upplönd og tekur Eyvindur við honum eftir orðsending konungs.	Now went Hreidar to away until he came to Uplands and took Eyvind with him after message the-king's	Now Hreidar went away, until he came to Uplands, and Eyvind received him as per the king's message.
Konungar höfðu sáttir orðið á það mál er áður var milli þeirra og var því sætt.	The-kings had agreed words of the matter that before was between them and was therefore settled	The kings had agreed words about the matter, which was between them, and it was therefore settled.
En hér verða þeir eigi ásáttir.	But here became they not place-about	But here they became not in agreement.
Þykir Magnúsi konungi þessir menn hafa sjálfir fyrirgert sér og valdið öllum sökum og þykir hirðmaður fallið hafa óheilagur	Thought Magnus the-king these men had themselves fore-done him and wielded all blame and thought court-man fallen had unholy	Magnus thought that these men had forgiven themselves and wielded all the blame, and thought that the court-man had fallen unholy.
en Haraldur konungur beiðir bóta fyrir hirðmann sinn og skildust nú með öngri sætt.	then Harald the-king asked compensation for court-man his and separated now with no settlement	But King Harald begged compensation for his court-man, and now they parted with no settlement.

The Tale of Hreiðarr the Fool (Old Icelandic)

Old Icelandic	Literal	English
6	**6**	**6**
Eigi liðu langar stundir áður Haraldur konungur spyr hvar Hreiðar er niður kominn, gerir síðan ferð sína og kemur á Upplönd til Eyvindar, hefir með sér sex tigu manna.	Not passed long while before Harald the-king learned where Hreidar then down came, made afterwards travelled he and came to Uplands to Eyvind, had with him six tens men	Not a long while had passed, before King Harald learned where Hreidar had come down to, and went afterwards to travel and come to Uplands to Eyvind, having with him sixty men.
Hann kemur þar um morgun snemma og ætlaði að koma á óvart.	He came there about morning early and intended to come to un-warned	He came there early in the morning and intended to come without warning.
En það var þó eigi því að Eyvindur þóttist vita fyrir að hann mundi koma og var hann á öngri stundu vanbúinn við.	But that was though not therefore that Eyvind thought knowing before that he would come and was he that no time unprepared against	But that was not to be, because Eyvind had thought before that he knew that he would come, and at no time was he unprepared against this.
Hafði hann stefnt liði að sér af launungu og var það í skógum þeim er nálægir voru bænum.	Had he located company that he of secretly and was that in the-woods they were near-lying were dwelling	He had located a company secretly, and they were in the woods, lying near the dwelling.
Skyldi Eyvindur gefa þeim mark ef Haraldur konungur kæmi og þóttist hann liðs þurfa.	Should Eyvind give them sign if Harald the-king came and thought he company needed	And Eyvind was to give them a sign, if King Harald came, and if he thought he needed company.
Það er sagt einhverju sinni áður Haraldur konungur kæmi að Hreiðar beiddist að Eyvindur skyldi fá honum silfur og nokkuð gull.	It was said once this after Harald the-king came that Hreidar asked that Eyvind should get him silver and some gold	It was said that once King Harald had arrived, Hreidar asked Eyvind to get him silver and some gold.
"Ertu hagur?"	"Are-you handy?"	"Are you handy?"
segir hann.	said he	he said.
Hreiðar svarar:	Hreidar answered:	Hreidar answered:
"Það sagði Magnús konungur mér.	"That said Magnus the-king to-me	"King Magnus said that to me.
En eigi má ég annað til vita því að ég hefi aldrei við leitað.	But not may I other to know because that I have never with sought	But I must know nothing else, for I have never sought.

The Tale of Hreiðarr the Fool (Old Icelandic)

Old Icelandic	Literal	English
En því mundi hann það segja að hann mundi vita og því trúi eg er hann sagði".	But because should he that say that he would know and therefore trust I what he said".	But because he said that, he should know, and therefore I trust what he said".
Eyvindur mælti:	Eyvind spoke:	Eyvind spoke:
"Þú ert undarlegur maður",	"You are a-strange man",	"You are a strange man",
segir hann,	said he,	he said.
"nú mun eg fá þér efnin.	"now should I give you materials	"Now should I get you the materials.
Skaltu fá mér silfrið ef ónýtt verður smíðað en njót sjálfur ellegar".	Shall-you get me silver if ruined becomes made then enjoy yourself otherwise".	You shall get silver from me, but if the construction becomes ruined, give it back to me, if not, enjoy yourself".
Hreiðar er byrgður í einu húsi og er hann þar að smíðinni.	Hreidar then closed in a house and was he there to smith	Hreidar was then kept in a house, and he began there his smithery.
Og áður en gert verði það er Hreiðar smíðaði þá kemur Haraldur konungur og er nú sem eg gat áður að Eyvindur er að öngu óbúinn og gerir hann konungi veislu góða.	And before then made was that which Hreidar making then came Harald the-king and was now as I got before that Eyvind was that none unprepared and made he the-king feast good	And before Hreidar finished what he was making, then came King Harald, and it was now as said before, that Eyvind was not unprepared, and he made the king a good feast.
Og nú er þeir sitja í drykkju þá fréttir konungur eftir ef Hreiðar sé þar - "og muntu hafa vináttu af mér í móti ef þú selur oss manninn".	And now were they sitting to drinking then news the-king afterwards of Hreidar seeing there "and shall-you have friendship of me in meeting if you sell us the-man".	And now when they were sitting drinking, then the King heard that Hreidar had been seen there, "and you shall have my friendship meeting if you sell us the man".
Eyvindur svarar:	Eyvind answered:	Eyvind answered:
"Eigi er hann hér nú",	"Not is he here now",	"He is not here now".
segir hann.	said he.	he said.
"Eg veit",	"I know",	"I know",
segir konungur, "að hann er og þarftu eigi dylja".	said the-king, "that he is and need-you not disguise".	said the king, "that he is, and you need not disguise it".
Eyvindur mælti:	Eyvind spoke:	Eyvind spoke:

The Tale of Hreiðarr the Fool (Old Icelandic)

Old Icelandic	Literal	English
"En þótt það sé þá geri eg eigi þann mun ykkar Magnúss konungs að eg selji þann mann í hendur þér er hann vill skýla láta", - gekk út síðan úr stofunni.	"But though that he then do I not then would you Magnus the-king that I sell then that-man in hand you then he will protect be", went out afterwards out-of the-room	"Even though he is, then I would not then betray King Magnus by selling that man to you and handing over the man he wishes to be protected", and with that he went out of the room.
Og er hann kemur út þá brýst Hreiðar á hurðina og kallar að hann vill á brott.	And when he came out then hammering Hreidar to the-door and called that he wished to away	And when he came out, then Hreidar began hammering on the door and calling that he wished to get out.
"Þegi þú",	"Silent you",	"Be quiet",
segir Eyvindur.	said Eyvind.	said Eyvind.
"Haraldur konungur er hér kominn og vill drepa þig".	"Harald the-king is here come and wishes to-kill you".	"King Harald has come here and he wishes to kill you".
Hreiðar brýst út eigi að síður og lést hitta vildu konung.	Hreidar hammering out not the less and let meet wiled the-king	Hreidar hammered on the door no less, and wished to meet the king.
Eyvindur sér þá að hann mun brjóta upp hurðina, gengur til og lýkur upp og mælti:	Eyvind himself then that he would break up the-door, going to and concluded up and spoke:	Eyvind saw then that he was going to break open the door, and went and unlocked it and said:
"Gramir munu taka þig",	"Anger shall take you",	"Anger shall take you",
segir hann, "er þú gengur til banans".	said he, "then you go to death".	he said, "then you go to your death".
Hreiðar gengur inn í stofuna og fyrir konung og kveður hann og mælti:	Hreidar went in to the-room and before the-king and spoke he and said:	Hreidar went into the room and before the king and spoke to him and said:
"Herra tak af mér reiðina því að eg em þér vel felldur fyrir margs sakir að gera það er þú vilt gera láta þó að eigi sé allríflegt í mannraunum eða því er við ber og mun eg þess ólatur er þú vilt mig til hafa sendan.	"Lord take off me anger because that I am to-you well situated for many reasons to do that which you wish done have though that not is all-abundant in human-trials or otherwise is with carrying and should I this not-forget when you wish me to have sent	"Lord, do not be angry with me, because I am pleased to do that which you wish to have done, even though it may not seem rich in human trials or so carried with, and I will not forget it, when you will have me sent for.

The Tale of Hreiðarr the Fool (Old Icelandic)

Old Icelandic	Literal	English
Hér er nú gripur er eg vil gefa þér", - setur á borðið fyrir hann en það var svín gert af silfri og gyllt.	Here is now treasure that I wish to-give you", set on table before him then that was a-pig made of silver and gold	Here is now a treasure, that I wish to give you", he set it on the table before him, and it was a pig made of silver and gold.
Þá mælti konungur er hann leit á svínið:	Then spoke the-king that he looked at the-pig:	Then the king spoke when he looked at the-pig:
"Þú ert hagur svo að trautt hefi eg séð jafnvel smíðað með því móti sem er".	"You are skilled so that scarcely have I seen equally-well smithery with this of such as".	"You are so skilled, that scarcely have I seen such craftsmanship as this".
Nú fer það með manna höndum.	Now passed that among the-men handed	Now it passed among people's hands.
Segir konungur að hann mun taka sættir af honum - "og er gott að senda þig til stórvirkja.	Said the-king that he would take settle of him "and was god that sending you to great-work	The king said that he would he would take settlement with him, "and it would be good to send you on great work.
Þú ert maður sterkur og ófælinn að því er eg hygg".	You are a-man strong and without-fear that therefore am I minded".	You are a strong man and without fear, and therefore I am minded".
Nú kemur svínið aftur fyrir konung.	Now came the-pig before in-front-of the-king	Now came the pig back to the king.
Tekur hann þá upp og hyggur að smíðinni enn vandlegar og sér þá að spenar eru á og það var gyltur, fleygir þegar í brott og sér að til háðs var gert og mælti:	Took he then up and considered that the-work then carefully and saw then that suckling was then and that was young-sow, threw then to away and he that to mockery was done and spoke:	He then picked it up and looked at the work then carefully, and then he saw that the pig was a suckling and a young-sow, then he threw it away, because he believed that it insulted him, and he spoke:
"Hafi þig allan tröll.	"Have you all monstrous	"Have you all, the devil.
Standi menn upp og drepi hann".	Stand men up and kill him".	Stand up men and kill him".
En Hreiðar tekur svínið og gengur út og fer þegar á brott þaðan og kom á fund Magnúss konungs og segir honum hvað í hefir gerst.	Then Hreidar took the-pig and went away and travelled straightaway to away from-there and came to meet Magnus the-king and told him what so had done	Then Hreidar took the pig, went away and travelled straightaway from there to meet King Magnus and told him how it had gone.

The Tale of Hreiðarr the Fool (Old Icelandic)

Old Icelandic	Literal	English
En í öðru lagi standa menn upp og út eftir honum og ætla drepa hann	Then with others lead standing men up and out after him and intended kill him	Then the others stood up and went out after him intending to kill him.
og er þeir koma út þá er Eyvindur þar fyrir og hefir fjölmenni mikið svo að ekki máttu þeir eftir Hreiðari halda og skilja þeir Eyvindur og Haraldur konungur við svo búið og líkar konungi illa.	and when they came out then was Eyvind there before and had followers many so that not may they after Hreidar held and parted they Eyvind and Harald the-king with so settled and liked the-king badly	And when they came outside, then Eyvind was there with many followers, so they could not go after Hreidar. Then Eyvind and King Harald parted, and the king was far from pleased.
Og er þeir hittast Magnús konungur og Hreiðar fréttir konungur eftir hvernug farið hefir.	And when they met Magnus the-king and Hreidar news the-king after how fared had	And when they met, King Magnus and Hreidar, the king asked for news of how it had gone.
En Hreiðar segir frá hið sanna og sýnir konungi svínið.	Then Hreidar told from the truth and showed the-king the-pig	Then Hreidar told the truth about what happened and showed the king the pig.
Magnús konungur mælti þá er hann hugði að svíninu:	Magnus the-king spoke then that he thought that the-pig:	King Magnus then spoke and said that he thought that the pig was:
"Geysihaglega er þetta smíðað	"Exceedingly-skilful was that crafted	"Exceedingly skilfully crafted.
en hefnt hefir Haraldur konungur frændi vor mjög minni háðungar en í þessu er og eigi ertu alláræðislítill og þó með öllu hugkvæmur".	but revenge had Harald the-king kinsman ours much less insult than in this has and not are-you very-timid and though with all ingenuity".	But King Harald, our kinsman, had revenge for much less of an insult than this, and you are not at all timid and though you are full of ingenuity".

7

Hreiðar var nú þar nakkvara stund með Magnúsi konungi.	Hreidar was now there some time with Magnus the-king	Hreidar was now there some time with Magnus the-king.
Og eitthvert sinn kemur hann að máli við konung og mælti:	And one occasion came he to speak with the-king and spoke:	And on one occasion he came to speak with the king and said:
"Það vildi eg konungur að þú veittir mér það er eg mun biðja þig".	"It wish I king that you grant me that which I may ask you".	"It is my wish, king, that you grant me that which I ask you".
"Hvað er það?"	"What is that?"	"What is that?"

The Tale of Hreiðarr the Fool (Old Icelandic)

Old Icelandic	Literal	English
spyr konungur.	asked the-king	asked the-king.
"Það herra",	"That lord",	"That, lord",
segir Hreiðar, "að þér hlýdduð kvæði er eg hefi ort um yður".	said Hreidar, "that you listen-to poem that I have worded about you".	said Hreidar, "that you listen-to poem, that I have worded about you".
"Hví skal eigi það?"	"Why should not that?"	"Why should not that?"
segir konungur.	said the-king	said the-king.
Nú kveður Hreiðar kvæðið og er það allundarlegt, fyrst kynlegast en því betra er síðar er.	Now recited Hreidar the-poem and was it all-wonderful, first strangely then since better then afterwards was	Now Hreidar recited the poem, and it was all wonderful, strange at first, but then it got better after that.
Og er lokið er kvæði mælti konungur:	And when ended was the-poem spoke the-king:	And when the poem had ended, the king spoke:
"Þetta kvæði sýnist mér undarlegt og þó gott að nestlokum.	"That poem seems to-me wonderful and though good as the-end	"That poem seems to be to be wonderful, particularly good at the end.
En kvæðið mun vera með þeim hætti sem ævi þín.	Then poem should be with the way as life yours	Then the poem should be the same way as your life.
Hún hefir fyrst verið með kynlegu móti og einrænlegu en hún mun þó vera því betur er meir líður á.	It has first been with strange meeting and eccentric but it shall though become therefore better the more passes so	First it has been strange and eccentric, but it shall become better the more passes.
Hér eftir skal eg og velja kvæðislaunin.	Here after shall I and will poem-reward	Here after I shall give you a poem's reward.
Hér er hólmur einn fyrir Noregi sá er eg vil þér gefa.	Here is small-island one along Norway so that I will you give	Here is a small island along Norway, so I will give it to you.
Hann er með góðum grösum og er það gott land þó að eigi sé mikið".	It is with good grass and is that good land though is not so large".	It is good with grass, and good land, though it is not so large".
Hreiðar mælti:	Hreidar spoke:	Hreidar spoke:
"Þar skal eg samtengja með Noreg og Ísland".	"There shall I unite with Norway and Iceland".	"There shall I unite with Norway and Iceland".
Konungur mælti:	The-king spoke:	The king spoke:

The Tale of Hreiðarr the Fool (Old Icelandic)

Old Icelandic	Literal	English
"Eigi veit eg hversu það fer.	"One-thing know I how-so that goes	"I know one thing about how it goes.
Hitt veit eg að margir menn munu búnir að kaupa að þér hólminn og gefa þér fé fyrir	This know I that many people shall offer to buy of you the-island and give you fee for	This I know, that many people shall offer to buy the island from you and give you wealth for.
en ráðlegra ætla eg vera að eg leysi til mín að eigi verði að bitbeini þér eða þeim er kaupa vilja.	but advisable suppose I be that I redeem to me that not becomes a bite-bone to-you or they who buy wish-to	But. I advise you to sell the island to me, so that it does not become a bone of contention to you, or those who wish to buy it.
Er nú og ekki vel felld vist þín vilgis lengi hér í Noregi því að eg þykist sjá hvern Haraldur konungur vill þinn hlut ef hann á að ráða sem hann mun ráða ef þú ert lengi í Noregi".	Then now also I well end hospitality yours very long here in Norway because that I think so who Harald the-king will your matter if he has the decision as he shall decide if you are long in Norway".	Then I will also end your very long stay here in Norway, because I think that King Harald will do to you, if he gets the chance, and he shall do what he wants if you stay here much longer".
Nú gaf Magnús konungur honum silfur fyrir hólminn og vill nú eigi þar hætta honum og fór Hreiðar út til Íslands og bjó norður í Svarfaðardal þar sem síðan heitir á Hreiðarsstöðum og gerist mikill maður fyrir sér.	Now gave Magnus the-king him silver for the-island and wished now not there endanger him and travelled Hreidar out to Iceland and settled north in Svarfardal there which afterwards is-named by Hreidar's-Place and became a-great man before himself	Now King Magnus gave him silver for the island and wished that he now not endanger himself, and Hreidar travelled to Iceland and settled north in Svarfardal, which was afterwards named Hreidar's Place, and he became a great man before himself.
Og fer hans ráð mjög eftir getu Magnúss konungs að þess betur er er meir líður fram hans ævi og hefir hann gert sér að mestum hluta þau kynjalæti er hann sló á sig hinn fyrra hlut ævinnar.	And went his advised much after could Magnus the-king that this better was that more passed from his life and had he done himself the most share then eccentricities that he struck to himself the last-years share of-life	And his life went much as King Magnus had advised, that his life would get better the more it passed, for he had made up for the greater share of eccentricities that he inflicted on himself in the first part of his life.
Bjó hann til elli í Svarfaðardal og eru margir menn frá honum komnir.	Lived he to old-age in Svarfardal and are many people from him coming	He lived to old age in Svarfardale and many people are descended from him.
Og lýkur hér þessi ræðu.	And concluded here this speech	And here this speech is concluded.

Word List (Old Icelandic to English)

Word List (Old Icelandic to English)

Old Icelandic	English

A, a

að	a, as, at, been, in, is, of, on, than, that, the, to, with
aðra	other
aðrir	others
af	of, of, off
afbragð	stood-out
afglapa	fool
afl	strength
afli	strength
aflið	strength
afskipti	dealings
aftur	back, before
aldregi	never
aldrei	never, never
aldri	age
alla	all
allan	all
alláræðislítill	very-timid
allgóð	all-good
allir	all
allnær	all-near
allra	all, all
allríflegt	all-abundant
alls	all
allstarsýnn	fixed-upon
allt	all, altogether
allundarlegt	all-wonderful
allur	all
allvel	all-well
allvel,	all-well
alþýðu	all-the-people, the-people
annað	other, other
annar	another
annarra	other
annarstaðar	any-other-place
annast	take-care-of
athlægi	the
auga	eye

Á, á

á	about, at, by, for, from, has, in, of, on, so, that, then, to
áðan	earlier
áður	after, before, returned
ágang	aggression
áheyrsli	to-hear
álpun	rough
ásáttir	place-about
átt	had, have, that
átti	had

Æ, æ

ætla	intended, suppose
ætlaði	intended
ætlar	intended, suppose
ætlun	suppose
ævi	life
ævinnar	of-life

B, b

báðir	both
bæði	both
bænum	dwelling, residence
bærist	bearing
banans	death
banni	banned
barður	beat
batna	better
beiddist	asked
beiðir	asked
beiðst	asked, best
ber	bear, carry, carrying
beri	bear
best	best
betra	better
betur	better

Word List (Old Icelandic to English)

Old Icelandic	English
biðja	ask, to-ask
bitbeini	bite-bone
bjó	lived, prepared, settled
Björgyn	Bergen
blásið	trumpet-blast
blíðlega	joyfully
borðið	table
borið	bear
bóta	compensation
bræðrum	brothers
bræður	brother, brothers
brátt	soon
breyttu	varied
brjóta	break
bróðir	brother
bróður	a-brother, brother
brögðóttur	tricky
brott	away
brottu	away, steep
brýst	hammering
bú	prepare
búa	dress
búið	settled
búinn	dressed, prepared
búning	clothing
búnir	offer, prepared
byrgður	closed

D, d

Old Icelandic	English
dæmd	to-deem
dála	bad
dauður	dead
dofna	numb
draga	draw
dregst	drawn
drepa	kill, to-kill
drepi	kill
drepið	kill
drepinn	killed
drykkju	drinking
dylja	disguise

E, e

Old Icelandic	English
eða	and, but, either, or
ef	if, of
efnin	materials
eftir	after, afterwards
eg	i, is
eiga	had, have, own
eigi	none, not, nothing, one-thing
einhverju	once
einkum	especially
einn	alone, one
einrænlegu	eccentric
eins	one's
einu	a
einum	alone, one
eirir	own
eitt	once, one
eitthvert	one
ekki	i, is-not, not
ekki,	not
ellegar	otherwise
elli	old-age
em	am
en	and, but, than, that, the, then, when
enda	and
engi	no, none, no-one
enn	but, that, then
er	am, am-i, are, as, be, being, but, has, i, in, is, that, the, then, to, to-be, was, were, what, when, where, which, who, whom, would
era	are
erindi	business
erindið	errand
ert	are
ertu	are-you
eru	are, they-are, was, were
eruð	are
Eyjafirði	Eyjafjord

Word List (Old Icelandic to English)

Old Icelandic	English
Eyvindar	Eyvind
Eyvindur	Eyvind

F, f

Old Icelandic	English
fá	get, give
fæ	give
fæðist	born
fær	capable
færa	bring
færð	can
færði	brought
færður	brought
færi	bring
fágar	cleaned
fagna	welcomed
fáir	few
fallið	fallen
fallin	fallen
fann	found
fara	go, going, to-be, to-go, travel, travelled, went, went
farar	journey
fari	travel, travelled
farið	fared, go, going
fastur	secure
fátt	few, little
fauk	drifted
fé	fee, money
feld	cloak
feldinum	cloak
felld	end, shed
felldur	situated
fellt	falling
fellur	fell
fenginn	given
fer	go, goes, passed, travelled, went
ferð	travel, travelled
ferðina	travelling
ferlegu	monstrous
finn	find
finna	find, found
finnast	meet, meet-up, met
finnst	found
finnumst	find
firna	criticised
fjandlegur	fiendish
fjárins	of-wealth
fjárskakka	uneven-share
fjölmenni	followers, followers-many
fjölmennið	many-people
fjölmennt	crowded
flesta	most
fleygir	threw
flokk	group
fluttir	brought
flytur	transport
föðurarf	inheritance
fór	travelled, went
för	going, travelled, travelling
förin	for-travelling, travelling
förina	sacrificing
forræði	self-control
förum	go, going, trading-voyages, travelling
föruneyti	companionship
föruneytis	company
forvitni	curious
fót	foot
frá	away-from, from
frændi	kinsman, kinsmen
fráleik	from-game
fráleikurinn	game, swiftness
fram	from
frammi	from
frávastur	swift
fréttir	news
fríðinda	good-things
fund	find, meet, visit
fundar	to-meet
fundarins	the-meeting
fundið	found
fundu	found
fúsastur	wished
fylgið	follow
fylgjusamur	follow-same

Word List (Old Icelandic to English)

Old Icelandic	English
fylgt	follow
fyrir	ahead, along, before, for, from, in-front-of
fyrirgert	fore-done
fyrr	before
fyrra	last-years
fyrst	first
fyrstu	first

G, g

Old Icelandic	English
gæfu	be-gifted
gæti	got
gætt	taken-care-of
gaf	gave
gafst	gave
gaman	fun, game
gamni	amuse
ganga	go, going, went
gat	got
gátu	got
gefa	gave, give, to-give
gefst	gave
gefur	give
gekk	went
geng	go
gengur	go, going, walked, went
ger	made
gera	did, do, done
geri	do
gerir	did, made
gerist	became
gerst	done, made
gert	did, done, made
get	guess, mention
getið	told
getu	could
getur	get
geysihaglega	exceedingly-skilful
ginna	mocking
ginningar	mocking
gjörla	completely
Glúmur	Glum
góða	good
góðan	good
góðum	good
góma	gums
gott	god, good
gramir	anger
grán	grey
grandi	injury
greipur	grasp
greitt	ready-to-serve
gripur	treasure
gropasamlega	grouped-together
grösum	grass
gull	gold
gyllt	gold
gyltur	young-sow

H, h

Old Icelandic	English
háðs	mockery
háðungar	insult
hæð	height
hægra	easy
hætta	conclude, endanger
hætti	way
haf	sea
hafa	had, have
hafði	had
hafi	have
hafir	have
hagur	benefit, handy, skilled
halda	held, rather
haldi	hold
haldist	rather
hálft	half
hálfu	half
handkrækjumst	hands-hook-us
hann	he, him, it, 0
hans	he, him, his
Harald	Harald
Haraldi	Harald
Haralds	Harald's
Haraldur	Harald, Harald's
harðleikið	hardness
hart	hard
háttung	risk

Word List (Old Icelandic to English)

Old Icelandic	English	Old Icelandic	English
hefði	having	hittir	found
hefi	have	hjá	beside, by
hefir	had, has, have	hlægi	ridicule
hefnt	revenge	hlæjandi	laughing
heftir	have	hlær	laughed
heilinn	brain	hleypur	ran
heill	a-complete, the-whole, whole	hljóp	ran
heim	home	hljóta	luck
heima	at-home	hló	laughed
heimil	home	hlotið	bound-to
heitir	is-named	hlut	matter, share
heldur	behold, rather	hluta	share
heljar	death	hlutar	share
helst	rather	hlutur	share
hendi	hand	hlýða	listened
hendur	hand	hlýdduð	listen-to
hentu	handed	hóf	in-moderation
hentur	suited	höfði	head
hér	here	höfðinu	head
herbergi	room	höfðu	had
herra	lord	hófi	measure
hest	horse	höfum	have
hesta	horse	hógvær	humble
hestinn	the-horse	hökulbrókum	ankle-breeches
hestum	horses	hólminn	the-island
hestur	a-horse	hólmur	small-island
hesturinn	horse's	hönd	hand
hét	promised, was-named	höndin	hand
heyra	heard	höndum	handed, seized
heyrði	heard	honum	he, him, it
heyrir	heard	horn	corners
heyrt	heard	hornblástur	trumpet-blast
hið	that, the, to	hræddur	worried
hinn	the	Hreiðar	Hreidar
hinnug	there	Hreiðari	Hreidar
hirðarinnar	court	Hreiðars	Hreidar
hirðinni	court, court-men	Hreiðarssonar	Son-of-Hreidar
hirðmaður	court-man	Hreiðarsstöðum	Hreidar's-Place
hirðmann	court-man	hríð	awhile
hirðmönnum	court-men	hring	a-ring
hirðvistar	court, court-visit	hrundu	teased
hitt	find, it, this	hrutu	fell
hitta	meet	hug	thought
hittast	met	hugði	thought
hitti	met	hugkvæmir	very-smart

Word List (Old Icelandic to English)

Old Icelandic	English
hugkvæmur	ingenuity
hugur	think
hún	it
hurðina	the-door
húsi	house
hvað	how, what
hvar	where
hve	how
hver	each, every, what
hvergi	nowhere
hverju	what
hverjum	each, everyone
hvern	each, who
hvernug	how, which
hversu	how-so
hví	why
hvíldar	rest
hvort	how, whether
hygg	minded
hyggðu	think
hyggur	considered, looked, think

I, i

illa	badly
illt	bad, badly, ill
inn	in
innast	do

Í, í

í	as, at, by, from, in, of, so, the, to, with
Ísland	Iceland
Íslands	Iceland
íslendingar	icelander

J, j

já	yes
jafnan	always, equally
jafnmæli	equal-speak
jafnt	equally
jafnvel	equally-well

K, k

kæja	disturbed
kæmi	came
kæmir	come
kæmist	come
kallaður	called
kallar	called
kann	can, know
kaupa	buy
kemur	came
kenna	knew
kjósa	choose
klæðum	clothes
kné	knees
kom	came, come
koma	came, come, coming, to-come
komi	come
komið	came, come
kominn	came, come, coming
komnir	coming
komu	came
konung	the-king
konunga	kings
konungar	kings, the-kings
konungi	the-king
konunginn	the-king
konungs	king, the-king, the-king's
konungur	king, the-king
krummur	hands
kvað	said, spoke
kvæði	poem, the-poem
kvæðið	poem, the-poem
kvæðislaunin	poem-reward
kveðju	greeting
kveður	greeted, recited, spoke
kykvendum	some-beast
kynjalæti	eccentricities
kynleg	strange

Word List (Old Icelandic to English)

Old Icelandic	English
kynlegast	strangely
kynlegu	strange

L, l

Old Icelandic	English
læti	noise
lætur	had, leaves
lagði	had
lagður	had, laid
lagi	lead
land	land
landi	the-land
langar	long
langt	long
lát	have
láta	allow, be, be-allowed, have, left
latlega	negligently
lattan	dissuade
látum	have
launungu	secretly
laust	let-go
leggi	take
leggja	allow, let
leggur	have, laid
leið	way
leiðast	carried-out, hand
leik	sport
leikmikill	playful
leikurinn	the-game
leit	looked
leitað	sought
lék	played
lends	land
lengi	long
lést	let
lét	had
létu	had
leyfa	allow
leyfi	leave
leyfir	leave
leyft	given-leave
leysi	redeem
liði	company
liðs	company
liðu	passed
líður	passed, passes
líkar	like, liked
líkast	like
líklegt	favourable
líkur	like
líst	appears
líta	company
lítið	little
lítill	a-little, small
lítils	little
litlu	a-little
litu	noticed
ljótari	uglier
ljótur	ugly
ljúga	lie
lofgjarnlega	praise-will
loft	lift
lögðu	had
lokið	ended
lokka	lure
lundhægur	even-spirit, tempered-even
lýkur	concluded

M, m

Old Icelandic	English
má	may
maður	a-man, man, people
maðurinn	a-man
mæl	say
mæla	discuss
mælgina	talking
mæli	speak
mælir	spoke
mælt	speaking, spoken
mælti	said, spoke
mæltir	speak
mæltu	spoke
mætti	may
Magnús	Magnus
Magnúsi	Magnus
Magnúss	Magnus, Magnus's
mál	matter, matters, way
máli	speak

Word List (Old Icelandic to English)

Old Icelandic	English
málið	discuss
málinu	the-matter
málugur	talkative
mann	man, that-man
manna	a-man, men, people, the-men
mannfátt	people-few
manni	of-the-people
manninn	the-man
manninum	the-people
mannraunum	human-trials
manns	man
marga	many
margir	many
margs	many
mark	sign
mart	many
mast	most
mátti	it-may
máttu	may, may-you
með	among, as, with
mega	may
meiddur	hurt
meir	further, more
meira	more
menn	men, people
mennskur	human
mér	i, me, mine, my, to-me
mest	most
mesta	most
mestum	most
miðlung	poorly
mig	i, me, much
mikið	large, many, much
mikil	much
mikill	a-great, great, tall
mikinn	great
miklum	much
milli	between
mín	me, mine
mína	mine
mínar	mine
minn	mine
minna	less
minni	less
míns	mine
mitt	me, mine, my
mjög	much
mönnum	men, people
mörgu	many-ways
mörgum	many
morgun	morning
morguninn	morning
mót	against
móti	meeting, of
mótið	meeting, meetings
mótinu	meeting
móts	meet, meetings
mun	could, may, must, shall, should, would
muna	should
mund	time
mundi	should, would
mundir	would
muni	should, would
munni	mouth
munt	shall-you, should-you
muntu	shall-you
munu	shall

N, n

Old Icelandic	English
naddar	studded
nær	near
nakkvað	some
nakkvara	some
nakkvarri	some
nálægir	near-lying
námu	took
nauðsyn	need
nema	except
nemur	took
nestlokum	the-end
niður	down
njót	enjoy
nokkuð	of-any, some, something
nokkur	somewhat
norður	north
Noreg	Norway

Word List (Old Icelandic to English)

Old Icelandic	English
Noregi	Norway
nú	now
nýkominn	newly-come
nýt	used
nytjar	use

O, o

ofar	above
ofsögum	off-said
oft	frequently
og	also, and
okkað	ours
okkarn	ours
okkur	ours, us, you
orð	words
orðið	words
orðsending	message
orðum	words
orðvar	discreet
ort	worded
oss	us

Ó, ó

óbúinn	unprepared
ófælinn	without-fear
ógreið	un-passable
óheilagur	unholy
óknáleik	prowess
ólatur	not-forget
ólið	unaccompanied
ólíkast	unlike
ólíklegt	unlikely
ómállatur	chatty, talkative
ónýtt	ruined
ósannlegt	untrue
ósýknlegur	un-innocent-looking
óvanur	un-accustomed
óvart	un-warned
óvísu	unknown

Ö, ö

öðru	others
öðrum	other, others
öllu	all
öllum	all
öngar	no
öngri	no
öngu	none
öxarsköft	axe-handles

P, p

peninga	money

R, r

ráð	advice, advised, decide
ráða	advice, advise, decide, decision
ráðlegra	advisable
ræða	discuss
ræðu	speech
rammur	frame
réði	decide
reið	rode
reiðar	ride
reiðast	anger
reiðfara	voyage
reiði	anger
reiðin	uproar
reiðina	anger
reiðingum	uproar
reiðist	angered, become-angry
reiður	angry
reikuð	roughly-handled
rennur	run
reyna	test
reynt	tried
rjáður	worried

Word List (Old Icelandic to English)

Old Icelandic	English

S, s

Old Icelandic	English
sá	saw, so, such, that
sæi	see
sæki	conviction
sæmilega	well-enough
sætt	settled, settlement
sættir	settle
sagði	said
sagt	said, told
sakar	conviction
sakir	reasons
sama	himself
saman	together
samdægris	same-day
samir	in-common
samtengja	unite
sanna	truth
sannast	true
satt	true
sáttarfundar	peace-meeting
sáttarfundur	peace-meeting
sáttir	agreed
sátu	sat
saurgar	dirty
sé	as, be, being, he, is, see, seeing, seen, so, you
séð	seen
sefur	sleeps
seg	tell
segir	said, say, told, 0
segja	said, say, told
seint	slowly
selji	sell
selur	sell
sem	as, how, like, such, which
senda	send, sending
sendan	sent
sendi	send, sent
senn	they, together
sér	he, him, himself, his, saw, so
sérð	saw, see
setur	set
séu	as
sex	six
síðan	after, afterwards, then
síðar	afterwards
síður	less
sig	him, himself, such, themselves
sigla	sailed
silfri	silver
silfrið	silver
silfur	silver
sín	theirs
sína	he, his
sinn	his, occasion
sinni	his, this
sínum	his
sitja	sit, sitting
sitt	his
sjá	saw, see, seemed, seen, so, to-see
sjálfan	myself
sjálfbjargi	self-supported
sjálfir	themselves
sjálfur	himself, self, yourself
skal	shall, should
skálpana	scabbards
skaltu	shall-you
skammt	short-distance
skap	mood
skapi	character
skauttogaður	roughly
skauttoguðu	pull-cloak, handle-roughly
skeindist	scratched
skerum	cut
skikkju	cloak
skikkjuna	cloak
skildi	parted
skildir	parted
skildust	separated
skilja	parted, understand
skilst	separate
skip	ship
skipa	exchange
skipast	changed

Word List (Old Icelandic to English)

Old Icelandic	English
skipdráttar	ship-launching
skjótt	swiftly
skógar	woods
skógum	the-woods
skömmu	recently
skortir	shortage
skrúðklæðin	costly-clothing
skulir	should
skulu	shall
skulum	shall, should
skýla	protect
skyldast	obliged
skyldi	should
skyldu	should
skýtur	throws
slíkt	such
sló	struck
smátt	small
smíðað	crafted, made, smithery
smíðaði	making
smíðinni	smith, the-work
snemma	early
sögðu	said
sögu	story
sökum	blame, sake
sönnu	true
sótti	took
spenar	suckling
spotti	small
spurði	asked
spyr	asked, learned
stað	place
staðinn	standing
stæði	stand
standa	stand, standing
standi	stand
stefnt	located
stendur	stood
sterkur	strong
stofuna	the-room
stofunni	the-room
stórvirkja	great-work
stukku	leapt
stund	awhile, time
stundir	while
stundu	time
stundum	awhile, sometimes
svaraði	answered
svarar	answered
Svarfaðardal	Svarfardal
sverðskónum	sword-studded
svín	a-pig
svínið	the-pig
svíninu	the-pig
svo	seen, so
sýnir	showed
sýnist	seemed, seems

T, t

Old Icelandic	English
tak	take
taka	take
tákna	betoken
táknar	taken
tal	talk
tala	talk
talað	told
tek	took
tekur	take, took
tíðinda	news
tíðindi	news
tíðir	wish
tigu	tens
til	to, until
tilgerðir	to-do
tjáir	express
tók	took
töluðu	talked
torsótt	difficulty
trautt	scarcely
treystist	we-trust
tröll	monstrous
trúi	trust
tvo	two
tvö	two

Word List (Old Icelandic to English)

Old Icelandic	English
Þ, þ	
þá	then
það	is, it, that, the, this
þaðan	from-there
þætti	seemed, seems
þættist	we-have
þangað	from-here, there
þann	he, then
þannug	thus
þar	then, there, they
þarftu	need-you
þars	there
þau	then
þaut	shrill
þegar	already, as-soon, as-soon-as, from-there, soon, straightaway, then, there, when
þegi	silent
þeim	the, them, they
þeir	their, they
þeirra	them, they
þenna	that
þér	to-you, you, your
þess	this
þessa	this
þessarar	this-kind-of
þessi	these, this
þessir	these
þessu	this
þessum	this
þetta	that, this
þeygi	yet-not
þig	you
þín	you, yours
þína	your, yours
þingið	assembly
þingsins	their-assembly
þinn	your, yours
þitt	the, your, yours
þó	though
Þórð	Thord
Þórðar	Thord's
Þórði	Thord
Þórður	Thord
Þorgrímsson	Son-of-Thorgrim
þótt	though, thought
þótti	thought
þóttist	thought
þraut	faltered
þreytti	tired
þrotinn	ended
þú	though, you
þurfa	need, needed
þvarr	decreased
þvegnar	to-wash
því	accordingly, because, before, for, otherwise, since, such, then, therefore, this
þvílíkt	therefore-like
þykir	felt, seemed, think, thought
þykist	seems, think, thought
þykja	to-think
þykjast	consider
U, u	
um	about, around
umbóta	put-right
umsjá	about, guidance
undan	away, away-from
undarlega	strange
undarlegt	wonderful
undarlegur	a-strange
undir	under
unga	young
unnið	done
uns	until
upp	up
upplönd	uplands
uppstert	upright
utan	out

Word List (Old Icelandic to English)

Old Icelandic	English
Ú, ú	
úr	out-of
út	away, out
úti	out
V, v	
vaðmál	homespun-cloth
vaðmálsklæði	wadding-clothes
vænleikur	handsome
vænn	handsome
vænsta	good
væri	was, were, will-be
væria	be
værir	be
væru	were
vaki	wake
vaknaðir	woken
valdið	wielded
vanbúinn	unprepared
vandamál	disputes
vandara	important
vandlega	closely
vandlegar	carefully
vant	difficult
var	aware, was, were
varla	hardly, scarcely
vasklegur	valiant
vega	ways
veggur	a-wall
vegið	slain
vegur	proceeded
veislu	feast
veistu	know-you
veit	knew, know, knows
veitt	given
veittir	grant
vel	well
vélir	wilful
velja	will
ver	be
vér	we
vera	be, become, being
verð	worth
verða	be, became, become, was
verði	became, become, becomes, was
verður	became, become, becomes, were
verið	been
verr	worse
verri	worse
verst	worse
vetri	winter
veturvistar	winter-provisions
vexti	grown
við	against, as, from, of, to, we, with
víðförull	widely-travelled
víginu	the-slaying
vil	will, wish
vildi	willed, wish, wished
vildir	would
vildu	wiled
vilgis	very
vilja	wish-to
vill	well, will, wished, wishes, would
vilt	will, wish
viltu	will-you, wish-you
vináttu	friendship
vindli	wind
vinveitt	friendly
virðir	worth
viskumaður	wise-man
vist	hospitality
víst	certainly
vistin	stay
vísu	certainly
vit	know
vita	know, knowing
viti	knowing
vitrari	wiser
vits	wits
viturlegra	wisely
vó	killed
vonir	custom
vopnum	weapons

Word List (Old Icelandic to English)

Old Icelandic	English
vor	ours
vorn	ours
voru	were

Y, y

yðarn	you
yður	you, your
yðvars	yours
yfir	about, over
ykkar	you
ykkur	you

Ý, ý

ýmsu	variously

Word List (English to Old Icelandic)

Word List (English to Old Icelandic)

English	Old Icelandic	English	Old Icelandic
		a-horse	hestur
		ankle-breeches	hökulbrókum
		awhile	hríð, hring, hrutu
		a-ring	hring
		always	jafnan
		allow	láta, láta, láta
		appears	líst
		a-little	lítill, lítils
		a-man	maður, maður, maðurinn

A, a

about	á, á, á, á	among	með
at	á, á, á	a-great	mikill
a	að, að	against	mót, móti
as	að, að, að, að, að, áðan, áður, áður	above	ofar
		also	og
after	áður, áður, ætla	axe-handles	öxarsköft
aggression	ágang	advice	ráð, ráð
age	aldri	advised	ráð
all	alla, allan, allgóð, allir, allnær, allra, allra, allríflegt, alls, allstarsýnn	advise	ráða
		advisable	ráðlegra
		angered	reiðist
		angry	reiður
all-good	allgóð	all-the-people	alþýðu
all-near	allnær	agreed	sáttir
all-abundant	allríflegt	answered	svaraði, svarar
altogether	allt	a-pig	svín
all-wonderful	allundarlegt	already	þegar
all-well	allvel, allvel	as-soon	þegar
all-the-people	alþýðu	as-soon-as	þegar
another	annar	assembly	þingið
any-other-place	annarstaðar	accordingly	því
asked	beiddist, beiðir, beiðst, beiðst, ber	around	um
		a-strange	undarlegur
ask	biðja	aware	var
a-brother	bróður	a-wall	veggur
away	brott, brottu, brýst, búa		

B, b

and	eða, eða, eða, ef	by	á, á, á
afterwards	eftir, eg, eg	been	að, að
alone	einn, einrænlegu	before	áður, ætla, ætlaði, ætlar, ævi
am	em, en		
am-i	er	back	aftur
are	er, er, er, er, er	both	báðir, bæði
are-you	ertu		
away-from	frá, frá		
ahead	fyrir		
along	fyrir		
amuse	gamni		
anger	gramir, grán, grandi, greipur		
a-complete	heill		
at-home	heima		

224

Word List (English to Old Icelandic)

English	*Old Icelandic*	English	*Old Icelandic*
bearing	bærist	carry	ber
banned	banni	carrying	ber
beat	barður	compensation	bóta
better	batna, beiddist, beiðir	clothing	búning
best	beiðst, ber	closed	byrgður
bear	ber, ber, ber	capable	fær
bite-bone	bitbeini	can	færð, færði
Bergen	Björgyn	cleaned	fágar
brothers	bræðrum, bræður	cloak	feld, feldinum, felld, fellt
brother	bræður, bræður, brjóta	criticised	firna
break	brjóta	crowded	fjölmennt
bad	dála, dauður	companionship	föruneyti
but	eða, eða, ef, efnin	company	föruneytis, forvitni, fót, frá
be	er, er, er, er, er, er, er, era	curious	forvitni
being	er, er, er	could	getu, getur
business	erindi	completely	gjörla
born	fæðist	conclude	hætta
bring	færa, færð	court	hirðarinnar, hirðinni, hirðinni
brought	færði, færður, færi	court-men	hirðinni, hirðmaður
be-gifted	gæfu	court-man	hirðmaður, hirðmann
became	gerist, gerst, gerst, gert	court-visit	hirðvistar
benefit	hagur	corners	horn
brain	heilinn	considered	hyggur
behold	heldur	came	kæmi, kæmir, kæmist, kallaður, kallar, kann, kann
beside	hjá		
bound-to	hlotið		
badly	illa, illt	come	kæmir, kæmist, kallaður, kallar, kann, kann, kaupa
buy	kaupa		
be-allowed	láta		
between	milli	called	kallaður, kallar
become-angry	reiðist	choose	kjósa
blame	sökum	clothes	klæðum
betoken	tákna	coming	koma, komi, komið
because	því	carried-out	leiðast
become	vera, vera, verða, verða	concluded	lýkur
becomes	verði, verður	chatty	ómállatur
		conviction	sæki, sakar
		character	skapi
		cut	skerum
		changed	skipast
		costly-clothing	skrúðklæðin
		crafted	smíðað
		consider	þykjast
		closely	vandlega

C, c

Word List (English to Old Icelandic)

English	Old Icelandic	English	Old Icelandic
carefully	vandlegar	exceedingly-skilful	geysihaglega
certainly	víst, vísu	easy	hægra
custom	vonir	endanger	hætta
		each	hver, hver, hverjum
		every	hver
		everyone	hverjum

D, d

		English	Old Icelandic
dealings	afskipti	equally	jafnan, jafnmæli
dwelling	bænum	equal-speak	jafnmæli
death	banans, banni	equally-well	jafnvel
dress	búa	eccentricities	kynjalæti
dressed	búinn	ended	lokið, lokka
dead	dauður	even-spirit	lundhægur
draw	draga	except	nema
drawn	dregst	enjoy	njót
drinking	drykkju	exchange	skipa
disguise	dylja	early	snemma
drifted	fauk	express	tjáir
did	gera, gera, gera		
do	gera, gera, geri		
done	gera, geri, gerir, gerir		

F, f

English	Old Icelandic
disturbed	kæja
dissuade	lattan
discuss	mæla, mætti, Magnús
down	niður
discreet	orðvar
decide	ráð, ráða, ráða
decision	ráða
dirty	saurgar
decreased	þvarr
difficulty	torsótt
disputes	vandamál
difficult	vant

English	Old Icelandic
for	á, á, á
from	á, á, á, að, að, að, að
fool	afglapa
fixed-upon	allstarsýnn
few	fáir, fallið
fallen	fallið, fallin
found	fann, fara, fara, farar, farið, farið
fared	farið
fee	fé
falling	fellt
fell	fellur, fenginn
find	finn, finna, finna, finnast, finnast
fiendish	fjandlegur
followers	fjölmenni
followers-many	fjölmenni
for-travelling	förin
foot	fót
from-game	fráleik
follow	fylgið, fylgjusamur
follow-same	fylgjusamur
fore-done	fyrirgert
first	fyrst, fyrstu
fun	gaman

E, e

English	Old Icelandic
earlier	áðan
eye	auga
either	eða
especially	einkum
eccentric	einrænlegu
errand	erindið
Eyjafjord	Eyjafirði
Eyvind	Eyvindar, Eyvindur
end	felld

Word List (English to Old Icelandic)

English	*Old Icelandic*	English	*Old Icelandic*
favourable	*líklegt*	grant	*veittir*
further	*meir*	grown	*vexti*
frequently	*oft*		
frame	*rammur*		
from-there	*þaðan, þangað*		
from-here	*þangað*		
faltered	*þraut*		
felt	*þykir*		
feast	*veislu*		
friendship	*vináttu*		
friendly	*vinveitt*		

H, h

English	*Old Icelandic*
has	*á, á, að*
had	*átt, átt, átti, auga, báðir, bæði, bænum, bærist, banans, banni, barður, batna, beiddist*
have	*átt, átti, auga, báðir, bæði, bænum, bærist, banans, banni, barður, batna, beiddist, beiðir*
hammering	*brýst*
height	*hæð*
handy	*hagur*
held	*halda*
hold	*haldi*
half	*hálft, hálfu*
hands-hook-us	*handkrækjumst*
he	*hann, hann, hann, hans, hans, hans, Harald*
him	*hann, hann, hans, hans, hans*
his	*hans, Harald, Haraldi, Haralds, Haraldur, Haraldur, harðleikið*
Harald	*Harald, Haraldi, Haralds*
Harald's	*Haralds, Haraldur*
hardness	*harðleikið*
hard	*hart*
having	*hefði*
home	*heim, heima*
hand	*hendi, hendur, hentu, hér, herra*
handed	*hentu, hér*
here	*hér*
horse	*hest, hesta*
horses	*hestum*
horse's	*hesturinn*
heard	*heyra, heyrði, heyrir, heyrt*

G, g

English	*Old Icelandic*
get	*fá, fá*
give	*fá, fæ, fæðist, fær*
go	*fara, fara, farar, farið, farið, farið, fátt*
going	*fara, farar, farið, farið, farið, fátt*
given	*fenginn, fer*
goes	*fer*
group	*flokk*
game	*fráleikurinn, fram*
good-things	*fríðinda*
got	*gæti, gaf, gafst*
gave	*gaf, gafst, gaman, gaman*
guess	*get*
Glum	*Glúmur*
good	*góða, góðan, góðum, góma, gott*
gums	*góma*
god	*gott*
grey	*grán*
grasp	*greipur*
grouped-together	*gropasamlega*
grass	*grösum*
gold	*gull, gyllt*
greeting	*kveðju*
greeted	*kveður*
given-leave	*leyft*
great	*mikill, mikinn*
great-work	*stórvirkja*
guidance	*umsjá*

Word List (English to Old Icelandic)

English	*Old Icelandic*	English	*Old Icelandic*
head	*höfði, höfðinu*		
humble	*hógvær*	**J, j**	
Hreidar	*Hreiðar, Hreiðari, Hreiðars*		
Hreidar's-Place	*Hreiðarsstöðum*	joyfully	*blíðlega*
house	*húsi*	journey	*farar*
how	*hvað, hve, hver, hver, hverjum*	**K, k**	
how-so	*hversu*		
hands	*krummur*	kill	*drepa, drepi, drepið*
human-trials	*mannraunum*	killed	*drepinn, drykkju*
hurt	*meiddur*	kinsman	*frændi*
human	*mennskur*	kinsmen	*frændi*
himself	*sama, samir, sáttir, saurgar*	know	*kann, kaupa, kemur, kenna*
homespun-cloth	*vaðmál*	knew	*kenna, kjósa*
handsome	*vænleikur, vænn*	knees	*kné*
hardly	*varla*	kings	*konunga, konungar*
hospitality	*vist*	king	*konungs, konungur*
		know-you	*veistu*
I, i		knows	*veit*
		knowing	*vita, viti*
in	*á, að, að, að, að*		
is	*að, áðan, áður, áður, ætla*	**L, l**	
intended	*ætla, ætlaði, ætlar*	life	*ævi*
if	*ef*	lived	*bjó*
i	*eg, eg, eiga, eiga, einkum*	little	*fátt, fauk, fé*
is-not	*ekki*	last-years	*fyrra*
inheritance	*föðurarf*	lord	*herra*
in-front-of	*fyrir*	laughing	*hlæjandi*
injury	*grandi*	laughed	*hlær, hljóta*
insult	*háðungar*	luck	*hljóta*
it	*hann, hans, hans, hans, Harald*	listened	*hlýða*
is-named	*heitir*	listen-to	*hlýdduð*
in-moderation	*hóf*	looked	*hyggur, í*
ingenuity	*hugkvæmur*	leaves	*lætur*
ill	*illt*	laid	*lagður, lagi*
Iceland	*Ísland, Íslands*	lead	*lagi*
icelander	*Íslendingar*	land	*land, langar*
it-may	*mátti*	long	*langar, langt, lát*
in-common	*samir*	left	*láta*
important	*vandara*	let-go	*laust*
		let	*leggja, leggur*
		leave	*leyfi, leyfir*

228

Word List (English to Old Icelandic)

English	*Old Icelandic*
like	*líkar, líkar, líkast, líklegt*
liked	*líkar*
lie	*ljúga*
lift	*loft*
lure	*lokka*
large	*mikið*
less	*minna, minni, míns*
learned	*spyr*
located	*stefnt*
leapt	*stukku*

M, m

English	*Old Icelandic*
materials	*efnin*
money	*fé, feld*
monstrous	*ferlegu, finn*
meet	*finnast, finnast, finnast, finnst*
meet-up	*finnast*
met	*finnast, finnst, finnumst*
many-people	*fjölmennið*
most	*flesta, flokk, fluttir, föðurarf, för*
made	*ger, gera, gera, gera, geri*
mention	*get*
mocking	*ginna, ginningar*
mockery	*háðs*
matter	*hlut, hlýða*
measure	*hófi*
minded	*hygg*
may	*má, maður, maður, maðurinn, mæla*
man	*maður, maðurinn, mæla*
Magnus	*Magnús, Magnúsi, Magnúss*
Magnus's	*Magnúss*
matters	*mál*
men	*manna, mannraunum, manns*
many	*marga, margir, margs, mart, mast, mátti*
may-you	*máttu*
more	*meir, meira*
me	*mér, mér, mér, mest*
mine	*mér, mér, mest, mesta, mestum, mig, mig*
my	*mér, mest*
much	*mig, mikið, mikið, mikið, mikil*
many-ways	*mörgu*
morning	*morgun, morguninn*
meeting	*móti, mótið, mótið*
meetings	*mótið, mótinu*
must	*mun*
mouth	*munni*
message	*orðsending*
myself	*sjálfan*
mood	*skap*
making	*smíðaði*

N, n

English	*Old Icelandic*
never	*aldregi, aldrei, aldrei*
numb	*dofna*
none	*eigi, eigi, eigi*
not	*eigi, eigi, eigi*
nothing	*eigi*
no	*engi, engi, engi*
no-one	*engi*
news	*fréttir, fund, fundar*
nowhere	*hvergi*
noise	*læti*
negligently	*latlega*
noticed	*litu*
near	*nær*
near-lying	*nálægir*
need	*nauðsyn, nemur*
north	*norður*
Norway	*Noreg, Noregi*
now	*nú*
newly-come	*nýkominn*
not-forget	*ólatur*
need-you	*þarftu*
needed	*þurfa*

O, o

Word List (English to Old Icelandic)

English	*Old Icelandic*	English	*Old Icelandic*
of	*á, á, á, á, á, á, að, að*	poorly	*miðlung*
on	*á, á*	prowess	*óknáleik*
other	*aðra, aðrir, áður, ætla, ætlar*	peace-meeting	*sáttarfundar, sáttarfundur*
others	*aðrir, áður, ætla*	pull-cloak, handle-roughly	*skauttoguðu*
of-life	*ævinnar*	parted	*skildi, skildir, skildust*
off	*af*	protect	*skýla*
offer	*búnir*	place	*stað*
or	*eða*	put-right	*umbóta*
own	*eiga, eigi*	proceeded	*vegur*
one-thing	*eigi*		
once	*einhverju, einn*		
one	*einn, eins, einum, eirir*		
one's	*eins*		
otherwise	*ellegar, elli*		
old-age	*elli*		
of-wealth	*fjárins*		
of-the-people	*manni*		
of-any	*nokkuð*		
off-said	*ofsögum*		
ours	*okkað, okkarn, okkur, okkur, okkur*		
occasion	*sinn*		
obliged	*skyldast*		
out-of	*úr*		
out	*út, utan, úti*		
over	*yfir*		

R, r

English	*Old Icelandic*
returned	*áður*
rough	*álpun*
residence	*bænum*
ready-to-serve	*greitt*
rather	*halda, haldist, háttung, hefnt*
risk	*háttung*
revenge	*hefnt*
room	*herbergi*
ridicule	*hlægi*
ran	*hleypur, hljóp*
rest	*hvíldar*
recited	*kveður*
redeem	*leysi*
ruined	*ónýtt*
rode	*reið*
ride	*reiðar*
roughly-handled	*reikuð*
run	*rennur*
reasons	*sakir*
roughly	*skauttogaður*
recently	*skömmu*

P, p

English	*Old Icelandic*
place-about	*ásáttir*
prepared	*bjó, bjó, blásið*
prepare	*bú*
passed	*fer, fer, fer*
promised	*hét*
poem	*kvæði, kvæði*
poem-reward	*kvæðislaunin*
playful	*leikmikill*
played	*lék*
passes	*líður*
praise-will	*lofgjarnlega*
people	*maður, mæl, mælgina, mæli*
people-few	*mannfátt*

S, s

English	*Old Icelandic*
so	*á, á, á, á, að, að, að*
suppose	*ætla, ætlar, ætlun*
stood-out	*afbragð*
strength	*afl, afli, aflið*
settled	*bjó, blásið, borðið*

Word List (English to Old Icelandic)

English	*Old Icelandic*	English	*Old Icelandic*
soon	brátt, breyttu	speech	ræðu
steep	brottu	saw	sá, sá, sá, sá
secure	fastur	such	sá, sá, sæi, sæmilega, sætt
shed	felld	see	sæi, sæmilega, sætt, sætt
situated	felldur	settlement	sætt
sacrificing	förina	settle	sættir
self-control	forræði	same-day	samdægris
swiftness	fráleikurinn	sat	sátu
swift	frávastur	seeing	sé
sea	haf	seen	sé, sé, sé, séð
skilled	hagur	sleeps	sefur
suited	hentur	slowly	seint
share	hlut, hluta, hlutar, hlutur	sell	selji, selur
small-island	hólmur	send	senda, senda
seized	höndum	sending	senda
Son-of-Hreidar	Hreiðarssonar	sent	sendan, sendi
said	kvað, kvað, kvæði, kvæði, kvæðið, kvæðið, kvæðislaunin	set	setur
		six	sex
spoke	kvað, kvæði, kvæði, kvæðið, kvæðið	sailed	sigla
		silver	silfri, silfrið, silfur
some-beast	kykvendum	sit	sitja
strange	kynleg, kynlegast, kynlegu	sitting	sitja
		seemed	sjá, sjá, sjá, sjá
strangely	kynlegast	self-supported	sjálfbjargi
secretly	launungu	self	sjálfur
sport	leik	scabbards	skálpana
sought	leitað	short-distance	skammt
small	lítill, litu, ljótari	scratched	skeindist
say	mæl, mælgina, mæli	separated	skildust
speak	mæli, mælir, mælt	separate	skilst
speaking	mælt	ship	skip
spoken	mælt	ship-launching	skipdráttar
sign	mark	swiftly	skjótt
shall	mun, mun, mun, muna, mund	shortage	skortir
should	mun, mun, muna, mund, mundi, mundi, mundir, muni, muni	struck	sló
		smithery	smíðað
		smith	smíðinni
shall-you	munt, munt, muntu	story	sögu
should-you	munt	sake	sökum
studded	naddar	suckling	spenar
some	nakkvað, nakkvara, nakkvarri, nálægir	standing	staðinn, stæði
		stand	stæði, standa, standa
something	nokkuð	stood	stendur
somewhat	nokkur	strong	sterkur

231

Word List (English to Old Icelandic)

English	*Old Icelandic*	English	*Old Icelandic*
sometimes	*stundum*	to-meet	*fundar*
Svarfardal	*Svarfaðardal*	the-meeting	*fundarins*
sword-studded	*sverðskónum*	taken-care-of	*gætt*
showed	*sýnir*	to-give	*gefa*
seems	*sýnist, tak, taka*	told	*getið, greitt, gripur, gyltur, hætti*
shrill	*þaut*		
straightaway	*þegar*	treasure	*gripur*
silent	*þegi*	the-whole	*heill*
Son-of-Thorgrim	*Þorgrímsson*	the-horse	*hestinn*
since	*því*	there	*hinnug, hitt, hlægi, hleypur, hljóp*
scarcely	*trautt, treystist*		
slain	*vegið*	this	*hitt, hlægi, hleypur, hljóp, hlut, hluta, hlutar, hlutur, hólminn, hólmur*
stay	*vistin*		

T, t

		the-island	*hólminn*
		teased	*hrundu*
that	*á, á, á, að, að, að, að, að, að, að, aðra*	thought	*hug, hugði, hugkvæmir, hugur, hurðina, hvað, hvar*
then	*á, á, að, að, að, að, að, að, að, aðra, aðrir*	think	*hugur, hurðina, hvað, hvar, hver*
to	*á, að, að, að, að, að, að*	the-door	*hurðina*
than	*að, að*	to-come	*koma*
the	*að, að, að, aðra, aðrir, áður, ætla, ætlar, ætlun, ævinnar*	the-king	*konung, konungar, konungi, konunginn, konungs*
		the-kings	*konungar*
to-hear	*áheyrsli*	the-king's	*konungs*
the-people	*alþýðu, annað*	the-poem	*kvæði, kvæðið*
take-care-of	*annast*	the-land	*landi*
to-ask	*biðja*	take	*leggi, leið, leik, leikmikill*
trumpet-blast	*blásið, borðið*		
table	*borðið*	the-game	*leikurinn*
tricky	*brögðóttur*	tempered-even	*lundhægur*
to-deem	*dæmd*	talking	*mælgina*
to-kill	*drepa*	the-matter	*málinu*
to-be	*er, er*	talkative	*málugur, mann*
they-are	*eru*	that-man	*mann*
to-go	*fara*	the-men	*manna*
travel	*fara, fara, fara*	the-man	*manninn*
travelled	*fara, fara, fara, fari, fari, fastur*	to-me	*mér*
		tall	*mikill*
travelling	*ferðina, fjárins, fjárskakka, fleygir*	time	*mund, mundi, mundi*
		took	*námu, nauðsyn, nemur, nestlokum, nokkuð, nokkuð*
threw	*fleygir*		
transport	*flytur*		
trading-voyages	*förum*	the-end	*nestlokum*

232

Word List (English to Old Icelandic)

English	Old Icelandic	English	Old Icelandic
test	reyna	ugly	ljótur
tried	reynt	used	nýt
together	saman, samdægris	use	nytjar
truth	sanna	unprepared	óbúinn, öðru
true	sannast, satt, sáttarfundar	un-passable	ógreið
tell	seg	unholy	óheilagur
they	senn, senn, sér, sér, sérð	us	okkur, okkur
		unaccompanied	ólið
themselves	sig, sigla	unlike	ólíkast
theirs	sín	unlikely	ólíklegt
to-see	sjá	untrue	ósannlegt
the-woods	skógum	un-innocent-looking	ósýknlegur
throws	skýtur	un-accustomed	óvanur
the-work	smíðinni	un-warned	óvart
the-room	stofuna, stofunni	unknown	óvísu
the-pig	svíníð, svíninu	uproar	reiðin, reiðingum
taken	táknar	unite	samtengja
talk	tal, tala	understand	skilja
thus	þannug	until	til, tilgerðir
them	þeim, þeim	under	undir
their	þeir	up	upp
to-you	þér	uplands	upplönd
this-kind-of	þessarar	upright	uppstert
these	þessi, þessi		
their-assembly	þingsins		
though	þó, Þórð, Þórðar	## V, v	
Thord	Þórð, Þórðar, Þórði		
Thord's	Þórðar	very-timid	alláræðislítill
tired	þreytti	varied	breyttu
to-wash	þvegnar	visit	fund
therefore	því	very-smart	hugkvæmir
therefore-like	þvílíkt	voyage	reiðfara
to-think	þykja	valiant	vasklegur
tens	tigu	very	vilgis
to-do	tilgerðir	variously	ýmsu
talked	töluðu		
trust	trúi		
two	tvo, tvö	## W, w	
the-slaying	víginu		
		with	að, aðra, aðrir, áður
## U, u		when	en, engi, engi
		was	er, er, er, er, er, er
uneven-share	fjárskakka	were	er, er, er, er, er, er, er
uglier	ljótari		

Word List (English to Old Icelandic)

English	*Old Icelandic*	English	*Old Icelandic*
what	er, er, er, er	wish-to	vilja
where	er, er	wishes	vill
which	er, er, er	will-you	viltu
who	er, er	wish-you	viltu
whom	er	wind	vindli
would	er, eru, eru, eru, fagna, fara, fara	wise-man	viskumaður
		wiser	vitrari
welcomed	fagna	wits	vits
went	fara, fara, fari, fari, fastur, felld, felldur	wisely	viturlegra
		weapons	vopnum
wished	fúsastur, gætt, ganga		
walked	gengur		
way	hætti, haf, hagur		
whole	heill		
was-named	hét		
worried	hræddur, Hreiðarssonar		

Y, y

English	*Old Icelandic*
young-sow	gyltur
yes	já
you	okkur, óknáleik, ólatur, ólið, ólíkast, ólíklegt, ómállatur, öngar, öngri, öngu
yourself	sjálfur
your	þér, þess, þessa, þessarar, þessi
yet-not	þeygi
yours	þín, þína, þína, þingsins, þinn
young	unga

English	*Old Icelandic*
why	hví
whether	hvort
without-fear	ófælinn
words	orð, orðið, orðum
worded	ort
well-enough	sæmilega
woods	skógar
while	stundir
we-have	þættist
wish	tíðir, tigu, til, til
we-trust	treystist
wonderful	undarlegt
wadding-clothes	vaðmálsklæði
will-be	væri
wake	vaki
woken	vaknaðir
wielded	valdið
ways	vega
well	vel, vélir
wilful	vélir
will	velja, vér, verð, verða
we	vér, verð
worth	verð, verða
worse	verr, verri, verst
winter	vetri
winter-provisions	veturvistar
widely-travelled	víðförull
willed	vildi
wiled	vildu

A Word Comparison of Old Norse and Old Icelandic Words

Old Norse	Old Icelandic	English	Old Norse	Old Icelandic	English
áðr	áður	after	brýzt	brýst	hammering
áðr	áður	before	búit	búið	settled
áðr	áður	returned	byrgðr	byrgður	closed
ætlan	ætlun	suppose	dæmð	dæmd	to-deem
af	að	of	dauðr	dauður	dead
aflit	aflið	strength	eigu	eiga	have
aftr	aftur	back	einrænligu	einrænlegu	eccentric
aftr	aftur	before	ek	eg	i
aldri	aldrei	never	ek	eg	is
aldrigi	aldregi	never	ekki	ekki,	not
allr	allur	all	elligar	ellegar	otherwise
allrífligt	allríflegt	all-abundant	engar	öngar	no
allundarligt	allundarlegt	all-wonderful	engri	öngri	no
allvel	allvel,	all-well	engu	öngu	none
annarr	annar	another	enn	en	but
annat	annað	other	erendi	erindi	business
at	að	a	erendit	erindið	errand
at	að	as	Eyvindr	Eyvindur	Eyvind
at	að	at	fær	færð	can
at	að	been	færðr	færður	brought
at	að	in	færr	fær	capable
at	að	is	fallit	fallið	fallen
at	að	of	fara	fari	travel
at	að	on	farit	farið	fared
at	að	than	farit	farið	going
at	að	that	fastr	fastur	secure
at	að	the	felldr	felldur	situated
at	að	to	fellr	fellur	fell
at	að	with	ferligu	ferlegu	monstrous
at	athlægi	the	ferr	fer	goes
barðr	barður	beat	ferr	fer	passed
beiðzt	beiðst	asked	ferr	fer	travelled
beiðzt	beiðst	best	ferr	fer	went
berr	ber	carry	fjandligr	fjandlegur	fiendish
berr	ber	carrying	fjölmennit	fjölmennið	many-people
betr	betur	better	flytr	flytur	transport
bezt	best	best	förna	förina	sacrificing
blásit	blásið	trumpet-blast	fráleikrinn	fráleikurinn	game
blíðlíga	blíðlega	joyfully	fráleikrinn	fráleikurinn	swiftness
borðit	borðið	table	frávastr	frávastur	swift
borit	borið	bear	fríðenda	fríðinda	good-things
bræðr	bræður	brothers	fundit	fundið	found
brögðóttr	brögðóttur	tricky	fúsastr	fúsastur	wished

A Word Comparison of Old Norse and Old Icelandic Words

Old Norse	Old Icelandic	English	Old Norse	Old Icelandic	English
fylgjusamr	fylgjusamur	follow-same	*hon*	hún	it
gefr	gefur	give	*hornblástr*	hornblástur	trumpet-blast
gengr	gengur	go	*hræddr*	hræddur	worried
gengr	gengur	going	*Hreiðarr*	Hreiðar	Hreidar
gengr	gengur	walked	*hugkvæmr*	hugkvæmur	ingenuity
gengr	gengur	went	*hugr*	hugur	think
gerik	geri	do	*hvárt*	hvort	how
gerla	gjörla	completely	*hvárt*	hvort	whether
gerr	ger	made	*hvat*	hvað	how
gerzt	gerst	done	*hvat*	hvað	what
gerzt	gerst	made	*hvé*	hve	how
getit	getið	told	*hvernig*	hvernug	how
getr	getur	get	*hvernig*	hvernug	which
geysihagliga	geysihaglega	exceedingly-skilful	*hverr*	hver	each
glíkligt	líklegt	favourable	*hverr*	hver	every
glíkr	líkur	like	*hverr*	hver	what
Glúmr	Glúmur	Glum	*hyggr*	hyggur	considered
greipr	greipur	grasp	*hyggr*	hyggur	looked
gripr	gripur	treasure	*hyggr*	hyggur	think
gropasamliga	gropasamlega	grouped-together	*inn*	hinn	the
gyltr	gyltur	young-sow	*ísinn*	sinn	his
hagr	hagur	benefit	*it*	hið	that
hagr	hagur	handy	*it*	hið	the
hagr	hagur	skilled	*it*	hið	to
Haraldr	Haraldur	Harald	*kallaðr*	kallaður	called
Haraldr	Haraldur	Harald's	*kemr*	kemur	came
harðleikit	harðleikið	hardness	*komit*	komið	came
heldr	heldur	behold	*komit*	komið	come
heldr	heldur	rather	*kómu*	komu	came
helzt	helst	rather	*konungr*	konungur	king
hendr	hendur	hand	*konungr*	konungur	the-king
hendu	hentu	handed	*korn*	kom	came
hentr	hentur	suited	*kvæðit*	kvæðið	poem
hestr	hestur	a-horse	*kvæðit*	kvæðið	the-poem
hestrinn	hesturinn	horse's	*kveðr*	kveður	greeted
heyrðak	heyrði	heard	*kveðr*	kveður	recited
hinnig	hinnug	there	*kveðr*	kveður	spoke
hirðmaðr	hirðmaður	court-man	*kynlig*	kynleg	strange
hleypr	hleypur	ran	*kynligast*	kynlegast	strangely
hlotit	hlotið	bound-to	*kynligu*	kynlegu	strange
hlutr	hlutur	share	*lætr*	lætur	had
hlýddið	hlýdduð	listen-to	*lætr*	lætur	leaves
hógværr	hógvær	humble	*lagðr*	lagður	had
hólmr	hólmur	small-island	*lagðr*	lagður	laid
			latliga	latlega	negligently

236

A Word Comparison of Old Norse and Old Icelandic Words

Old Norse	Old Icelandic	English	Old Norse	Old Icelandic	English
leggja	leggi	take	myndi	mundi	would
leggr	leggur	have	myndir	mundir	would
leggr	leggur	laid	nemr	nemur	took
leikrinn	leikurinn	the-game	niðr	niður	down
leitat	leitað	sought	nökkur	nokkur	somewhat
leysa	leysi	redeem	nökkura	nakkvara	some
lézt	lést	let	nökkurri	nakkvarri	some
líðr	líður	passed	nökkut	nakkvað	some
líðr	líður	passes	nökkut	nokkuð	of-any
líkr	líkur	like	nökkut	nokkuð	some
lítit	lítið	little	nökkut	nokkuð	something
lízt	líst	appears	norðr	norður	north
ljótr	ljótur	ugly	Nóreg	Noreg	Norway
lofgjarnliga	lofgjarnlega	praise-will	Nóregi	Noregi	Norway
lokit	lokið	ended	óheilagr	óheilagur	unholy
lundhægr	lundhægur	even-spirit	ok	og	also
lundhægr	lundhægur	tempered-even	ok	og	and
lýkr	lýkur	concluded	okkart	okkað	ours
maðr	maður	a-man	okkr	okkur	ours
maðr	maður	man	okkr	okkur	us
maðr	maður	people	okkr	okkur	you
maðrinn	maðurinn	a-man	ökulbrókum	hökulbrókum	ankle-breeches
mælik	mæli	speak	ólatr	ólatur	not-forget
mælir	mælti	spoke	ólíkligt	ólíklegt	unlikely
málit	málið	discuss	ómállatr	ómállatur	chatty
málugr	málugur	talkative	ómállatr	ómállatur	talkative
margt	mart	many	ór	úr	out-of
mazt	mast	most	orðit	orðið	words
meiddr	meiddur	hurt	orðvarr	orðvar	discreet
mennskr	mennskur	human	ósannligt	ósannlegt	untrue
miðlungi	miðlung	poorly	ósýknligr	ósýknlegur	un-innocent-looking
mik	mig	i	óvanr	óvanur	un-accustomed
mik	mig	me	penninga	peninga	money
mik	mig	much	ráðligra	ráðlegra	advisable
mikit	mikið	large	rammi	rammur	frame
mikit	mikið	many	reiðr	reiður	angry
mikit	mikið	much	reiðumst	reiðist	become-angry
mjök	mjög	much	rennr	rennur	run
morgin	morgun	morning	rjáðr	rjáður	worried
morgininn	morguninn	morning	sæja	sæi	see
mótit	mótið	meeting	sæmiliga	sæmilega	well-enough
mótit	mótið	meetings	sagða	sagði	said
muna	muni	should	sakar	sakir	reasons
muntu	munt	should-you	sáttarfundr	sáttarfundur	peace-meeting
myndi	mundi	should			

A Word Comparison of Old Norse and Old Icelandic Words

Old Norse	Old Icelandic	English	Old Norse	Old Icelandic	English
sé	séu	as	þannig	þannug	thus
sefr	sefur	sleeps	þat	það	is
selja	selji	sell	þat	það	it
selr	selur	sell	þat	það	that
sér	sérð	saw	þat	það	the
sér	sérð	see	þat	það	this
sét	séð	seen	þ-at	það	it
setr	setur	set	þeira	þeirra	them
síðr	síður	less	þeira	þeirra	they
sik	sig	him	þik	þig	you
sik	sig	himself	þingit	þingið	assembly
sik	sig	such	Þórðr	Þórði	Thord
sik	sig	themselves	Þórðr	Þórður	Thord
silfr	silfur	silver	þykkir	þykir	felt
silfrit	silfrið	silver	þykkir	þykir	seemed
sinn	sinni	his	þykkir	þykir	think
sjálfr	sjálfur	himself	þykkir	þykir	thought
sjálfr	sjálfur	self	þykkist	þykist	seems
sjálfr	sjálfur	yourself	þykkist	þykist	think
skauttogaðr	skauttogaður	roughly	þykkist	þykist	thought
skilði	skildi	parted	þykkja	þykja	to-think
skilðir	skildir	parted	þykkjast	þykjast	consider
skilðust	skildust	separated	þykkjumst	þykist	think
skyldi	skyldu	should	tíðenda	tíðinda	news
skýtr	skýtur	throws	tíðendi	tíðindi	news
smíðat	smíðað	crafted	treystumst	treystist	we-trust
smíðat	smíðað	made	tvá	tvo	two
smíðat	smíðað	smithery	tvau	tvö	two
spyrr	spyr	asked	undarliga	undarlega	strange
spyrr	spyr	learned	undarligr	undarlegur	a-strange
srterkr	sterkur	strong	undarligt	undarlegt	wonderful
stæða	stæði	stand	unnit	unnið	done
stendr	stendur	stood	unz	uns	until
sterkr	sterkur	strong	útan	utan	out
svá	svo	seen	vá	vó	killed
svá	svo	so	vælir	vélir	wilful
svínit	svínið	the-pig	vænleikr	vænleikur	handsome
sýndi	sýnir	showed	væri	væru	were
talat	talað	told	valdit	valdið	wielded
tekr	tekur	take	vandliga	vandlega	closely
tekr	tekur	took	vandligar	vandlegar	carefully
þættist	þóttist	thought	vánir	vonir	custom
þættumst	þættist	we-have	vápnum	vopnum	weapons
þangat	þangað	from-here	várn	vorn	ours
þangat	þangað	there	varr	var	aware

A Word Comparison of Old Norse and Old Icelandic Words

Old Norse	Old Icelandic	English
várr	vor	ours
váru	voru	were
vaskligr	vasklegur	valiant
veggr	veggur	a-wall
vegit	vegið	slain
vegr	vegur	proceeded
veizlu	veislu	feast
veiztu	veistu	know-you
verðr	verður	became
verðr	verður	become
verðr	verður	becomes
verðr	verður	were
verit	verið	been
vetrvistar	veturvistar	winter-provisions
vilda	vildi	willed
vilda	vildi	wish
vilda	vildi	wished
vill	vilt	will
vill	vilt	wish
villt	vilt	wish
villtu	viltu	will-you
villtu	viltu	wish-you
vit	við	we
vitrligra	viturlegra	wisely
vizkumaðr	viskumaður	wise-man
yðr	yður	you
yðr	yður	your
yðvarn	yðarn	you
ykkr	ykkur	you

The Tale of Star-Oddi's Dream (*Old Norse*)

Old Norse	Literal	English
1	**1**	**1**
Þórðr hét maðr, er bjó í Múla norðr í Reykjardal.	Thord was-named a-man, who lived at Muli in-the-north in Reykjardal.	There was a man named Thord who lived at Muli in the north, in Reykjardal.
Þar var á vist með honum sá maðr, er Oddi hét ok var Helgason.	There was in hospitality with him so a-man, who Oddi named and was Son-of-Helgi.	There was a man living with him named Oddi who was the son of Helgi.
Hann var kallaðr Stjörnu-Oddi.	He was called Star-Oddi.	He was called Star-Oddi.
Hann var rímkænn maðr, svá at engi maðr var hans maki honum samtíða á öllu Íslandi, ok at mörgu var hann annars vitr.	He was calendar-computation-wise a-man, so that no man was his match him contemporary in all Iceland, and that many was he otherwise wise.	He was skilled in the art of calendar computation, such that no man in all of Iceland was a match for him, and he was also wise in many other things.
Ekki var hann skáld né kvæðinn.	Not was he poet nor poetry.	He was not a poet, nor did he know much poetry.
Þess er ok einkum getit um hans ráð, at þat höfðu menn fyrir satt, at hann lygi aldri, ef hann vissi satt at segja, ok at öllu var hann ráðvandr kallaðr ok tryggðarmaðr inn mesti.	This was also particularly told about his statements, that it had people before the-truth, that he lied never, if he knew the-truth to say, and that all was he honest called and faithful-man the most.	It was also particularly said about him of his statements that people held them to be the truth, that he never lied if he knew the truth to tell, and that he was the most honest and faithful man.
Félítill var hann ok ekki mikill verkmaðr.	Fee-little was he and not much working-man.	He was poor and not an especially good worker.
Frá því er at segja, at um þenna mann, Odda, gerðist undarligr atburðr.	From therefore is to say, that about this man, Oddi, happened extraordinary events.	The story goes that extraordinary events happened to this man Oddi.
Hann fór heiman út til Flateyjar, er Þórðr, húsbóndi hans, sendi hann þessa ferð á vit fiska, ok er eigi annars getit en þeim fórst vel til eyjarinnar.	He travelled home out-from to Flatey, when Thord, housemaster his, sent him this journey to to fishing, and was not anything-else told-of but they travelled well to the-island.	He travelled out from his home to Flatey when his housemaster Thord sent him on a journey to go fishing, and nothing else is told except that the journey to the island went well.
Þar var hann í góðum beina.	There was he in good assistance.	He was well looked after there.

The Tale of Star-Oddi's Dream (Old Norse)

Old Norse	Literal	English
Ekki er frá því sagt, hverr þar bjó.	Not was from therefore said, who there lived.	It was not said who lived there.
En frá því er at segja, at um kveldit, er menn fóru í rekkju, var vel búit um Odda ok hægliga,	Then from therefore was it said, that about evening, were people going to bed, was well preparations about Oddi and comfortable,	Then from there it was said that about one evening people were going to bed, as preparations were made to make Oddi comfortable.
en við þat, er Oddi var farmóðr ok veittr hógligr umbúnaðr, þá sofnar hann brátt, ok dreymði hann þegar, at hann þóttist staddr vera heima í Múla, ok svá þótti honum sem þar væri kominn maðr til gistingar, ok þótti honum sem menn færi í rekkju um kveldit.	and with that, was Oddi was travel-weary and given comfortably soft-bed-prepared, then slept he soon, and dreamed he straightaway, that he though stood was home in Muli, and so seemed to-him that there was come a-man to guest, and thought he as people went to bed about evening.	And with Oddi being travel-weary, he was given a comfortable and soft bed that had been prepared for him, and he soon fell asleep and dreamed straightaway that he stood at home in Muli, and it seemed to him that a man had come as a guest, and that people were going to bed in the evening.
Þótti honum gestrinn vera beðinn skemmtanar, en hann tók til ok sagði sögu ok hóf á þessa leið:	Seemed to-him the-guest was asking entertainment, and he took to of the-saga telling and began in this way:	It seemed to him that the guest had asked for some entertainment, and he took to telling a saga, which began in this way.

2

Hróðbjartr hefir konungr heitit.	Hrodbjart had king dominion.	Hrodbart had the rule of a king.
Hann réð austr fyrir Gautlandi.	He ruled east for Götaland.	He ruled over east Götaland.
Hann var kvángaðr maðr.	He was married man.	He was a married man.
Hildiguðr hét kona hans.	Hildigunn named wife his.	His wife was named Hildigunn.
Þau áttu sér einn son barna, er Geirviðr er nefndr.	They had themselves only son child, was Geirvid was named.	They had an only child whose was named Geirvid.
Hann var snemma vænn ok vitmikill ok at öllum hlutum mannaðr um fram sína jafnaldra, en barn var hann at aldri, er sagan gerðist.	He was soon handsome and knowing-much and in all things brought-up about from his equal-age, but child was he of age, when the-saga begins.	He grew up to be handsome and wise in all things more than those his age, but he was a child when the saga begins.

The Tale of Star-Oddi's Dream (Old Norse)

Old Norse	Literal	English
Frá því er at segja, at konungrinn Hróðbjartr hafði settan til landstjórnar yfir þriðjung ríkis síns jarl þann, er Hjörvarðr hét.	From therefore is to say, that this-king Hrodbjart had appointed to governing over a-third-of kingdom his earl then, was Hjorvard named.	From there is to say that this King Hrodbjart had appointed an earl to govern over a third of the kingdom who was named Hjorvard.
Hann var ok kvángaðr, ok hét kona hans Hjörguðr,	He was also married, and named wife his Hjorgunn,	He was also married and his wife was named Hjorgunn.
Þau áttu eina dóttur barna.	They had only daughter child.	They had a daughter who was an only child.
Sú hét Hléguðr.	So named Hlegunn.	She was named Hlegunn.
Frá henni er svá sagt, at hon var ólát í æsku sinni, ok var ávallt því ódælli sem hon var eldri.	From her is so said, that she was un-courteous in youth hers, and was always therefore un-pleasant as she was older.	It is said of her that she was discourteous in her youth and got more unpleasant as she got older.
Þat var ok sagt, at hon vildi ekki kvennasið fága í sínu athæfi.	It was also said, that she willed not woman's-customs cultivate in her behaviour.	It was also said that she did not wish to cultivate womanly traditions in her behaviour.
Þat var hennar venja jafnan, at hon gekk í herklæðum ok með vápnum, ok ef hana skildi á við menn, þá veitti hon þeim annathvárt áverka stóra eða líflát, þegar henni líkaði eigi.	It was her way always, that she went in war-clothes and with weapons, and if she should then against people, then gave her them either-way injury great or life-less, as-soon-as she liked not.	It was always her way that she went about in armour with weapons, and if people went against her in any way she gave them either a great injury or death as soon as she did not like them.
En við þenna hennar ójafnað þá þótti Hjörvarði jarli, föður hennar, eigi mega við sæma hennar vandræði ok sagði henni þá ljósliga, at hann mundi eigi þann veg lengr láta fram fara, ok kvað henni eigi hlýða mundu, nema um batnaði nökkurs háttar,	Then with this her unequal then thought Hjorvard the-earl, father hers, not may with the-same her difficulty and told her then lightly, that he may not then way longer let from go, and said she not obey would, except about bettering somewhat kind,	Then with this overbearing behaviour, her father earl Hjorvard felt that he may not tolerate her disruptions any more, and told her plainly that it could not go on any longer, and that she should do somewhat better,
"eða elligar far í brott sem skjótast ór minni hirð",	"or otherwise travel to away as soonest from my court",	or otherwise leave my court as soon as possible.

The Tale of Star-Oddi's Dream (Old Norse)

Old Norse	Literal	English
En þegar Hléguðr jarlsdóttir verðr þessa áheyrsla af feðr sínum, at hann vildi hana láta í burt fara af sinni hirð, þá svarar hon því máli svá, at hon kvað sik þar ekki dvelja, ok beiddi hon þá föður sinn, at hann skyldi fá henni langskip þrjú, alskipuð bæði at mönnum ok herklæðum, ok búa at öllu sem bezt með góðum liðskosti, svá at henni þætti vel skipuð,	Then as-soon-as Hlegunn the-earl's-daughter became of-this to-hear of father hers, that he willed her leave to away travel from his court, then answered she therefore saying so, that she spoke herself there not dwell, and asked she then father hers, that he should give her longships three, fully-prepared both in men and war-clothes, and prepare that all as best with good provisions, so that she seemed well prepared,	Then as soon as the earl's daughter Hlegunn came to hear of her father, that he wished her to travel away from his court, then she answered therefore declaring, that she did not wish to stay there and asked her father to give her three longships fully prepared with men and armour, and prepared with the best provisions so that she was well prepared.
ok ef svá væri gert sem hon beiddi hér um þetta mál, þá talði hon sér mundu vel líka, þótt hon færi í braut við svá búit.	and if so would-be done as she asked she about that matter, then said she herself would well like, thought she travel to away with so prepared.	And if it would be done as she asked in this matter then she said she would like to travel away as she was prepared.
Hjörvarðr jarl vildi gjarna þetta til vinna, at hon kæmist á braut sem skjótast, því at honum þótti, sem var, mikil vandræði af standa hennar ráði.	Hjorvard the-earl willed gladly this to grant, that she comes to away as quickly, therefore that he thought, that was, much difficulty of standing her conduct.	Earl Hjorvard was glad to grant this so that she would go away as soon as possible, for he thought there was great difficulty with her conduct if she stayed.
Síðan lét hann búa at öllu þrjú langskip sem bezt.	Then had he prepared to all three longships as best.	Then he had prepared all three longships as best as possible.
En þegar þetta lið var búit, þá ferr Hléguðr jarlsdóttir ór landi með þessu liði ok lagðist síðan í hernað ok víking ok aflaði sér svá fjár ok frama.	Then as-soon-as the crew were prepared, then travelled Hlegunn the-earl's-daughter out-of land with this crew and lay afterwards to raiding and viking and obtained herself such wealth and fame.	Then as soon as the crew were ready Hlegunn the earl's daughter travelled out of the land with this crew and went raiding and viking and obtained such wealth and fame for herself.
Svá er sagt, at hon kom eigi í land, meðan faðir hennar lifði.	So was said, that she came not to land, while father hers lived.	So it was said that she did not come back to the land while her father lived.

The Tale of Star-Oddi's Dream (Old Norse)

Old Norse	Literal	English
En í annan stað er þar til at taka sögunnar, at þá er Geirviðr, sonr Hróðbjarts konungs, var átta vetra gamall, tók Hróðbjartr konungr sótt, ok verðr þat lítil frásaga, því at sóttin leiðir svá til lands, at konungrinn andast.	But in another place is there to of take the-saga, that then was Geirvid, son Hrodbjart's king, was eight winters old, took Hrodbjart king sickness, and became that little from-to-say, accordingly that sickness took so to the-lands, that the-king died.	But to take the saga to another place, then King Hrodbjart's son Geirvid was eight winters old, Hrodbjart took ill, and there was little to say of it, but a sickness took to the land and the king died.
Þat þótti öllum hans ástvinum ok virkðamönnum inn mesti skaði, sem var, at missa slíks höfðingja ok bar út í frá öllu landsfólkinu.	That thought all of-him beloved and chosen-man the most harm, as was, that missed such chieftains and there out to from all lands-folk.	Everyone thought this a great harm as he was beloved by his chosen companions, chieftains, and people of the land.
Síðan var fengit at virðuligri veizlu ok þar til boðit öllum inum ríkustum mönnum ok inum beztum höfðingjum, er í váru landinu.	Afterwards was got then worthy feast and there to invited all the kingdom's people and the best chieftains, that in were the-land.	Afterwards a worthy feast was prepared, and all of the kingdom's people and the best chieftains in the land were invited.
Þar með var ok til boðit hverjum manni, þeim er veizluna vildi sækja, bæði innan lands ok útan, svá at engi skyldi þar óboðit koma.	Then with was also to invited each person, they of feast willed seek, both within lands and without, so that none should there uninvited come.	With that, everyone who wished to attend was also invited, both within the land and without, so that no one should come uninvited.
En síðan þessi veizla var saman sett með því fjölmenni, er þangat sótti, þá var þar erfi drukkit eftir Hróðbjart konung með miklum veg ok sóma, svá sem byrjaði hans tígn ok sómasamligri virðingu.	Then after the feast were together set with because followers, were there attending, then was there a-toast drunk after Hrodbjart the-king with much way and honour, so as began his prestige and respectable worthiness.	Then after the feast was held with the many followers who attended there, a toast was drunk for King Hrodbjart, in such a way that honoured his prestige and respectable worthiness.
En er erfinu var lokit, þá var konungrinn heygðr at fornum sið eftir því, sem þá var tízka til við göfga menn.	Then as the-toast was ended, then was the-king buried in ancient traditions after according-to, as then was fashion to with noble men.	Then when the toast had ended, the king was buried according to ancient traditions that were then fashionable with noble men.

The Tale of Star-Oddi's Dream (Old Norse)

Old Norse	Literal	English
3	**3**	**3**
Nú er svá at segja, at eftir þessi miklu tíðendi, er þar í landi höfðu gerzt, þá sýndist þat öllum inum vitrustum mönnum ok inum beztum vinum konungsins at taka annan mann til konungs ok landstjórnar í stað þvílíks höfðingja, sem þá var við misst.	Now is so to say, that after this much news, was there in the-land had done, then seemed that all the-others wise people and the best friends the-king's to take another person to king and governing the place such-like chieftains, as then were with lost.	Now the saga goes that after this there was much news in the land that all the wise people and the king's best friends had to take another person as king and for the chieftains to cover the place as such a leader had been lost.
En svá var mikil ástúð öllum landsmönnum á Hróðbjarti konungi, meðan hann lifði, at menn vildu ekki annat en velja Geirvið, son hans, til konungs ok láta eigi konungdóminn ganga ór hans ætt.	But so was great affection of-all lands-people to Hrodbjart the-king, while he lived, that people willed not another to choose Geirvid, son his, to king and allowed not kingdom going out-of his lineage.	But so great was the affection of all the people of the land to King Hrodbjart while he lived that no one wanted to choose other than Geirvid his son as king and not to let the kingdom pass out of his lineage.
Þótt Geirviðr væri ungr at aldri eða hann þætti þá enn lítt til landráða fallinn í þann tíma, vildi þó allt landsfólkit til þessa hætta með umsjá dróttningar, móður hans, með því at hon var in vitrasta kona ok vel at sér í alla staði.	Thought Geirvid was young in age and he thought then that little to land-ruling disposed in that time, willed though all the-land's-people to this conclude with supervision queen, mother his, with accordingly that she was the wisest woman and well to herself in all places.	Though Geirvid was young in age and seemed little disposed to ruling the land at that time, all the people of the land wished it, with supervision of his mother the queen accordingly, as she was the wisest woman and capable in all ways.
En er svá fór fram um hríð, at svá ungr maðr skyldi höfðingi vera ok stjórna mörgu fólki sem Geirviðr var, þá gerðist brátt landsstjórnin lítil, sem líkligt var.	But when so went from about awhile, that so young man should chieftain be and ruling many folk as Geirvid was, then became soon the-government little, as likely was.	But when this had been so for a while, with such a young man as Geirvid being a ruler and governing many people, then the government became weak, as was likely.
Þat gerðist ok, at hirðin fátkaðist, fyrir því at margir váru þeir af hans hirðmönnum, at aðra iðn lögðu fyrir sik.	It became also, that courtiers few, because therefore that many were they of his court-men, that other crafts laid for themselves.	It also came about that he courtiers were fewer because many of his court men found themselves other jobs.
Sumir lögðust í víking, aðrir réðust í kaupferðir til ýmissa landa.	Some laid to viking-raids, others appointed to merchant-voyages to various lands.	Some went on viking raids, others were appointed on merchant voyages to various lands.

The Tale of Star-Oddi's Dream (Old Norse)

Old Norse	Literal	English
Nú með því at á þessu þótti mikit mein, sem nú var frá sagt, þá gerðust þó mörg önnur óhægendi í ríki þessa ins unga konungs.	Now with therefore that of this thought much harm, as how was from said, then made though many others inconvenience in the-kingdom this the young king.	Now with this being thought of as much harm, as before said, then there were other inconveniences in the kingdom of this young kind.
Þess er við getit í sögunni, at illvirkjar tveir lögðust út á skóg þann, er Jöruskógr heitir.	This was with told-of in the-saga, that evil-doers two camped out in forest then, was Battle-forest named.	It was told of in this saga that two evil doers camped out in the forest which was then named Battle Forest.
Þat var í ríki þessa ins unga manns.	It was in kingdom this the young man's.	This was in the young man's kingdom.
Þessir víkingar drápu menn til fjár sér ok váru náliga berserkir.	These vikings killed people for wealth as also were nearly berserkers.	These vikings killed men for money and were virtually berserkers.
Annarr þeira hét Garpr, en annarr Gnýr.	One of-them named Garp, and the-other Gny.	One of them was named Garp, and the other Gny.
Svá er sagt, at mönnum hlýddi aldri fám at fara saman.	So is said, that people followed never few to travel together.	So it was said that people never travelled in small numbers together.
Jafnan váru menn vanir at fara á skóginn með fjölmenni at leita illvirkjanna ok ráða þá af, en þeir urðu aldrigi hittir, þó at þeira væri leita farit með fjölmenni.	Always were people friends that travelled to the-forest with followers-many to search for-the-evil-doers and prevail then of, which they became never found, though that they were searching travelling with followers-many.	People were always travelling with friends to the forest with followers to search for these evil doers and defeat them, but they were never found, even though many people were searching for them.
Slíku ferr fram, til þess er Geirviðr konungr er tólf vetra.	So it-went from, to this that Geirvid the-king was twelve winters.	So it went on until King Geirvid was twelve winters old.
Ok þá er hann var svá aldrs kominn, þá var hann svá mikill maðr vexti ok sterkr at afli sem þeir menn margir, sem fullkomnir váru at aldri ok atgervi náliga, eftir því sem þeir bezt váru á sik komnir fyrir allra hluta sakir.	And then when he was so of-age come, then was he so much a-man grown and strong in strength as they men many, as fully-come were to age and deeds closely, after accordingly which they best were in himself come before all things sake.	And then when he had come of age, he was a great man in height and strength, as much as many men who had come of age, and almost like those who were at their peak in all things.

The Tale of Star-Oddi's Dream (Old Norse)

Old Norse	Literal	English
Þat var eitthvert sinn, þá er Geirviðr konungr sat yfir borðum með allri hirð sinni, þá tók hann til orða ok mælti svá:	Then was some-time one-day, then that Geirvid the-king sat over the-tables with all retainers his, then took he to words and spoke so:	Then one day King Geirvid sat at the table with his retainers, and took to words and said:
Nú er svá sem yðr er kunnigt, öllum mínum mönnum, at ek hefi ungr verit hér til at aldri, ok svá hefi ek haft litla orku, ok því hefir af mér staðit lítil stjórn í ríkinu.	Now is so as you that known, all my men, that I have young been forces to that age, and so have I had little power, and therefore have of me stood little control in the-kingdom.	Now it is well known to you, all my people, that I have been young and have had little power, and therefore I have had little control over the kingdom.
Hefi ek þat ok oft heyrt, sem ván er at.	Have I that and often heard, as expected was it.	And I have often heard, as was expected,
Má þat ok eigi mjök undrast, þó at hér til hafi af mér lítil stjórn staðit fyrir sakir æsku minnar.	May it also not much wonder, though that forces to have of me little control placed before the-sake-of youth mine.	It may also not be much to wonder that I have had little force of control for the sake of my youth.
En þó er ek nú svá aldrskominn, at mér er nú mál at reyna mik ok vita, at nökkut vili mitt ráð þroskast ok meir hefjast en áðr er, þar sem ek er nú orðinn maðr tólf vetra gamall.	However though am I now so come-of-age, that to-me is now matter to test myself and know, that something wish mine decide develop and more start then after that, there was I am now become a-man twelve winters old.	However, now that I have come of age, there is now the matter to test myself and I wish to know something whether it is decided that my rule will develop and become more after than it was at the start, now that I am a man of twelve winters old.
Eru ok margir ekki betr mannaðir á mínum aldri.	Are and many not better mannered at my age.	There are many my age who are not better mannered than me.
Nú vil ek ok því lýsa fyrir öllum yðr, mínum þegnum ok virkðavinum, at ek ætla mér at fara til móts við berserkina, þá Garp ok Gný, er liggja á Jöruskógi ok gera þar mörg illvirki.	Now will I also therefore show for all of-you, my subjects and friends, that I intend me to travel to meet with berserkers, then Garp and Gny, who camped in Battle-forest and do there many outrages.	Now therefore I wish to show all of you, my subjects and friends, that I intend to travel to meet with the berserkers, Garp and Gny, who camp in Battle Forest and do many outrages there.
Ætla ek ok til þess at koma eigi aftr svá, at þeir sé á lífi, ok skal ek þá yfirkoma eða þeir mik ella",	Intend I also to this that come not back so, so-as they are of alive, and shall I then overcome or they me or-else",	I also do not intend to come back so long as they are alive, and either I shall over come them, or they me".

The Tale of Star-Oddi's Dream (Old Norse)

Old Norse	Literal	English
En er Geirviðr konungr hafði þetta mælt, þá svarar fyrst máli hans dróttningin, móðir hans, ok þar með allir hans beztu menn, ok mæltu náliga allir sem eins manns munni ok báðu konung fara fjölmennan á fund stigamannanna ok með miklum viðbúnaði, ef hann vildi fara.	And when Geirvid the-king had this spoke, then answered first speech his the-queen, mother his, and there with all his best people, and spoke almost all as one man's mouth and asked the-king travel followers-many to find the-robbing-men and with much preparation, if he wished to-travel.	And when King Geirvid had spoken, the first to answer his speech was his mother the queen, along with his best people, and all spoke almost with one voice and asked that the king travel with many followers to find the robbing men and with much preparation if he wished to travel.
Geirviðr konungr svarar:	Geirvid the-king answered:	King Geirvid answered:
Hugsat hefi ek þetta mál áðr nökkut fyrir mér en ek kvæða upp, ok sýnist mér á þá leið sem í þessari ferð megi mér þá engi frami kaupast, þótt ek fá nát berserkjunum, enda leita ek þeira með miklu liði alvápnuðu,	Think have I this matter before some-time for me that I announced up, and seems to-me that then passes so in this journey may for-me then not courage redeem, though I get protection the-berserkers, with seeking I them with much company all-weaponed,	I have been thinking about this matter for some time before I announced it and it seems to me that if it so passes on my journey, I may not redeem courage if I have the protection from the berserkers while seeking them with a great company all armed.
en þat er þá nökkur svívirðing, ef þeir fást þá eigi ok koma ek við þat aftr, ok verðr þá ósnöfrmannliga minnar handar, ef svá tekst.	but it is then somewhat disgraceful, if them get then not and come I with it returning, and became then un-alert my hand, if so takes.	But then it is a disgrace if they are not caught, and I will come to return, and then it will have been feeble for my hand if it it ends like that.
Nú hefi ek hina leið ætlat ferðina at fara með annan mann á þeira fund, ok mun þá skipta gæfa með oss, hverr þá skal verða várr skilnaðr.	Now have I then company intend travelling that travel with another person that they find, and should then exchange good-fortune with us, each then shall become our parting.	Now I intend to travel with another person to find them, and it should then exchange good fortune between us and we shall se how we part.
Má þá ok verða, ef vill, at nökkur svá fremð fylgi ferðinni.	May then also be, if will, that something so honour follows the-journey.	May it then also become, if willing, that some honour follows this journey.
Skal nú ok á þat ráð hætta, hversu sem til vill takast.	Shall now also to that decide conclude, how-so as to will take.	That shall now decide and conclude how it may turn out.

The Tale of Star-Oddi's Dream (Old Norse)

Old Norse	Literal	English
Er nú ok fyrir því upp borit þetta mál fyrir yðr, at ek vil nú vita, hverr fúsastr er til þessarar ferðar með mér, ok er nú þat ráð, at nökkurr vakni við, sá er til vill ráðast, ok svari sá nú mínu máli, enda skuluð þér þat vita hér með, at nú er þetta mál fullgert fyrir mína hönd, at ek mun þó fara þessa ferð, þótt ek fara einn saman ok verði engi til at fylgja mér",	Is now also before because up brought this matter before you, that I wish no to-know, who willing that to this journey with me, and is now that decision, to someone wake against, so that to wish arrange, and answer so now my speech, and should you it know here with, that now is this matter full-done before my hand, that I should though travel this journey, though I travel one the-same and be none to that follow me",	Now, therefore, this matter has been brought before you that I now want to know who is most willing to go on this journey with me, and it is now the plan that someone will wake up, whoever may decide, and he will now answer my question, and you shall do so. Know herewith that now this matter is settled on my behalf that I will still go on this journey even though I go alone and there will be no one to follow me".
En við þessi ummæli konungs, þá er þat sagt, at dróttning sjálf fyrst at upphafi latti á alla vega þessar ferðar ok sagði, sem var, allbráðliga stofnat, þar sem við heljarmenn var at eiga, er illvirkjarnir váru, svá mikit sem þar var í ábyrgð, er konungrinn var sjálfr, því at öllum þótti viss ván, at hann mundi látast fyrir þeim ok fá minna hlut í þeira skiptum, ef svá yrði sem líkligt mundi þykkja fyrir sakir æsku konungs þeira, en harðfengi berserkjanna.	And with these about-words the-king's, then was it said, that the-queen herself first to became discouraged to all ways this journey and said, that was, all-un-forethought planned, there as with accursed-men was that only, were criminals were, so much as there was in responsibility, was the-king's was himself, therefore to all thought aware expecting, that he would die before them and get less lot of there exchanged, if so became as likely would regarded for sake youth the-king's they, which toughness the-berserkers.	And with these words from the king, then it was said that the queen herself was the first to discourage this expedition in every respect, and she said it had been planned with little forethought, with these accursed men who were criminals, as much as there was a responsibility for the king himself, all expected that he would get the worst of it and die because of them, if it became as was likely, for the sake of the king's youth and the toughness of the berserkers.
Allir vinir konungs löttu ákafliga fararinnar ok þótti konungr út seldr, ef hann færi við annan mann.	All friends the-king's dissuaded extremely of-the-journey and thought the-king out sold, if he journeyed with another man.	All the king's friends were extremely discouraging of the journey and thought that the king would be done for if he went with only one other man.
Konungr svarar, at ekki mundi tjóa at letja hann.	The-king answered, that not would avail to discourage him.	The king answered that it would be to no avail to try and discourage him.
Ok er allir skildu, at konungr mundi eigi letjast láta, þá verðr til ok svarar máli konungs sá, er Dagfinnr hét.	And when all knew, that the-king would not discouraged allow, then became to also answer the-matter the-king's so, that Dagfinn named.	And when all understood that the king would not be discouraged, then cane an answer to the king's case, who was named Dagfinn.

The Tale of Star-Oddi's Dream (Old Norse)

Old Norse	Literal	English
Hann var hirðmaðr konungs ok konungsskáld.	He was court-man the-king's and the-king's-poet.	He was the king's court man and the king's poet.
"Herra", segir hann, "engan mann veit ek þér meiri sæmð eiga at launa í alla staði en mik.	"Lord", said he, "no person know I to-you more honour have to reward in all places than me.	"Lord," said he, "I know of no man more honorable to you in all things than me.
Er ek ok því skyldari at skiljast aldri við þik, er þú ert í meira háska staddr, ef þér vilið þiggja mitt föruneyti ok fylgð, ok er ek til þessar farar albúinn, þegar þér vilið",	Am I also therefore obliged to separate never with you, that you are the more danger placed, if you wish accept my companionship and follow, and that I to this travel all-prepared, as-soon-as you wish",	I am therefore more obliged to never part with you when you are in more danger if you want to accept my entourage and escort, and I am ready for this journey whenever you want".

4

Old Norse	Literal	English
En þegar þessi maðr, Dagfinnr, var nefndr í sögunni, þá er frá því at segja, er mjök er undarligt, at þá brá því við í drauminum Odda, at hann Oddi sjálfr þóttist vera þessi maðr, Dagfinnr, en gestrinn, sá er söguna sagði, er nú ór sögunni ok drauminum, en þá þóttist hann sjálfr sjá ok vita allt þat, er heðan af er í drauminum.	Then as-soon-as this man, Dagfinn, was named in the-saga, then was from accordingly to say, that much was wonder-like, that then drew therefore with in the-dream Oddi's, that he Oddi himself thought was this man, Dagfinn, but the-guest, so was the-saga telling, was now out-of the-saga and the-dream, and then thought he himself so and knew all that, was from-here of for in the-dream.	But when this man, Dagfinn, was mentioned in the story, it is very strange to say that in Oddi's dream it happened that Oddi himself thought he was this man, Dagfinn, but the guest who told the story is now out of the story and the dream, but then he thought he saw and knew all that is henceforth in the dream.
En nú síðan er drauminn svá at segja sem honum þótti sjálfum fyrir sik bera, Odda, þá þóttist hann vera Dagfinnr ok ráðast í ferðina með konunginum Geirviði.	Then now after in the-dream so to say as he thought himself before himself borne, Oddi, then thought he was Dagfinn and arranging to travel with the-king Geirvid.	But now since the dream is, so to speak, that Oddi then he thought he was Dagfinn and embarked on the journey with King Geirvid.

The Tale of Star-Oddi's Dream (Old Norse)

Old Norse	Literal	English
En er þeir váru albúnir, þá riðu þeir tveir saman með vápnum sínum, til þess er þeir kómu á Jöruskóg, þangat sem illvirkjanna var ván, en þar var svá við vaxit, at gata var breið um skóginn,	Then when they were all-prepared, then rode they two together with weapons theirs, to this that they came to Battle-forest, from-there as the-evil-doers were expecting, then they were so trees grown, that the-way was broad about the-forest,	Then when they were ready the two rode together with their weapons until they came to Battle Forest, where the evil doers were waiting, then the trees were so grown that there was a wide path through the forest.
ok er þeir kómu mjök langt í skóginn, þá er þess getit, at þar varð fyrir þeim hóll einn mjök hár.	and when they came much long in the-forest, then is this told-of, that there was before them hill one much high.	And when they came very far into the forest, it is told that there was a very high hill before them.
Hann var brattr öllum megin.	It was broad all sides.	It was steep on all sides.
Síðan gengu þeir upp á hólinn ok vildu þaðan sjást um ok vita, hverra tíðenda þeir mætti vissir verða.	Afterwards went they up by the-hill and wished then t-look about and know, what news they may know to-be.	Then they went up the hill and from there wanted to look around and know what tidings they might become.
Margt smágrjót var á hóli þessum.	Many small-stones were on hill this.	Many small stones were on this hill.
Þaðan sá þeir víða.	From-there saw they widely.	From there they saw widely.
Þeir geta at líta, hvar ganga tveir menn.	They could to look, where going two men.	They could see where the two men were walking.
Þeir váru miklir vexti ok gengu þegar þangat at hólinum, sem þeir konungr stóðu.	They were great grown and went they from-there to the-hill, as they the-king stood.	They were tall and they immediately walked to the hill where the king stood.
Þessir menn váru báðir vel vápnaðir.	These men were both well weaponed.	These men were both well armed.
En þegar þeir konungr ok Dagfinnr sá þessa menn, þá þóttust þeir vita, at þar váru þeir komnir, Garpr ok Gnýr.	Then as-soon-as they the-king and Dagfinn saw these men, then thought they knew, that there were they coming, Garp and Gny.	But when the king and Dagfinn saw these men, they thought they knew that Garp and Gny had come there.
Þá mælti Dagfinnr:	Then spoke Dagfinn:	Then Dagfinn said,

The Tale of Star-Oddi's Dream (Old Norse)

Old Norse	Literal	English
Herra, ek vil yðr kunnigt gera, at ek er eigi mjök vanr vápnaskipti, ok kann ek lítt at treysta hug mínum né vápnfimi.	Lord, I wish to-you know be, that I am not much accustomed weapons-exchange, and can I a-little to trust mind mine nor weapon-nimble.	Lord, I want to let you know that I am not very accustomed to exchanging arms, and I can scarcely trust my mind or my agility.
Nú vil ek, at þér kjósið um tvá kosti, hvárt þér vilið heldr, at ek ráðist mót berserkjunum með þér, eða villtu, at ek sjá til yðvarrar sameignar af hólinum ok kunna ek frá at segja öðrum mönnum",	Now wish I, that you choose about two benefits, either you wish rather, that I determine-to meet the-berserkers with you, or will-you, that I see that your fight of the-hill and know I from to say to-other people",	Now I want you to choose two options, whether you want me to attack the berserkers with you or you want me to see to your fight from the hill and I can tell other people what happened".
Konungr svarar:	The-king answered:	The king answered:
Ef þér lér nökkut tveggja huga um þetta mál, þá þykkir mér einsætt, at þú sér hér á hólinum ok sjáir heðan til sameignar várrar ok komir eigi nær við vár vápnaskipti",	If you lean somewhat two minds about this matter, then seems to-me evident, that you are here on the-hill and look from-here to the-fight aware and come not near with our weapons-exchange",	If you lean somewhat in two minds about this matter, I think it is decided that you are here on the hill and see from here to the fight and do not come any closer to our exchange of arms.
Dagfinnr tekr þat ráð, sem konungr mælti, ok dvaldist eftir á hólinum ok kemr hvergi nær, ok þykkir honum þat allráðligt, en konungrinn sjálfr ræðst ofan af hólinum í móti stigamönnum.	Dagfinn took this advice, as the-king spoke, and dwelled afterwards on the-hill and came each near, and seemed to-him that advisable, what the-king himself decided over of the-hill in meeting the-robbers.	Dagfinn took the advice which the king had said and stayed on the hill, and came nowhere near, and he thought it wise, but the king himself attacked from the top of the hill against the robbers.
Þar kann eigi glöggliga frá at segja, hversu högg fóru með þeim, ok mun ek þar gera skjóta frásögu, því at þat er þar frá lykðum at segja, at svá skipti hamingjan með þeim, því at konungi var lagit líf ok lykka, at hann bar af báðum illvirkjunum, ok létust þeir af stórum sárum, er konungr hafði þeim veitt.	There known not clearly from to say, how-so blows went between them, and should I there do short from-saying, because that it was there from completion to say, that so exchanged graciousness with them, because that the-king was granted life and luck, that he bore of both evil-doers, and had they of great wounds, that the-king had them given.	It is not clear from there how the blows went with them, and I will make a quick account of it, for it is from there to say that their happiness that was so important to them was exchanged, for the king was given life and happiness, that he bore from both evil doers. and they died of the great wounds which the king had inflicted on them.

The Tale of Star-Oddi's Dream (Old Norse)

Old Norse	Literal	English
Ok eftir þat er illvirkjarnir váru fallnir, þá gengu þeir konungr ok Dagfinnr fram á götuna lengra ok kómu þar at farandi, er stígr lítill lá af þjóðbrautinni í skóginn.	And afterwards that when the-evil-doers were fallen, then went they the-king and Dagfinn from to path longer and came there to travel, where climbed little lying of the-highway in the-forest.	And after the evildoers had fallen, the king and Dagfinn went further out into the path, and came to a place where a small path lay from the highway into the forest.
Þeir höfðu litla stund gengit þann inn litla stíg, áðr brátt gerðist rjóðr mjök mikit í mörkinni, ok stóð þar eitt hús.	They had little awhile gone then the little path, before soon became clearing much greatly in the-border, and stood there one house.	They had walked the small path for a short time before soon there was a lot of clearing in the border and a house stood there.
Þat hús var hátt ok rammgert ok læst ok grafinn lykill í dyrigætti.	The house was tall and firmly-built and locked and the-key buried in doorway.	That house was tall and firmly built, and firmly locked with a key buried in the doorway.
Þeir luku upp húsinu ok gengu þar inn.	They unlocked up the-house and went they in.	They opened the house and went inside.
Þat hús var vel innan búit ok var náliga fullt af alls kyns auðæfum.	The house was well inside prepared and was nearly full of all kinds-of wealthy-treasures.	That house was well furnished and was almost full of all kinds of riches.
Þar váru þeir um nóttina, ok skorti þar hvárki góðan drykk né dýran mat, en um morgininn fóru þeir heimleiðis, ok huldu áðr hræ útilegumannanna.	They were there about the-night, and shortage of neither good drink nor fine food, then about morning travelled they homeward, and covering after corpses the-outlaw-men.	They were there during the night and there was no shortage of good drinks or expensive food, but in the morning they went home and hid the carcasses of the outlaw men before.
En er konungrinn kom heim til ríkis síns, þá varð hann frægr mjök víða um lönd af sínu þrekvirki ok ágætum sigri, ök urðu allir vinir konungsins ok frændr honum fegnir, er hann kom heim með göfugligum sigri, ok þóttust menn hann náliga ór helju heimt hafa, sem var.	Then when the-king came home to kingdom his, then was he famous much with about the-land of his brave-deeds and wonderful victory, and became all friends the-king's and kinsmen his celebrated, that he came home with noble-like victory, and thought people he nearly out-of Hel drawn had, as was.	But when the king came home to his kingdom, he became famous in many lands for his endurance and excellent victory, and all the king's friends and relatives rejoiced when he came home with a noble victory, and it was thought that people had almost recovered him from hell, which they were.

The Tale of Star-Oddi's Dream (Old Norse)

Old Norse	Literal	English
5	**5**	**5**
Nú eftir þenna atburð allan saman lét konungr þings kveðja, ok kemr þar mikit fjölmenni saman.	Now after these events all together had the-king an-assembly called, and came there great many-followers together.	Now after all these events, the king called an assembly and a great many people gathered there.
En er saman var sett þetta it fjölmenna þing, þá sagði konungr þar þessi miklu tíðendi, ok þótti öllum þetta in mesta frægð, sem var, er Geirviðr konungr hafði einn sigr borit af slíkum kempum.	Then when together were sat that the many-men the-assembly, then said the-king there this great news, and thought all this the most fame, which was, that Geirvid the-king had one victory carried of such champion.	And when this large assembly was convened, the king there told this great news, and it was considered by all to be the greatest fame, which was that King Geirvid had won one such a battle.
Síðan bað Geirviðr, at menn skyldi vitja til þess húss, er illvirkjarnir höfðu í borit þat mikla fé, ok skyldi þar hverr taka sitt fé, þat er misst hafði,	Afterwards invited Geirvid, that people should visit to the house, where the-evil-doers had in bore that much wealth, and should there each take his wealth, that was missed had,	Then Geirvid asked that men should visit the house in which the evildoers had brought much money, and that each should take his money which he had lost.
en allir gáfu konungi upp sitt fé, þat sem hverr átti, ok sögðu þat bezt komit, at hann hefði, ok kváðu hann fullu kostat hafa.	but all have the-king up their wealth, that which each had, and said that best came, to him have, and said he fully earned had.	But they all gave to the king what they had, and said that it was best for him to have it, and said that he had earned it in full.
Síðan lét konungr sækja féit ok kastaði á sinni eigu.	Afterwards had the-king sought the-treasure and cast to his ownership.	Then the king fetched the money and cast it into his possession.
Eftir þat lét konungr taka til húsgerðar, ok gerðu menn konungi haug þann, er hann skyldi sitja á.	After that had the-king taken to house-builder, and made people the-king a-mound then, that he should sit on.	After that the king had a house built, and the people made a mound for the king to sit on.
Þá var konungr settr á stól þann, er stóð á hauginum, ok hófu menn hann svá einkum til tígnar ok gáfu honum þá enn af nýju dýrar presentur ok dýrkuðu hann, sem þeir höfðu framast föng á.	Then was the-king sat on throne then, as place on the-mound, and had people him so especially to princely and gave him then but of new precious presents and adored him, as they had foremost possessions of.	Then the king was placed on the throne that stood on the mound, and the people began to honor him, and gave him again expensive gifts, and worshiped him whom they had bestowed.

254

The Tale of Star-Oddi's Dream (Old Norse)

Old Norse	Literal	English
Þess er við getit, þar sem Dagfinnr skáld er, honum kom í hug, at engi mundi skyldari til konunginn at sæma með kvæði en svá sem hann var.	This is with told-of, that as Dagfinn the-poet was, he came to mind, that none would obliged to the-king to honour with a-poem than such as he was.	This is told of Dagfinn the poet, that it occurred to him that no one would be more obliged to the king to honour with a poem than he was.
Síðan gengr Dagfinnr á hauginn upp til konungsins ok fell á kné fyrir hann ok laut honum ok kvaddi hann virðuliga ok sagði honum, at hann hefði kvæði ort um konunginn, ok bað, at hann mundi hlýða.	Afterwards went Dagfinn on the-mound up to the-king and fell to knee before him and place his and greeted him worthily and said to-him, that he had a-poem worded about the-king, and asked, that he would listen.	Then Dagfinn went to the mound up to the king and fell on his knees before him and bowed to him and greeted him respectfully and told him that he had written a poem about the king and asked him to listen.
Konungr játti því blíðliga.	King said accordingly joyfully.	The king agreed joyfully.
Síðan tók Dagfinnr til ok flutti kvæðit, ok var þat flokkr.	Then took Dagfinn to and brought the-poem, and was it flokk.	Then Dagfinn took over and performed the poem, and it was a flokk.
Ok er lokit var kvæðinu, þá þakkar konungr vel ok allir þeir, er við váru staddir, ok sögðu vel ort ok svá sem sæmði tígn ok virðing konungs þeira.	And when ended was the-poem, then thanked the-king well and all there, was with were standing, and said well worded and so as honour prestige and worthy king they.	And when the poem was finished, the king thanked well and all those who were present and said it was well written and so they honored the prestige and worthiness of their king.
Ok sem konungr heyrði, at allir létu vel yfir ok lofuðu mjök kvæðit, þá vildi hann sér láta ok verða stórmannliga ok launa höfðingliga ok vill gefa skáldinu gullhring mikinn, er hann hafði á arminum,	And as the-king heard, that all had all over and praised much the-poem, then willed he himself to-have and worthy great-man-like and reward nobly and wanted-to give the-poet a-gold-ring great, that he had on arm,	And when the king heard that everyone had praised the poem very much, he wanted to be generous and reward the poet with a large gold ring that he had on his arm.
en Dagfinnr vildi eigi hringinn þiggja ok sagði svá, at honum var mikil aufúsa á því at hafa sóma ok virðing af konunginum, en fé kvaðst hann eigi þurfa at þiggja af honum ok kallaði sik ekki skorta, meðan hann heldi honum heilum,	but Dagfinn wished not the-ring accept and said so, that he was great gratitude that therefore to have honour and worth of the-king, that treasure said he not needed to accept of him and claimed himself not shortage, while he held him whole,	But Dagfinn did not wish to accept the ring and said that he was very grateful to have the honour and respect of the king, but he said he did not need to accept it from him because he had no shortage of anything as long as he kept him safe,
"en þeir eru margir aðrir, er þar sjá til fjárins, sem þér eruð",	"but there are many others, that there look to wealth, as to-you are",	but there are any others who look for wealth while looking to you.

The Tale of Star-Oddi's Dream (Old Norse)

Old Norse	Literal	English
Konungi líkar þetta vel.	The-king liked this well.	This pleased the king.

6

Old Norse	Literal	English
Þessu næst er at segja frá þeim tíðendum, at Hjörguðr, kona Hjörvarðar jarls, tók sótt hættliga, ok þarf þar eigi at gera mikinn orðahjaldr, at þessi sótt leiðir Hjörgunni til bana.	This next was to say from they news, that Hjorgunn, wife-of Hjorvard the-earl, took sickness dangerously, and needed there not to do much word-struggle, that this sickness took Hjorgunn to death.	The next thing to tell of news was that Hjorgunn, the wife of Earl Hjorvard, took a dangerous sickness and there is no need to struggle with words to say that this sickness took Hjorgunn to her death.
Síðan var hon erfð ok út borin ok gert eftir hana sem tízka var til í fornum sið eftir ríkar konur.	Afterwards was she honoured and out brought and made after her as fashion was to in ancient traditions after rich women.	Afterwards she was honoured and brought out and so it was done for her in the fashion of ancient traditions of wealthy women.
Jarli þótti mikill skaði eftir dróttning sína, sem ván var, ok harmaði hana mjök ok svá margir aðrir út í frá.	The-earl thought much harm after the-queen himself, as expected was, and mourned her much and so many others out in from.	The earl thought great harm to his queen, which was expected, and mourned her greatly, along with so many others from then on.
Eigi höfðu liðit langir tímar, áðr vinir hans fýstu, at hann skyldi fá sér annarrar konu.	Not had passed long time, before friends his urged, that he should get himself another wife.	It had not been long before his friends wanted him to have another wife.
Hann spurði, hvar þeir sæi honum kvánfang þat, er honum væri virðing í at fá.	He asked, where they saw him a-match that, was to-him being worthy in to get.	He asked where they saw for him a wife that he would be honored to receive.
Þeir tölðu ráðligt, at hann bæði til handa sér Hildigunnar dróttningar, ok sögðu honum mikit uppheldi at þeim ráðahag, ef hann næðist.	They told advice, that he ask for the-hand he Hildigunn the-queen, and said to-him much advancement that they marriage-proposal, if he reached.	They thought it advisable for him to ask for the hand of Queen Hildigunn, and said that there would be much advancement for him if such a marriage could be achieved.
Ok er þetta var oft tját fyrir jarli, þá sýndist á þá leið, því at hann var vitr maðr.	And was that was often expressed before the-earl, then seemed to then laid, therefore that he was wise man.	And when this was often told to the earl, he saw things the same way, because he was a wise man.
Síðan hefir hann upp orð sín ok biðr Hildigunnar dróttningar sér til eiginkonu.	Afterwards had he up worded his and invited Hildigunn the-queen herself to wife.	Then he raised his words and asked Queen Hildigunn to marry him.

The Tale of Star-Oddi's Dream (Old Norse)

Old Norse	Literal	English
Hon var þá enn ekki meir en fertug kona at aldri, ok þótti kostrinn vera inn merkiligsti fyrir allra hluta sakir.	She was then was not more than forty woman in age, and thought distinguished was the remarkable before all things sake.	She was still no more than forty women at the time and was considered the most remarkable option for all intents and purposes.
Ok hvárt sem um þetta var talat lengr eða skemr, þá var þat at ráði gert, at dróttning var gift Hjörvarði jarli með ráði konungs, sonar hennar.	And how as about this was told longer or shorter, then was it that decision made, that the-queen was married Hjorvard the-earl with consent the-king, son hers.	And whether this was talked about longer or shorter, it was decided that the queen should marry Earl Hjorvard, with the consent of her son the king.
Síðan var fengit at virðuligri veizlu ok drukkit brúðhlaup Hjörvarðar jarls ok Hildigunnar dróttningar með miklum veg ok margs konar sóma.	Afterwards was got a worthy feast and drank the-wedding Hjorvard the-earl and Hildigunn the-queen with much way and many kinds-of honour.	Then a worthy feast was held, and the wedding of Earl Hjörvarður and Queen Hildigunn was drunk with great prestige and many honours.
Ok er veizlunni var lokit, þá ferr hverr heim til sinna heimkynna.	And when the-feast was concluded, then travelled each home to their households.	And when the feast was over, everyone went home to their households.
Brátt takast þar miklar ástir í millum þeira, ok eru samfarar þeira sæmiligar ok eigi langar, áðr en þau áttu dóttur.	Soon took there much love in between them, and was interaction theirs honourable and not long, after then they had a-daughter.	Soon there was much love between them and their interaction was honourable, and it was not long after that they had a daughter.
Hon var nefnd Hlaðreið.	She was named Hladreid.	She was named Hladreid.
Svá er sagt, at samför þeira jarls ok dróttningar var eigi löng þaðan í frá, er þau höfðu Hlaðreiði getit, áðr þau tíðendi gerðust, at jarl tekr sótt, ok leiðir hon svá til lands, at hann andast af þeiri sótt.	So was said, that togetherness theirs the-earl and the-queen was not long from-there to from, when they had Hladreid told, before the news made, that earl took sickness, and led it so to the-land, that he died of that sickness.	So it was said that the togetherness of the earl and the queen did not last long after they had Hladreid, before the news came that the earl had taken ill, and so it led through the land, and he died of that sickness.
Þat þótti vera skaði mikill, því at hann var virðuligr höfðingi.	It thought was harm much, because that he was worthy chieftain.	It was thought a great harm because he was a worthy chieftain.
Eftir þessi tíðendi setti Geirviðr konungr sína menn yfir ríkit, þat er jarl hafði átt, ok eignaði sér.	After this the-news set Geirvid the-king his men over the-kingdom, that the earl had owned, and owned himself.	After these tidings King Geirvid put his men over the kingdom which the earl had owned and appropriated.

The Tale of Star-Oddi's Dream (Old Norse)

Old Norse	Literal	English
Þessi tíðendi spyrjast víða, sem ván var, fráfall þvílíks höfðingja.	This news was-heard widely, as expected was, death such-like a-chieftain.	These tidings were widely learned of, as was to be expected, from the demise of such a ruler.
Þar kemr, at þessi tíðendi koma fyrir Hlégunni, dóttur Hjörvarðar jarls, at faðir hennar er andaðr, þar sem hon er í hernaði ok brýtr undir sik víkinga.	There came, to this news came before Hlegunn, daughter Hjorvard the-earl, that father hers had died, there as she was about raiding and subduing under herself vikings.	There came these tidings to Hlegunn, the daughter of Earl Hjorvard, that her father was dead, as she was at war and subduing vikings.
Bregðr henni svá við tíðendin, at hon snýr öllu sínu liði til Gautlands ok herjar þar.	Reaction hers so with news, that she turned all her company to Götaland and raided there.	She reacted to the news by turning all her army towards Götaland and raided there.
Ok svá kemr því máli, at hon lagði undir sik allt þat ríki, er átt hafði faðir hennar.	And so came therefore the-matter, that she had under herself all that kingdom, which owned had father hers.	And then it came to pass that she subdued all the kingdom which her father had possessed.
Síðan sendir hon menn á fund Geirviðar konungs ok bað svá segja honum sín orð, at hann skyldi annathvárt gera at unna henni hálfs ríkis ok landráða við sjálfan sik eða ella skyldi hann búa sik ok sína menn ok koma til móts við hana með sinn her í sund þau, er heita Síldasund, ok berjast við hana þar, ok hefði þat þeira sigr ok gagn, er meiri gæfu stýrði.	Afterwards sent she men to find Geirvid the-king and asked to say to-him her words, that he should another-either do to grant her half the-kingdom and land-ruling with herself his or either should he prepare himself and his men and come to meet with her with her army in a-sound there, was named Herring-sound, and battle with her there, and had that there victory and won, was more luck guided.	Afterwards she sent men to find Geirvid and asked them to tell him her words, that he should either grant her half the kingdom and authority to rule or prepare himself and his men to come to meet with her army in a sound that was named Herringsound and battle with her there, and that victory would be won by whoever had the most luck.

7

Nú er þar til at taka, at sendimenn fóru, þeir er Hléguðr sendi.	Now is there to to take, the messengers travelled, they that Hlegunn sent.	Now we take to the messengers that Hlegunn had sent.
Þat váru skjaldmeyjar.	They were shield-maidens.	They were shield-maidens.
Þær fóru á konungs fund ok báru upp sín erendi fyrir konunginn.	They went to the-king meet and brought up their errand before the-king.	They went to meet the king and presented their message to the king.

The Tale of Star-Oddi's Dream (Old Norse)

Old Norse	Literal	English
Ok er hann heyrði kostaboð Hlégunnar, þá svarar hann skjótt á þessa leið:	And when he heard choice-bid Hlegunn's, then answered he quickly to this laid:	And when he heard Hlegunn's offer, he answered quickly in this way:
Því skjótara skal kjósa sem kostir eru ójafnari, ok vil ek miklu heldr berjast við hana en láta ríki mitt fyrir ágangi hennar",	Because shorter shall choices which choose they-are unequal, and will I much rather fight with her than lose kingdom mine before aggression hers",	I shall sooner choose the more unequal option, and I would much rather fight against it than leave my kingdom to its invasion.
Sendimenn fóru aftr á fund Hlégunnar ok segja henni til svá búins, ok líkaði henni þeira för forkunnliga vel.	Sending-men travelled returning to meet Hlegunn and said to-her to so prepared, and liked her their journey exceedingly well.	The messengers went back to meet Hlegunn and told her what had happened and she was pleased with their journey very much.
Nú er þat at segja, at Geirviðr konungr safnar herliði um allt sitt ríki, ok skal hverr maðr fara í þessa herför, er skildi má valda eða skafti skjóta.	Now is it to say, that Geirvid the-king gathered war-company about all his kingdom, and shall each man travel to this warfare, who shield may wield or spear throw.	Now it is said that King Geirvid gathered armies all over his kingdom, and every man should go on this campaign whether he can carry a shield or throw a spear.
Þess er við at geta, at höfði sá gekk einum megin hjá sundunum, er Hofshöfði heitir, ok skyldi þar hittast lið konungsins allt við höfðann.	This is with to get, that headland that went one side near the-sound, was Temple-Head named, and should there meet company the-king's all with headland.	It is now worth getting that the headland that went on one side near the sound was named Temple-Head and the king and his forces were all to meet at the headland.
En er Geirviðr konungr var albúinn, þá leiddi hann alþýðu til skips.	And when Geirvid the-king was all-ready, then led he the-people to the-ships.	But when King Geirvid was ready, he led the people to the ships.
Þar var í ferð með konungi Dagfinnr skáld.	There was on the-journey with the-king Dagfinn the-poet.	The poet Dagfinn was on the journey there with the king.
En í ofangöngunni til skipanna, þá varð sá atburðr, er geta verðr, þó at lítils vægis þykki vera, at losnaði skóþvengr Dagfinns skálds.	But in over-going to the-ships, then was seen happening, which could worth, though that little weight thought being, that loosened shoe-thong Dagfinn's the-poet.	But in the passage to the ships, the event that can be mentioned, even though it is considered to be of little importance, was that the poet Dagfinn's shoelace came loose.
Ok síðan bindr hann þvenginn, ok þá vaknaði hann ok var þá Oddi, sem ván var, en eigi Dagfinnr.	And after tied he thong, and then woke he and was then Oddi, as expected was, and not Dagfinn.	And then he tied the shoelace, and then he awoke, and it was Odd, as was expected, but not Dagfinn.

The Tale of Star-Oddi's Dream (Old Norse)

Old Norse	Literal	English
Eftir þenna fyrirburð gekk Oddi út ok hugði at stjörnum, sem hann átti venju til jafnan, er hann sá út um nætr, þá er sjá mátti stjörnur.	After these visions went Oddi out and thought that the-stars, which he had habitually to always, that he saw out about night, then was saw might stars.	After these visions Oddi went out and thought about the stars which he had always seen many of at night.
Þá minntist hann á drauminn ok mundi allan nema kvæðit, þat er hann þóttist ort haf a í drauminum, nema þessar vísur sem hér eru ritnar:	Then remembered he the dream and thought everything except the-poem, that which he thought worded had so in the-dream, except this verse which here they-are written:	Then he remembered the dream and remembered everything except the poem he thought he had written in the dream except these verses written here:
Váru austr á Jöruskógi barmar tveir, böls of fylldir, ok til fjár fyrða næmdu við morðráð mörgu sinni.	They-were east in Battle-forest brothers two, spite about filled, and to wealth treasure took with murder many times.	There were in the east at Battle Forest two brothers filled with spite and for wealth they took treasure with murder many times.
En sá gramr, er gera bræðir, hefr tírgjarn tindótt hjarta, ok böðfrækn báða felldi Garp ok Gný Geirviðr konungr.	But that warrior, that made the-brothers, had fame-ambition toothed heart, and valiant both felled Garp and Gny Geirvid the-king.	But that anger that the brothers made had fame ambition with toothed heart and valiant felled both Garp and Gny King Geirvid.
Réð jafngjarn auði at skipta Róðbjarts sonr, rekka mærði af því fé, fyrða kindir, er svikmenni safnat höfðu.	Ruling equally riches to divide Hrodbjart's son, unfolded praise of for wealth, among-people kin, that the-wicked gathered had.	Ruling equally dividing the riches Hrodbjart's son, unfolded praise of that wealth among people and kinsmen that the wicked had collected.
Lét gunndjarfr gefna hringa seggja ætt siklingr Gauta, svát hirðmenn höfðu allir	Had the-treasurer given rings say descendants the-king Of-Goths, so-that court-men had all	the treasurer had given rings say descendants of the king of the Goths so that the court men had all

The Tale of Star-Oddi's Dream (Old Norse)

Old Norse	Literal	English
haukstóls hengiskafla.	hawk-seat mound-of-snow.	a hawk's seat on a mound of snow.
Mun Dagfinnr dýrra mála við lofsorð lúka kvæði. Njóti vel vegs ok landa gramr göfugr gauzkrar þjóðar.	Must Dagfinn dear words with praise conclude the-poem. Appreciate well glory and land warrior noble of-the-Goths king.	Dagfinn must with dear words and with praise conclude the poem. Enjoy well glory and land noble warrior king of the Goths.

8

En sem Oddi hafði úti verit slíka stund sem honum vel líkaði, fór hann inn í rekkju sína ok sofnaði þegar, ok dreymði hann þat sem it fyrra sinn ok hann hafði vaknat frá.	And as Oddi had out been such awhile as he well liked, fared he in to bed his and slept immediately, and dreamed he that which the first his and he had woken from.	But as Oddi had been outside for a moment which he liked well, he went into his bed and fell asleep at once, and dreamed it as the first time he had woken up from.
Þóttist hann þá hafa bundit skóþvenginn ok vera Dagfinnr ok skynda til skipanna.	Seemed to-him then had bound shoe-thong and was Dagfinn and hurrying to-the-ships.	He then thought he had tied the shoelace and was Dagfinn and hurried to the ships.
Svá þótti honum í drauminum sem hann skyldi vera skipstjórnarmaðr.	So seemed to-him in-the-dream as he should be ship-steering-man.	In his dream, he thought he was a captain.
Ok þegar þeir váru búnir til ferðar, fóru þeir með skipaflotann, til þess er þeir kómu við höfðann, ok hittist þar allt lið konungs, ok lögðu síðan fram í sundin Síldasund.	And as-soon-as they were ready to voyage, travel they with ship-fleet, to this that they came with headland, and met there all company the-king's, and laid then from to-the-sound Herring-sound.	And when they were ready to go, they took the fleet until they came to the head, and there met all the king's army, and then put into the channel Herring-sound.
Þá er ok sagt, at þar var komin Hléguðr skjaldmær ok lá þar fyrir í sundunum með skipaflota sinn ok hafði ógrynni liðs ok albúin til orrostu.	Then is also said, that there was coming Hlegunn shield-maiden and lying there before the sound with ship-fleet hers and had mass company and all-prepared to battle.	It is also said that Hlegunn, a shield-bearer, had arrived there and lay there in the channels with her fleet of ships, and had an innumerable army ready for battle.

The Tale of Star-Oddi's Dream (Old Norse)

Old Norse	Literal	English
Síðan lögðu hvárir í mót öðrum, ok laust saman með þeim snarpri sókn, ok var þar inn harðasti bardagi, ok réðst brátt mikit mannfall í hvártveggja liði, en þó hafði eigi lengi staðit bardaginn, áðr en mannfallit hneig í lið konungs, ok hruðust hans skip mjök.	Afterwards laid each to meet each-other, and loosed together with they roughly attacked, and was there the hardest battle, and had soon much people-felled in each-way company, but though had none longer stood the-battle, before the people-felling strain to company the-king's, and cleared his ships much.	Then they put up a fight against each other, and a sharp attack broke out with them, and there was the hardest battle, and soon many casualties were inflicted on both sides, but the battle had not lasted long before the casualty fell to the king's army, and his ships were greatly wrecked.
Þess er ok getit, at Hléguðr varð ekki sén í orrostunni um daginn, ok hugðu menn þó drjúgt at af konungsmönnum, ok þótti þat undarligt.	It is also told-of, that Hlegunn was not seen in the-battle about the-day, and thought men though straight to of the-king's-men, and thought that wonder-like.	It is also mentioned that Hlegunn was not seen in the battle that day, and yet many of the king's men thought of it, and thought it strange.
En er slíku hafði fram farit langa hríð um daginn, þá leitaðist Dagfinnr um með sinni list, ok sá hann þá Hlégunni, ok var þá komin á konungsskipit, ok var þá orðin skipan mikil á hennar hag.	And when such had from gone long while about the-day, then sought Dagfinn about with his skills, and saw he then Hlegunn, and was then come to the-king's-ship, and was then become the-ship great about her circumstance.	But when such a thing had taken place for a long time that day, Dagfinn sought with his art, and he then saw Hlegunn, and had then come to the king's ship, and by then there had been a great order in her favour.
Honum sýndist á henni ylgjarhöfuð geysimikit ok tröllsligt ok biti með því höfuðin af konungsmönnum.	To-him seemed that her she-wolf's-head exceedingly-great and trollish and bit with against heads of the-king's-men.	It seemed to him that her head was a wolf's head, huge and trollish, and that it bit the heads of the king's men.
En er Dagfinnr sá þessi undr, þá steig hann af því skipi, er hann stýrði.	Then when Dagfinn saw this wonder, then leapt he off then the-ship, that he steered.	But when Dagfinn saw this miracle, he got off the ship he was steering.
Þat lá fjarri konungsskipinu.	It lay far-away the-king's-ship.	It was far from the king's ship.
Síðan hljóp hann hvert af öðru, unz hann kom á konungsskipit,	Afterwards ran he each of others, until he came to the-king's-ship,	Then he ran one by one until he came to the king's ship.
en þegar hann kom á fund konungs, þá sagði Dagfinnr, hvat títt var ok hvat stór endemi váru við.	then as-soon-as he came to find the-king, then said Dagfinn, what report was and that great unheard-of was against.	But when he came to meet the king, then Dagfinn said what was to report and what a great unheard of thing they were up against.

The Tale of Star-Oddi's Dream (Old Norse)

Old Norse	Literal	English
Síðan vísaði Dagfinnr konungi til, hvar Hléguðr var, at hann mætti sjá hana, en konungr fekk hana eigi sét sakir fjölkynngi hennar, en hitt sá hann, at menn hans fellu tugum saman.	Afterwards pointed-out Dagfinn the-king to, where Hlegunn was, that he may see her, but the-king got her not seen for-the-sake-of sorcery hers, but found saw he, that men his fell tens together.	Then Dagfinn referred to the king where Hlegunn was, that he might see her, but the king could not see her because of her witchcraft, but he saw that his men fell together by the dozens.
Þá bað Dagfinnr konunginn sjá undir hönd sér ina vinstri, ok svá gerði hann.	Then asked Dagfinn the-king look under hand his the left, and so did he.	Then King Dagfinn asked the king to see under his left hand, and so he did.
En er konungr fór svá með, þá sá hann Hlégunni.	And when the-king did so with, then saw he Hlegunn.	But when the king went with him, he saw Hlegunn.
Síðan gengu þeir báðir saman aftan til siglu.	Afterwards went they both together aft to sail.	Afterwards went they both together aft to sail.
Þá hljóp konungrinn fram með brugðnu sverði, ok þegar hann kemr í höggfæri við Hlégunni, þá höggr hann til hennar með sverðinu, ok kemr höggit á hálsinn, ok hjó hann af henni höfuðit, ok fell þat útbyrðis.	Then ran the-king forwards with drawn sword, and as-soon-as he came to striking-distance with Hlegunn, then struck he to her with sword, and came the-blow to neck, and hewed he off her head, and fell it overboard.	Then the king ran forward with a drawn sword, and when he came under attack with Hlegunn, he struck her with the sword, and the blow came on her neck, and he cut off her head, and it fell overboard.
En er hon var fallin, þá bauð konungrinn kost þeim mönnum, er fylgt höfðu Hlégunni, hvárt þeir vildi heldr halda bardaga upp við hann eða ganga honum til handa.	And when she was fallen, then offered the-king choice they the-people, who followed had Hlegunn, each they willed rather hold battle up with him or go him to hand.	But when she had fallen, the king offered the men who had followed Hlegunn whether they would rather fight him or go to his hand.
En þeir köru skjótt at ganga á konungs vald.	Then they chose quickly to go to the-king's power.	But they soon chose to enter into the king's power.
Ok síðan er Geirviðr lagði á braut ór þeim bardaga, þá lagði hann undir sik allt landit ok setr þar yfir sýslumenn ok friðaði svá allt ríkit.	And afterwards when Geirvid had to away from them the-battle, then had he under his all land and set there over stewards and peace so all the-kingdom.	And since King Geirviður set out from that battle, he conquered the whole country and placed it over the magistrates, and then pacified the whole kingdom.
Síðan helt konungr heim, ok var ger í mót honum dýrðlig veizla.	Afterwards held the-king home, and was made to meet him glorious feast.	Then the king returned home, and a glorious feast was held for him.
Eftir þat var kvatt þings, ok var þat þing allfjölmennt.	After it was summoned assembly, and was the assembly all-many-people.	After that an assembly was convened and that assembly was very crowded.

The Tale of Star-Oddi's Dream (Old Norse)

Old Norse	Literal	English
Var konungrinn Geirviðr settr þá enn á stól af nýju ok hafiðr upp á inn sama haug sem fyrr ok nú til konungs tekinn ok ríkisstjórnar yfir allt Gautland.	Was the-king Geirvid set then was on throne of new and raised up in the same mound as before and now to the-king taken and governor over all Götaland.	King Geirviður was then again put on a chair again and raised on the same mound as before and now taken to the king and the government over all of Götaland.
Gekk þá annarr höfðingi at öðrum upp á hauginn ok gerði til konungsins veg ok sóma, hverr eftir slíku, sem framast hafði föng ok færi á.	Went then one chieftain to another up to the-mound and made to the-king way and honour, each after such, as foremost had power and means of.	Then another chieftain went up to the hill, and made a way for the king, and honored each one according to all that he had.
Dagfinni skáldi kom þat í hug, at engi átti konunginum meiri virðing at launa í alla staði en hann.	Dagfinn the-poet came to the thought, that none had the-king more worthiness to repay in all places than him.	The poet Dagfinn thought that no one had more respect for the king in all respects than he.
Gekk hann síðan upp á hauginn ok kvaddi konunginn vel ok hæverskliga.	Went he then up on the-mound and greeted the-king well and modestly.	He then went up to the mound and greeted the king kindly and modestly.
Konungr tók glaðliga kveðju hans.	King took gladly greeting his.	The king gladly accepted his greeting.
Dagfinnr sagði konunginum deili á því, at hann hafði þá enn ort kvæði um hann af nýju, ok bað, at hann skyldi hlýða, ok kvaðst þá vilja færa kvæðit.	Dagfinn told the-king shared that accordingly, that he had then one worded a-poem about him of new, and asked, that he should listen, and spoke then willed bring the-poem.	Dagfinn told the king that he had written a poem about him again, and asked him to listen, and said he would bring the poem.
Konungrinn svarar, at hann kvaðst gjarna hlýða vilja.	The-king answered, that he said gladly listen willed.	The king replied that he will gladly listen.
Tók þá Dagfinnr ok flutti kvæðit, ok var þat þrítug drápa, er hann þóttist ort hafa.	Took then Dagfinn and brought the-poem, and was it thirty drapa, which he thought worded had.	Then Dagfinn took and recited the poem, and it was thirty stanza drapa which he thought he had written.

The Tale of Star-Oddi's Dream (Old Norse)

Old Norse	Literal	English
En er kvæðinu var lokit, þá þakkaði konungr þat allvel ok dró digran gullhring af hendi sér ok gaf Dagfinni at skáldskaparlaunum, en Dagfinnr vildi eigi þiggja hringinn ok sagðist allt ærit hafa, meðan hann heldi konunginum heilum,	And when the-poem was concluded, then thanked the-king it well and drew a-thick gold-ring of hand his and gave Dagfinn the poet's-reward, but Dagfinn willed not accept the-ring and said all abundance had, as-long-as he held the-king whole,	But when the poem was finished, the king thanked him very well and took a huge gold ring from his hand and gave Dagfinn a poet's reward, but Dagfinn did not want to accept the ring and said he had abundance as long as he kept the king whole.
en Geirviðr konungr lét þat þá í ljós við Dagfinn, at hann skyldi hans sóma meira gera í alla staði heldr en hvers manns annars í sínu ríki, ok bauð honum þat, at hann mundi afla honum kvánfangs, ok sagði svá, at hann mundi þá konu fá honum til handa, er hann vildi helzt kjósa náliga, þess er kostr var í því landi.	but Geirvid the-king had it then to light with Dagfinn, that he should him honour more do than all places rather than each man other in his kingdom, and offered him that, to him would gain him a-match, and said so, that he would then a-wife get him to hand, that he willed rather choose nearly, this as choice was in then the-land.	But King Geirvid then made it clear to Dagfinn that he should do him more honour in all respects than any other man in his kingdom, and offered him that he would give him a wife, and said that he would get a woman for him, which he preferred to choose, close by in the land whom Dagfinn most wanted to marry.
Dagfinnr tók þessu máli vel, sem ván var, er konungrinn vildi svá mikinn gera hans sóma, ok svarar:	Dagfinn took this matter well, as expected was, as the-king willed so much to-do him honour, and answered:	Dagfinn took this matter well, as was to be hoped, since the king wished so much to do him honour, and answered:
Ef þetta skal allt efna af yðvarri hendi við mik, sem nú er um mælt, þá er ekki því at leyna, at er sá kostrinn, at gjarna munda ek mér unna ok þú átt ok mest undir sjálfum þér",	If this shall all be-carried-out of your hand with me, as now is about spoken, then is not because that concealing, that is so choice, that gladly would I to-me love and you have and the-most under yourself to-you",	If all this is to be done by your hand with me, as is now said, then it is no secret that the choice is that I would gladly treat myself and you have and most of all under yourself.
Konungr mælti:	King spoke:	The king said,
Hver er sú kona, er þú talar til?"	Who is this woman, that you speak to?"	Who is the woman you are talking to?
Dagfinnr svarar:	Dagfinn answered:	Dagfinn answered:
Þat er Hlaðreið, systir þín.	It is Hladreid, sister yours.	It is Hladreid, your sister.
Hon er svá kvenna, at mér er mestr hugr á at fá, ella hygg ek, at fyrir muni farast um kvánföngin",	She is so the-woman, that to-me is the-greatest thinking that to marry, otherwise think I, that for should go about a-match",	She's so the woman that I'm most interested in marrying, otherwise I think about the match going".

The Tale of Star-Oddi's Dream (Old Norse)

Old Norse	Literal	English
Konungr sagði, at þat skyldi ok eigi undan draga við Dagfinn, er honum þótti sinn sómi vaxa við.	The-king said, that it should and not under drawn with Dagfinn, that he thought his honour grow with.	The king said that nothing should be denied to Dagfinn which he thought would increase his honour.
Hlaðreið konungssystir var þá gjafvaxta ok þó ung mjök at aldri, en kvenna var hon fegrst ok fríðust ok hezt at sér ger um alla hluti.	Hladreid the-king's-sister was then of-marriage-grown and though young much in age, but woman was she fairest and most-beautiful and the-best that herself made about all things.	Hlaðreið, the king's sister, was then gifted and yet very young, but of women she was the most fair and beautiful and the best at everything.
En hvárt sem þetta mál var talat lengr eðr skemr, þá ræðst þat af, að Hlaðreið var föstnuð Dagfinni skáldi.	And how as this matter was told longer or shorter, then decided it of, that Hladreid was betrothed-to Dagfinn the-poet.	But whether this matter was discussed longer or shorter, it was determined that Hladreid was engaged to the poet Dagfinn.
Síðan var þar fengit at boði, ok var þar ger in vegligasta veizla í alla staði með inum heztum tilföngum, því at ekki vantaði til, þat er hafa þurfti.	Afterwards was there got to announced, and was there done the greatest feast in all places with the best means, because that not lacking to, this was had need.	Then it was announced and there was the most successful feast in all respects with the best resources because there was no shortage of what was needed.
Þar var ok allt it hezta mannval, þat er í var landinu.	There were also all the best people, that were in were the-land.	There was also all the best selection of people in the country.
Var nú drukkit brúðhlaup þeira með inni mestu sæmð ok prýði.	Was now drunk the-wedding they with the most honour and finery.	Their wedding was now drunk with the greatest honour and splendor.
En er veizluna þraut, þá fór hverr til sinna heimkynna, er þangat hafði sótt.	And when the-feast finished, then travelled each to their households, that from-there had attended.	But when the feast ended, everyone who had gone there went to their own home.
En með þeim Dagfinni ok Hlaðreiði tókust brátt miklar ástir, ok var þeira samför einkar góð.	And between them Dagfinn and Hladreid took soon much love, and were they together very good.	And between Dagfinn and Hladreidi, they soon fell in love and their relationship was very good.
En er svá kurteisliga var komit ráðahag Dagfinns sem nú er frá sagt, þá var lokit drauminum, ok vaknaði hann þá, er Oddi var raunar.	But when so courtly was come marriage Dagfinn's as now was from said, then was ended the-dream, and awoke he then, that Oddi was actually.	But when in such a courtly fashion had Dagfinn's marriage taken place, as related, the dream ended, and he awoke that was actually Oddi.

The Tale of Star-Oddi's Dream (Old Norse)

Old Norse	Literal	English
# 9	# 9	# 9
Síðan hugði Oddi at um draum sinn ok mundi gersamliga drauminn allan, bæði inn fyrra ok svá inn síðara, ok minntist síðan á drápuna, þá er hann þóttist síðar kveðit hafa, ok mundi hann eigi fleira í kvæðinu heldr en þessar ellifu vísur, sem nú eru hér ritnar ok þetta er upphaf at:	Afterwards thought Oddi that about dream his and remembered completely the-dream all, both the first and so the latter, and remembered afterwards the drapa, then that he thought afterwards recited had, and would he not more of the-poem rather than these eleven verses, as now they-are here written and this is beginning of:	Then Odd thought of his dream and remembered the whole dream, both the first and then the second, and then remembered the drapa when he was thought to have recited later and he remembered no more in the poem than these eleven verses now written here and this is the beginning of:
Geirviðr of nam greiða gang, svát skreið ór þangi,	Geirvid of took ready going, so glided through seaweed,	Geirvid took ready going as gliding through seaweed
ok byrsóta beitti barð út of lágarða, ok seglhættu sóttu snarpir meðr ór veðri,	and windswept biting ship out about the-surf, and sail-danger attended sharply between with the-weather,	and windswept biting a ship out and about in the surf. and danger attended the sails sharp with the weather,
blés við hún, und Höfða,	blew with her, under Temple-Head,	blew against her under Temple Head,
harðan vegg of seggjum.	hard wall with men.	a hardened wall of men.
Skeið náði þá skríða	Sheathed-sword caught then action	The sheathed sword then caught ation
skjót of bylgjur ljótar. Fóru dyggir drengir á dýrmörum hlýra. Þar sák frægra fyrða för prúðligsta görva. Þó er gotneskra gumna Geirviðr konungr þeira.	launched about waves hideous. Travelled virtuous warriors in treasured bows. There saw famous fighters went most-prolific clearly. Yet of Gothic men Geirvid the-king theirs.	launched about hideous waves. Virtuous warriors travelled in treasured bows. There I saw famous fighters going most prolific and clearly. Yet of the Gothic men Geirvid is their king.
Sigldum Hofs fyrir höfða	We-sailed Temple before headland	We sailed to Temple Head before the Headland
herðendr skipa ferðum göndul, grams, með landi,	hardy the-ship's course Göndul, warriors, with land,	hardy, the ship's course, Gondul, the warriors, with the land,
gótt ráð var þat dróttar, unz í Síldasundi sigrgöfgaðir vigrum hjuggu horskir seggir hjörs andskota börva.	good advice was that right, ours in Herring-sound victory-gift-gods spears striking brave said sword enemies trees.	good advice that was right, until in Herring-sound victorious god gifted spears striking bravely said the enemy sword trees.

The Tale of Star-Oddi's Dream (Old Norse)

Old Norse	Literal	English
Ok skjaldmeyja skjóma	And shield-maidens shimmering	And shield-maidens shimmering
skerðendr ok svá gerðu,	diminished and so doing,	did so diminish
at varfærir véar	with caution the-gods	with the caution of the gods
í vág fyrir lágu.	in inlet before laying-to.	in the inlet before laying-to.
Gátu ljónar líta	Could the-men see	The men could see
leiðangrs flota breiðan.	expedition fleet wide.	the expedition fleet wide.
Hilmis fór und hjálmi	Helmsman went under the-helm	The helmsman went under the helm,
hirð, sú er vörn of firrðisk.	court-men, so were defended over the-firth.	The court men, so were defended over the firth.
Brátt vöknuðu virðar	Soon awoke men	Soon awoke men
at vígboði þjóðar,	that battle-bidding great-river,	to the battle-bidding people
þá er Hlégunnar hestar	then were Hlegunn's horses	then were Hlegunn's horses
hafrastar mjök þustu	eagerly most flailing	eagerly most flailing
ok snarráðir sóttu	and quickly attended	and quickly attended
siklings vinir þingat.	the-king's friends assembled.	the king's friends assembled.
Þó er gotneskra gumna	Yet of Gothic men	And yet of all the Gothic men,
Geirviðr konungr þeira.	Geirvid king theirs.	Geirvid was their king.
Ok hnigsólar Högna	And stricken-sun Hogni's	And Hogni's stricken sun
hríð æxti þá síðan	awhile increased then after	increased awhile, then afterwards
blóðísunga beiðir,	blood-helmeted demanded,	the blood-helmeted demanded,
bragna konr, af magni,	heroes descended, of strength,	heroes descended, of strength,
en vígroða víða	then warfare wide	then warfare wide
varp af rómu snarpri.	thrown of battle rough.	thrown of battle rough.
Sjár varð dökkr af dreyra,	The-sea became dark of gore,	The sea became dark with gore
drótt þá er hríðmál sótti.	people then were storm encountered.	people then were storm encountered.
Svipun gerðisk þar sverða,	Swooping came there swords,	Swooping came there swords,
saman kómu þar rómu,	together came there a-roar,	together came there a-roar
göndul varð fyrir grundu,	Göndul became before ground,	Göndul fell to the ground,
grams drótt því vel sótti.	warriors right because well attended.	warriors right because that well attended.
Geirviðr of vá geiri,	Geirvid too guarded spears,	Geirvid too guarded spears,
geirvaldr, í hlökk þeiri.	spear-guardian, in looking-forward there.	spear-guardian in looking-forward there.
Blóðár sá ek í blóði.	Bloodied saw I in blood.	Bloodied, saw I in blood.
Blóð stökk of skor þjóða.	Blood leapt about across people.	Blood leapt about across the people.
Gerði hríð af hörðu	Made awhile of hordes	Made awhile of hordes

The Tale of Star-Oddi's Dream (Old Norse)

Old Norse	Literal	English
hirð sú, er fylkir stýrði.	court-men so, were commanded steered.	court-men so were commanding steered.
Margr er gramr af gengi göfugr tíginna jöfra. *Spyrkat ek frægra fyrða ferð snjallari verða.* *Þó er gotneskra gumna Geirviðr konungr þeira.*	Many were warriors of going noble high-born ruler. Learned I fame among-people journey most-valiant becomes. Though are Gothic men Geirvid the-king theirs.	Many were warriors of going noble high-born rulers. Learned I fame among-people journey most-valiant becomes. And yet of all the Gothic men, Geirvid was their king.
Hlégunnar leit ek hingat harðráðar ódáðir. *Ýfð með ylgjar höfði eiskranlig réð geisa.* *Trölls kjafta sá ek tyggja tönnum hold af mönnum.* *Með hnitgeirum hváfta herða sókn of gerði.*	Hlegunn sought I here hard-headed abhorrence. Bristling with wolf's head rage fixed furiously. Trolls jaws saw I chewing teeth the-bodies of men. With battle-spears wafting hard attack with done.	Hlegunn sought I here hard-headed abhorrence bristling with wolf's head rage fixed furiously. Troll's jaws saw I chewing teeth the-bodies of men. With battle-spears wafting a hard attack was done.
Annat sté ek af öðru Áta skíð of víði, unz glæsimar Gylfa gekk með hilmis rekkum, *ok ek siklingi sagðak, sýslu ægis geisla hvé grimmhuguð gerði Gerðr of vígaferði.*	One stepped I to another Stain wood about wood, until gleaming Gylfi went with the-helmsman upright, and I the-king told, realm Aegir's gleam how grimly done Made too slayings.	I stepped from one to another stained wood about wood until gleaming Gylfi went with the helmsman upright and I told the king the realm of Aegir's gleam how grimly done made too slayings.
Gramr leit hitt, hvar hafði *Hörn hvergymis stjörnu höfuð á hauka stofni heiðingja sér brúðar.* *Ásynju lét elda örvígr konungr hníga flóðs af fyllar meiði frægr, hinn er ekki vægði.*	Warrior sought to-meet, where had Angled each star had upon hawk stem wolf her bride. The-goddesses had flames un-swinging the-king felled flood of full beam far-famed, that was no mercy.	The warrior sought to meet where had each star anged had upon her hawk stem the wolf her bride. The Goddesses had flames unswinging the king felled flood of full beam far-famed, that was no mercy.
Nú er draum þessum lokit, er Stjörnu-Odda dreymði, eftir því sem hann sjálfr hefir sagt,	Now is the-dream this concluded, that Star-Oddi dreamed, after according as he himself has said,	Now this dream is over that Star-Oddi dreamed according to what he himself has said.

The Tale of Star-Oddi's Dream (Old Norse)

Old Norse	Literal	English
ok má víst undarligr ok fáheyrðr þykkja þessi fyrirburðr, en þó þykkir flestum líkligt, at hann muni þat eina sagt hafa, er honum hafi svá þótt verða í drauminum, því at Oddi var reiknaðr bæði fróðr ok sannsögull.	and may vision wonder-like and unusual seem this vision, but though seems most likely, that he would that only told have, what he had so thought happened in the-dream, because that Oddi was counted both wise and truthful.	And this phenomenon may be considered strange and unheard of, but most people still think that he will have said the only thing that seemed to him to be the case in the dream, because Oddur was considered both knowledgeable and truthful.
Má ok ekki undrast, þótt kveðskaprinn sé stirðr, því at í svefni var kveðit.	May also not wonder, thought poetry-making being stiff-footed, because that in sleep was recited.	It is not surprising that the poetry is stiff because it was recited in sleep.

Word List (Old Norse to English)

Word List (Old Norse to English)

Old Norse	English

A, a

Old Norse	English
a	so
að	that
aðra	other
aðrir	others
af	from, of, of, off, to
afla	gain
aflaði	obtained
afli	strength
aftan	aft
aftr	back, returning
albúin	all-prepared
albúinn	all-prepared, all-ready
albúnir	all-prepared
aldri	age, age, never, never
aldrigi	never
aldrs	of-age
aldrskominn	come-of-age
alla	all, all
allan	all, everything
allbráðliga	all-un-forethought
allfjölmennt	all-many-people
allir	all, all
allra	all, all
allráðligt	advisable
allri	all
alls	all
allt	all, all
allvel	well
alskipuð	fully-prepared
alþýðu	the-people
alvápnuðu	all-weaponed
andaðr	died
andast	died, died
andskota	enemies
annan	another, another
Annarr	one, one, the-other
annarrar	another
annars	anything-else, other, otherwise
annat	another, one
annathvárt	another-either, either-way
arminum	arm
at	a, in, it, of, so-as, that, the, then, to, with
atburð	events
atburðr	events, happening
atgervi	deeds
athæfi	behaviour
auðæfum	wealthy-treasures
auði	riches
aufúsa	gratitude
austr	east

Á, á

Old Norse	English
á	about, at, by, in, of, on, that, the, then, to, upon
ábyrgð	responsibility
áðr	after, before
ágætum	wonderful
ágangi	aggression
áheyrsla	to-hear
ákafliga	extremely
ástir	love, love
ástúð	affection
ástvinum	beloved
Ásynju	the-goddesses
Áta	stain
átt	have, owned
átta	eight
átti	had
áttu	had
ávallt	always
áverka	injury

Æ, æ

Old Norse	English
ægis	Aegir's (name)
ærit	abundance
æsku	youth
ætla	intend

Word List (Old Norse to English)

Old Norse	English
ætlat	intend
ætt	descendants, lineage
æxti	increased

B, b

Old Norse	English
bað	asked, invited
báða	both
báðir	both
báðu	asked
báðum	both
bæði	ask, both
bana	death
bar	bore, there
barð	ship
bardaga	battle, the-battle
bardagi	battle
bardaginn	the-battle
barmar	brothers
barn	child
barna	child
báru	brought
batnaði	bettering
bauð	offered
beðinn	asking
beiddi	asked
beiðir	demanded
beina	assistance
beitti	biting
bera	borne
berjast	battle, fight
berserkina	berserkers
berserkir	berserkers
berserkjanna	the-berserkers
berserkjunum	the-berserkers
betr	better
bezt	best
beztu	best
beztum	best
biðr	invited
bindr	tied
biti	bit
bjó	lived
blés	blew
blíðliga	joyfully
Blóð	blood
Blóðár	bloodied
blóði	blood
blóðísunga	blood-helmeted
böðfrækn	valiant
boði	announced
boðit	invited
böls	spite
borðum	the-tables
borin	brought
borit	bore, brought, carried
börva	trees
brá	drew
bræðir	the-brothers
bragna	heroes
brátt	soon
brattr	broad
braut	away
Bregðr	reaction
breið	broad
breiðan	wide
brott	away
brúðar	bride
brúðhlaup	the-wedding
brugðnu	drawn
brýtr	subduing
búa	prepare, prepared
búins	prepared
búit	preparations, prepared
bundit	bound
búnir	ready
burt	away
bylgjur	waves
byrjaði	began
byrsóta	windswept

D, d

Old Norse	English
Dagfinn	Dagfinn (name)
Dagfinni	Dagfinn (name)
Dagfinnr	Dagfinn (name)
Dagfinns	Dagfinn's (name)
daginn	the-day
deili	shared

Word List (Old Norse to English)

Old Norse	English
digran	a-thick
dökkr	dark
dóttur	a-daughter, daughter
draga	drawn
drápa	drapa
drápu	killed
drápuna	drapa
draum	dream, the-dream
drauminn	dream, the-dream
drauminum	the-dream
drengir	warriors
dreymði	dreamed
dreyra	gore
drjúgt	straight
dró	drew
drótt	people, right
dróttar	right
dróttning	the-queen
dróttningar	queen, the-queen
dróttningin	the-queen
drukkit	drank, drunk
drykk	drink
dvaldist	dwelled
dvelja	dwell
dyggir	virtuous
dýran	fine
dýrar	precious
dýrðlig	glorious
dyrigætti	doorway
dýrkuðu	adored
dýrmörum	treasured
dýrra	dear

E, e

Old Norse	English
eða	and, or
eðr	or
ef	if
efna	be-carried-out
eftir	after, afterwards
eiga	have, only
eigi	none, not
eiginkonu	wife
eignaði	owned
eigu	ownership
eina	only
einkar	very
einkum	especially, particularly
einn	one, only
eins	one
einsætt	evident
einum	one
eiskranlig	rage
eitt	one
eitthvert	some-time
ek	I
ekki	no, not
elda	flames
eldri	older
ella	either, or-else, otherwise
ellifu	eleven
elligar	otherwise
en	and, but, however, than, that, the, then, to, what, which
enda	and, with
endemi	unheard-of
engan	no
engi	no, none, not
enn	but, one, that, was
er	am, are, as, for, had, in, is, of, that, the, was, were, what, when, where, which, who
erendi	errand
erfð	honoured
erfi	a-toast
erfinu	the-toast
ert	are
Eru	are, they-are, was
eruð	are
eyjarinnar	the-island

F, f

Old Norse	English
fá	get, give, marry
faðir	father
færa	bring

273

Word List (Old Norse to English)

Old Norse	English
færi	journeyed, means, travel, went
fága	cultivate
fáheyrðr	unusual
fallin	fallen
fallinn	disposed
fallnir	fallen
fám	few
far	travel
fara	go, to-travel, travel, travelled
farandi	travel
farar	travel
fararinnar	of-the-journey
farast	go
farit	gone, travelling
farmóðr	travel-weary
fást	get
fátkaðist	few
fé	treasure, wealth
feðr	father
fegnir	celebrated
fegrst	fairest
féit	the-treasure
fekk	got
Félítill	fee-little
fell	fell
felldi	felled
fellu	fell
fengit	got
ferð	journey, the-journey
ferðar	journey, voyage
ferðina	travel, travelling
ferðinni	the-journey
ferðum	course
ferr	it-went, travelled
fertug	forty
firrðisk	the-firth
fiska	fishing
fjár	wealth
fjárins	wealth
fjarri	far-away
fjölkynngi	sorcery
fjölmenna	many-men
fjölmennan	followers-many
fjölmenni	followers, followers-many, many-followers
Flateyjar	Flatey (place)
fleira	more
flestum	most
flóðs	flood
flokkr	flokk
flota	fleet
flutti	brought
föður	father
fólki	folk
föng	possessions, power
fór	did, fared, travelled, went
för	journey, went
forkunnliga	exceedingly
fornum	ancient
fórst	travelled
fóru	going, travel, travelled, went
föruneyti	companionship
föstnuð	betrothed-to
Frá	from
frægð	fame
frægr	famous, far-famed
frægra	fame, famous
frændr	kinsmen
fráfall	death
fram	forwards, from
frama	fame
framast	foremost
frami	courage
frásaga	from-to-say
frásögu	from-saying
fremð	honour
friðaði	peace
fríðust	most-beautiful
fróðr	wise
fullgert	full-done
fullkomnir	fully-come
fullt	full
fullu	fully
fund	find, meet
fúsastr	willing
fylgð	follow
fylgi	follows

274

Word List (Old Norse to English)

Old Norse	English
fylgja	follow
fylgt	followed
fylkir	commanded
fyllar	full
fylldir	filled
fyrða	among-people, fighters, treasure
fyrir	because, before, for
fyrirburð	visions
fyrirburðr	vision
fyrr	before
fyrra	first
fyrst	first
fýstu	urged

G, g

Old Norse	English
gæfa	good-fortune
gæfu	luck
gaf	gave
gáfu	gave, have
gagn	won
gamall	old
gang	going
ganga	go, going
Garp	Garp (name)
Garpr	Garp (name)
gata	the-way
Gátu	could
Gauta	of-Goths
Gautland	Götaland (place)
Gautlandi	Götaland (place)
Gautlands	Götaland (place)
gauzkrar	of-the-Goths
gefa	give
gefna	given
geiri	spears
geirvaldr	spear-guardian
Geirvið	Geirvid (name)
Geirviðar	Geirvid (name)
Geirviði	Geirvid (name)
Geirviðr	Geirvid (name)
geisa	furiously
geisla	gleam
gekk	went
gengi	going
gengit	gone
gengr	went
gengu	went
ger	done, made
gera	be, do, made, to-do
gerði	did, done, made
gerðisk	came
gerðist	became, begins, happened
Gerðr	made
gerðu	doing, made
gerðust	made
gersamliga	completely
gert	done, made
gerzt	done
gestrinn	the-guest
geta	could, get
getit	told, told-of
geysimikit	exceedingly-great
gift	married
gistingar	guest
gjafvaxta	of-marriage-grown
gjarna	gladly
glaðliga	gladly
glæsimar	gleaming
glöggliga	clearly
Gný	Gny (name)
Gnýr	Gny (name)
góð	good
góðan	good
góðum	good
göfga	noble
göfugligum	noble-like
göfugr	noble
göndul	Göndul (place)
görva	clearly
gotneskra	Gothic (name)
gótt	good
götuna	path
grafinn	the-key
gramr	warrior, warriors
grams	warriors
greiða	ready
grimmhuguð	grimly
grundu	ground

Word List (Old Norse to English)

Old Norse	English
gullhring	a-gold-ring, gold-ring
gumna	men
gunndjarfr	the-treasurer
Gylfa	Gylfi (name)

H, h

Old Norse	English
hægliga	comfortable
hætta	conclude
hættliga	dangerously
hæverskliga	modestly
haf	had
hafa	had, have
hafði	had
hafi	had, have
hafiðr	raised
hafrastar	eagerly
haft	had
hag	circumstance
halda	hold
hálfs	half
hálsinn	neck
hamingjan	graciousness
hana	her, she
handa	hand, the-hand
handar	hand
Hann	he, him, it, to-him
hans	him, his, of-him
hár	high
harðan	hard
harðasti	hardest
harðfengi	toughness
harðráðar	hard-headed
harmaði	mourned
háska	danger
hátt	tall
háttar	kind
haug	a-mound, mound
hauginn	the-mound
hauginum	the-mound
hauka	hawk
haukstóls	hawk-seat
heðan	from-here
hefði	had, have
hefi	have

Old Norse	English
hefir	had, has, have
hefjast	start
hefr	had
heiðingja	wolf
heilum	whole
heim	home
heima	home
heiman	home
heimkynna	households
heimleiðis	homeward
heimt	drawn
heita	named
heitir	named
heitit	dominion
heldi	held
heldr	rather
Helgason	son-of-Helgi (name)
heljarmenn	accursed-men
helju	Hel (place)
helt	held
helzt	rather
hendi	hand
hengiskafla	mound-of-snow
hennar	her, hers
henni	her, hers, she, to-her
her	army
hér	forces, here, she
herða	hard
herðendr	hardy
herför	warfare
herjar	raided
herklæðum	war-clothes
herliði	war-company
hernað	raiding
hernaði	raiding
Herra	lord
hestar	horses
hét	named, was-named
heygðr	buried
heyrði	heard
heyrt	heard
hezt	the-best
hezta	best
heztum	best
Hildiguðr	Hildigunn (name)

Word List (Old Norse to English)

Old Norse	English
Hildigunnar	Hildigunn (name)
Hilmis	helmsman, the-helmsman
hina	then
hingat	here
hinn	that
hirð	court, court-men, retainers
hirðin	courtiers
hirðmaðr	court-man
hirðmenn	court-men
hirðmönnum	court-men
hitt	found, to-meet
hittast	meet
hittir	found
hittist	met
hjá	near
hjálmi	the-helm
hjarta	heart
hjó	hewed
Hjörguðr	Hjorgunn (name)
Hjörgunni	Hjorgunn (name)
hjörs	sword
Hjörvarðar	Hjorvard (name)
Hjörvarði	Hjorvard (name)
Hjörvarðr	Hjorvard (name)
hjuggu	striking
Hlaðreið	Hladreid (name)
Hlaðreiði	Hladreid (name)
Hléguðr	Hlegunn (name)
Hlégunnar	Hlegunn (name), Hlegunn's (name)
Hlégunni	Hlegunn (name)
hljóp	ran
hlökk	looking-forward
hlut	lot
hluta	things
hluti	things
hlutum	things
hlýða	listen, obey
hlýddi	followed
hlýra	bows
hneig	strain
hníga	felled
hnigsólar	stricken-sun
hnitgeirum	battle-spears
hóf	began
höfða	headland, Temple-Head (place)
höfðann	headland
höfði	head, headland
höfðingi	chieftain
höfðingja	a-chieftain, chieftains
höfðingjum	chieftains
höfðingliga	nobly
höfðu	had
Hofs	temple
Hofshöfði	Temple-Head (place)
hófu	had
höfuð	had
höfuðin	heads
höfuðit	head
högg	blows
höggfæri	striking-distance
höggit	the-blow
höggr	struck
hógligr	comfortably
Högna	Hogni's (name)
hold	the-bodies
hóli	hill
hólinn	the-hill
hólinum	the-hill
hóll	hill
hon	her, it, she
hönd	hand
honum	he, he, him, him, his, his, to-him
hörðu	hordes
Hörn	angled
horskir	brave
hræ	corpses
hríð	awhile, while
hríðmál	storm
hringa	rings
hringinn	the-ring
Hróðbjart	Hrodbjart (name)
Hróðbjarti	Hrodbjart (name)
Hróðbjartr	Hrodbjart (name)
Hróðbjarts	Hrodbjart's (name)
hruðust	cleared
hug	mind, thought
huga	minds

Word List (Old Norse to English)

Old Norse	English
hugði	thought
hugðu	thought
hugr	thinking
Hugsat	think
hulðu	covering
hún	her
hús	house
húsbóndi	housemaster
húsgerðar	house-builder
húsinu	the-house
húss	house
hváfta	wafting
hvar	where
hvárir	each
hvárki	neither
hvárt	each, either, how
hvártveggja	each-way
hvat	that, what
hvé	how
Hver	who
hvergi	each
hvergymis	each
hverjum	each
hverr	each, who
hverra	what
hvers	each
hversu	how-so
hvert	each
hygg	think

I, i

Old Norse	English
iðn	crafts
illvirki	outrages
illvirkjanna	for-the-evil-doers, the-evil-doers
illvirkjar	evil-doers
illvirkjarnir	criminals, the-evil-doers
illvirkjunum	evil-doers
in	the
ina	the
inn	in, the
innan	inside, within
inni	the
ins	the
inum	the, the-others
it	the

Í, í

Old Norse	English
í	about, at, in, of, on, than, the, to
Íslandi	Iceland (place)

J, j

Old Norse	English
jafnaldra	equal-age
jafnan	always
jafngjarn	equally
jarl	earl, the-earl
jarli	the-earl
jarls	the-earl
jarlsdóttir	the-earl's-daughter
játti	said
jöfra	ruler
Jöruskóg	Battle-forest (place)
Jöruskógi	Battle-forest (place)
Jöruskógr	Battle-forest (place)

K, k

Old Norse	English
kæmist	comes
kallaði	claimed
kallaðr	called
kann	can, known
kastaði	cast
kaupast	redeem
kaupferðir	merchant-voyages
kempum	champion
kemr	came
kindir	kin
kjafta	jaws
kjósa	choices, choose
kjósið	choose
kné	knee
kom	came
koma	came, come

Word List (Old Norse to English)

Old Norse	English
komin	come, coming
kominn	come
komir	come
komit	came, come
komnir	come, coming
kómu	came
kona	wife, wife-of, woman
konar	kinds-of
konr	descended
konu	a-wife, wife
konung	the-king
konungdóminn	kingdom
konungi	the-king
konunginn	the-king
konunginum	the-king
konungr	king, the-king
konungrinn	the-king, the-king's, this-king
konungs	king, the-king, the-king's
konungsins	the-king, the-king's
konungsmönnum	the-king's-men
konungsskáld	the-king's-poet
konungsskipinu	the-king's-ship
konungsskipit	the-king's-ship
konungssystir	the-king's-sister
konur	women
köru	chose
kost	choice
kostaboð	choice-bid
kostat	earned
kosti	benefits
kostir	choose
kostr	choice
kostrinn	choice, distinguished
kunna	know
kunnigt	know, known
kurteisliga	courtly
kvað	said, spoke
kvaddi	greeted
kvaðst	said, spoke
kváðu	said
kvæða	announced
kvæði	a-poem, the-poem
kvæðinn	poetry
kvæðinu	the-poem
kvæðit	the-poem
kvánfang	a-match
kvánfangs	a-match
kvánföngin	a-match
kvángaðr	married
kvatt	summoned
kveðit	recited
kveðja	called
kveðju	greeting
kveðskaprinn	poetry-making
kveldit	evening
kvenna	the-woman, woman
kvennasið	woman's-customs
kyns	kinds-of

L, l

Old Norse	English
lá	lay, lying
læst	locked
lágarða	the-surf
lagði	had
lagðist	lay
lagit	granted
lágu	laying-to
land	land
landa	land, lands
landi	land, the-land
landinu	the-land, the-land
landit	land
landráða	land-ruling
lands	lands, the-land, the-lands
landsfólkinu	lands-folk
landsfólkit	the-land's-people
landsmönnum	lands-people
landsstjórnin	the-government
landstjórnar	governing
langa	long
langar	long
langir	long
langskip	longships
langt	long
láta	allow, allowed, leave, let, lose, to-have
látast	die

Word List (Old Norse to English)

Old Norse	English
latti	discouraged
launa	repay, reward
laust	loosed
laut	place
leið	company, laid, passes, way
leiðangrs	expedition
leiddi	led
leiðir	led, took
leit	sought
leita	search, searching, seeking
leitaðist	sought
lengi	longer
lengr	longer
lengra	longer
lér	lean
lét	had
letja	discourage
letjast	discouraged
létu	had
létust	had
leyna	concealing
lið	company, crew
liði	company, crew
liðit	passed
liðs	company
liðskosti	provisions
líf	life
lifði	lived
lífi	alive
líflát	life-less
liggja	camped
líka	like
líkaði	liked
líkar	liked
líkligt	likely
list	skills
líta	look, see
lítil	little
lítill	little
lítils	little
litla	little
lítt	a-little, little
ljónar	the-men
ljós	light
ljósliga	lightly
ljótar	hideous
lofsorð	praise
lofuðu	praised
lögðu	laid
lögðust	camped, laid
lokit	concluded, ended
lönd	the-land
löng	long
losnaði	loosened
löttu	dissuaded
lúka	conclude
luku	unlocked
lygi	lied
lykðum	completion
lykill	buried
lykka	luck
lýsa	show

M, m

Old Norse	English
Má	may
maðr	a-man, man
mælt	spoke, spoken
mælti	spoke
mæltu	spoke
mærði	praise
mætti	may
magni	strength
maki	match
mál	matter
mála	words
máli	matter, saying, speech, the-matter
mann	man, man, person
mannaðir	mannered
mannaðr	brought-up
mannfall	people-felled
mannfallit	people-felling
manni	person
manns	man, man's
mannval	people
margir	many
Margr	many
margs	many

Word List (Old Norse to English)

Old Norse	English
Margt	many
mat	food
mátti	might
með	between, with
meðan	as-long-as, while
meðr	between
mega	may
megi	may
megin	side, sides
meiði	beam
mein	harm
meir	more
meira	more
meiri	more
menn	men, people
mér	for-me, me, to-me
merkiligsti	remarkable
mest	the-most
mesta	most
mesti	most
mestr	the-greatest
mestu	most
mik	me, myself
mikil	great, much
mikill	much
mikinn	great, much
mikit	great, greatly, much
mikla	much
miklar	much
miklir	great
miklu	great, much
miklum	much
millum	between
mína	my
minna	less
minnar	mine, my
minni	my
minntist	remembered
mínu	my
mínum	mine, my
missa	missed
misst	lost, missed
mitt	mine, my
mjök	most, much
móðir	mother
móður	mother
mönnum	men, people, the-people
morðráð	murder
mörg	many
morgininn	morning
mörgu	many
mörkinni	the-border
mót	meet
móti	meeting
móts	meet
Múla	Muli (place)
Mun	must, should
munda	would
mundi	may, remembered, thought, would
mundu	would
muni	should, would
munni	mouth

N, n

Old Norse	English
náði	caught
næðist	reached
næmdu	took
nær	near
næst	next
nætr	night
náliga	almost, closely, nearly
nam	took
nát	protection
né	nor
nefnd	named
nefndr	named
nema	except
Njóti	appreciate
nökkur	something, somewhat
nökkurr	someone
nökkurs	somewhat
nökkut	something, sometime, somewhat
norðr	in-the-north
nóttina	the-night
nú	how, no, now
nýju	new

Word List (Old Norse to English)

Old Norse	English

O, o

Old Norse	English
Odda	Oddi (name), Oddi's (name)
Oddi	Oddi (name)
of	about, of, over, too, with
ofan	over
ofangöngunni	over-going
oft	often
ok	also, and, of
orð	worded, words
orða	words
orðahjaldr	word-struggle
orðin	become
orðinn	become
orku	power
orrostu	battle
orrostunni	the-battle
ort	worded
oss	us

Ó, ó

Old Norse	English
óboðit	uninvited
ódáðir	abhorrence
ódælli	un-pleasant
ógrynni	mass
óhægendi	inconvenience
ójafnað	unequal
ójafnari	unequal
ólát	un-courteous
ór	from, out-of, through, with
ósnöfrmannliga	un-alert

Ö, ö

Old Norse	English
öðru	another, others
öðrum	another, each-other, to-other
ök	and
öllu	all
öllum	all, of-all
önnur	others
örvígr	un-swinging

P, p

Old Norse	English
presentur	presents
prúðligsta	most-prolific
prýði	finery

R, r

Old Norse	English
ráð	advice, decide, decision, statements
ráða	prevail
ráðahag	marriage, marriage-proposal
ráðast	arrange, arranging
ráði	conduct, consent, decision
ráðist	determine-to
ráðligt	advice
ráðvandr	honest
ræðst	decided
rammgert	firmly-built
raunar	actually
réð	fixed, ruled, ruling
réðst	had
réðust	appointed
reiknaðr	counted
rekka	unfolded
rekkju	bed
rekkum	upright
Reykjardal	Reykjardal (place)
reyna	test
riðu	rode
ríkar	rich
ríki	kingdom, the-kingdom
ríkinu	the-kingdom
ríkis	kingdom, the-kingdom
ríkisstjórnar	governor
ríkit	the-kingdom
ríkustum	kingdom's
rímkænn	calendar-computation-wise

Word List (Old Norse to English)

Old Norse	English
ritnar	written
rjóðr	clearing
Róðbjarts	Hrodbjart's (name)
rómu	a-roar, battle

S, s

Old Norse	English
sá	saw, seen, so, that
sæi	saw
sækja	seek, sought
sæma	honour, the-same
sæmð	honour
sæmði	honour
sæmiligar	honourable
safnar	gathered
safnat	gathered
sagan	the-saga
sagðak	told
sagði	said, telling, the-saga, told, told
sagðist	said
sagt	said, said, told
sák	saw
sakir	for-the-sake-of, sake, the-sake-of
sama	same
saman	the-same, together
sameignar	fight, the-fight
samfarar	interaction
samför	together, togetherness
samtíða	contemporary
sannsögull	truthful
sárum	wounds
sat	sat
satt	the-truth
sé	are, being
seggir	said
seggja	say
seggjum	men
segir	said
segja	said, say
seglhættu	sail-danger
seldr	sold
sem	as, so, that, was, which
sén	seen
sendi	sent
sendimenn	messengers, sending-men
sendir	sent
sér	are, as, he, her, herself, himself, his, themselves
sét	seen
setr	set
sett	sat, set
settan	appointed
setti	set
settr	sat, set
sið	traditions
síðan	after, afterwards, then
síðar	afterwards
síðara	latter
Sigldum	we-sailed
siglu	sail
sigr	victory
sigrgöfgaðir	victory-gift-gods
sigri	victory
sik	herself, himself, his, themselves
siklingi	the-king
siklingr	the-king
siklings	the-king's
Síldasund	Herring-sound (place)
Síldasundi	Herring-sound (place)
sín	her, his, their
sína	himself, his
sinn	her, hers, his, one-day
sinna	their
sinni	hers, his, times
síns	his
sínu	her, his
sínum	hers, theirs
sitja	sit
sitt	his, their
sjá	look, saw, see, so
sjáir	look
sjálf	herself

Word List (Old Norse to English)

Old Norse	English
sjálfr	himself
sjálfum	himself, yourself
Sjár	the-sea
sjást	t-look
skaði	harm
skafti	spear
skal	shall
skáld	poet, the-poet
skáldi	the-poet
skáldinu	the-poet
skálds	the-poet
skáldskaparlaunum	poet's-reward
Skeið	sheathed-sword
skemmtanar	entertainment
skemr	shorter
skerðendr	diminished
skíð	wood
skildi	shield
skilði	should
skilðu	knew
skiljast	separate
skilnaðr	parting
skip	ships
skipa	the-ship's
skipaflota	ship-fleet
skipaflotann	ship-fleet
skipan	the-ship
skipanna	the-ships
skipi	the-ship
skips	the-ships
skipstjórnarmaðr	ship-steering-man
skipta	divide, exchange
skipti	exchanged
skiptum	exchanged
skipuð	prepared
skjaldmær	shield-maiden
skjaldmeyja	shield-maidens
skjaldmeyjar	shield-maidens
skjóma	shimmering
skjót	launched
skjóta	short, throw
skjótara	shorter
skjótast	quickly, soonest
skjótt	quickly
skóg	forest

Old Norse	English
skóginn	the-forest
skor	across
skorta	shortage
skorti	shortage
skóþvenginn	shoe-thong
skóþvengr	shoe-thong
skreið	glided
skríða	action
skuluð	should
skyldari	obliged
skyldi	should
skynda	hurrying
slíka	such
slíks	such
Slíku	so, such
slíkum	such
smágrjót	small-stones
snarpir	sharply
snarpri	rough, roughly
snarráðir	quickly
snemma	soon
snjallari	most-valiant
snýr	turned
sofnaði	slept
sofnar	slept
sögðu	said
sögu	telling
söguna	the-saga
sögunnar	the-saga
sögunni	the-saga
sókn	attack, attacked
sóma	honour
sómasamligri	respectable
sómi	honour
son	son
sonar	son
sonr	son
sótt	attended, sickness
sótti	attended, attending, encountered
sóttin	sickness
sóttu	attended
spurði	asked
spyrjast	was-heard
Spyrkat	learned
stað	place

Word List (Old Norse to English)

Old Norse	English
staddir	standing
staddr	placed, stood
staði	places
staðit	placed, stood
standa	standing
sté	stepped
steig	leapt
sterkr	strong
stíg	path
stigamannanna	the-robbing-men
stigamönnum	the-robbers
stígr	climbed
stirðr	stiff-footed
stjórn	control
stjórna	ruling
stjörnu	star
stjörnum	the-stars
Stjörnu-Odda	Star-Oddi (name)
Stjörnu-Oddi	Star-Oddi (name)
stjörnur	stars
stóð	place, stood
stóðu	stood
stofnat	planned
stofni	stem
stökk	leapt
stól	throne
stór	great
stóra	great
stórmannliga	great-man-like
stórum	great
stund	awhile
stýrði	guided, steered
Sú	so, this
Sumir	some
sund	a-sound
sundin	the-sound
sundunum	sound, the-sound
svá	so, such, to
svarar	answer, answered
svari	answer
svát	so, so-that
svefni	sleep
sverða	swords
sverði	sword
sverðinu	sword
svikmenni	the-wicked
Svipun	swooping
svívirðing	disgraceful
sýndist	seemed
sýnist	seems
sýslu	realm
sýslumenn	stewards
systir	sister

T, t

Old Norse	English
taka	take, taken
takast	take, took
talar	speak
talat	told
talði	said
tekinn	taken
tekr	took
tekst	takes
tíðenda	news
tíðendi	news, the-news
tíðendin	news
tíðendum	news
tíginna	high-born
tígn	prestige
tígnar	princely
til	for, that, to
tilföngum	means
tíma	time
tímar	time
tindótt	toothed
tírgjarn	fame-ambition
títt	report
tízka	fashion
tját	expressed
tjóa	avail
tók	took
tókust	took
tölðu	told
tólf	twelve
tönnum	teeth
treysta	trust
Trölls	trolls
tröllsligt	trollish
tryggðarmaðr	faithful-man

Word List (Old Norse to English)

Old Norse	English
tugum	tens
tvá	two
tveggja	two
tveir	two
tyggja	chewing

Þ, þ

Old Norse	English
þá	then
Þaðan	from-there, then
Þær	they
þætti	seemed, thought
þakkaði	thanked
þakkar	thanked
þangat	from-there, there
þangi	seaweed
þann	that, then
þar	of, that, then, there, they
þarf	needed
þat	it, that, the, then, they, this, to
þau	the, there, they
þegar	as-soon-as, immediately, straightaway, they
þegnum	subjects
þeim	them, they
þeir	them, there, they
þeira	of-them, their, theirs, them, there, they
þeiri	that, there
þenna	these, this
þér	to-you, you
Þess	it, the, this
þessa	of-this, these, this
þessar	these, this
þessarar	this
þessari	this
þessi	the, these, this
Þessir	these
þessu	this
þessum	this
þetta	that, the, this
þiggja	accept
þik	you
þín	yours
þing	assembly, the-assembly
þingat	assembled
þings	an-assembly, assembly
þjóða	people
þjóðar	great-river, king
þjóðbrautinni	the-highway
þó	though, yet
Þórðr	Thord (name)
þótt	though, thought
þótti	seemed, thought
Þóttist	seemed, though, thought
þóttust	thought
þraut	finished
þrekvirki	brave-deeds
þriðjung	a-third-of
þrítug	thirty
þrjú	three
þroskast	develop
þú	you
þurfa	needed
þurfti	need
þustu	flailing
þvenginn	thong
því	according, accordingly, according-to, against, because, for, then, therefore
þvílíks	such-like
þvít	because
þykki	thought
þykkir	seemed, seems
þykkja	regarded, seem

U, u

Old Norse	English
um	about
umbúnaðr	soft-bed-prepared
ummæli	about-words
umsjá	supervision
und	under

Word List (Old Norse to English)

Old Norse	English
undan	under
undarligr	extraordinary, wonder-like
undarligt	wonder-like
undir	under
undr	wonder
undrast	wonder
ung	young
unga	young
ungr	young
unna	grant, love
unz	ours, until
upp	up
upphaf	beginning
upphafi	became
uppheldi	advancement
urðu	became

Ú, ú

Old Norse	English
út	out, out-from
útan	without
útbyrðis	overboard
úti	out
útilegumannanna	the-outlaw-men

V, v

Old Norse	English
vá	guarded
vægði	mercy
vægis	weight
vænn	handsome
væri	being, was, were, would-be
vág	inlet
vaknaði	awoke, woke
vaknat	woken
vakni	wake
vald	power
valda	wield
ván	expected, expecting
vandræði	difficulty
vanir	friends
vanr	accustomed
vantaði	lacking
vápnaðir	weaponed
vápnaskipti	weapons-exchange
vápnfimi	weapon-nimble
vápnum	weapons
var	was, were
vár	our
varð	became, was
varfærir	caution
varp	thrown
várr	our
várrar	aware
Váru	they-were, was, were
vaxa	grow
vaxit	grown
véar	the-gods
veðri	the-weather
veg	way
vega	ways
vegg	wall
vegligasta	greatest
vegs	glory
veit	know
veitt	given
veitti	gave
veittr	given
veizla	feast
veizlu	feast
veizluna	feast, the-feast
veizlunni	the-feast
vel	all, well
velja	choose
venja	way
venju	habitually
vera	be, being, was
verða	be, become, becomes, happened, to-be, worthy
verði	be
verðr	became, worth
verit	been
verkmaðr	working-man
vetra	winters
vexti	grown
við	against, trees, with
víða	wide, widely, with

Word List (Old Norse to English)

Old Norse	English
viðbúnaði	preparation
víði	wood
vígaferði	slayings
vígboði	battle-bidding
vígroða	warfare
vigrum	spears
víking	viking, viking-raids
víkinga	vikings
víkingar	vikings
vil	will, wish
vildi	willed, wished
vildu	willed, wished
vili	wish
vilið	wish
vilja	willed
vill	wanted-to, will, wish
villtu	will-you
vinir	friends
vinna	grant
vinstri	left
vinum	friends
virðar	men
virðing	worth, worthiness, worthy
virðingu	worthiness
virðuliga	worthily
virðuligr	worthy
virðuligri	worthy
virkðamönnum	chosen-man
virkðavinum	friends
vísaði	pointed-out
viss	aware
vissi	knew
vissir	know
vist	hospitality
víst	vision
vísur	verse, verses
vit	to
vita	knew, know, to-know
vitja	visit
vitmikill	knowing-much
vitr	wise
vitrasta	wisest
vitrustum	wise
vöknuðu	awoke
vörn	defended

Y, y

Old Norse	English
yðr	of-you, to-you, you
yðvarrar	your
yðvarri	your
yfir	over
yfirkoma	overcome
ylgjar	wolf's
ylgjarhöfuð	she-wolf's-head
yrði	became

Ý, ý

Old Norse	English
Ýfð	bristling
ýmissa	various

Word List (English to Old Norse)

English	Old Norse

A, a

English	Old Norse
a	at
abhorrence	ódáðir
about	á, í, of, um
about-words	ummæli
abundance	ærit
accept	þiggja
according	því
accordingly	því
according-to	því
accursed-men	heljarmenn
accustomed	vanr
a-chieftain	höfðingja
across	skor
action	skríða
actually	raunar
a-daughter	dóttur
adored	dýrkuðu
advancement	uppheldi
advice	ráð, ráðligt
advisable	allráðligt
Aegir's (name)	ægis
affection	ástúð
aft	aftan
after	áðr, eftir, síðan
afterwards	eftir, síðan, síðar
against	því, við
age	aldri
aggression	ágangi
a-gold-ring	gullhring
a-little	lítt
alive	lífi
all	alla, allan, allir, allra, allri, alls, allt, öllu, öllum, vel
all-many-people	allfjölmennt
allow	láta
allowed	láta
all-prepared	albúin, albúinn, albúnir
all-ready	albúinn
all-un-forethought	allbráðliga
all-weaponed	alvápnuðu
almost	náliga
also	ok
always	ávallt, jafnan
am	er
a-man	maðr
a-match	kvánfang, kvánfangs, kvánföngin
among-people	fyrða
a-mound	haug
an-assembly	þings
ancient	fornum
and	eða, en, enda, ok, ök
angled	Hörn
announced	boði, kvæða
another	annan, annarrar, annat, öðru, öðrum
another-either	annathvárt
answer	svarar, svari
answered	svarar
anything-else	annars
a-poem	kvæði
appointed	réðust, settan
appreciate	Njóti
are	er, ert, Eru, eruð, sé, sér
arm	arminum
army	her
a-roar	rómu
arrange	ráðast
arranging	ráðast
as	er, sem, sér
ask	bæði
asked	bað, báðu, beiddi, spurði
asking	beðinn
as-long-as	meðan
a-sound	sund
assembled	þingat
assembly	þing, þings
assistance	beina
as-soon-as	þegar
at	á, í
a-thick	digran

Word List (English to Old Norse)

English	Old Norse
a-third-of	þriðjung
a-toast	erfi
attack	sókn
attacked	sókn
attended	sótt, sótti, sóttu
attending	sótti
avail	tjóa
aware	várrar, viss
away	braut, brott, burt
awhile	hríð, stund
a-wife	konu
awoke	vaknaði, vöknuðu

B, b

English	Old Norse
back	aftr
battle	bardaga, bardagi, berjast, orrostu, rómu
battle-bidding	vígboði
Battle-forest (place)	Jöruskóg, Jöruskógi, Jöruskógr
battle-spears	hnitgeirum
be	gera, vera, verða, verði
beam	meiði
became	gerðist, upphafi, urðu, varð, verðr, yrði
be-carried-out	efna
because	fyrir, því, þvít
become	orðin, orðinn, verða
becomes	verða
bed	rekkju
been	verit
before	áðr, fyrir, fyrr
began	byrjaði, hóf
beginning	upphaf
begins	gerðist
behaviour	athæfi
being	sé, væri, vera
beloved	ástvinum
benefits	kosti
berserkers	berserkina, berserkir
best	bezt, beztu, beztum, hezta, heztum
betrothed-to	föstnuð
better	betr
bettering	batnaði
between	með, meðr, millum
bit	biti
biting	beitti
blew	blés
blood	Blóð, blóði
blood-helmeted	blóðísunga
bloodied	Blóðár
blows	högg
bore	bar, borit
borne	bera
both	báða, báðir, báðum, bæði
bound	bundit
bows	hlýra
brave	horskir
brave-deeds	þrekvirki
bride	brúðar
bring	færa
bristling	Ýfð
broad	brattr, breið
brothers	barmar
brought	báru, borin, borit, flutti
brought-up	mannaðr
buried	heygðr, lykill
but	en, enn
by	á

C, c

English	Old Norse
calendar-computation-wise	rímkænn
called	kallaðr, kveðja
came	gerðisk, kemr, kom, koma, komit, kómu
camped	liggja, lögðust
can	kann
carried	borit
cast	kastaði
caught	náði
caution	varfærir
celebrated	fegnir
champion	kempum
chewing	tyggja
chieftain	höfðingi

Word List (English to Old Norse)

English	Old Norse	English	Old Norse
chieftains	höfðingja, höfðingjum	covering	hulðu
child	barn, barna	crafts	iðn
choice	kost, kostr, kostrinn	crew	lið, liði
choice-bid	kostaboð	criminals	illvirkjarnir
choices	kjósa	cultivate	fága
choose	kjósa, kjósið, kostir, velja		
chose	köru		

D, d

English	Old Norse
chosen-man	virkðamönnum
circumstance	hag
claimed	kallaði
cleared	hruðust
clearing	rjóðr
clearly	glöggliga, görva
climbed	stígr
closely	náliga
come	koma, komin, kominn, komir, komit, komnir
come-of-age	aldrskominn
comes	kæmist
comfortable	hægliga
comfortably	hógligr
coming	komin, komnir
commanded	fylkir
companionship	föruneyti
company	leið, lið, liði, liðs
completely	gersamliga
completion	lykðum
concealing	leyna
conclude	hætta, lúka
concluded	lokit
conduct	ráði
consent	ráði
contemporary	samtíða
control	stjórn
corpses	hræ
could	Gátu, geta
counted	reiknaðr
courage	frami
course	ferðum
court	hirð
courtiers	hirðin
courtly	kurteisliga
court-man	hirðmaðr
court-men	hirð, hirðmenn, hirðmönnum

English	Old Norse
Dagfinn (name)	Dagfinn, Dagfinni, Dagfinnr
Dagfinn's (name)	Dagfinns
danger	háska
dangerously	hættliga
dark	dökkr
daughter	dóttur
dear	dýrra
death	bana, fráfall
decide	ráð
decided	ræðst
decision	ráð, ráði
deeds	atgervi
defended	vörn
demanded	beiðir
descendants	ætt
descended	konr
determine-to	ráðist
develop	þroskast
did	fór, gerði
die	látast
died	andaðr, andast
difficulty	vandræði
diminished	skerðendr
discourage	letja
discouraged	latti, letjast
disgraceful	svívirðing
disposed	fallinn
dissuaded	löttu
distinguished	kostrinn
divide	skipta
do	gera
doing	gerðu
dominion	heitit
done	ger, gerði, gert, gerzt
doorway	dyrigætti
drank	drukkit

291

Word List (English to Old Norse)

English	Old Norse
drapa	drápa, drápuna
drawn	brugðnu, draga, heimt
dream	draum, drauminn
dreamed	dreymði
drew	brá, dró
drink	drykk
drunk	drukkit
dwell	dvelja
dwelled	dvaldist

E, e

English	Old Norse
each	hvárir, hvárt, hvergi, hvergymis, hverjum, hverr, hvers, hvert
each-other	öðrum
each-way	hvártveggja
eagerly	hafrastar
earl	jarl
earned	kostat
east	austr
eight	átta
either	ella, hvárt
either-way	annathvárt
eleven	ellifu
encountered	sótti
ended	lokit
enemies	andskota
entertainment	skemmtanar
equal-age	jafnaldra
equally	jafngjarn
errand	erendi
especially	einkum
evening	kveldit
events	atburð, atburðr
everything	allan
evident	einsætt
evil-doers	illvirkjar, illvirkjunum
exceedingly	forkunnliga
exceedingly-great	geysimikit
except	nema
exchange	skipta
exchanged	skipti, skiptum
expected	ván
expecting	ván
expedition	leiðangrs
expressed	tját
extraordinary	undarligr
extremely	ákafliga

F, f

English	Old Norse
fairest	fegrst
faithful-man	tryggðarmaðr
fallen	fallin, fallnir
fame	frægð, frægra, frama
fame-ambition	tírgjarn
famous	frægr, frægra
far-away	fjarri
fared	fór
far-famed	frægr
fashion	tízka
father	faðir, feðr, föður
feast	veizla, veizlu, veizluna
fee-little	Félítill
fell	fell, fellu
felled	felldi, hníga
few	fám, fátkaðist
fight	berjast, sameignar
fighters	fyrða
filled	fylldir
find	fund
fine	dýran
finery	prýði
finished	þraut
firmly-built	rammgert
first	fyrra, fyrst
fishing	fiska
fixed	réð
flailing	þustu
flames	elda
Flatey (place)	Flateyjar
fleet	flota
flokk	flokkr
flood	flóðs
folk	fólki
follow	fylgð, fylgja
followed	fylgt, hlýddi
followers	fjölmenni

Word List (English to Old Norse)

English	Old Norse
followers-many	fjölmennan, fjölmenni
follows	fylgi
food	mat
for	er, fyrir, því, til
forces	hér
foremost	framast
forest	skóg
for-me	mér
for-the-evil-doers	illvirkjanna
for-the-sake-of	sakir
forty	fertug
forwards	fram
found	hitt, hittir
friends	vanir, vinir, vinum, virkðavinum
from	af, Frá, fram, ór
from-here	heðan
from-saying	frásögu
from-there	Þaðan, þangat
from-to-say	frásaga
full	fullt, fyllar
full-done	fullgert
fully	fullu
fully-come	fullkomnir
fully-prepared	alskipuð
furiously	geisa

G, g

English	Old Norse
gain	afla
Garp (name)	Garp, Garpr
gathered	safnar, safnat
gave	gaf, gáfu, veitti
Geirvid (name)	Geirvið, Geirviðar, Geirviði, Geirviðr
get	fá, fást, geta
give	fá, gefa
given	gefna, veitt, veittr
gladly	gjarna, glaðliga
gleam	geisla
gleaming	glæsimar
glided	skreið
glorious	dýrðlig
glory	vegs
Gny (name)	Gný, Gnýr

English	Old Norse
go	fara, farast, ganga
going	fóru, gang, ganga, gengi
gold-ring	gullhring
Göndul (place)	göndul
gone	farit, gengit
good	góð, góðan, góðum, gótt
good-fortune	gæfa
gore	dreyra
got	fekk, fengit
Götaland (place)	Gautland, Gautlandi, Gautlands
Gothic (name)	gotneskra
governing	landstjórnar
governor	ríkisstjórnar
graciousness	hamingjan
grant	unna, vinna
granted	lagit
gratitude	aufúsa
great	mikil, mikinn, mikit, miklir, miklu, stór, stóra, stórum
greatest	vegligasta
greatly	mikit
great-man-like	stórmannliga
great-river	þjóðar
greeted	kvaddi
greeting	kveðju
grimly	grimmhuguð
ground	grundu
grow	vaxa
grown	vaxit, vexti
guarded	vá
guest	gistingar
guided	stýrði
Gylfi (name)	Gylfa

H, h

English	Old Norse
habitually	venju
had	átti, áttu, er, haf, hafa, hafði, hafi, haft, hefði, hefir, hefr, höfðu, hófu, höfuð, lagði, lét, létu, létust, réðst

Word List (English to Old Norse)

English	Old Norse	*English*	Old Norse
half	hálfs	*Hjorvard (name)*	Hjörvarðar, Hjörvarði, Hjörvarðr
hand	handa, handar, hendi, hönd	*Hladreid (name)*	Hlaðreið, Hlaðreiði
handsome	vænn	*Hlegunn (name)*	Hléguðr, Hlégunnar, Hlégunni
happened	gerðist, verða	*Hlegunn's (name)*	Hlégunnar
happening	atburðr	*Hogni's (name)*	Högna
hard	harðan, herða	*hold*	halda
hardest	harðasti	*home*	heim, heima, heiman
hard-headed	harðráðar	*homeward*	heimleiðis
hardy	herðendr	*honest*	ráðvandr
harm	mein, skaði	*honour*	fremð, sæma, sæmð, sæmði, sóma, sómi
has	hefir	*honourable*	sæmiligar
have	átt, eiga, gáfu, hafa, hafi, hefði, hefi, hefir	*honoured*	erfð
hawk	hauka	*hordes*	hörðu
hawk-seat	haukstóls	*horses*	hestar
he	Hann, honum, sér	*hospitality*	vist
head	höfði, höfuðit	*house*	hús, húss
headland	höfða, höfðann, höfði	*house-builder*	húsgerðar
heads	höfuðin	*households*	heimkynna
heard	heyrði, heyrt	*housemaster*	húsbóndi
heart	hjarta	*how*	hvárt, hvé, nú
Hel (place)	helju	*however*	En
held	heldi, helt	*how-so*	hversu
helmsman	Hilmis	*Hrodbjart (name)*	Hróðbjart, Hróðbjarti, Hróðbjartr
her	hana, hennar, henni, hon, hún, sér, sín, sinn, sínu	*Hrodbjart's (name)*	Hróðbjarts, Róðbjarts
here	hér, hingat	*hurrying*	skynda
heroes	bragna		
Herring-sound (place)	Síldasund, Síldasundi		
hers	hennar, henni, sinn, sinni, sínum		

I, i

English	Old Norse
herself	sér, sik, sjálf
hewed	hjó
hideous	ljótar	*I*	ek
high	hár	*Iceland (place)*	Íslandi
high-born	tíginna	*if*	ef
Hildigunn (name)	Hildiguðr, Hildigunnar	*immediately*	þegar
hill	hóli, hóll	*in*	á, at, er, í, inn
him	hann, hans, honum	*inconvenience*	óhægendi
himself	sér, sik, sína, sjálfr, sjálfum	*increased*	æxti
		injury	áverka
his	hans, honum, sér, sik, sín, sína, sinn, sinni, síns, sínu, sitt	*inlet*	vág
		inside	innan
		intend	ætla, ætlat
Hjorgunn (name)	Hjörguðr, Hjörgunni	*interaction*	samfarar
		in-the-north	norðr

Word List (English to Old Norse)

English	Old Norse
invited	bað, biðr, boðit
is	er
it	at, Hann, hon, þat, Þess
it-went	ferr

J, j

jaws	kjafta
journey	ferð, ferðar, för
journeyed	færi
joyfully	blíðliga

K, k

killed	drápu
kin	kindir
kind	háttar
kinds-of	konar, kyns
king	konungr, konungs, þjóðar
kingdom	konungdóminn, ríki, ríkis
kingdom's	ríkustum
kinsmen	frændr
knee	kné
knew	skilðu, vissi, vita
know	kunna, kunnigt, veit, vissir, vita
knowing-much	vitmikill
known	kann, kunnigt

L, l

lacking	vantaði
laid	leið, lögðu, lögðust
land	land, landa, landi, landit
land-ruling	landráða
lands	landa, lands
lands-folk	landsfólkinu
lands-people	landsmönnum
latter	síðara
launched	skjót

English	Old Norse
lay	lá, lagðist
laying-to	lágu
lean	lér
leapt	steig, stökk
learned	Spyrkat
leave	láta
led	leiddi, leiðir
left	vinstri
less	minna
let	láta
lied	lygi
life	líf
life-less	líflát
light	ljós
lightly	ljósliga
like	líka
liked	líkaði, líkar
likely	líkligt
lineage	ætt
listen	hlýða
little	lítil, lítill, lítils, litla, lítt
lived	bjó, lifði
locked	læst
long	langa, langar, langir, langt, löng
longer	lengi, lengr, lengra
longships	langskip
look	líta, sjá, sjáir
looking-forward	hlökk
loosed	laust
loosened	losnaði
lord	Herra
lose	láta
lost	misst
lot	hlut
love	ástir, unna
luck	gæfu, lykka
lying	lá

M, m

made	ger, gera, gerði, Gerðr, gerðu, gerðust, gert

Word List (English to Old Norse)

English	Old Norse
man	maðr, mann, manns
mannered	mannaðir
man's	manns
many	margir, Margr, margs, Margt, mörg, mörgu
many-followers	fjölmenni
many-men	fjölmenna
marriage	ráðahag
marriage-proposal	ráðahag
married	gift, kvángaðr
marry	fá
mass	ógrynni
match	maki
matter	mál, máli
may	Má, mætti, mega, megi, mundi
me	mér, mik
means	færi, tilföngum
meet	fund, hittast, mót, móts
meeting	móti
men	gumna, menn, mönnum, seggjum, virðar
merchant-voyages	kaupferðir
mercy	vægði
messengers	sendimenn
met	hittist
might	mátti
mind	hug
minds	huga
mine	minnar, mínum, mitt
missed	missa, misst
modestly	hæverskliga
more	fleira, meir, meira, meiri
morning	morgininn
most	flestum, mesta, mesti, mestu, mjök
most-beautiful	fríðust
most-prolific	prúðligsta
most-valiant	snjallari
mother	móðir, móður
mound	haug
mound-of-snow	hengiskafla
mourned	harmaði
mouth	munni
much	mikil, mikill, mikinn, mikit, mikla, miklar, miklu, miklum, mjök
Muli (place)	Múla
murder	morðráð
must	Mun
my	mína, minnar, minni, mínu, mínum, mitt
myself	mik

N, n

English	Old Norse
named	heita, heitir, hét, nefnd, nefndr
near	hjá, nær
nearly	náliga
neck	hálsinn
need	þurfti
needed	þarf, þurfa
neither	hvárki
never	aldri, aldrigi
new	nýju
news	tíðenda, tíðendi, tíðendin, tíðendum
next	næst
night	nætr
no	ekki, engan, engi, nú
noble	göfga, göfugr
noble-like	göfugligum
nobly	höfðingliga
none	eigi, engi
nor	né
not	eigi, Ekki, engi
now	Nú

O, o

English	Old Norse
obey	hlýða
obliged	skyldari
obtained	aflaði
Oddi (name)	Odda, Oddi
Oddi's (name)	Odda
of	á, af, at, er, í, of, ok, þar
of-age	aldrs

Word List (English to Old Norse)

English	Old Norse
of-all	öllum
off	af
offered	bauð
of-Goths	Gauta
of-him	hans
of-marriage-grown	gjafvaxta
often	oft
of-the-Goths	gauzkrar
of-the-journey	fararinnar
of-them	þeira
of-this	þessa
of-you	yðr
old	gamall
older	eldri
on	á, í
one	Annarr, Annat, einn, eins, einum, eitt, enn
one-day	sinn
only	eiga, eina, einn
or	eða, eðr
or-else	ella
other	aðra, annars
others	aðrir, öðru, önnur
otherwise	annars, ella, elligar
our	vár, várr
ours	unz
out	út, úti
out-from	út
out-of	ór
outrages	illvirki
over	of, ofan, yfir
overboard	útbyrðis
overcome	yfirkoma
over-going	ofangöngunni
owned	átt, eignaði
ownership	eigu

P, p

English	Old Norse
particularly	einkum
parting	skilnaðr
passed	liðit
passes	leið
path	götuna, stíg
peace	friðaði
people	drótt, mannval, menn, mönnum, þjóða
people-felled	mannfall
people-felling	mannfallit
person	mann, manni
place	laut, stað, stóð
placed	staddr, staðit
places	staði
planned	stofnat
poet	skáld
poetry	kvæðinn
poetry-making	kveðskaprinn
poet's-reward	skáldskaparlaunum
pointed-out	vísaði
possessions	föng
power	föng, orku, vald
praise	lofsorð, mærði
praised	lofuðu
precious	dýrar
preparation	viðbúnaði
preparations	búit
prepare	búa
prepared	búa, búins, búit, skipuð
presents	presentur
prestige	tígn
prevail	ráða
princely	tígnar
protection	nát
provisions	liðskosti

Q, q

English	Old Norse
queen	dróttningar
quickly	skjótast, skjótt, snarráðir

R, r

English	Old Norse
rage	eiskranlig
raided	herjar
raiding	hernað, hernaði
raised	hafiðr

Word List (English to Old Norse)

English	Old Norse	English	Old Norse
ran	hljóp	searching	leita
rather	heldr, helzt	seaweed	þangi
reached	næðist	see	líta, sjá
reaction	Bregðr	seek	sækja
ready	búnir, greiða	seeking	leita
realm	sýslu	seem	þykkja
recited	kveðit	seemed	sýndist, þætti, þótti, Þóttist, þykkir
redeem	kaupast		
regarded	þykkja	seems	sýnist, þykkir
remarkable	merkiligsti	seen	sá, sén, sét
remembered	minntist, mundi	sending-men	Sendimenn
repay	launa	sent	sendi, sendir
report	títt	separate	skiljast
respectable	sómasamligri	set	setr, sett, setti, settr
responsibility	ábyrgð	shall	skal
retainers	hirð	shared	deili
returning	aftr	sharply	snarpir
reward	launa	she	hana, henni, hér, hon
Reykjardal (place)	Reykjardal	sheathed-sword	Skeið
rich	ríkar	she-wolf's-head	ylgjarhöfuð
riches	auði	shield	skildi
right	drótt, dróttar	shield-maiden	skjaldmær
rings	hringa	shield-maidens	skjaldmeyja, skjaldmeyjar
rode	riðu		
rough	snarpri	shimmering	skjóma
roughly	snarpri	ship	barð
ruled	réð	ship-fleet	skipaflota, skipaflotann
ruler	jöfra		
ruling	Réð, stjórna	ships	skip
		ship-steering-man	skipstjórnarmaðr
		shoe-thong	skóþvenginn, skóþvengr

S, s

English	Old Norse	English	Old Norse
said	játti, kvað, kvaðst, kváðu, sagði, sagðist, sagt, seggir, segir, segja, sögðu, talði	short	skjóta
		shortage	skorta, skorti
		shorter	skemr, skjótara
		should	mun, muni, skilði, skuluð, skyldi
sail	siglu	show	lýsa
sail-danger	seglhættu	sickness	sótt, sóttin
sake	sakir	side	megin
same	sama	sides	megin
sat	sat, sett, settr	sister	systir
saw	sá, sæi, sák, sjá	sit	sitja
say	seggja, segja	skills	list
saying	máli	slayings	vígaferði
search	leita	sleep	svefni

298

Word List (English to Old Norse)

English	Old Norse	English	Old Norse
slept	sofnaði, sofnar	straight	drjúgt
small-stones	smágrjót	straightaway	þegar
so	a, sá, sem, sjá, Slíku, Sú, svá, svát	strain	hneig
		strength	afli, magni
so-as	at	stricken-sun	hnigsólar
soft-bed-prepared	umbúnaðr	striking	hjuggu
sold	seldr	striking-distance	höggfæri
some	Sumir	strong	sterkr
someone	nökkurr	struck	höggr
something	nökkur, nökkut	subduing	brýtr
some-time	eitthvert, nökkut	subjects	þegnum
somewhat	nökkur, nökkurs, nökkut	such	slíka, slíks, slíku, slíkum, svá
son	son, sonar, sonr	such-like	þvílíks
son-of-Helgi (name)	Helgason	summoned	kvatt
soon	brátt, snemma	supervision	umsjá
soonest	skjótast	swooping	Svipun
sorcery	fjölkynngi	sword	hjörs, sverði, sverðinu
so-that	svát	swords	sverða
sought	leit, leitaðist, sækja		
sound	sundunum		
speak	talar		
spear	skafti		

T, t

English	Old Norse
spear-guardian	geirvaldr
spears	geiri, vigrum
speech	máli
spite	böls
spoke	kvað, kvaðst, mælt, mælti, mæltu
spoken	mælt
stain	Áta
standing	staddir, standa
star	stjörnu
Star-Oddi (name)	Stjörnu-Odda, Stjörnu-Oddi
stars	stjörnur
start	hefjast
statements	ráð
steered	stýrði
stem	stofni
stepped	sté
stewards	sýslumenn
stiff-footed	stirðr
stood	staddr, staðit, stóð, stóðu
storm	hríðmál

English	Old Norse
take	taka, takast
taken	taka, tekinn
takes	tekst
tall	hátt
teeth	tönnum
telling	sagði, sögu
temple	Hofs
Temple-Head (place)	Höfða, Hofshöfði
tens	tugum
test	reyna
than	en, í
thanked	þakkaði, þakkar
that	á, að, at, en, enn, er, hinn, hvat, sá, sem, þann, þar, þat, þeiri, þetta, til
the	á, at, en, er, í, in, ina, inn, inni, ins, inum, it, Þat, þau, þess, þessi, þetta
the-assembly	þing
the-battle	bardaga, bardaginn, orrostunni

Word List (English to Old Norse)

English	Old Norse	*English*	Old Norse
the-berserkers	berserkjanna, berserkjunum	*the-land*	landi, landinu, lands, lönd
the-best	hezt	*the-lands*	lands
the-blow	höggit	*the-land's-people*	landsfólkit
the-bodies	hold	*them*	þeim, þeir, þeira
the-border	mörkinni	*the-matter*	máli
the-brothers	bræðir	*the-men*	ljónar
the-day	daginn	*the-most*	mest
the-dream	draum, drauminn, drauminum	*the-mound*	hauginn, hauginum
		themselves	sér, sik
the-earl	jarl, jarli, jarls	*then*	á, at, En, hina, Síðan, þá, þaðan, þann, Þar, Þat, því
the-earl's-daughter	jarlsdóttir		
the-evil-doers	illvirkjanna, illvirkjarnir		
the-feast	veizluna, veizlunni	*the-news*	tíðendi
the-fight	sameignar	*the-night*	nóttina
the-firth	firrðisk	*the-other*	annarr
the-forest	skóginn	*the-others*	inum
the-goddesses	Ásynju	*the-outlaw-men*	útilegumannanna
the-gods	véar	*the-people*	alþýðu, mönnum
the-government	landsstjórnin	*the-poem*	kvæði, kvæðinu, kvæðit
the-greatest	mestr		
the-guest	gestrinn	*the-poet*	skáld, skáldi, skáldinu, skálds
the-hand	handa		
the-helm	hjálmi	*the-queen*	dróttning, dróttningar, dróttningin
the-helmsman	hilmis		
the-highway	þjóðbrautinni	*there*	bar, þangat, Þar, þau, þeir, þeira, þeiri
the-hill	hólinn, hólinum		
the-house	húsinu	*therefore*	því
their	sín, sinna, sitt, þeira	*the-ring*	hringinn
theirs	sínum, þeira	*the-robbers*	stigamönnum
the-island	eyjarinnar	*the-robbing-men*	stigamannanna
the-journey	ferð, ferðinni	*the-saga*	sagan, sagði, söguna, sögunnar, sögunni
the-key	grafinn		
the-king	konung, konungi, konunginn, konunginum, konungr, konungrinn, konungs, konungsins, siklingi, siklingr	*the-sake-of*	sakir
		the-same	sæma, saman
		these	þenna, þessa, þessar, þessi, Þessir
		the-sea	Sjár
		the-ship	skipan, skipi
		the-ships	skipanna, skips
the-kingdom	ríki, ríkinu, ríkis, ríkit	*the-ship's*	skipa
the-king's	konungrinn, konungs, konungsins, siklings	*the-sound*	sundin, sundunum
		the-stars	stjörnum
the-king's-men	konungsmönnum	*the-surf*	lágarða
the-king's-poet	konungsskáld	*the-tables*	borðum
the-king's-ship	konungsskipinu, konungsskipit	*the-toast*	erfinu
the-king's-sister	konungssystir	*the-treasure*	féit

Word List (English to Old Norse)

English	Old Norse	*English*	Old Norse
the-treasurer	gunndjarfr	*to-him*	hann, honum
the-truth	satt	*to-know*	vita
the-way	gata	*told*	getit, sagðak, sagði, sagt, talat, tölðu
the-weather	veðri		
the-wedding	brúðhlaup	*told-of*	getit
the-wicked	svikmenni	*to-me*	mér
the-woman	kvenna	*to-meet*	hitt
they	Þær, þar, Þat, Þau, þegar, þeim, þeir, þeira	*too*	of
		took	leiðir, næmdu, nam, takast, tekr, tók, tókust
they-are	eru		
they-were	Váru	*toothed*	tindótt
things	hluta, hluti, hlutum	*to-other*	öðrum
think	Hugsat, hygg	*to-travel*	fara
thinking	hugr	*toughness*	harðfengi
thirty	þrítug	*to-you*	þér, yðr
this	sú, þat, þenna, Þess, þessa, þessar, þessarar, þessari, þessi, þessu, þessum, þetta	*traditions*	sið
		travel	færi, far, fara, farandi, farar, ferðina, fóru
		travelled	fara, ferr, fór, fórst, fóru
this-king	konungrinn	*travelling*	farit, ferðina
thong	þvenginn	*travel-weary*	farmóðr
Thord (name)	Þórðr	*treasure*	fé, fyrða
though	þó, þótt, þóttist	*treasured*	dýrmörum
thought	hug, hugði, hugðu, mundi, þætti, þótt, þótti, þóttist, þóttust, þykki	*trees*	börva, við
		trollish	tröllsligt
		trolls	Trölls
		trust	treysta
three	þrjú	*truthful*	sannsögull
throne	stól	*turned*	snýr
through	ór	*twelve*	tólf
throw	skjóta	*two*	tvá, tveggja, tveir
thrown	varp		
tied	bindr		
time	tíma, tímar		
times	sinni		
t-look	sjást		
to	á, af, at, en, í, svá, þat, til, vit		

U, u

English	Old Norse
un-alert	ósnöfrmannliga
un-courteous	ólát
under	und, undan, undir
to-be	verða
unequal	ójafnað, ójafnari
to-do	gera
unfolded	rekka
together	saman, samför
unheard-of	endemi
togetherness	samför
uninvited	óboðit
to-have	láta
unlocked	luku
to-hear	áheyrsla
un-pleasant	ódælli
to-her	henni

Word List (English to Old Norse)

English	Old Norse	English	Old Norse
un-swinging	örvígr	way	leið, veg, venja
until	unz	ways	vega
unusual	fáheyrðr	wealth	fé, fjár, fjárins
up	upp	wealthy-treasures	auðæfum
upon	á	weaponed	vápnaðir
upright	rekkum	weapon-nimble	vápnfimi
urged	fýstu	weapons	vápnum
us	oss	weapons-exchange	vápnaskipti
		weight	vægis
		well	allvel, vel
		went	færi, fór, för, fóru, gekk, gengr, gengu

V, v

English	Old Norse	English	Old Norse
valiant	böðfrækn	were	er, væri, var, váru
various	ýmissa	we-sailed	Sigldum
verse	vísur	what	en, er, hvat, hverra
verses	vísur	when	er
very	einkar	where	er, hvar
victory	sigr, sigri	which	en, er, sem
victory-gift-gods	sigrgöfgaðir	while	hríð, meðan
viking	víking	who	er, Hver, hverr
viking-raids	víking	whole	heilum
vikings	víkinga, víkingar	wide	breiðan, víða
virtuous	dyggir	widely	víða
vision	fyrirburðr, víst	wield	valda
visions	fyrirburð	wife	eiginkonu, kona, konu
visit	vitja	wife-of	kona
voyage	ferðar	will	vil, vill
		willed	vildi, vildu, vilja
		willing	fúsastr
		will-you	villtu
		windswept	byrsóta
		winters	vetra

W, w

English	Old Norse	English	Old Norse
wafting	hváfta	wise	fróðr, vitr, vitrustum
wake	vakni	wisest	vitrasta
wall	vegg	wish	vil, vili, vilið, vill
wanted-to	vill	wished	vildi, vildu
war-clothes	herklæðum	with	at, enda, með, of, ór, við, víða
war-company	herliði	within	innan
warfare	herför, vígroða	without	útan
warrior	gramr	woke	vaknaði
warriors	drengir, gramr, grams	woken	vaknat
was	enn, er, eru, sem, væri, var, varð, váru, vera	wolf	heiðingja
was-heard	spyrjast	wolf's	ylgjar
was-named	hét	woman	kona, kvenna
waves	bylgjur	woman's-customs	kvennasið

Word List (English to Old Norse)

English	Old Norse
women	konur
won	gagn
wonder	undr, undrast
wonderful	ágætum
wonder-like	undarligr, undarligt
wood	skíð, víði
worded	orð, ort
words	mála, orð, orða
word-struggle	orðahjaldr
working-man	verkmaðr
worth	verðr, virðing
worthily	virðuliga
worthiness	virðing, virðingu
worthy	verða, virðing, virðuligr, virðuligri
would	munda, mundi, mundu, muni
would-be	væri
wounds	sárum
written	ritnar

Y, y

English	Old Norse
yet	Þó
you	þér, þik, þú, yðr
young	ung, unga, ungr
your	yðvarrar, yðvarri
yours	þín
yourself	sjálfum
youth	æsku

The Tale of Star-Oddi's Dream (*Old Icelandic*)

Old Icelandic	Literal	English
1	**1**	**1**
Þórður hét maður er bjó í Múla norður í Reykjardal.	Thord was-named a-man who lived at Muli in-the-north in Reykjardal.	There was a man named Thord who lived at Muli in the north, in Reykjardal.
Þar var á vist með honum sá maður er Oddi hét og var Helgason.	There was in hospitality with him so a-man who Oddi named and was Son-of-Helgi.	There was a man living with him named Oddi who was the son of Helgi.
Hann var kallaður Stjörnu-Oddi.	He was called Star-Oddi.	He was called Star-Oddi.
Hann var rímkænn maður svo að engi maður var hans maki honum samtíða á öllu Íslandi og að mörgu var hann annars vitur.	He was calendar-computation-wise a-man so that no man was his match him contemporary in all Iceland and that many was he otherwise wise.	He was skilled in the art of calendar computation, such that no man in all of Iceland was a match for him, and he was also wise in many other things.
Ekki var hann skáld né kvæðinn.	Not was he poet nor poetry.	He was not a poet, nor did he know much poetry.
Þess er og einkum getið um hans ráð að það höfðu menn fyrir satt að hann lygi aldrei ef hann vissi satt að segja og að öllu var hann ráðvandur kallaður og tryggðarmaður hinn mesti.	This was also particularly told about his statements that it had people before the-truth that he lied never if he knew the-truth to say and that all was he honest called and faithful-man the most.	It was also particularly said about him of his statements that people held them to be the truth, that he never lied if he knew the truth to tell, and that he was the most honest and faithful man.
Félítill var hann og ekki mikill verkmaður.	Fee-little was he and not much working-man.	He was poor and not an especially good worker.
Frá því er að segja að um þenna mann Odda gerðist undarlegur atburður.	From therefore is to say that about this man Oddi happened extraordinary events.	The story goes that extraordinary events happened to this man Oddi.
Hann fór heiman út til Flateyjar er Þórður húsbóndi hans sendi hann þessa ferð á vit fiska og er eigi annars getið en þeim fórst vel til eyjarinnar.	He travelled home out-from to Flatey when Thord housemaster his sent him this journey to to fishing and was not anything-else told-of but they travelled well to the-island.	He travelled out from his home to Flatey when his housemaster Thord sent him on a journey to go fishing, and nothing else is told except that the journey to the island went well.
Þar var hann í góðum beina.	There was he in good assistance.	He was well looked after there.

The Tale of Star-Oddi's Dream (Old Icelandic)

Old Icelandic	Literal	English
Ekki er frá því sagt hver þar bjó.	Not was from therefore said who there lived.	It was not said who lived there.
En frá því er að segja að um kveldið er menn fóru í rekkju var vel búið um Odda og hæglega.	Then from therefore was it said that about evening were people going to bed was well preparations about Oddi and comfortable.	Then from there it was said that about one evening people were going to bed, as preparations were made to make Oddi comfortable.
En við það er Oddi var farmóður og veittur hóglegur umbúnaður þá sofnar hann brátt og dreymdi hann þegar að hann þóttist staddur vera heima í Múla og svo þótti honum sem þar væri kominn maður til gistingar og þótti honum sem menn færu í rekkju um kveldið.	And with that was Oddi was travel-weary and given comfortably soft-bed-prepared then slept he soon and dreamed he straightaway that he though stood was home in Muli and so seemed to-him that there was come a-man to guest and thought he as people went to bed about evening.	And with Oddi being travel-weary, he was given a comfortable and soft bed that had been prepared for him, and he soon fell asleep and dreamed straightaway that he stood at home in Muli, and it seemed to him that a man had come as a guest, and that people were going to bed in the evening.
Þótti honum gesturinn vera beðinn skemmtanar en hann tók til og sagði sögu og hóf á þessa leið.	Seemed to-him the-guest was asking entertainment and he took to of the-saga telling and began in this way.	It seemed to him that the guest had asked for some entertainment, and he took to telling a saga, which began in this way.

2

Old Icelandic	Literal	English
Hróðbjartur hefir konungur heitið.	Hrodbjart had king dominion.	Hrodbart had the rule of a king.
Hann réð austur fyrir Gautlandi.	He ruled east for Götaland.	He ruled over east Götaland.
Hann var kvongaður maður.	He was married man.	He was a married man.
Hildigunnur hét kona hans.	Hildigunn named wife his.	His wife was named Hildigunn.
Þau áttu sér einn son barna er Geirviður er nefndur.	They had themselves only son child was Geirvid was named.	They had an only child whose was named Geirvid.
Hann var snemma vænn og vitmikill og að öllum hlutum mannaður um fram sína jafnaldra en barn var hann að aldri er sagan gerðist.	He was soon handsome and knowing-much and in all things brought-up about from his equal-age but child was he of age when the-saga begins.	He grew up to be handsome and wise in all things more than those his age, but he was a child when the saga begins.

The Tale of Star-Oddi's Dream (Old Icelandic)

Old Icelandic	Literal	English
Frá því er að segja að konungurinn Hróðbjartur hafði settan til landstjórnar yfir þriðjung ríkis síns jarl þann er Hjörvarður hét.	From therefore is to say that this-king Hrodbjart had appointed to governing over a-third-of kingdom his earl then was Hjorvard named.	From there is to say that this King Hrodbjart had appointed an earl to govern over a third of the kingdom who was named Hjorvard.
Hann var og kvongaður og hét kona hans Hjörgunnur.	He was also married and named wife his Hjorgunn.	He was also married and his wife was named Hjorgunn.
Þau áttu eina dóttur barna.	They had only daughter child.	They had a daughter who was an only child.
Sú hét Hlégunnur.	So named Hlegunn.	She was named Hlegunn.
Frá henni er svo sagt að hún var ólát í æsku sinni og var ávallt því ódælli sem hún var eldri.	From her is so said that she was un-courteous in youth hers and was always therefore unpleasant as she was older.	It is said of her that she was discourteous in her youth and got more unpleasant as she got older.
Það var og sagt að hún vildi ekki kvenna sið fága í sínu athæfi.	It was also said that she willed not woman customs cultivate in her behaviour.	It was also said that she did not wish to cultivate womanly traditions in her behaviour.
Það var hennar venja jafnan að hún gekk í herklæðum og með vopnum og ef hana skildi á við menn þá veitti hún þeim annaðhvort áverka stóra eða líflát þegar henni líkaði eigi.	It was her way always that she went in war-clothes and with weapons and if she should then against people then gave her them either-way injury great or life-less as-soon-as she liked not.	It was always her way that she went about in armour with weapons, and if people went against her in any way she gave them either a great injury or death as soon as she did not like them.
En við þenna hennar ójafnað þá þótti Hjörvarði jarli föður hennar eigi mega við sæma hennar vandræði og sagði henni þá ljóslega að hann mundi eigi þann veg lengur láta fram fara og kvað henni eigi hlýða mundu nema um batnaði nokkurs háttar	Then with this her unequal then thought Hjorvard the-earl father hers not may with-the-same her difficulty and told her then lightly that he may not then way longer let from go and said she not obey would except about bettering somewhat kind	Then with this overbearing behaviour, her father earl Hjorvard felt that he may not tolerate her disruptions any more, and told her plainly that it could not go on any longer, and that she should do somewhat better,
"eða ellegar far í brott sem skjótast úr minni hirð".	"or otherwise travel to away as soonest from my court".	or otherwise leave my court as soon as possible.

The Tale of Star-Oddi's Dream (Old Icelandic)

Old Icelandic	Literal	English
En þegar Hlégunnur jarlsdóttir verður þessa áheyrsla af föður sínum að hann vildi hana láta í burt fara af sinni hirð þá svarar hún því máli svo að hún kvað sig þar ekki dvelja og beiddi hún þá föður sinn að hann skyldi fá henni langskip þrjú alskipuð bæði að mönnum og herklæðum og búa að öllu sem best með góðum liðskosti svo að henni þætti vel skipuð.	Then as-soon-as Hlegunn the-earl's-daughter became of-this to-hear of father hers that he willed her leave to away travel from his court then answered she therefore saying so that she spoke herself there not dwell and asked she then father hers that he should give her longships three fully-prepared both in men and war-clothes and prepare that all as best with good provisions so that she seemed well prepared.	Then as soon as the earl's daughter Hlegunn came to hear of her father, that he wished her to travel away from his court, then she answered therefore declaring, that she did not wish to stay there and asked her father to give her three longships fully prepared with men and armour, and prepared with the best provisions so that she was well prepared.
Og ef svo væri gert sem hún beiddi hér um þetta mál þá taldi hún sér mundu vel líka þótt hún færi í braut við svo búið.	And if so would-be done as she asked she about that matter then said she herself would well like thought she travel to away with so prepared.	And if it would be done as she asked in this matter then she said she would like to travel away as she was prepared.
Hjörvarður jarl vildi gjarna þetta til vinna að hún kæmist á braut sem skjótast því að honum þótti, sem var, mikil vandræði af standa hennar ráði.	Hjorvard the-earl willed gladly this to grant that she comes to away as quickly therefore that he thought that was much difficulty of standing her conduct.	Earl Hjorvard was glad to grant this so that she would go away as soon as possible, for he thought there was great difficulty with her conduct if she stayed.
Síðan lét hann búa að öllu þrjú langskip sem best.	Then had he prepared to all three longships as best.	Then he had prepared all three longships as best as possible.
En þegar þetta lið var búið þá fer Hlégunnur jarlsdóttir úr landi með þessu liði og lagðist síðan í hernað og víking og aflaði sér svo fjár og frama.	Then as-soon-as the crew were prepared then travelled Hlegunn the-earl's-daughter out-of land with this crew and lay afterwards to raiding and viking and obtained herself such wealth and fame.	Then as soon as the crew were ready Hlegunn the earl's daughter travelled out of the land with this crew and went raiding and viking and obtained such wealth and fame for herself.
Svo er sagt að hún kom eigi í land meðan faðir hennar lifði.	So was said that she came not to land while father hers lived.	So it was said that she did not come back to the land while her father lived.

The Tale of Star-Oddi's Dream (Old Icelandic)

Old Icelandic	Literal	English
En í annan stað er þar til að taka sögunnar að þá er Geirviður son Hróðbjarts konungs var átta vetra gamall tók Hróðbjartur konungur sótt og verður það lítil frásaga því að sóttin leiðir svo til lands að konungurinn andast.	But in another place is there to of take the-saga that then was Geirvid son Hrodbjart's king was eight winters old took Hrodbjart king sickness and became that little from-to-say accordingly that sickness took so to the-lands that the-king died.	But to take the saga to another place, then King Hrodbjart's son Geirvid was eight winters old, Hrodbjart took ill, and there was little to say of it, but a sickness took to the land and the king died.
Það þótti öllum hans ástvinum og virktamönnum hinn mesti skaði, sem var, að missa slíks höfðingja og þar út í frá öllu landsfólkinu.	That thought all of-him beloved and chosen-man the most harm, as was, that missed such chieftains and there out to from all lands-folk.	Everyone thought this a great harm as he was beloved by his chosen companions, chieftains, and people of the land.
Síðan var fengið að virðulegri veislu og þar til boðið öllum hinum ríkustum mönnum og hinum bestum höfðingjum er í voru landinu.	Afterwards was got then worthy feast and there to invited all the kingdom's people and the best chieftains that in were the-land.	Afterwards a worthy feast was prepared, and all of the kingdom's people and the best chieftains in the land were invited.
Þar með var og til boðið hverjum manni þeim er veisluna vildi sækja, bæði innan lands og utan svo að engi skyldi þar óboðið koma.	Then with was also to invited each person they of feast willed seek, both within lands and without so that none should there uninvited come.	With that, everyone who wished to attend was also invited, both within the land and without, so that no one should come uninvited.
En síðan þessi veisla var saman sett með því fjölmenni er þangað sótti þá var þar erfi drukkið eftir Hróðbjart konung með miklum veg og sóma svo sem byrjaði hans tign og sómasamlegri virðingu.	Then after the feast were together set with because followers were there attending then was there a-toast drunk after Hrodbjart the-king with much way and honour so as began his prestige and respectable worthiness.	Then after the feast was held with the many followers who attended there, a toast was drunk for King Hrodbjart, in such a way that honoured his prestige and respectable worthiness.
En er erfinu var lokið þá var konungurinn heygður að fornum sið eftir því sem þá var tíska til við göfga menn.	Then as the-toast was ended then was the-king buried in ancient traditions after according-to as then was fashion to with noble men.	Then when the toast had ended, the king was buried according to ancient traditions that were then fashionable with noble men.

The Tale of Star-Oddi's Dream (Old Icelandic)

Old Icelandic	Literal	English
3	**3**	**3**
Nú er svo að segja að eftir þessi miklu tíðindi er þar í landi höfðu gerst þá sýndist það öllum hinum vitrustum mönnum og hinum bestum vinum konungsins að taka annan mann til konungs og landstjórnar í stað þvílíks höfðingja sem þá var við misst.	Now is so to say that after this much news was there in the-land had done then seemed that all the-others wise people and the best friends the-king's to take another person to king and governing the place such-like chieftains as then were with lost.	Now the saga goes that after this there was much news in the land that all the wise people and the king's best friends had to take another person as king and for the chieftains to cover the place as such a leader had been lost.
En svo var mikil ástúð öllum landsmönnum á Hróðbjarti konungi meðan hann lifði að menn vildu ekki annað en velja Geirvið son hans til konungs og láta eigi konungdóminn ganga úr hans ætt.	But so was great affection of-all lands-people to Hrodbjart the-king while he lived that people willed not another to choose Geirvid son his to king and allowed not kingdom going out-of his lineage.	But so great was the affection of all the people of the land to King Hrodbjart while he lived that no one wanted to choose other than Geirvid his son as king and not to let the kingdom pass out of his lineage.
Þótt Geirviður væri ungur að aldri eða hann þætti þá enn lítt til landráða fallinn í þann tíma vildi þó allt landsfólkið til þessa hætta með umsjá drottningar móður hans með því að hún var hin vitrasta kona og vel að sér í alla staði.	Thought Geirvid was young in age and he thought then that little to land-ruling disposed in that time willed though all the-land's-people to this conclude with supervision queen mother his with accordingly that she was the wisest woman and well to herself in all places.	Though Geirvid was young in age and seemed little disposed to ruling the land at that time, all the people of the land wished it, with supervision of his mother the queen accordingly, as she was the wisest woman and capable in all ways.
En er svo fór fram um hríð að svo ungur maður skyldi höfðingi vera og stjórna mörgu fólki sem Geirviður var þá gerðist brátt landstjórnin lítil, sem líklegt var.	But when so went from about awhile that so young man should chieftain be and ruling many folk as Geirvid was then became soon the-government little, as likely was.	But when this had been so for a while, with such a young man as Geirvid being a ruler and governing many people, then the government became weak, as was likely.
Það gerðist og að hirðin fáttkaðist fyrir því að margir voru þeir af hans hirðmönnum að aðra iðn lögðu fyrir sig.	It became also that courtiers few because therefore that many were they of his court-men that other crafts laid for themselves.	It also came about that he courtiers were fewer because many of his court men found themselves other jobs.
Sumir lögðust í víking, aðrir réðust í kaupferðir til ýmissa landa.	Some laid to viking-raids, others appointed to merchant-voyages to various lands.	Some went on viking raids, others were appointed on merchant voyages to various lands.

The Tale of Star-Oddi's Dream (Old Icelandic)

Old Icelandic	Literal	English
Nú með því að á þessu þótti mikið mein sem nú var frá sagt þá gerðust þó mörg önnur óhægindi í ríki þessa hins unga konungs.	Now with therefore that of this thought much harm as how was from said then made though many others inconvenience in the-kingdom this the young king.	Now with this being thought of as much harm, as before said, then there were other inconveniences in the kingdom of this young kind.
Þess er við getið í sögunni að illvirkjar tveir lögðust út á skóg þann er Jöruskógur heitir.	This was with told-of in the-saga that evil-doers two camped out in forest then was Battle-forest named.	It was told of in this saga that two evil doers camped out in the forest which was then named Battle Forest.
Það var í ríki þessa hins unga manns.	It was in kingdom this the young man's.	This was in the young man's kingdom.
Þessir víkingar drápu menn til fjár sér og voru nálega berserkir.	These vikings killed people for wealth as also were nearly berserkers.	These vikings killed men for money and were virtually berserkers.
Annar þeirra hét Garpur en annar Gnýr.	One of-them named Garp and the-other Gny.	One of them was named Garp, and the other Gny.
Svo er sagt að mönnum hlýddi aldrei fám að fara saman.	So is said that people followed never few to travel together.	So it was said that people never travelled in small numbers together.
Jafnan voru menn vanir að fara á skóginn með fjölmenni að leita illvirkjanna og ráða þá af en þeir urðu aldregi hittir þó að þeirra væri leita farið með fjölmenni.	Always were people friends that travelled to the-forest with followers-many to search for-the-evil-doers and prevail then of which they became never found though that they were searching travelling with followers-many.	People were always travelling with friends to the forest with followers to search for these evil doers and defeat them, but they were never found, even though many people were searching for them.
Slíku fer fram til þess er Geirviður konungur er tólf vetra.	So it-went from to this that Geirvid the-king was twelve winters.	So it went on until King Geirvid was twelve winters old.
Og þá er hann var svo aldurs kominn þá var hann svo mikill maður vexti og sterkur að afli sem þeir menn margir sem fullkomnir voru að aldri og atgervi nálega eftir því sem þeir best voru á sig komnir fyrir allra hluta sakir.	And then when he was so of-age come then was he so much a-man grown and strong in strength as they men many as fully-come were to age and deeds closely after accordingly which they best were in himself come before all things sake.	And then when he had come of age, he was a great man in height and strength, as much as many men who had come of age, and almost like those who were at their peak in all things.

The Tale of Star-Oddi's Dream (Old Icelandic)

Old Icelandic	Literal	English
Það var eitthvert sinn þá er Geirviður konungur sat yfir borðum með allri hirð sinni, þá tók hann til orða og mælti svo:	Then was some-time one-day then that Geirvid the-king sat over the-tables with all retainers his, then took he to words and spoke so:	Then one day King Geirvid sat at the table with his retainers, and took to words and said:
"Nú er svo sem yður er kunnigt öllum mínum mönnum að eg hefi ungur verið hér til að aldri og svo hefi eg haft litla orku og því hefir af mér staðið lítil stjórn í ríkinu.	"Now is so as you that known all my men that I have young been forces to that age and so have I had little power and therefore have of me stood little control in the-kingdom.	Now it is well known to you, all my people, that I have been young and have had little power, and therefore I have had little control over the kingdom.
Hefi eg það og oft heyrt sem von er að.	Have I that and often heard as expected was it.	And I have often heard, as was expected,
Má það og eigi mjög undrast þó að hér til hafi af mér lítil stjórn staðið fyrir sakir æsku minnar.	May it also not much wonder though that forces to have of me little control placed before the-sake-of youth mine.	It may also not be much to wonder that I have had little force of control for the sake of my youth.
En þó er eg nú svo aldurs kominn að mér er nú mál að reyna mig og vita að nokkuð vilji mitt ráð þroskast og meir hefjast en áður er þar sem eg er nú orðinn maður tólf vetra gamall.	However though am I now so of-age come that to-me is now matter to test myself and know that something wish mine decide develop and more start then after that there was I am now become a-man twelve winters old.	However, now that I have come of age, there is now the matter to test myself and I wish to know something whether it is decided that my rule will develop and become more after than it was at the start, now that I am a man of twelve winters old.
Eru og margir ekki betur mannaðir á mínum aldri.	Are and many not better mannered at my age.	There are many my age who are not better mannered than me.
Nú vil eg og því lýsa fyrir öllum yður, mínum þegnum og virktavinum, að eg ætla mér að fara til móts við berserkina, þá Garp og Gný, er liggja á Jöruskógi og gera þar mörg illvirki.	Now will I also therefore show for all of-you, my subjects and friends, that I intend me to travel to meet with berserkers, then Garp and Gny, who camped in Battle-forest and do there many outrages.	Now therefore I wish to show all of you, my subjects and friends, that I intend to travel to meet with the berserkers, Garp and Gny, who camp in Battle Forest and do many outrages there.
Ætla eg og til þess að koma eigi aftur svo að þeir séu á lífi og skal eg þá yfirkoma eða þeir mig ella".	Intend I also to this that come not back so so-as they are of alive and shall I then overcome or they me or-else".	I also do not intend to come back so long as they are alive, and either I shall over come them, or they me".

The Tale of Star-Oddi's Dream (Old Icelandic)

Old Icelandic	Literal	English
En er Geirviður konungur hafði þetta mælt þá svarar fyrst máli hans drottningin móðir hans og þar með allir hans bestu menn og mæltu nálega allir sem eins manns munni og báðu konung fara fjölmennan á fund stigamannanna og með miklum viðbúnaði ef hann vildi fara.	And when Geirvid the-king had this spoke then answered first speech his the-queen mother his and there with all his best people and spoke almost all as one man's mouth and asked the-king travel followers-many to find the-robbing-men and with much preparation if he wished to-travel.	And when King Geirvid had spoken, the first to answer his speech was his mother the queen, along with his best people, and all spoke almost with one voice and asked that the king travel with many followers to find the robbing men and with much preparation if he wished to travel.
Geirviður konungur svarar:	Geirvid the-king answered:	King Geirvid answered:
"Hugsað hefi eg þetta mál áður nokkuð fyrir mér en eg kvæði upp og sýnist mér á þá leið sem í þessari ferð megi mér þá engi frami kaupast þótt eg fái náð berserkjunum enda leita eg þeirra með miklu liði alvopnuðu.	"Think have I this matter before some-time for me that I announced up and seems to-me that then passes so in this journey may for-me then not courage redeem though I get protection the-berserkers with seeking I them with much company all-weaponed.	I have been thinking about this matter for some time before I announced it and it seems to me that if it so passes on my journey, I may not redeem courage if I have the protection from the berserkers while seeking them with a great company all armed.
En það er þá nokkur svívirðing ef þeir fást þá eigi og komi eg við það aftur og verður þá ósnöfurmannlega minnar handar ef svo tekst.	But it is then somewhat disgraceful if them get then not and come I with it returning and became then un-alert my hand if so takes.	But then it is a disgrace if they are not caught, and I will come to return, and then it will have been feeble for my hand if it it ends like that.
Nú hefi eg hina leið ætlað ferðina að fara með annan mann á þeirra fund og mun þá skipta gæfa með oss hver þá skal verða vor skilnaður.	Now have I then company intend travelling that travel with another person that they find and should then exchange good-fortune with us each then shall become our parting.	Now I intend to travel with another person to find them, and it should then exchange good fortune between us and we shall se how we part.
Má þá og verða ef vill að nokkur svo fremd fylgi ferðinni.	May then also be if will that something so honour follows the-journey.	May it then also become, if willing, that some honour follows this journey.
Skal nú og á það ráð hætta hversu sem til vill takast.	Shall now also to that decide conclude how-so as to will take.	That shall now decide and conclude how it may turn out.

The Tale of Star-Oddi's Dream (Old Icelandic)

Old Icelandic	Literal	English
Er nú og fyrir því upp borið þetta mál fyrir yður að eg vil nú vita hver fúsastur er til þessarar ferðar með mér og er nú það ráð að nokkur vakni við, sá er til vill ráðast, og svari sá nú mínu máli enda skuluð þér það vita hér með að nú er þetta mál fullgert fyrir mína hönd að eg mun þó fara þessa ferð þótt eg fari einn saman og verði engi til að fylgja mér".	Is now also before because up brought this matter before you that I wish no to-know who willing that to this journey with me and is now that decision to someone wake against, so that to wish arrange, and answer so now my speech and should you it know here with that now is this matter full-done before my hand that I should though travel this journey though I travel one the-same and be none to that follow me".	Now, therefore, this matter has been brought before you that I now want to know who is most willing to go on this journey with me, and it is now the plan that someone will wake up, whoever may decide, and he will now answer my question, and you shall do so. Know herewith that now this matter is settled on my behalf that I will still go on this journey even though I go alone and there will be no one to follow me".
En við þessi ummæli konungs þá er það sagt að drottning sjálf fyrst að upphafi latti á alla vega þessar ferðar og sagði, sem var, allóráðlega stofnað þar sem við heljarmenn var að eiga er illvirkjarnir voru, svo mikið sem þar var í ábyrgð er konungurinn var sjálfur því að öllum þótti vís von að hann mundi látast fyrir þeim og fá minna hlut í þeirra skiptum ef svo yrði sem líklegt mundi þykja fyrir sakir æsku konungs þeirra en harðfengi berserkjanna.	And with these about-words the-king's then was it said that the-queen herself first to became discouraged to all ways this journey and said, that was, all-un-forethought planned there as with accursed-men was that only were criminals were, so much as there was in responsibility was the-king's was himself therefore to all thought aware expecting that he would die before them and get less lot of there exchanged if so became as likely would regarded for sake youth the-king's they which toughness the-berserkers.	And with these words from the king, then it was said that the queen herself was the first to discourage this expedition in every respect, and she said it had been planned with little forethought, with these accursed men who were criminals, as much as there was a responsibility for the king himself, all expected that he would get the worst of it and die because of them, if it became as was likely, for the sake of the king's youth and the toughness of the berserkers.
Allir vinir konungs löttu ákaflega fararinnar og þótti konungur út seldur ef hann færi við annan mann.	All friends the-king's dissuaded extremely of-the-journey and thought the-king out sold if he journeyed with another man.	All the king's friends were extremely discouraging of the journey and thought that the king would be done for if he went with only one other man.
Konungur svarar að ekki mundi tjóa að letja hann.	The-king answered that not would avail to discourage him.	The king answered that it would be to no avail to try and discourage him.
Og er allir skildu að konungur mundi eigi letjast láta þá verður til og svarar máli konungs sá er Dagfinnur hét.	And when all knew that the-king would not discouraged allow then became to also answer the-matter the-king's so that Dagfinn named.	And when all understood that the king would not be discouraged, then cane an answer to the king's case, who was named Dagfinn.

The Tale of Star-Oddi's Dream (Old Icelandic)

Old Icelandic	Literal	English
Hann var hirðmaður konungs og konungsskáld.	He was court-man the-king's and the-king's-poet.	He was the king's court man and the king's poet.
"Herra", segir hann, "engan mann veit eg þér meiri sæmd eiga að launa í alla staði en mig.	"Lord", said he, "no person know I to-you more honour have to reward in all places than me.	"Lord," said he, "I know of no man more honorable to you in all things than me.
Er eg og því skyldari að skiljast aldrei við þig er þú ert í meira háska staddur ef þér viljið þiggja mitt föruneyti og fylgd og er eg til þessar farar albúinn þegar þér viljið".	Am I also therefore obliged to separate never with you that you are the more danger placed if you wish accept my companionship and follow and that I to this travel all-prepared as-soon-as you wish".	I am therefore more obliged to never part with you when you are in more danger if you want to accept my entourage and escort, and I am ready for this journey whenever you want".

4

En þegar þessi maður, Dagfinnur, var nefndur í sögunni þá er frá því að segja er mjög er undarlegt að þá brá því við í drauminum Odda að hann Oddi sjálfur þóttist vera þessi maður, Dagfinnur, en gesturinn sá er söguna sagði er nú úr sögunni og drauminum en þá þóttist hann sjálfur sjá og vita allt það er héðan af er í drauminum.	Then as-soon-as this man, Dagfinn, was named in the-saga then was from accordingly to say that much was wonder-like that then drew therefore with in the-dream Oddi's that he Oddi himself thought was this man, Dagfinn, but-the-guest so was the-saga telling was now out-of the-saga and the-dream and then thought he himself so and knew all that was from-here of for in the-dream.	But when this man, Dagfinn, was mentioned in the story, it is very strange to say that in Oddi's dream it happened that Oddi himself thought he was this man, Dagfinn, but the guest who told the story is now out of the story and the dream, but then he thought he saw and knew all that is henceforth in the dream.
En nú síðan er drauminn svo að segja sem honum þótti sjálfum fyrir sig bera, Odda, þá þóttist hann vera Dagfinnur og ráðast í ferðina með konunginum Geirviði.	Then now after in the-dream so to say as he thought himself before himself borne, Oddi, then thought he was Dagfinn and arranging to travel with the-king Geirvid.	But now since the dream is, so to speak, that Oddi then he thought he was Dagfinn and embarked on the journey with King Geirvid.
En er þeir voru albúnir þá riðu þeir tveir saman með vopnum sínum til þess er þeir komu á Jöruskóg þangað sem illvirkjanna var von en þar var svo viður vaxið að gata var breið um skóginn.	Then when they were all-prepared then rode they two together with weapons theirs to this that they came to Battle-forest from-there as the-evil-doers were expecting then they were so trees grown that the-way was broad about the-forest.	Then when they were ready the two rode together with their weapons until they came to Battle Forest, where the evil doers were waiting, then the trees were so grown that there was a wide path through the forest.

The Tale of Star-Oddi's Dream (Old Icelandic)

Old Icelandic	Literal	English
Og er þeir komu mjög langt í skóginn þá er þess getið að þar varð fyrir þeim hóll einn mjög hár.	And when they came much long in the-forest then is this told-of that there was before them hill one much high.	And when they came very far into the forest, it is told that there was a very high hill before them.
Hann var brattur öllum megin.	It was broad all sides.	It was steep on all sides.
Síðan gengu þeir upp á hólinn og vildu þaðan sjást um og vita hverra tíðinda þeir mættu vísir verða.	Afterwards went they up by the-hill and wished then t-look about and know what news they may know to-be.	Then they went up the hill and from there wanted to look around and know what tidings they might become.
Mart smágrjót var á hóli þessum.	Many small-stones were on hill this.	Many small stones were on this hill.
Þaðan sáu þeir víða.	From-there saw they widely.	From there they saw widely.
Þeir geta að líta hvar ganga tveir menn.	They could to look where going two men.	They could see where the two men were walking.
Þeir voru miklir vexti og gengu þegar þangað að hólinum sem þeir konungur stóðu.	They were great grown and went they from-there to the-hill as they the-king stood.	They were tall and they immediately walked to the hill where the king stood.
Þessir menn voru báðir vel vopnaðir.	These men were both well weaponed.	These men were both well armed.
En þegar þeir konungur og Dagfinnur sáu þessa menn þá þóttust þeir vita að þar voru þeir komnir Garpur og Gnýr.	Then as-soon-as they the-king and Dagfinn saw these men then thought they knew that there were they coming Garp and Gny.	But when the king and Dagfinn saw these men, they thought they knew that Garp and Gny had come there.
Þá mælti Dagfinnur:	Then spoke Dagfinn:	Then Dagfinn said,
"Herra, eg vil yður kunnigt gera að eg er eigi mjög vanur vopnaskipti og kann eg lítt að treysta hug mínum né vopnfimi.	"Lord, I wish to-you know be that I am not much accustomed weapons-exchange and can I a-little to trust mind mine nor weapon-nimble.	Lord, I want to let you know that I am not very accustomed to exchanging arms, and I can scarcely trust my mind or my agility.
Nú vil eg að þér kjósið um tvo kosti, hvort þér viljið heldur að eg ráðist í mót berserkjunum með þér eða viltu að eg sjái til yðvarrar sameignar af hólinum og kunni eg frá að segja öðrum mönnum".	Now wish I that you choose about two benefits, either you wish rather that I determine to meet the-berserkers with you or will-you that I see that your fight of the-hill and know I from to say to-other people".	Now I want you to choose two options, whether you want me to attack the berserkers with you or you want me to see to your fight from the hill and I can tell other people what happened".

The Tale of Star-Oddi's Dream (Old Icelandic)

Old Icelandic	Literal	English
Konungur svarar:	The-king answered:	The king answered:
"Ef þér lér nokkuð tveggja huga um þetta mál þá þykir mér einsætt að þú sért hér á hólinum og sjáir héðan til sameignar vorrar og komir eigi nær við vor vopnaskipti".	"If you lean somewhat two minds about this matter then seems to-me evident that you are here on the-hill and look from-here to the-fight aware and come not near with our weapons-exchange".	If you lean somewhat in two minds about this matter, I think it is decided that you are here on the hill and see from here to the fight and do not come any closer to our exchange of arms.
Dagfinnur tekur það ráð sem konungur mælti og dvaldist eftir á hólinum og kemur hvergi nær og þykir honum það allráðlegt en konungurinn sjálfur ræðst ofan af hólinum í móti stigamönnunum.	Dagfinn took this advice as the-king spoke and dwelled afterwards on the-hill and came each near and seemed to-him that advisable what the-king himself decided over of the-hill in meeting the-robbers.	Dagfinn took the advice which the king had said and stayed on the hill, and came nowhere near, and he thought it wise, but the king himself attacked from the top of the hill against the robbers.
Þar kann eigi glögglega frá að segja hversu högg fóru með þeim og mun eg þar gera skjóta frásögu því að það er þar frá lyktum að segja að svo skipti hamingjan með þeim, því að konungi varð lagið líf og lykka, að hann bar af báðum illvirkjunum og létust þeir af stórum sárum er konungur hafði þeim veitt.	There known not clearly from to say how-so blows went between them and should I there do short from-saying because that it was there from completion to say that so exchanged graciousness with them, because that the-king was granted life and luck, that he bore of both evil-doers and had they of great wounds that the-king had them given.	It is not clear from there how the blows went with them, and I will make a quick account of it, for it is from there to say that their happiness that was so important to them was exchanged, for the king was given life and happiness, that he bore from both evil doers. and they died of the great wounds which the king had inflicted on them.
Og eftir það er illvirkjarnir voru fallnir þá gengu þeir konungur og Dagfinnur fram á götuna lengra og komu þar að farandi er stígur lítill lá af þjóðbrautinni í skóginn.	And afterwards that when the-evil-doers were fallen then went they the-king and Dagfinn from to path longer and came there to travel where climbed little lying of the-highway in the-forest.	And after the evildoers had fallen, the king and Dagfinn went further out into the path, and came to a place where a small path lay from the highway into the forest.
Þeir höfðu litla stund gengið þann hinn litla stíg áður brátt gerðist rjóður mjög mikið í mörkinni og stóð þar eitt hús.	They had little awhile gone then the little path before soon became clearing much greatly in the-border and stood there one house.	They had walked the small path for a short time before soon there was a lot of clearing in the border and a house stood there.
Það hús var hátt og rammgert og rammlega læst og grafinn lykill í dyragætti.	The house was tall and firmly-built and firmly locked and the-key buried in doorway.	That house was tall and firmly built, and firmly locked with a key buried in the doorway.

The Tale of Star-Oddi's Dream (Old Icelandic)

Old Icelandic	Literal	English
Þeir luku upp húsinu og gengu þar inn.	They unlocked up the-house and went they in.	They opened the house and went inside.
Það hús var vel innan búið og var nálega fullt af allskyns auðæfum.	The house was well inside prepared and was nearly full of all-kinds-of wealthy-treasures.	That house was well furnished and was almost full of all kinds of riches.
Þar voru þeir um nóttina og skorti þar hvorki góðan drykk né dýran mat en um morguninn fóru þeir heimleiðis og huldu áður hræ útilegumannanna.	They were there about the-night and shortage of neither good drink nor fine food then about morning travelled they homeward and covering after corpses the-outlaw-men.	They were there during the night and there was no shortage of good drinks or expensive food, but in the morning they went home and hid the carcasses of the outlaw men before.
En er konungurinn kom heim til ríkis síns þá varð hann frægur mjög víða um lönd af sínu þrekvirki og ágætum sigri og urðu allir vinir konungsins og frændur honum fegnir er hann kom heim með göfuglegum sigri og þóttust menn hann nálega úr helju heimt hafa, sem var.	Then when the-king came home to kingdom his then was he famous much with about the-land of his brave-deeds and wonderful victory and became all friends the-king's and kinsmen his celebrated that he came home with noble-like victory and thought people he nearly out-of Hel drawn had, as was.	But when the king came home to his kingdom, he became famous in many lands for his endurance and excellent victory, and all the king's friends and relatives rejoiced when he came home with a noble victory, and it was thought that people had almost recovered him from hell, which they were.

5

Nú eftir þenna atburð allan saman lét konungur þings kveðja og kemur þar mikið fjölmenni saman.	Now after these events all together had the-king an-assembly called and came there great many-followers together.	Now after all these events, the king called an assembly and a great many people gathered there.
En er saman var sett þetta hið fjölmenna þing þá sagði konungur þar þessi miklu tíðindi og þótti öllum þetta hin mesta frægð, sem var, er Geirviður konungur hafði einn sigur borið af slíkum kempum.	Then when together were sat that the many-men the-assembly then said the-king there this great news and thought all this the most fame, which was, that Geirvid the-king had one victory carried of such champion.	And when this large assembly was convened, the king there told this great news, and it was considered by all to be the greatest fame, which was that King Geirvid had won one such a battle.

The Tale of Star-Oddi's Dream (Old Icelandic)

Old Icelandic	Literal	English
Síðan bað Geirviður að menn skyldu vitja til þess húss er illvirkjarnir höfðu í borið það mikla fé og skyldi þar hver taka sitt fé það er misst hafði.	Afterwards invited Geirvid that people should visit to the house where the-evil-doers had in bore that much wealth and should there each take his wealth that was missed had.	Then Geirvid asked that men should visit the house in which the evildoers had brought much money, and that each should take his money which he had lost.
En allir gáfu konungi upp sitt fé það sem hver átti og sögðu það best komið að hann hefði og kváðu hann fullu kostað hafa.	But all have the-king up their wealth that which each had and said that best came to him have and said he fully earned had.	But they all gave to the king what they had, and said that it was best for him to have it, and said that he had earned it in full.
Síðan lét konungur sækja féið og kastaði á sinni eigu.	Afterwards had the-king sought the-treasure and cast to his ownership.	Then the king fetched the money and cast it into his possession.
Eftir það lét konungur taka til húsgerðar og gerðu menn konungi haug þann er hann skyldi sitja á.	After that had the-king taken to house-builder and made people the-king a-mound then that he should sit on.	After that the king had a house built, and the people made a mound for the king to sit on.
Þá var konungur settur á stól þann er stóð á hauginum og hófu menn hann svo einkum til tignar og gáfu honum þá enn af nýju dýrar presentur og dýrkuðu hann sem þeir höfðu framast föng á.	Then was the-king sat on throne then as place on the-mound and had people him so especially to princely and gave him then but of new precious presents and adored him as they had foremost possessions of.	Then the king was placed on the throne that stood on the mound, and the people began to honor him, and gave him again expensive gifts, and worshiped him whom they had bestowed.
Þess er við getið þar sem Dagfinnur skáld er, honum kom í hug að engi mundi skyldari til konunginn að sæma með kvæði en svo sem hann var.	This is with told-of that as Dagfinn the-poet was, he came to mind that none would obliged to the-king to honour with a-poem than such as he was.	This is told of Dagfinn the poet, that it occurred to him that no one would be more obliged to the king to honour with a poem than he was.
Síðan gengur Dagfinnur á hauginn upp til konungsins og féll á kné fyrir hann og laut honum og kvaddi hann virðulega og sagði honum að hann hefði kvæði ort um konunginn og bað að hann mundi hlýða.	Afterwards went Dagfinn on the-mound up to the-king and fell to knee before him and place his and greeted him worthily and said to-him that he had a-poem worded about the-king and asked that he would listen.	Then Dagfinn went to the mound up to the king and fell on his knees before him and bowed to him and greeted him respectfully and told him that he had written a poem about the king and asked him to listen.
Konungur játti því blíðlega.	King said accordingly joyfully.	The king agreed joyfully.
Síðan tók Dagfinnur til og flutti kvæðið og var það flokkur.	Then took Dagfinn to and brought the-poem and was it flokk.	Then Dagfinn took over and performed the poem, and it was a flokk.

The Tale of Star-Oddi's Dream (Old Icelandic)

Old Icelandic	Literal	English
Og er lokið var kvæðinu þá þakkar konungur vel og allir þeir er við voru staddir og sögðu vel ort og svo sem sæmdi tign og virðing konungs þeirra.	And when ended was the-poem then thanked the-king well and all there was with were standing and said well worded and so as honour prestige and worthy king they.	And when the poem was finished, the king thanked well and all those who were present and said it was well written and so they honored the prestige and worthiness of their king.
Og sem konungur heyrði að allir létu vel yfir og lofuðu mjög kvæðið þá vildi hann sér láta og verða stórmannlega og launa höfðinglega og vill gefa skáldinu gullhring mikinn er hann hafði á arminum.	And as the-king heard that all had all over and praised much the-poem then willed he himself to-have and worthy great-man-like and reward nobly and wanted-to give the-poet a-gold-ring great that he had on arm.	And when the king heard that everyone had praised the poem very much, he wanted to be generous and reward the poet with a large gold ring that he had on his arm.
En Dagfinnur vildi eigi hringinn þiggja og sagði svo að honum var mikil öfúsa á því að hafa sóma og virðing af konunginum en fé kvaðst hann eigi þurfa að þiggja af honum og kallaði sig ekki skorta meðan hann héldi honum heilum	But Dagfinn wished not the-ring accept and said so that he was great gratitude that therefore to have honour and worth of the-king that treasure said he not needed to accept of him and claimed himself not shortage while he held him whole	But Dagfinn did not wish to accept the ring and said that he was very grateful to have the honour and respect of the king, but he said he did not need to accept it from him because he had no shortage of anything as long as he kept him safe,
"en þeir eru margir aðrir er þar sjá til fjárins sem þér eruð".	"but there are many others that there look to wealth as to-you are".	but there are any others who look for wealth while looking to you.
Konungi líkar þetta vel.	The-king liked this well.	This pleased the king.

6

Þessu næst er að segja frá þeim tíðindum að Hjörgunnur kona Hjörvarðar jarls tók sótt hættlega og þarf þar eigi að gera mikinn orðahjaldur að þessi sótt leiðir Hjörgunni til bana.	This next was to say from they news that Hjorgunn wife-of Hjorvard the-earl took sickness dangerously and needed there not to do much word-struggle that this sickness took Hjorgunn to death.	The next thing to tell of news was that Hjorgunn, the wife of Earl Hjorvard, took a dangerous sickness and there is no need to struggle with words to say that this sickness took Hjorgunn to her death.
Síðan var hún erfð og út borin og gert eftir hana sem tíska var til í fornum sið eftir ríkar konur.	Afterwards was she honoured and out brought and made after her as fashion was to in ancient traditions after rich women.	Afterwards she was honoured and brought out and so it was done for her in the fashion of ancient traditions of wealthy women.

The Tale of Star-Oddi's Dream (Old Icelandic)

Old Icelandic	Literal	English
Jarli þótti mikill skaði eftir drottning sína, sem von var, og harmaði hana mjög og svo margir aðrir út í frá.	The-earl thought much harm after the-queen himself, as expected was, and mourned her much and so many others out in from.	The earl thought great harm to his queen, which was expected, and mourned her greatly, along with so many others from then on.
Eigi höfðu liðið langir tímar áður vinir hans fýstu að hann skyldi fá sér annarrar konu.	Not had passed long time before friends his urged that he should get himself another wife.	It had not been long before his friends wanted him to have another wife.
Hann spurði hvar þeir sæju honum kvonfang það er honum væri virðing í að fá.	He asked where they saw him a-match that was to-him being worthy in to get.	He asked where they saw for him a wife that he would be honored to receive.
Þeir töldu ráðlegt að hann bæði til handa sér Hildigunnar drottningar og sögðu honum mikið uppheldi að þeim ráðahag ef hann næðist.	They told advice that he ask for the-hand he Hildigunn the-queen and said to-him much advancement that they marriage-proposal if he reached.	They thought it advisable for him to ask for the hand of Queen Hildigunn, and said that there would be much advancement for him if such a marriage could be achieved.
Og er þetta var oft tjáð fyrir jarli þá sýndist á þá leið því að hann var vitur maður.	And was that was often expressed before the-earl then seemed to then laid therefore that he was wise man.	And when this was often told to the earl, he saw things the same way, because he was a wise man.
Síðan hefir hann upp orð sín og biður Hildigunnar drottningar sér til eiginkonu.	Afterwards had he up worded his and invited Hildigunn the-queen herself to wife.	Then he raised his words and asked Queen Hildigunn to marry him.
Hún var þá enn ekki meir en fertug kona að aldri og þótti kosturinn vera hinn merkilegasti fyrir allra hluta sakir.	She was then was not more than forty woman in age and thought distinguished was the remarkable before all things sake.	She was still no more than forty women at the time and was considered the most remarkable option for all intents and purposes.
Og hvort sem um þetta var talað lengur eða skemur þá var það að ráði gert að drottning var gift Hjörvarði jarli með ráði konungs sonar hennar.	And how as about this was told longer or shorter then was it that decision made that the-queen was married Hjorvard the-earl with consent the-king son hers.	And whether this was talked about longer or shorter, it was decided that the queen should marry Earl Hjorvard, with the consent of her son the king.
Síðan var fengið að virðulegri veislu og drukkið brúðhlaup Hjörvarðar jarls og Hildigunnar drottningar með miklum veg og margskonar sóma.	Afterwards was got a worthy feast and drank the-wedding Hjorvard the-earl and Hildigunn the-queen with much way and many-kinds-of honour.	Then a worthy feast was held, and the wedding of Earl Hjörvarður and Queen Hildigunn was drunk with great prestige and many honours.

The Tale of Star-Oddi's Dream (Old Icelandic)

Old Icelandic	Literal	English
Og er veislunni var lokið þá fer hver heim til sinna heimkynna.	And when the-feast was concluded then travelled each home to their households.	And when the feast was over, everyone went home to their households.
Brátt takast þar miklar ástir í millum þeirra og eru samfarar þeirra sæmilegar og eigi langar áður en þau áttu dóttur.	Soon took there much love in between them and was interaction theirs honourable and not long after then they had a-daughter.	Soon there was much love between them and their interaction was honourable, and it was not long after that they had a daughter.
Hún var nefnd Hlaðreið.	She was named Hladreid.	She was named Hladreid.
Svo er sagt að samför þeirra jarls og drottningar var eigi löng þaðan í frá er þau höfðu Hlaðreiði getið áður þau tíðindi gerðust að jarl tekur sótt og leiðir hún svo til lands að hann andast af þeirri sótt.	So was said that togetherness theirs the-earl and the-queen was not long from-there to from when they had Hladreid told before the news made that earl took sickness and led it so to the-land that he died of that sickness.	So it was said that the togetherness of the earl and the queen did not last long after they had Hladreid, before the news came that the earl had taken ill, and so it led through the land, and he died of that sickness.
Það þótti vera skaði mikill því að hann var virðulegur höfðingi.	It thought was harm much because that he was worthy chieftain.	It was thought a great harm because he was a worthy chieftain.
Eftir þessi tíðindi setti Geirviður konungur sína menn yfir ríkið það er jarl hafði átt og eignaði sér.	After this the-news set Geirvid the-king his men over the-kingdom that the earl had owned and owned himself.	After these tidings King Geirvid put his men over the kingdom which the earl had owned and appropriated.
Þessi tíðindi spyrjast víða, sem von var, fráfall þvílíks höfðingja.	This news was-heard widely, as expected was, death such-like a-chieftain.	These tidings were widely learned of, as was to be expected, from the demise of such a ruler.
Þar kemur að þessi tíðindi koma fyrir Hlégunni dóttur Hjörvarðar jarls, að faðir hennar er andaður, þar sem hún er í hernaði og brýtur undir sig víkinga.	There came to this news came before Hlegunn daughter Hjorvard the-earl, that father hers had died, there as she was about raiding and subduing under herself vikings.	There came these tidings to Hlegunn, the daughter of Earl Hjorvard, that her father was dead, as she was at war and subduing vikings.
Bregður henni svo við tíðindin að hún snýr öllu sínu liði til Gautlands og herjar þar.	Reaction hers so with news that she turned all her company to Götaland and raided there.	She reacted to the news by turning all her army towards Götaland and raided there.
Og svo kemur því máli að hún lagði undir sig allt það ríki er átt hafði faðir hennar.	And so came therefore the-matter that she had under herself all that kingdom which owned had father hers.	And then it came to pass that she subdued all the kingdom which her father had possessed.

The Tale of Star-Oddi's Dream (Old Icelandic)

Old Icelandic	Literal	English
Síðan sendir hún menn á fund Geirviðar konungs og bað svo segja honum sín orð að hann skyldi annaðhvort gera að unna henni hálfs ríkis og landráða við sjálfan sig eða ella skyldi hann búa sig og sína menn og koma til móts við hana með sinn her í sund þau er heita Síldasund og berjast við hana þar og hefði það þeirra sigur og gagn er meiri gæfu stýrði.	Afterwards sent she men to find Geirvid the-king and asked to say to-him her words that he should another-either do to grant her half the-kingdom and land-ruling with herself his or either should he prepare himself and his men and come to meet with her with her army in a-sound there was named Herring-sound and battle with her there and had that there victory and won was more luck guided.	Afterwards she sent men to find Geirvid and asked them to tell him her words, that he should either grant her half the kingdom and authority to rule or prepare himself and his men to come to meet with her army in a sound that was named Herringsound and battle with her there, and that victory would be won by whoever had the most luck.

7

Nú er þar til að taka að sendimenn fóru þeir er Hlégunnur sendi.	Now is there to to take the messengers travelled they that Hlegunn sent.	Now we take to the messengers that Hlegunn had sent.
Það voru skjaldmeyjar.	They were shield-maidens.	They were shield-maidens.
Þær fóru á konungs fund og báru upp sín erindi fyrir konunginn.	They went to the-king meet and brought up their errand before the-king.	They went to meet the king and presented their message to the king.
Og er hann heyrði kostaboð Hlégunnar þá svarar hann skjótt á þessa leið:	And when he heard choice-bid Hlegunn's then answered he quickly to this laid:	And when he heard Hlegunn's offer, he answered quickly in this way:
"Því skjótara skal kjósa sem kostir eru ójafnari og vil eg miklu heldur berjast við hana en láta ríki mitt fyrir ágangi hennar".	"Because shorter shall choices which choose they-are unequal and will I much rather fight with her than lose kingdom mine before aggression hers".	I shall sooner choose the more unequal option, and I would much rather fight against it than leave my kingdom to its invasion.
Sendimenn fóru aftur á fund Hlégunnar og segja henni til svo búins og líkaði henni þeirra för forkunnlega vel.	Sending-men travelled returning to meet Hlegunn and said to-her to so prepared and liked her their journey exceedingly well.	The messengers went back to meet Hlegunn and told her what had happened and she was pleased with their journey very much.

The Tale of Star-Oddi's Dream (Old Icelandic)

Old Icelandic	Literal	English
Nú er það að segja að Geirviður konungur safnar herliði um allt sitt ríki og skal hver maður fara í þessa herför er skildi má valda eða skafti skjóta.	Now is it to say that Geirvid the-king gathered war-company about all his kingdom and shall each man travel to this warfare who shield may wield or spear throw.	Now it is said that King Geirvid gathered armies all over his kingdom, and every man should go on this campaign whether he can carry a shield or throw a spear.
Þess er við að geta að höfði sá gekk einum megin hjá sundunum er Hofshöfði heitir og skyldi þar hittast lið konungsins allt við höfðann.	This is with to get that headland that went one side near the-sound was Temple-Head named and should there meet company the-king's all with headland.	It is now worth getting that the headland that went on one side near the sound was named Temple-Head and the king and his forces were all to meet at the headland.
En er Geirviður konungur var albúinn þá leiddi hann alþýða til skips.	And when Geirvid the-king was all-ready then led he the-people to the-ships.	But when King Geirvid was ready, he led the people to the ships.
Þar var í ferð með konungi Dagfinnur skáld.	There was on the-journey with the-king Dagfinn the-poet.	The poet Dagfinn was on the journey there with the king.
En í ofangöngunni til skipanna þá varð sá atburður er geta verður, þó að lítils vægis þyki vera, að losnaði skóþvengur Dagfinns skálds.	But in over-going to the-ships then was seen happening which could worth, though that little weight thought being, that loosened shoe-thong Dagfinn's the-poet.	But in the passage to the ships, the event that can be mentioned, even though it is considered to be of little importance, was that the poet Dagfinn's shoelace came loose.
Og síðan bindur hann þvenginn og þá vaknaði hann og var þá Oddi, sem von var, en eigi Dagfinnur.	And after tied he thong and then woke he and was then Oddi, as expected was, and not Dagfinn.	And then he tied the shoelace, and then he awoke, and it was Odd, as was expected, but not Dagfinn.
Eftir þenna fyrirburð gekk Oddi út og hugði að stjörnum sem hann átti venju til jafnan er hann sá út um nætur þá er sjá mátti stjörnur.	After these visions went Oddi out and thought that the-stars which he had habitually to always that he saw out about night then was saw might stars.	After these visions Oddi went out and thought about the stars which he had always seen many of at night.
Þá minntist hann á drauminn og mundi allan nema kvæðið það er hann þóttist ort hafa í drauminum nema þessar vísur sem hér eru ritnar:	Then remembered he the dream and thought everything except the-poem that which he thought worded had in the-dream except this verse which here they-are written:	Then he remembered the dream and remembered everything except the poem he thought he had written in the dream except these verses written here:
Voru austr *á Jöruskógi* *barmar tveir*	They-were east in Battle-forest brothers two	There were in the east at Battle Forest two brothers

The Tale of Star-Oddi's Dream (Old Icelandic)

Old Icelandic	Literal	English
böls um fylltir	spite about filled	filled with spite
og til fjár	and to wealth	and for wealth
fyrðar næmdu	treasure took	they took treasure
við morðráð	with murder	with murder
mörgu sinni.	many times.	many times.
En sá gramr	But that warrior	But that anger
er gera bræðir	that made the-brothers	that the brothers made
hefir tírgjarn	had fame-ambition	had fame ambition
tindótt hjarta	toothed heart	with toothed heart
og böðfrækn	and valiant	and valiant
báða felldi	both felled	felled both
Garp og Gný	Garp and Gny	Garp and Gny
Geirviðr konungr.	Geirvid the-king.	King Geirvid.
Réð jafngjarn	Ruling equally	Ruling equally
auði að skipta	riches to divide	dividing the riches
Roðbjartssonr,	Son-of-Hrodbjart,	Hrodbjart's son,
rekka mærði	unfolded praise	unfolded praise
af því fé	of for wealth	of that wealth
fyrða kindir	among-people kin	among people and kinsmen
er svikmenni	that the-wicked	that the wicked
safnað höfðu.	gathered had.	had collected.
Lét gunndjarfr	Had the-treasurer	the treasurer had
gefna hringa	given rings	given rings
seggja ætt	say descendants	say descendants
siklingr Gauta	the-king Of-Goths	of the king of the Goths
svo að hirðmenn	so that court-men	so that the court men
höfðu allir	had all	had all
haukastóls	hawk-seat	a hawk's seat
hengiskafla.	mound-of-snow.	on a mound of snow.
Mun Dagfinnr	Must Dagfinn	Dagfinn must
dýrra málma	dear words	with dear words
við lofsorð	with praise	and with praise
lúka kvæði.	conclude the-poem.	conclude the poem.
Njóti vel	Appreciate well	Enjoy well
vegs og landa	glory and land	glory and land
gramr göfugr	warrior noble	noble warrior
gauskrar þjóðar.	of-the-Goths king.	king of the Goths.

The Tale of Star-Oddi's Dream (Old Icelandic)

Old Icelandic	Literal	English
8	**8**	**8**
En sem Oddi hafði úti verið slíka stund sem honum vel líkaði fór hann inn í rekkju sína og sofnaði þegar og dreymdi hann það sem hið fyrra sinn og hann hafði vaknað frá.	And as Oddi had out been such awhile as he well liked fared he in to bed his and slept immediately and dreamed he that which the first his and he had woken from.	But as Oddi had been outside for a moment which he liked well, he went into his bed and fell asleep at once, and dreamed it as the first time he had woken up from.
Þóttist hann þá hafa bundið skóþvenginn og vera Dagfinnur og skynda til skipanna.	Seemed to-him then had bound shoe-thong and was Dagfinn and hurrying to the-ships.	He then thought he had tied the shoelace and was Dagfinn and hurried to the ships.
Svo þótti honum í drauminum sem hann skyldi vera skipstjórnarmaður.	So seemed to-him in the-dream as he should be ship-steering-man.	In his dream, he thought he was a captain.
Og þegar þeir voru búnir til ferðar fóru þeir með skipaflotann til þess er þeir komu við höfðann og hittist þar allt lið konungs og lögðu síðan fram í sundin Síldasund.	And as-soon-as they were ready to voyage travel they with ship-fleet to this that they came with headland and met there all company the-king's and laid then from to the-sound Herring-sound.	And when they were ready to go, they took the fleet until they came to the head, and there met all the king's army, and then put into the channel Herring-sound.
Þá er og sagt að þar var komin Hlégunnur skjaldmær og lá þar fyrir í sundunum með skipaflota sinn og hafði ógrynni liðs og albúin til orustu.	Then is also said that there was coming Hlegunn shield-maiden and lying there before the sound with ship-fleet hers and had mass company and all-prepared to battle.	It is also said that Hlegunn, a shield-bearer, had arrived there and lay there in the channels with her fleet of ships, and had an innumerable army ready for battle.
Síðan lögðu hvorir í mót öðrum og laust saman með þeim snarpri sókn og var þar hinn harðasti bardagi og réðst brátt mikið mannfall í hvortveggja liði en þó hafði eigi lengi staðið bardaginn áður en mannfallið hneig í lið konungs og hruðust hans skip mjög.	Afterwards laid each to meet each-other and loosed together with they roughly attacked and was there the hardest battle and had soon much people-felled in each-way company but though had none longer stood the-battle before the people-felling strain to company the-king's and cleared his ships much.	Then they put up a fight against each other, and a sharp attack broke out with them, and there was the hardest battle, and soon many casualties were inflicted on both sides, but the battle had not lasted long before the casualty fell to the king's army, and his ships were greatly wrecked.

The Tale of Star-Oddi's Dream (Old Icelandic)

Old Icelandic	Literal	English
Þess er og getið að Hlégunnur varð ekki sén í orustunni um daginn og hugðu menn þó drjúgt að af konungsmönnum og þótti það undarlegt.	It is also told-of that Hlegunn was not seen in the-battle about the-day and thought men though straight to of the-king's-men and thought that wonder-like.	It is also mentioned that Hlegunn was not seen in the battle that day, and yet many of the king's men thought of it, and thought it strange.
En er slíku hafði fram farið langa hríð um daginn þá leitaðist Dagfinnur um með sinni list og sá hann þá Hlégunni og var þá komin á konungsskipið og var þá orðin skipan mikil á hennar hag.	And when such had from gone long while about the-day then sought Dagfinn about with his skills and saw he then Hlegunn and was then come to the-king's-ship and was then become the-ship great about her circumstance.	But when such a thing had taken place for a long time that day, Dagfinn sought with his art, and he then saw Hlegunn, and had then come to the king's ship, and by then there had been a great order in her favour.
Honum sýndist á henni ylgjarhöfuð geysimikið og tröllslegt og biti með því höfuðin af konungsmönnum.	To-him seemed that her she-wolf's-head exceedingly-great and trollish and bit with against heads of the-king's-men.	It seemed to him that her head was a wolf's head, huge and trollish, and that it bit the heads of the king's men.
En er Dagfinnur sá þessi undur þá steig hann af því skipi er hann stýrði.	Then when Dagfinn saw this wonder then leapt he off then the-ship that he steered.	But when Dagfinn saw this miracle, he got off the ship he was steering.
Það lá fjarri konungsskipinu.	It lay far-away the-king's-ship.	It was far from the king's ship.
Síðan hljóp hann hvert af öðru uns hann kom á konungsskipið.	Afterwards ran he each of others until he came to the-king's-ship.	Then he ran one by one until he came to the king's ship.
En þegar hann kom á fund konungs þá sagði Dagfinnur hvað títt var og hvað stór endemi voru við.	Then as-soon-as he came to find the-king then said Dagfinn what report was and that great unheard-of was against.	But when he came to meet the king, then Dagfinn said what was to report and what a great unheard of thing they were up against.
Síðan vísaði Dagfinnur konungi til hvar Hlégunnur var, að hann mætti sjá hana, en konungur fékk hana eigi séð sakir fjölkynngi hennar en hitt sá hann að menn hans féllu tugum saman.	Afterwards pointed-out Dagfinn the-king to where Hlegunn was, that he may see her, but the-king got her not seen for-the-sake-of sorcery hers but found saw he that men his fell tens together.	Then Dagfinn referred to the king where Hlegunn was, that he might see her, but the king could not see her because of her witchcraft, but he saw that his men fell together by the dozens.
Þá bað Dagfinnur konunginn sjá undir hönd sér hina vinstri og svo gerði hann.	Then asked Dagfinn the-king look under hand his the left and so did he.	Then King Dagfinn asked the king to see under his left hand, and so he did.

The Tale of Star-Oddi's Dream (Old Icelandic)

Old Icelandic	Literal	English
En er konungur fór svo með þá sá hann Hlégunni.	And when the-king did so with then saw he Hlegunn.	But when the king went with him, he saw Hlegunn.
Síðan gengu þeir báðir saman aftan til siglu.	Afterwards went they both together aft to sail.	Afterwards went they both together aft to sail.
Þá hljóp konungurinn fram með brugðnu sverði og þegar hann kemur í höggfæri við Hlégunni þá höggur hann til hennar með sverðinu og kemur höggið á hálsinn og hjó hann af henni höfuðið og féll það útbyrðis.	Then ran the-king forwards with drawn sword and as-soon-as he came to striking-distance with Hlegunn then struck he to her with sword and came the-blow to neck and hewed he off her head and fell it overboard.	Then the king ran forward with a drawn sword, and when he came under attack with Hlegunn, he struck her with the sword, and the blow came on her neck, and he cut off her head, and it fell overboard.
En er hún var fallin þá bauð konungurinn kost þeim mönnum er fylgt höfðu Hlégunni hvort þeir vildu heldur halda bardaga upp við hann eða ganga honum til handa.	And when she was fallen then offered the-king choice they the-people who followed had Hlegunn each they willed rather hold battle up with him or go him to hand.	But when she had fallen, the king offered the men who had followed Hlegunn whether they would rather fight him or go to his hand.
En þeir kjöru skjótt að ganga á konungs vald.	Then they chose quickly to go to the-king's power.	But they soon chose to enter into the king's power.
Og síðan er Geirviður konungur lagði á braut úr þeim bardaga þá lagði hann undir sig allt landið og setur þar yfir sýslumenn og friðaði svo allt ríkið.	And afterwards when Geirvid the-king had to away from them the-battle then had he under his all land and set there over stewards and peace so all the-kingdom.	And since King Geirviður set out from that battle, he conquered the whole country and placed it over the magistrates, and then pacified the whole kingdom.
Síðan hélt konungur heim og var ger í mót honum dýrðleg veisla.	Afterwards held the-king home and was made to meet him glorious feast.	Then the king returned home, and a glorious feast was held for him.
Eftir það var kvatt þings og var það þing allfjölmennt.	After it was summoned assembly and was the assembly all-many-people.	After that an assembly was convened and that assembly was very crowded.
Var konungurinn Geirviður settur þá enn á stól af nýju og hafiður upp á hinn sama haug sem fyrr og nú til konungs tekinn og ríkisstjórnar yfir allt Gautland.	Was the-king Geirvid set then was on throne of new and raised up in the same mound as before and now to the-king taken and governor over all Götaland.	King Geirviður was then again put on a chair again and raised on the same mound as before and now taken to the king and the government over all of Götaland.

The Tale of Star-Oddi's Dream (Old Icelandic)

Old Icelandic	Literal	English
Gekk þá annar höfðingi að öðrum upp á hauginn og gerði til konungsins veg og sóma hver eftir slíku sem framast hafði föng og færi á.	Went then one chieftain to another up to the-mound and made to the-king way and honour each after such as foremost had power and means of.	Then another chieftain went up to the hill, and made a way for the king, and honored each one according to all that he had.
Dagfinni skáldi kom það í hug að engi átti konunginum meiri virðing að launa í alla staði en hann.	Dagfinn the-poet came to the thought that none had the-king more worthiness to repay in all places than him.	The poet Dagfinn thought that no one had more respect for the king in all respects than he.
Gekk hann síðan upp á hauginn og kvaddi konunginn vel og hæversklega.	Went he then up on the-mound and greeted the-king well and modestly.	He then went up to the mound and greeted the king kindly and modestly.
Konungur tók glaðlega kveðju hans.	King took gladly greeting his.	The king gladly accepted his greeting.
Dagfinnur sagði konunginum deili á því að hann hafði þá enn ort kvæði um hann af nýju og bað að hann skyldi hlýða og kvaðst þá vilja færa kvæðið.	Dagfinn told the-king shared that accordingly that he had then one worded a-poem about him of new and asked that he should listen and spoke then willed bring the-poem.	Dagfinn told the king that he had written a poem about him again, and asked him to listen, and said he would bring the poem.
Konungurinn svarar að hann kvaðst gjarna hlýða vilja.	The-king answered that he said gladly listen willed.	The king replied that he will gladly listen.
Tók þá Dagfinnur og flutti kvæðið og var það þrítug drápa er hann þóttist ort hafa.	Took then Dagfinn and brought the-poem and was it thirty drapa which he thought worded had.	Then Dagfinn took and recited the poem, and it was thirty stanza drapa which he thought he had written.
En er kvæðinu var lokið þá þakkaði konungur það allvel og dró digran gullhring af hendi sér og gaf Dagfinni að skáldskaparlaunum en Dagfinnur vildi eigi þiggja hringinn og sagðist allt ærið hafa meðan hann héldi konunginum heilum.	And when the-poem was concluded then thanked the-king it well and drew a-thick gold-ring of hand his and gave Dagfinn the poet's-reward but Dagfinn willed not accept the-ring and said all abundance had as-long-as he held the-king whole.	But when the poem was finished, the king thanked him very well and took a huge gold ring from his hand and gave Dagfinn a poet's reward, but Dagfinn did not want to accept the ring and said he had abundance as long as he kept the king whole.

The Tale of Star-Oddi's Dream (Old Icelandic)

Old Icelandic	Literal	English
En Geirviður konungur lét það þá í ljós við Dagfinn að hann skyldi hans sóma meira gera í alla staði heldur en hvers manns annars í sínu ríki og bauð honum það að hann mundi afla honum kvonfangs og sagði svo að hann mundi þá konu fá honum til handa er hann vildi helst kjósa, nálega þess er kostur var í því landi.	But Geirvid the-king had it then to light with Dagfinn that he should him honour more do than all places rather than each man other in his kingdom and offered him that to him would gain him a-match and said so that he would then a-wife get him to hand that he willed rather choose, nearly this as choice was in then the-land.	But King Geirvid then made it clear to Dagfinn that he should do him more honour in all respects than any other man in his kingdom, and offered him that he would give him a wife, and said that he would get a woman for him, which he preferred to choose, close by in the land whom Dagfinn most wanted to marry.
Dagfinnur tók þessu máli vel, sem von var, er konungurinn vildi svo mikinn gera hans sóma og svarar:	Dagfinn took this matter well, as expected was, as the-king willed so much to-do him honour and answered:	Dagfinn took this matter well, as was to be hoped, since the king wished so much to do him honour, and answered:
"Ef þetta skal allt efna af yðvarri hendi við mig sem nú er um mælt þá er ekki því að leyna að er sá kosturinn að gjarna mundi eg mér unna og þú átt og mest undir sjálfum þér".	"If this shall all be-carried-out of your hand with me as now is about spoken then is not because that concealing that is so choice that gladly would I to-me love and you have and the-most under yourself to-you".	If all this is to be done by your hand with me, as is now said, then it is no secret that the choice is that I would gladly treat myself and you have and most of all under yourself.
Konungur mælti:	King spoke:	The king said,
"Hver er sú kona er þú talar til?"	"Who is this woman that you speak to?"	Who is the woman you are talking to?
Dagfinnur svarar:	Dagfinn answered:	Dagfinn answered:
"Það er Hlaðreið systir þín.	"It is Hladreid sister yours.	It is Hladreid, your sister.
Hún er svo kvenna að mér er mestur hugur á að fá ella hygg eg að fyrir muni farast um kvonföngin".	She is so the-woman that to-me is the-greatest thinking that to marry otherwise think I that for should go about a-match".	She's so the woman that I'm most interested in marrying, otherwise I think about the match going".
Konungur sagði að það skyldi og eigi undan draga við Dagfinn er honum þótti sinn sómi vaxa við.	The-king said that it should and not under drawn with Dagfinn that he thought his honour grow with.	The king said that nothing should be denied to Dagfinn which he thought would increase his honour.

The Tale of Star-Oddi's Dream (Old Icelandic)

Old Icelandic	Literal	English
Hlaðreið konungssystir var þá gjafvaxta og þó ung mjög að aldri en kvenna var hún fegurst og fríðust og best að sér ger um alla hluti.	Hladreid the-king's-sister was then of-marriage-grown and though young much in age but woman was she fairest and most-beautiful and the-best that herself made about all things.	Hlaðreið, the king's sister, was then gifted and yet very young, but of women she was the most fair and beautiful and the best at everything.
En hvort sem þetta mál var talað lengur eða skemur þá ræðst það af að Hlaðreið var föstnuð Dagfinni skáldi.	And how as this matter was told longer or shorter then decided it of that Hladreid was betrothed-to Dagfinn the-poet.	But whether this matter was discussed longer or shorter, it was determined that Hladreid was engaged to the poet Dagfinn.
Síðan var þar fengið að boði og var þar ger hin veglegasta veisla í alla staði með hinum bestum tilföngum því að ekki vantaði til það er hafa þurfti.	Afterwards was there got to announced and was there done the greatest feast in all places with the best means because that not lacking to this was had need.	Then it was announced and there was the most successful feast in all respects with the best resources because there was no shortage of what was needed.
Þar var og allt hið besta mannval það er í var landinu.	There were also all the best people that were in were the-land.	There was also all the best selection of people in the country.
Var nú drukkið brúðhlaup þeirra með hinni mestu sæmd og prýði.	Was now drunk the-wedding they with the most honour and finery.	Their wedding was now drunk with the greatest honour and splendor.
En er veisluna þraut þá fór hver til sinna heimkynna er þangað hafði sótt.	And when the-feast finished then travelled each to their households that from-there had attended.	But when the feast ended, everyone who had gone there went to their own home.
En með þeim Dagfinni og Hlaðreiði tókust brátt miklar ástir og var þeirra samför einkar góð.	And between them Dagfinn and Hladreid took soon much love and were they together very good.	And between Dagfinn and Hladreidi, they soon fell in love and their relationship was very good.
En er svo kurteislega var komið ráðahag Dagfinns sem nú er frá sagt þá var lokið drauminum og vaknaði hann þá, er Oddi var raunar.	But when so courtly was come marriage Dagfinn's as now was from said then was ended the-dream and awoke he then, that Oddi was actually.	But when in such a courtly fashion had Dagfinn's marriage taken place, as related, the dream ended, and he awoke that was actually Oddi.

The Tale of Star-Oddi's Dream (Old Icelandic)

Old Icelandic	Literal	English
9	**9**	**9**
Síðan hugði Oddi að um draum sinn og mundi gersamlega drauminn allan, bæði hinn fyrra og svo hinn síðara, og minntist síðan á drápuna þá er hann þóttist síðar kveðið hafa og mundi hann eigi fleira í kvæðinu heldur en þessar ellefu vísur sem nú eru hér ritnar og þetta er upphaf að:	Afterwards thought Oddi that about dream his and remembered completely the-dream all, both the first and so the latter, and remembered afterwards the drapa then that he thought afterwards recited had and would he not more of the-poem rather than these eleven verses as now they-are here written and this is beginning of:	Then Odd thought of his dream and remembered the whole dream, both the first and then the second, and then remembered the drapa when he was thought to have recited later and he remembered no more in the poem than these eleven verses now written here and this is the beginning of:
Geirviðr of nam greiða *gang svo að skreið úr þangi* *og byrsóta beitti* *barð út um lágarða.* *Og seglhættu sóttu* *snarpir meðr úr veðri,* *blés við hún, und höfða,* *harðan vegg of seggjum.*	Geirvid of took ready going so that glided through seaweed and windswept biting ship out about the-surf. And sail-danger attended sharply between with the-weather, blew with her, under Temple-Head, hard wall with men.	Geirvid took ready going as gliding through seaweed and windswept biting a ship out and about in the surf. and danger attended the sails sharp with the weather, blew against her under Temple Head, a hardened wall of men.
Skeið náði þá skríða *skjót um bylgjur ljótar.* *Fóru dyggir drengir* *á dýrmörum hlýra.* *Þar sá eg frægra fyrða* *för prúðlegsta görva.* *Þó er gotneskra gumna* *Geirviðr konungr þeira.*	Sheathed-sword caught then action launched about waves hideous. Travelled virtuous warriors in treasured bows. There saw I famous fighters went most-prolific clearly. Yet of Gothic men Geirvid the-king theirs.	The sheathed sword then caught ation launched about hideous waves. Virtuous warriors travelled in treasured bows. There I saw famous fighters going most prolific and clearly. Yet of the Gothic men Geirvid is their king.
Sigldum Hofs fyrir höfða *herðendr, skipaferðum,* *Göndul, grams, með landi,* *gott ráð var það dróttar,* *uns í Síldasundi* *sigrgöfgaðir vigrum* *hjuggu horskir seggir* *hjörs andskota börva.*	We-sailed Temple before headland hardy, ship's-course, Göndul, warriors, with land, good advice was that right, ours in Herring-sound victory-gift-gods spears striking brave said sword enemies trees.	We sailed to Temple Head before the Headland hardy, the ship's course, Gondul, the warriors, with the land, good advice that was right, until in Herring-sound victorious god gifted spears striking bravely said the enemy sword trees.

The Tale of Star-Oddi's Dream (Old Icelandic)

Old Icelandic	Literal	English
Og skjaldmeyja skjóma skerðendr svo gerðu að varfærir véar í vág fyrir lágu. Gátu ljónar líta leiðangrs flota breiðan. Hilmis fór und hjálmi, hirð, sú er vörn of firrðist.	And shield-maidens shimmering diminished so doing with caution the-gods in inlet before laying-to. Could the-men see expedition fleet wide. Helmsman went under the-helm, court-men, so were defended over the-firth.	And shield-maidens shimmering did so diminish with the caution of the gods in the inlet before laying-to. The men could see the expedition fleet wide. The helmsman went under the helm, The court men, so were defended over the firth.
Brátt vöknuðu virðar að vígboði þjóðar þá er Hlégunnar hestar hafrastar mjög þustu og snarráðir sóttu siklings vinir þingað. Þó er gotneskra gumna Geirviðr konungr þeira.	Soon awoke men that battle-bidding great-river then were Hlegunn's horses eagerly most flailing and quickly attended the-king's friends assembled. Yet of Gothic men Geirvid king theirs.	Soon awoke men to the battle-bidding people then were Hlegunn's horses eagerly most flailing and quickly attended the king's friends assembled. And yet of all the Gothic men, Geirvid was their king.
Og hnigsólar Högna hríð æxti þá síðan blóðísunga beiðir, bragna konr, af magni, en vígroða víða varp af rómu snarpri. Sjár varð dökkr af dreyra drótt þá er hríðmál sótti.	And stricken-sun Hogni's awhile increased then after blood-helmeted demanded, heroes descended, of strength, then warfare wide thrown of battle rough. The-sea became dark of gore people then were storm encountered.	And Hogni's stricken sun increased awhile, then afterwards the blood-helmeted demanded, heroes descended, of strength, then warfare wide thrown of battle rough. The sea became dark with gore people then were storm encountered.
Svipan gerðist þar sverða, saman kómu þar rómu, Göndul varð fyrir grundu, grams drótt því að vel sótti. Geirviðr of vó geiri, geirvaldr, í Hlökk þeiri. Blóðár sá eg í blóði. Blóð stökk um skör þjóða.	Swooping came there swords, together came there a-roar, Göndul became before ground, warriors right because that well attended. Geirvid too guarded spears, spear-guardian, in Looking-forward there. Bloodied saw I in blood. Blood leapt about across people.	Swooping came there swords, together came there a-roar Göndul fell to the ground, warriors right because that well attended. Geirvid too guarded spears, spear-guardian in looking-forward there. Bloodied, saw I in blood. Blood leapt about across the people.
Gerði hríð af hörðu hirð sú er fylkir stýrði.	Made awhile of hordes court-men so were commanded steered.	Made awhile of hordes court-men so were commanding steered.

The Tale of Star-Oddi's Dream (Old Icelandic)

Old Icelandic	Literal	English
Margr er gramr af gengi göfugr tiginna jöfra. Spyrkat eg frægra fyrða ferð snjallari verða. Þó er gotneskra gumna Geirviðr konungr þeira.	Many were warriors of going noble high-born ruler. Learned I fame among-people journey most-valiant becomes. Though are Gothic men Geirvid the-king theirs.	Many were warriors of going noble high-born rulers. Learned I fame among-people journey most-valiant becomes. And yet of all the Gothic men, Geirvid was their king.
Hlégunnar leit eg hingað harðráðar ódáðir. Ýfð með ylgjar höfði eiskranleg réð geisa. Trölls kjafta sá eg tyggja tönnum hold af mönnum. Með hnitgeirum hvofta harða sókn of gerði.	Hlegunn sought I here hard-headed abhorrence. Bristling with wolf's head rage fixed furiously. Trolls jaws saw I chewing teeth the-bodies of men. With battle-spears wafting hard attack with done.	Hlegunn sought I here hard-headed abhorrence bristling with wolf's head rage fixed furiously. Troll's jaws saw I chewing teeth the-bodies of men. With battle-spears wafting a hard attack was done.
Annað sté eg af öðru Áta skíð um víði uns glæsimar Gylfa gekk með hilmis rekkum og eg siklingi sagðag sýslu ægis geisla hve grimmhuguð gerði Gerðr of vígaferði.	One stepped I to another Stain wood about wood until gleaming Gylfi went with the-helmsman upright and I the-king told realm Aegir's gleam how grimly done Made too slayings.	I stepped from one to another stained wood about wood until gleaming Gylfi went with the helmsman upright and I told the king the realm of Aegir's gleam how grimly done made too slayings.
Gramr leit hitt hvar hafði Hörn hvergymis stjörnu höfuð á hauka stofni heiðingja sér brúðar. Ásynju lét elda ósvífr konungr hníga flóðs af fyllar meiði frægr, hinn er ekki vægði.	Warrior sought to-meet where had Angled each star had upon hawk stem wolf her bride. The-goddesses had flames un-swinging the-king felled flood of full beam far-famed, that was no mercy.	The warrior sought to meet where had each star anged had upon her hawk stem the wolf her bride. The Goddesses had flames unswinging the king felled flood of full beam far-famed, that was no mercy.
Nú er draum þessum lokið er Stjörnu-Odda dreymdi eftir því sem hann sjálfur hefir sagt.	Now is the-dream this concluded that Star-Oddi dreamed after according as he himself has said.	Now this dream is over that Star-Oddi dreamed according to what he himself has said.

The Tale of Star-Oddi's Dream (Old Icelandic)

Old Icelandic	Literal	English
Og má víst undarlegur og fáheyrður þykja þessi fyrirburður en þó þykir flestum líklegt að hann muni það eina sagt hafa er honum hafi svo þótt verða í drauminum því að Oddi var reiknaður bæði fróður og sannsögull.	And may vision wonder-like and unusual seem this vision but though seems most likely that he would that only told have what he had so thought happened in the-dream because that Oddi was counted both wise and truthful.	And this phenomenon may be considered strange and unheard of, but most people still think that he will have said the only thing that seemed to him to be the case in the dream, because Oddur was considered both knowledgeable and truthful.
Má og ekki undrast þótt kveðskapurinn sé stirður því að í svefni var kveðið.	May also not wonder thought poetry-making being stiff-footed because that in sleep was recited.	It is not surprising that the poetry is stiff because it was recited in sleep.

Word List (Old Icelandic to English)

Old Icelandic	English
A, a	
að	a, in, it, of, so-as, that, the, then, to, with
aðra	other
aðrir	others
af	from, of, of, off, to
afla	gain
aflaði	obtained
afli	strength
aftan	aft
aftur	back, returning
albúin	all-prepared
albúinn	all-prepared, all-ready
albúnir	all-prepared
aldregi	never
aldrei	never, never
aldri	age, age
aldurs	of-age, of-age
alla	all, all
allan	all, everything
allfjölmennt	all-many-people
allir	all, all
allóráðlega	all-un-forethought
allra	all, all
allráðlegt	advisable
allri	all
allskyns	all-kinds-of
allt	all, all
allvel	well
alskipuð	fully-prepared
alþýða	the-people
alvopnuðu	all-weaponed
andaður	died
andast	died, died
andskota	enemies
annað	another, one
annaðhvort	another-either, either-way
annan	another, another
annar	one, one, the-other
annarrar	another
annars	anything-else, other, otherwise
arminum	arm
atburð	events
atburður	events, happening
atgervi	deeds
athæfi	behaviour
auðæfum	wealthy-treasures
auði	riches
austr	east
austur	east
Á, á	
á	about, at, by, in, of, on, that, the, then, to, upon
ábyrgð	responsibility
áður	after, before
ágætum	wonderful
ágangi	aggression
áheyrsla	to-hear
ákaflega	extremely
ástir	love, love
ástúð	affection
ástvinum	beloved
ásynju	the-goddesses
áta	stain
átt	have, owned, owned
átta	eight
átti	had
áttu	had
ávallt	always
áverka	injury
Æ, æ	
ægis	Aegir's (name)
ærið	abundance
æsku	youth
ætla	intend

Word List (Old Icelandic to English)

Old Icelandic	English
ætlað	intend
ætt	descendants, lineage
æxti	increased

B, b

Old Icelandic	English
bað	asked, invited
báða	both
báðir	both
báðu	asked
báðum	both
bæði	ask, both
bana	death
bar	bore
barð	ship
bardaga	battle, the-battle
bardagi	battle
bardaginn	the-battle
barmar	brothers
barn	child
barna	child
báru	brought
batnaði	bettering
bauð	offered
beðinn	asking
beiddi	asked
beiðir	demanded
beina	assistance
beitti	biting
bera	borne
berjast	battle, fight
berserkina	berserkers
berserkir	berserkers
berserkjanna	the-berserkers
berserkjunum	the-berserkers
best	best, the-best
besta	best
bestu	best
bestum	best
betur	better
biður	invited
bindur	tied
biti	bit
bjó	lived
blés	blew
blíðlega	joyfully
blóð	blood
blóðár	bloodied
blóði	blood
blóðísunga	blood-helmeted
böðfrækn	valiant
boði	announced
boðið	invited
böls	spite
borðum	the-tables
borið	bore, brought, carried
borin	brought
börva	trees
brá	drew
bræðir	the-brothers
bragna	heroes
brátt	soon
brattur	broad
braut	away
bregður	reaction
breið	broad
breiðan	wide
brott	away
brúðar	bride
brúðhlaup	the-wedding
brugðnu	drawn
brýtur	subduing
búa	prepare, prepared
búið	preparations, prepared
búins	prepared
bundið	bound
búnir	ready
burt	away
bylgjur	waves
byrjaði	began
byrsóta	windswept

D, d

Old Icelandic	English
dagfinn	Dagfinn (name)
dagfinni	Dagfinn (name)
dagfinnr	Dagfinn (name)
dagfinns	Dagfinn's (name)
dagfinnur	Dagfinn (name)

Word List (Old Icelandic to English)

Old Icelandic	English
daginn	the-day
deili	shared
digran	a-thick
dökkr	dark
dóttur	a-daughter, daughter
draga	drawn
drápa	drapa
drápu	killed
drápuna	drapa
draum	dream, the-dream
drauminn	dream, the-dream
drauminum	the-dream
drengir	warriors
dreymdi	dreamed
dreyra	gore
drjúgt	straight
dró	drew
drótt	people, right
dróttar	right
drottning	the-queen
drottningar	queen, the-queen
drottningin	the-queen
drukkið	drank, drunk
drykk	drink
dvaldist	dwelled
dvelja	dwell
dyggir	virtuous
dyragætti	doorway
dýran	fine
dýrar	precious
dýrðleg	glorious
dýrkuðu	adored
dýrmörum	treasured
dýrra	dear

E, e

Old Icelandic	English
eða	and, or
ef	if
efna	be-carried-out
eftir	after, afterwards
eg	I
eiga	have, only
eigi	none, not
eiginkonu	wife
eignaði	owned
eigu	ownership
eina	only
einkar	very
einkum	especially, particularly
einn	one, only
eins	one
einsætt	evident
einum	one
eiskranleg	rage
eitt	one
eitthvert	some-time
ekki	no, not
elda	flames
eldri	older
ella	either, or-else, otherwise
ellefu	eleven
ellegar	otherwise
en	and, but, however, than, that, the, then, to, what, which
enda	and, with
endemi	unheard-of
engan	no
engi	no, none, not
enn	but, one, that, was
er	am, are, as, for, had, in, is, of, that, the, was, were, what, when, where, which, who
erfð	honoured
erfi	a-toast
erfinu	the-toast
erindi	errand
ert	are
eru	are, they-are, was
eruð	are
eyjarinnar	the-island

F, f

Old Icelandic	English
fá	get, give, marry
faðir	father

Word List (Old Icelandic to English)

Old Icelandic	English
færa	bring
færi	journeyed, means, travel
færu	went
fága	cultivate
fáheyrður	unusual
fái	get
fallin	fallen
fallinn	disposed
fallnir	fallen
fám	few
far	travel
fara	go, to-travel, travel, travelled
farandi	travel
farar	travel
fararinnar	of-the-journey
farast	go
fari	travel
farið	gone, travelling
farmóður	travel-weary
fást	get
fáttkaðist	few
fé	treasure, wealth
fegnir	celebrated
fegurst	fairest
féið	the-treasure
fékk	got
félítill	fee-little
féll	fell
félldi	felled
féllu	fell
fengið	got
fer	it-went, travelled
ferð	journey, the-journey
ferðar	journey, voyage
ferðina	travel, travelling
ferðinni	the-journey
fertug	forty
firrðist	the-firth
fiska	fishing
fjár	wealth
fjárins	wealth
fjarri	far-away
fjölkynngi	sorcery
fjölmenna	many-men
fjölmennan	followers-many
fjölmenni	followers, followers-many, many-followers
flateyjar	Flatey (place)
fleira	more
flestum	most
flóðs	flood
flokkur	flokk
flota	fleet
flutti	brought
föður	father
fólki	folk
föng	possessions, power
fór	did, fared, travelled, went
för	journey, went
forkunnlega	exceedingly
fornum	ancient
fórst	travelled
fóru	going, travel, travelled, went
föruneyti	companionship
föstnuð	betrothed-to
frá	from
frægð	fame
frægr	far-famed
frægra	fame, famous
frægur	famous
frændur	kinsmen
fráfall	death
fram	forwards, from
frama	fame
framast	foremost
frami	courage
frásaga	from-to-say
frásögu	from-saying
fremd	honour
friðaði	peace
fríðust	most-beautiful
fróður	wise
fullgert	full-done
fullkomnir	fully-come
fullt	full
fullu	fully
fund	find, meet

Word List (Old Icelandic to English)

Old Icelandic	English
fúsastur	willing
fylgd	follow
fylgi	follows
fylgja	follow
fylgt	followed
fylkir	commanded
fyllar	full
fylltir	filled
fyrða	among-people, fighters
fyrðar	treasure
fyrir	because, before, for
fyrirburð	visions
fyrirburður	vision
fyrr	before
fyrra	first
fyrst	first
fýstu	urged

G, g

Old Icelandic	English
gæfa	good-fortune
gæfu	luck
gaf	gave
gáfu	gave, have
gagn	won
gamall	old
gang	going
ganga	go, going
garp	Garp (name)
garpur	Garp (name)
gata	the-way
gátu	could
gauskrar	of-the-Goths
gauta	of-Goths
gautland	Götaland (place)
gautlandi	Götaland (place)
gautlands	Götaland (place)
gefa	give
gefna	given
geiri	spears
geirvaldr	spear-guardian
geirvið	Geirvid (name)
geirviðar	Geirvid (name)
geirviði	Geirvid (name)
geirviðr	Geirvid (name)
geirviður	Geirvid (name)
geisa	furiously
geisla	gleam
gekk	went
gengi	going
gengið	gone
gengu	went
gengur	went
ger	done, made
gera	be, do, made, to-do
gerði	did, done, made
gerðist	became, begins, came, happened
gerðr	made
gerðu	doing, made
gerðust	made
gersamlega	completely
gerst	done
gert	done, made
gesturinn	the-guest
geta	could, get
getið	told, told-of
geysimikið	exceedingly-great
gift	married
gistingar	guest
gjafvaxta	of-marriage-grown
gjarna	gladly
glaðlega	gladly
glæsimar	gleaming
glögglega	clearly
gný	Gny (name)
gnýr	Gny (name)
góð	good
góðan	good
góðum	good
göfga	noble
göfuglegum	noble-like
göfugr	noble
göndul	Göndul (place)
görva	clearly
gotneskra	Gothic (name)
gott	good
götuna	path
grafinn	the-key
gramr	warrior, warriors

Word List (Old Icelandic to English)

Old Icelandic	English
grams	warriors
greiða	ready
grimmhuguð	grimly
grundu	ground
gullhring	a-gold-ring, gold-ring
gumna	men
gunndjarfr	the-treasurer
gylfa	Gylfi (name)

H, h

Old Icelandic	English
hæglega	comfortable
hætta	conclude
hættlega	dangerously
hæversklega	modestly
hafa	had, have
hafði	had
hafi	had, have
hafiður	raised
hafrastar	eagerly
haft	had
hag	circumstance
halda	hold
hálfs	half
hálsinn	neck
hamingjan	graciousness
hana	her, she
handa	hand, the-hand
handar	hand
hann	he, him, it, to-him
hans	him, his, of-him
hár	high
harða	hard
harðan	hard
harðasti	hardest
harðfengi	toughness
harðráðar	hard-headed
harmaði	mourned
háska	danger
hátt	tall
háttar	kind
haug	a-mound, mound
hauginn	the-mound
hauginum	the-mound
hauka	hawk

Old Icelandic	English
haukastóls	hawk-seat
héðan	from-here
hefði	had, have
hefi	have
hefir	had, has, have
hefjast	start
heiðingja	wolf
heilum	whole
heim	home
heima	home
heiman	home
heimkynna	households
heimleiðis	homeward
heimt	drawn
heita	named
heitið	dominion
heitir	named
héldi	held
heldur	rather
helgason	son-of-Helgi (name)
heljarmenn	accursed-men
helju	Hel (place)
helst	rather
hélt	held
hendi	hand
hengiskafla	mound-of-snow
hennar	her, hers
henni	her, hers, she, to-her
her	army
hér	forces, here, she
herðendr	hardy
herför	warfare
herjar	raided
herklæðum	war-clothes
herliði	war-company
hernað	raiding
hernaði	raiding
herra	lord
hestar	horses
hét	named, was-named
heygður	buried
heyrði	heard
heyrt	heard
hið	the
hildigunnar	Hildigunn (name)

Word List (Old Icelandic to English)

Old Icelandic	English	*Old Icelandic*	English
hildigunnur	Hildigunn (name)	hneig	strain
hilmis	helmsman, the-helmsman	hníga	felled
		hnigsólar	stricken-sun
hin	the	hnitgeirum	battle-spears
hina	the, then	hóf	began
hingað	here	höfða	headland, Temple-Head (place)
hinn	that, the		
hinni	the	höfðann	headland
hins	the	höfði	head, headland
hinum	the, the-others	höfðingi	chieftain
hirð	court, court-men, retainers	höfðingja	a-chieftain, chieftains
		höfðingjum	chieftains
hirðin	courtiers	höfðinglega	nobly
hirðmaður	court-man	höfðu	had
hirðmenn	court-men	hofs	temple
hirðmönnum	court-men	hofshöfði	Temple-Head (place)
hitt	found, to-meet	hófu	had
hittast	meet	höfuð	had
hittir	found	höfuðið	head
hittist	met	höfuðin	heads
hjá	near	högg	blows
hjálmi	the-helm	höggfæri	striking-distance
hjarta	heart	höggið	the-blow
hjó	hewed	höggur	struck
hjörgunni	Hjorgunn (name)	hóglegur	comfortably
hjörgunnur	Hjorgunn (name)	högna	Hogni's (name)
hjörs	sword	hold	the-bodies
hjörvarðar	Hjorvard (name)	hóli	hill
hjörvarði	Hjorvard (name)	hólinn	the-hill
hjörvarður	Hjorvard (name)	hólinum	the-hill
hjuggu	striking	hóll	hill
hlaðreið	Hladreid (name)	hönd	hand
hlaðreiði	Hladreid (name)	honum	he, him, his, to-him
hlégunnar	Hlegunn (name), Hlegunn's (name)	hörðu	hordes
		hörn	angled
hlégunni	Hlegunn (name)	horskir	brave
hlégunnur	Hlegunn (name)	hræ	corpses
hljóp	ran	hríð	awhile, while
hlökk	looking-forward	hríðmál	storm
hlut	lot	hringa	rings
hluta	things	hringinn	the-ring
hluti	things	hróðbjart	Hrodbjart (name)
hlutum	things	hróðbjarti	Hrodbjart (name)
hlýða	listen, obey	hróðbjarts	Hrodbjart's (name)
hlýddi	followed	hróðbjartur	Hrodbjart (name)
hlýra	bows	hruðust	cleared

Word List (Old Icelandic to English)

Old Icelandic	English	Old Icelandic	English
hug	mind, thought	**Í, í**	
huga	minds		
hugði	thought	í	about, at, in, of, on, than, the, to
hugðu	thought		
hugsað	think	íslandi	Iceland (place)
hugur	thinking		
huldu	covering	**J, j**	
hún	her, it, she		
hús	house	jafnaldra	equal-age
húsbóndi	housemaster	jafnan	always
húsgerðar	house-builder	jafngjarn	equally
húsinu	the-house	jarl	earl, the-earl
húss	house	jarli	the-earl
hvað	that, what	jarls	the-earl
hvar	where	jarlsdóttir	the-earl's-daughter
hve	how	játti	said
hver	each, who	jöfra	ruler
hvergi	each	jöruskóg	Battle-forest (place)
hvergymis	each	jöruskógi	Battle-forest (place)
hverjum	each	jöruskógur	Battle-forest (place)
hverra	what		
hvers	each	**K, k**	
hversu	how-so		
hvert	each	kæmist	comes
hvofta	wafting	kallaði	claimed
hvorir	each	kallaður	called
hvorki	neither	kann	can, known
hvort	each, either, how	kastaði	cast
hvortveggja	each-way	kaupast	redeem
hygg	think	kaupferðir	merchant-voyages
		kempum	champion
I, i		kemur	came
		kindir	kin
iðn	crafts	kjafta	jaws
illvirki	outrages	kjöru	chose
illvirkjanna	for-the-evil-doers, the-evil-doers	kjósa	choices, choose
		kjósið	choose
illvirkjar	evil-doers	kné	knee
illvirkjarnir	criminals, the-evil-doers	kom	came
		koma	came, come
illvirkjunum	evil-doers	komi	come
inn	in	komið	came, come
innan	inside, within	komin	come, coming

342

Word List (Old Icelandic to English)

Old Icelandic	English
kominn	come
komir	come
komnir	come, coming
komu	came
kómu	came
kona	wife, wife-of, woman
konr	descended
konu	a-wife, wife
konung	the-king
konungdóminn	kingdom
konungi	the-king
konunginn	the-king
konunginum	the-king
konungr	king, the-king
konungs	king, the-king, the-king's
konungsins	the-king, the-king's
konungsmönnum	the-king's-men
konungsskáld	the-king's-poet
konungsskipið	the-king's-ship
konungsskipinu	the-king's-ship
konungssystir	the-king's-sister
konungur	king, the-king
konungurinn	the-king, the-king's, this-king
konur	women
kost	choice
kostaboð	choice-bid
kostað	earned
kosti	benefits
kostir	choose
kostur	choice
kosturinn	choice, distinguished
kunni	know
kunnigt	know, known
kurteislega	courtly
kvað	said, spoke
kvaddi	greeted
kvaðst	said, spoke
kváðu	said
kvæði	announced, a-poem, the-poem
kvæðið	the-poem
kvæðinn	poetry
kvæðinu	the-poem
kvatt	summoned
kveðið	recited
kveðja	called
kveðju	greeting
kveðskapurinn	poetry-making
kveldið	evening
kvenna	the-woman, woman
kvonfang	a-match
kvonfangs	a-match
kvonföngin	a-match
kvongaður	married

L, l

Old Icelandic	English
lá	lay, lying
læst	locked
lágarða	the-surf
lagði	had
lagðist	lay
lagið	granted
lágu	laying-to
land	land
landa	land, lands
landi	land, the-land
landið	land
landinu	the-land
landráða	land-ruling
lands	lands, the-land, the-lands
landsfólkið	the-land's-people
landsfólkinu	lands-folk
landsmönnum	lands-people
landstjórnar	governing
landstjórnin	the-government
langa	long
langar	long
langir	long
langskip	longships
langt	long
láta	allow, allowed, leave, let, lose, to-have
látast	die
latti	discouraged
launa	repay, reward
laust	loosed
laut	place

Word List (Old Icelandic to English)

Old Icelandic	English
leið	company, laid, passes, way
leiðangrs	expedition
leiddi	led
leiðir	led, took
leit	sought
leita	search, searching, seeking
leitaðist	sought
lengi	longer
lengra	longer
lengur	longer
lér	lean
lét	had
letja	discourage
letjast	discouraged
létu	had
létust	had
leyna	concealing
lið	company, crew
liði	company, crew
liðið	passed
liðs	company
liðskosti	provisions
líf	life
lifði	lived
lífi	alive
líflát	life-less
liggja	camped
líka	like
líkaði	liked
líkar	liked
líklegt	likely
list	skills
líta	look, see
lítil	little
lítill	little
lítils	little
litla	little
lítt	a-little, little
ljónar	the-men
ljós	light
ljóslega	lightly
ljótar	hideous
lofsorð	praise
lofuðu	praised
lögðu	laid
lögðust	camped, laid
lokið	concluded, ended
lönd	the-land
löng	long
losnaði	loosened
löttu	dissuaded
lúka	conclude
luku	unlocked
lygi	lied
lykill	buried
lykka	luck
lyktum	completion
lýsa	show

M, m

Old Icelandic	English
má	may
maður	a-man, man
mælt	spoke, spoken
mælti	spoke
mæltu	spoke
mærði	praise
mætti	may
mættu	may
magni	strength
maki	match
mál	matter
máli	matter, saying, speech, the-matter
málma	words
mann	man, person
mannaðir	mannered
mannaður	brought-up
mannfall	people-felled
mannfallið	people-felling
manni	person
manns	man, man's
mannval	people
margir	many
margr	many
margskonar	many-kinds-of
mart	many
mat	food
mátti	might

Word List (Old Icelandic to English)

Old Icelandic	English
með	between, with
meðan	as-long-as, while
meðr	between
mega	may
megi	may
megin	side, sides
meiði	beam
mein	harm
meir	more
meira	more
meiri	more
menn	men, people
mér	for-me, me, to-me
merkilegasti	remarkable
mest	the-most
mesta	most
mesti	most
mestu	most
mestur	the-greatest
mig	me, myself
mikið	great, greatly, much
mikil	great, much
mikill	much
mikinn	great, much
mikla	much
miklar	much
miklir	great
miklu	great, much
miklum	much
millum	between
mína	my
minna	less
minnar	mine, my
minni	my
minntist	remembered
mínu	my
mínum	mine, my
missa	missed
misst	lost, missed
mitt	mine, my
mjög	most, much
mjög	much
móðir	mother
móður	mother
mönnum	men, people, the-people
morðráð	murder
mörg	many
mörgu	many
morguninn	morning
mörkinni	the-border
mót	meet
móti	meeting
móts	meet
múla	Muli (place)
mun	must, should
mundi	may, remembered, thought, would
mundu	would
muni	should, would
munni	mouth

N, n

Old Icelandic	English
náð	protection
náði	caught
næðist	reached
næmdu	took
nær	near
næst	next
nætur	night
nálega	almost, closely, nearly
nam	took
né	nor
nefnd	named
nefndur	named
nema	except
njóti	appreciate
nokkuð	something, sometime, somewhat
nokkur	someone, something, somewhat
nokkurs	somewhat
norður	in-the-north
nóttina	the-night
nú	how, no, now
nýju	new

O, o

Word List (Old Icelandic to English)

Old Icelandic	English
odda	Oddi (name), Oddi's (name)
oddi	Oddi (name)
of	of, over, too, with
ofan	over
ofangöngunni	over-going
oft	often
og	also, and, of
orð	worded, words
orða	words
orðahjaldur	word-struggle
orðin	become
orðinn	become
orku	power
ort	worded
orustu	battle
orustunni	the-battle
oss	us

Ó, ó

Old Icelandic	English
óboðið	uninvited
ódáðir	abhorrence
ódælli	un-pleasant
ógrynni	mass
óhægindi	inconvenience
ójafnað	unequal
ójafnari	unequal
ólát	un-courteous
ósnöfurmannlega	un-alert
ósvífr	un-swinging

Ö, ö

Old Icelandic	English
öðru	another, others
öðrum	another, each-other, to-other
öfúsa	gratitude
öllu	all
öllum	all, of-all
önnur	others

P, p

Old Icelandic	English
presentur	presents
prúðlegsta	most-prolific
prýði	finery

R, r

Old Icelandic	English
ráð	advice, decide, decision, statements
ráða	prevail
ráðahag	marriage, marriage-proposal
ráðast	arrange, arranging
ráði	conduct, consent, decision
ráðist	determine
ráðlegt	advice
ráðvandur	honest
ræðst	decided
rammgert	firmly-built
rammlega	firmly
raunar	actually
réð	fixed, ruled, ruling
réðst	had
réðust	appointed
reiknaður	counted
rekka	unfolded
rekkju	bed
rekkum	upright
reykjardal	Reykjardal (place)
reyna	test
riðu	rode
ríkar	rich
ríki	kingdom, the-kingdom
ríkið	the-kingdom
ríkinu	the-kingdom
ríkis	kingdom, the-kingdom
ríkisstjórnar	governor
ríkustum	kingdom's
rímkænn	calendar-computation-wise
ritnar	written
rjóður	clearing

Word List (Old Icelandic to English)

Old Icelandic	English
roðbjartssonr	Son-of-Hrodbjart (name)
rómu	a-roar, battle

S, s

Old Icelandic	English
sá	saw, seen, so, that
sæju	saw
sækja	seek, sought
sæma	honour, the-same
sæmd	honour
sæmdi	honour
sæmilegar	honourable
safnað	gathered
safnar	gathered
sagan	the-saga
sagðag	told
sagði	said, telling, the-saga, told, told
sagðist	said
sagt	said, said, told
sakir	for-the-sake-of, sake, the-sake-of
sama	same
saman	the-same, together
sameignar	fight, the-fight
samfarar	interaction
samför	together, togetherness
samtíða	contemporary
sannsögull	truthful
sárum	wounds
sat	sat
satt	the-truth
sáu	saw
sé	being
séð	seen
seggir	said
seggja	say
seggjum	men
segir	said
segja	said, say
seglhættu	sail-danger
seldur	sold
sem	as, so, that, was, which
sén	seen
sendi	sent
sendimenn	messengers, sending-men
sendir	sent
sér	as, he, her, herself, himself, his, themselves
sért	are
sett	sat, set
settan	appointed
setti	set
settur	sat, set
setur	set
séu	are
sið	customs, traditions
síðan	after, afterwards, then
síðar	afterwards
síðara	latter
sig	herself, himself, his, themselves
sigldum	we-sailed
siglu	sail
sigrgöfgaðir	victory-gift-gods
sigri	victory
sigur	victory
siklingi	the-king
siklingr	the-king
siklings	the-king's
síldasund	Herring-sound (place)
síldasundi	Herring-sound (place)
sín	her, his, their
sína	himself, his
sinn	her, hers, his, one-day
sinna	their
sinni	hers, his, times
síns	his
sínu	her, his
sínum	hers, theirs
sitja	sit
sitt	his, their
sjá	look, saw, see, so
sjái	see

Word List (Old Icelandic to English)

Old Icelandic	English	Old Icelandic	English
sjáir	look	skóg	forest
sjálf	herself	skóginn	the-forest
sjálfum	himself, yourself	skör	across
sjálfur	himself	skorta	shortage
sjár	the-sea	skorti	shortage
sjást	t-look	skóþvenginn	shoe-thong
skaði	harm	skóþvengur	shoe-thong
skafti	spear	skreið	glided
skal	shall	skríða	action
skáld	poet, the-poet	skuluð	should
skáldi	the-poet	skyldari	obliged
skáldinu	the-poet	skyldi	should
skálds	the-poet	skyldu	should
skáldskaparlaunum	poet's-reward	skynda	hurrying
skeið	sheathed-sword	slíka	such
skemmtanar	entertainment	slíks	such
skemur	shorter	slíku	so, such
skerðendr	diminished	slíkum	such
skíð	wood	smágrjót	small-stones
skildi	shield, should	snarpir	sharply
skildu	knew	snarpri	rough, roughly
skiljast	separate	snarráðir	quickly
skilnaður	parting	snemma	soon
skip	ships	snjallari	most-valiant
skipaferðum	ship's-course	snýr	turned
skipaflota	ship-fleet	sofnaði	slept
skipaflotann	ship-fleet	sofnar	slept
skipan	the-ship	sögðu	said
skipanna	the-ships	sögu	telling
skipi	the-ship	söguna	the-saga
skips	the-ships	sögunnar	the-saga
skipstjórnarmaður	ship-steering-man	sögunni	the-saga
skipta	divide, exchange	sókn	attack, attacked
skipti	exchanged	sóma	honour
skiptum	exchanged	sómasamlegri	respectable
skipuð	prepared	sómi	honour
skjaldmær	shield-maiden	son	son
skjaldmeyja	shield-maidens	sonar	son
skjaldmeyjar	shield-maidens	sótt	attended, sickness
skjóma	shimmering	sótti	attended, attending, encountered
skjót	launched		
skjóta	short, throw	sóttin	sickness
skjótara	shorter	sóttu	attended
skjótast	quickly, soonest	spurði	asked
skjótt	quickly	spyrjast	was-heard
		spyrkat	learned

348

Word List (Old Icelandic to English)

Old Icelandic	English	*Old Icelandic*	English
stað	place	*svipan*	swooping
staddir	standing	*svívirðing*	disgraceful
staddur	placed, stood	*svo*	so, such, to
staði	places	*sýndist*	seemed
staðið	placed, stood	*sýnist*	seems
standa	standing	*sýslu*	realm
sté	stepped	*sýslumenn*	stewards
steig	leapt	*systir*	sister
sterkur	strong		
stíg	path		
stigamannanna	the-robbing-men		
stigamönnunum	the-robbers		

T, t

Old Icelandic	English
stígur	climbed
stirður	stiff-footed
stjórn	control
stjórna	ruling
stjörnu	star
stjörnum	the-stars
stjörnu-odda	Star-Oddi (name)
stjörnu-oddi	Star-Oddi (name)
stjörnur	stars
stóð	place, stood
stóðu	stood
stofnað	planned
stofni	stem
stökk	leapt
stól	throne
stór	great
stóra	great
stórmannlega	great-man-like
stórum	great
stund	awhile
stýrði	guided, steered
sú	so, this
sumir	some
sund	a-sound
sundin	the-sound
sundunum	sound, the-sound
svarar	answer, answered
svari	answer
svefni	sleep
sverða	swords
sverði	sword
sverðinu	sword
svikmenni	the-wicked

Old Icelandic	English
taka	take, taken
takast	take, took
talað	told
talar	speak
taldi	said
tekinn	taken
tekst	takes
tekur	took
tíðinda	news
tíðindi	news, the-news
tíðindin	news
tíðindum	news
tiginna	high-born
tign	prestige
tignar	princely
til	for, that, to
tilföngum	means
tíma	time
tímar	time
tindótt	toothed
tírgjarn	fame-ambition
tíska	fashion
títt	report
tjáð	expressed
tjóa	avail
tók	took
tókust	took
töldu	told
tólf	twelve
tönnum	teeth
treysta	trust
trölls	trolls
tröllslegt	trollish
tryggðarmaður	faithful-man

Word List (Old Icelandic to English)

Old Icelandic	English
tugum	tens
tveggja	two
tveir	two
tvo	two
tyggja	chewing

Þ, þ

Old Icelandic	English
þá	then
það	it, that, the, then, they, this, to
þaðan	from-there, then
þær	they
þætti	seemed, thought
þakkaði	thanked
þakkar	thanked
þangað	from-there, there
þangi	seaweed
þann	that, then
þar	of, that, then, there, they
þarf	needed
þau	the, there, they
þegar	as-soon-as, immediately, straightaway, they
þegnum	subjects
þeim	them, they
þeir	them, there, they
þeira	theirs
þeiri	there
þeirra	of-them, their, theirs, them, there, they
þeirri	that
þenna	these, this
þér	to-you, you
þess	it, the, this
þessa	of-this, these, this
þessar	these, this
þessarar	this
þessari	this
þessi	the, these, this
þessir	these
þessu	this
þessum	this
þetta	that, the, this
þig	you
þiggja	accept
þín	yours
þing	assembly, the-assembly
þingað	assembled
þings	an-assembly, assembly
þjóða	people
þjóðar	great-river, king
þjóðbrautinni	the-highway
þó	though, yet
Þórður	Thord (name)
þótt	though, thought
þótti	seemed, thought
þóttist	seemed, though, thought
þóttust	thought
þraut	finished
þrekvirki	brave-deeds
þriðjung	a-third-of
þrítug	thirty
þrjú	three
þroskast	develop
þú	you
þurfa	needed
þurfti	need
þustu	flailing
þvenginn	thong
því	according, accordingly, according-to, against, because, for, then, therefore
þvílíks	such-like
þyki	thought
þykir	seemed, seems
þykja	regarded, seem

U, u

Old Icelandic	English
um	about
umbúnaður	soft-bed-prepared
ummæli	about-words
umsjá	supervision

Word List (Old Icelandic to English)

Old Icelandic	English
und	under
undan	under
undarlegt	wonder-like
undarlegur	extraordinary, wonder-like
undir	under
undrast	wonder
undur	wonder
ung	young
unga	young
ungur	young
unna	grant, love
uns	ours, until
upp	up
upphaf	beginning
upphafi	became
uppheldi	advancement
urðu	became
utan	without

Ú, ú

Old Icelandic	English
úr	from, out-of, through, with
út	out, out-from
útbyrðis	overboard
úti	out
útilegumannanna	the-outlaw-men

V, v

Old Icelandic	English
vægði	mercy
vægis	weight
vænn	handsome
væri	being, was, were, would-be
vág	inlet
vaknað	woken
vaknaði	awoke, woke
vakni	wake
vald	power
valda	wield
vandræði	difficulty
vanir	friends
vantaði	lacking
vanur	accustomed
var	was, were
varð	became, was
varfærir	caution
varp	thrown
vaxa	grow
vaxið	grown
véar	the-gods
veðri	the-weather
veg	way
vega	ways
vegg	wall
veglegasta	greatest
vegs	glory
veisla	feast
veislu	feast
veisluna	feast, the-feast
veislunni	the-feast
veit	know
veitt	given
veitti	gave
veittur	given
vel	all, well
velja	choose
venja	way
venju	habitually
vera	be, being, was
verða	be, become, becomes, happened, to-be, worthy
verði	be
verður	became, worth
verið	been
verkmaður	working-man
vetra	winters
vexti	grown
við	against, with
víða	wide, widely, with
viðbúnaði	preparation
víði	wood
viður	trees
vígaferði	slayings
vígboði	battle-bidding
vígroða	warfare
vigrum	spears

Word List (Old Icelandic to English)

Old Icelandic	English
víking	viking, viking-raids
víkinga	vikings
víkingar	vikings
vil	will, wish
vildi	willed, wished
vildu	willed, wished
vilja	willed
vilji	wish
viljið	wish
vill	wanted-to, will, wish
viltu	will-you
vinir	friends
vinna	grant
vinstri	left
vinum	friends
virðar	men
virðing	worth, worthiness, worthy
virðingu	worthiness
virðulega	worthily
virðulegri	worthy
virðulegur	worthy
virktamönnum	chosen-man
virktavinum	friends
vís	aware
vísaði	pointed-out
vísir	know
vissi	knew
vist	hospitality
víst	vision
vísur	verse, verses
vit	to
vita	knew, know, to-know
vitja	visit
vitmikill	knowing-much
vitrasta	wisest
vitrustum	wise
vitur	wise
vó	guarded
vöknuðu	awoke
von	expected, expected, expecting
vopnaðir	weaponed
vopnaskipti	weapons-exchange
vopnfimi	weapon-nimble
vopnum	weapons
vor	our
vörn	defended
vorrar	aware
voru	they-were, was, were, were

Y, y

Old Icelandic	English
yður	of-you, to-you, you
yðvarrar	your
yðvarri	your
yfir	over
yfirkoma	overcome
ylgjar	wolf's
ylgjarhöfuð	she-wolf's-head
yrði	became

Ý, ý

Old Icelandic	English
ýfð	bristling
ýmissa	various

Word List (English to Old Icelandic)

Word List (English to Old Icelandic)

English	*Old Icelandic*

A, a

English	*Old Icelandic*
a	*að*
abhorrence	*ódáðir*
about	*á, í, um*
about-words	*ummæli*
abundance	*ærið*
accept	*þiggja*
according	*því*
accordingly	*því*
according-to	*því*
accursed-men	*heljarmenn*
accustomed	*vanur*
a-chieftain	*höfðingja*
across	*skör*
action	*skríða*
actually	*raunar*
a-daughter	*dóttur*
adored	*dýrkuðu*
advancement	*uppheldi*
advice	*ráð, ráðlegt*
advisable	*allráðlegt*
Aegir's (name)	*ægis*
affection	*ástúð*
aft	*aftan*
after	*áður, eftir, síðan*
afterwards	*eftir, síðan, síðar*
against	*því, við*
age	*aldri*
aggression	*ágangi*
a-gold-ring	*gullhring*
a-little	*lítt*
alive	*lífi*
all	*alla, allan, allir, allra, allri, allt, öllu, öllum, vel*
all-kinds-of	*allskyns*
all-many-people	*allfjölmennt*
allow	*láta*
allowed	*láta*
all-prepared	*albúin, albúinn, albúnir*
all-ready	*albúinn*
all-un-forethought	*allóráðlega*
all-weaponed	*alvopnuðu*
almost	*nálega*
also	*og*
always	*ávallt, jafnan*
am	*er*
a-man	*maður*
a-match	*kvonfang, kvonfangs, kvonföngin*
among-people	*fyrða*
a-mound	*haug*
an-assembly	*þings*
ancient	*fornum*
and	*eða, en, enda, og*
angled	*hörn*
announced	*boði, kvæði*
another	*annað, annan, annarrar, öðru, öðrum*
another-either	*annaðhvort*
answer	*svarar, svari*
answered	*svarar*
anything-else	*annars*
a-poem	*kvæði*
appointed	*réðust, settan*
appreciate	*njóti*
are	*er, ert, eru, eruð, sért, séu*
arm	*arminum*
army	*her*
a-roar	*rómu*
arrange	*ráðast*
arranging	*ráðast*
as	*er, sem, sér*
ask	*bæði*
asked	*bað, báðu, beiddi, spurði*
asking	*beðinn*
as-long-as	*meðan*
a-sound	*sund*
assembled	*þingað*
assembly	*þing, þings*
assistance	*beina*
as-soon-as	*þegar*
at	*á, í*

Word List (English to Old Icelandic)

English	Old Icelandic	English	Old Icelandic
a-thick	digran	better	betur
a-third-of	þriðjung	bettering	batnaði
a-toast	erfi	between	með, meðr, millum
attack	sókn	bit	biti
attacked	sókn	biting	beitti
attended	sótt, sótti, sóttu	blew	blés
attending	sótti	blood	blóð, blóði
avail	tjóa	blood-helmeted	blóðísunga
aware	vís, vorrar	bloodied	blóðár
away	braut, brott, burt	blows	högg
awhile	hríð, stund	bore	bar, borið
a-wife	konu	borne	bera
awoke	vaknaði, vöknuðu	both	báða, báðir, báðum, bæði

B, b

		bound	bundið
back	aftur	bows	hlýra
battle	bardaga, bardagi, berjast, orustu, rómu	brave	horskir
		brave-deeds	þrekvirki
battle-bidding	vígboði	bride	brúðar
Battle-forest (place)	jöruskóg, jöruskógi, jöruskógur	bring	færa
		bristling	ýfð
battle-spears	hnitgeirum	broad	brattur, breið
be	gera, vera, verða, verði	brothers	barmar
		brought	báru, borið, borin, flutti
beam	meiði		
became	gerðist, upphafi, urðu, varð, verður, yrði	brought-up	mannaður
		buried	heygður, lykill
be-carried-out	efna	but	en, enn
because	fyrir, því	by	á
become	orðin, orðinn, verða		
becomes	verða	## C, c	
bed	rekkju		
been	verið	calendar-computation-wise	rímkænn
before	áður, fyrir, fyrr	called	kallaður, kveðja
began	byrjaði, hóf	came	gerðist, kemur, kom, koma, komið, komu, kómu
beginning	upphaf		
begins	gerðist		
behaviour	athæfi	camped	liggja, lögðust
being	sé, væri, vera	can	kann
beloved	ástvinum	carried	borið
benefits	kosti	cast	kastaði
berserkers	berserkina, berserkir	caught	náði
best	best, besta, bestu, bestum	caution	varfærir
		celebrated	fegnir
betrothed-to	föstnuð		

354

Word List (English to Old Icelandic)

English	Old Icelandic	English	Old Icelandic
champion	kempum	court-men	hirð, hirðmenn, hirðmönnum
chewing	tyggja	covering	huldu
chieftain	höfðingi	crafts	iðn
chieftains	höfðingja, höfðingjum	crew	lið, liði
child	barn, barna	criminals	illvirkjarnir
choice	kost, kostur, kosturinn	cultivate	fága
choice-bid	kostaboð	customs	sið
choices	kjósa		
choose	kjósa, kjósið, kostir, velja		

D, d

English	Old Icelandic
chose	kjöru
chosen-man	virktamönnum
circumstance	hag
claimed	kallaði
cleared	hruðust
clearing	rjóður
clearly	glögglega, görva
climbed	stígur
closely	nálega
come	koma, komi, komið, komin, kominn, komir, komnir
comes	kæmist
comfortable	hæglega
comfortably	hóglegur
coming	komin, komnir
commanded	fylkir
companionship	föruneyti
company	leið, lið, liði, liðs
completely	gersamlega
completion	lyktum
concealing	leyna
conclude	hætta, lúka
concluded	lokið
conduct	ráði
consent	ráði
contemporary	samtíða
control	stjórn
corpses	hræ
could	gátu, geta
counted	reiknaður
courage	frami
court	hirð
courtiers	hirðin
courtly	kurteislega
court-man	hirðmaður

English	Old Icelandic
Dagfinn (name)	dagfinn, dagfinni, dagfinnr, dagfinnur
Dagfinn's (name)	dagfinns
danger	háska
dangerously	hættlega
dark	dökkr
daughter	dóttur
dear	dýrra
death	bana, fráfall
decide	ráð
decided	ræðst
decision	ráð, ráði
deeds	atgervi
defended	vörn
demanded	beiðir
descendants	ætt
descended	konr
determine	ráðist
develop	þroskast
did	fór, gerði
die	látast
died	andaður, andast
difficulty	vandræði
diminished	skerðendr
discourage	letja
discouraged	latti, letjast
disgraceful	svívirðing
disposed	fallinn
dissuaded	löttu
distinguished	kosturinn
divide	skipta
do	gera
doing	gerðu
dominion	heitið

355

Word List (English to Old Icelandic)

English	Old Icelandic
done	ger, gerði, gerst, gert
doorway	dyragætti
drank	drukkið
drapa	drápa, drápuna
drawn	brugðnu, draga, heimt
dream	draum, drauminn
dreamed	dreymdi
drew	brá, dró
drink	drykk
drunk	drukkið
dwell	dvelja
dwelled	dvaldist

E, e

English	Old Icelandic
each	hver, hvergi, hvergymis, hverjum, hvers, hvert, hvorir, hvort
each-other	öðrum
each-way	hvortveggja
eagerly	hafrastar
earl	jarl
earned	kostað
east	austr, austur
eight	átta
either	ella, hvort
either-way	annaðhvort
eleven	ellefu
encountered	sótti
ended	lokið
enemies	andskota
entertainment	skemmtanar
equal-age	jafnaldra
equally	jafngjarn
errand	erindi
especially	einkum
evening	kveldið
events	atburð, atburður
everything	allan
evident	einsætt
evil-doers	illvirkjar, illvirkjunum
exceedingly	forkunnlega
exceedingly-great	geysimikið
except	nema
exchange	skipta
exchanged	skipti, skiptum
expected	von
expecting	von
expedition	leiðangrs
expressed	tjáð
extraordinary	undarlegur
extremely	ákaflega

F, f

English	Old Icelandic
fairest	fegurst
faithful-man	tryggðarmaður
fallen	fallin, fallnir
fame	frægð, frægra, frama
fame-ambition	tírgjarn
famous	frægra, frægur
far-away	fjarri
fared	fór
far-famed	frægr
fashion	tíska
father	faðir, föður
feast	veisla, veislu, veisluna
fee-little	félítill
fell	féll, féllu
felled	felldi, hníga
few	fám, fáttkaðist
fight	berjast, sameignar
fighters	fyrða
filled	fylltir
find	fund
fine	dýran
finery	prýði
finished	braut
firmly	rammlega
firmly-built	rammgert
first	fyrra, fyrst
fishing	fiska
fixed	réð
flailing	bustu
flames	elda
Flatey (place)	flateyjar
fleet	flota
flokk	flokkur

Word List (English to Old Icelandic)

English	*Old Icelandic*
flood	*flóðs*
folk	*fólki*
follow	*fylgd, fylgja*
followed	*fylgt, hlýddi*
followers	*fjölmenni*
followers-many	*fjölmennan, fjölmenni*
follows	*fylgi*
food	*mat*
for	*er, fyrir, því, til*
forces	*hér*
foremost	*framast*
forest	*skóg*
for-me	*mér*
for-the-evil-doers	*illvirkjanna*
for-the-sake-of	*sakir*
forty	*fertug*
forwards	*fram*
found	*hitt, hittir*
friends	*vanir, vinir, vinum, virktavinum*
from	*af, frá, fram, úr*
from-here	*héðan*
from-saying	*frásögu*
from-there	*þaðan, þangað*
from-to-say	*frásaga*
full	*fullt, fyllar*
full-done	*fullgert*
fully	*fullu*
fully-come	*fullkomnir*
fully-prepared	*alskipuð*
furiously	*geisa*

G, g

gain	*afla*
Garp (name)	*garp, garpur*
gathered	*safnað, safnar*
gave	*gaf, gáfu, veitti*
Geirvid (name)	*geirvið, geirviðar, geirviði, geirviðr, geirviður*
get	*fá, fái, fást, geta*
give	*fá, gefa*
given	*gefna, veitt, veittur*
gladly	*gjarna, glaðlega*

English	*Old Icelandic*
gleam	*geisla*
gleaming	*glæsimar*
glided	*skreið*
glorious	*dýrðleg*
glory	*vegs*
Gny (name)	*gný, gnýr*
go	*fara, farast, ganga*
going	*fóru, gang, ganga, gengi*
gold-ring	*gullhring*
Göndul (place)	*göndul*
gone	*farið, gengið*
good	*góð, góðan, góðum, gott*
good-fortune	*gæfa*
gore	*dreyra*
got	*fékk, fengið*
Götaland (place)	*gautland, gautlandi, gautlands*
Gothic (name)	*gotneskra*
governing	*landstjórnar*
governor	*ríkisstjórnar*
graciousness	*hamingjan*
grant	*unna, vinna*
granted	*lagið*
gratitude	*öfúsa*
great	*mikið, mikil, mikinn, miklir, miklu, stór, stóra, stórum*
greatest	*veglegasta*
greatly	*mikið*
great-man-like	*stórmannlega*
great-river	*þjóðar*
greeted	*kvaddi*
greeting	*kveðju*
grimly	*grimmhuguð*
ground	*grundu*
grow	*vaxa*
grown	*vaxið, vexti*
guarded	*vó*
guest	*gistingar*
guided	*stýrði*
Gylfi (name)	*gylfa*

H, h

Word List (English to Old Icelandic)

English	Old Icelandic	English	Old Icelandic
		hill	hóli, hóll
habitually	venju	him	hann, hans, honum
had	átti, áttu, er, hafa, hafði, hafi, haft, hefði, hefir, höfðu, hófu, höfuð, lagði, lét, létu, létust, réðst	himself	sér, sig, sína, sjálfum, sjálfur
		his	hans, honum, sér, sig, sín, sína, sinn, sinni, síns, sínu, sitt
half	hálfs	Hjorgunn (name)	hjörgunni, hjörgunnur
hand	handa, handar, hendi, hönd	Hjorvard (name)	hjörvarðar, hjörvarði, hjörvarður
handsome	vænn	Hladreid (name)	hlaðreið, hlaðreiði
happened	gerðist, verða	Hlegunn (name)	hlégunnar, hlégunni, hlégunnur
happening	atburður		
hard	harða, harðan	Hlegunn's (name)	hlégunnar
hardest	harðasti	Hogni's (name)	högna
hard-headed	harðráðar	hold	halda
hardy	herðendr	home	heim, heima, heiman
harm	mein, skaði	homeward	heimleiðis
has	hefir	honest	ráðvandur
have	átt, eiga, gáfu, hafa, hafi, hefði, hefi, hefir	honour	fremd, sæma, sæmd, sæmdi, sóma, sómi
hawk	hauka	honourable	sæmilegar
hawk-seat	haukastóls	honoured	erfð
he	hann, honum, sér	hordes	hörðu
head	höfði, höfuðið	horses	hestar
headland	höfða, höfðann, höfði	hospitality	vist
heads	höfuðin	house	hús, húss
heard	heyrði, heyrt	house-builder	húsgerðar
heart	hjarta	households	heimkynna
Hel (place)	helju	housemaster	húsbóndi
held	héldi, hélt	how	hve, hvort, nú
helmsman	hilmis	however	en
her	hana, hennar, henni, hún, sér, sín, sinn, sínu	how-so	hversu
		Hrodbjart (name)	hróðbjart, hróðbjarti, hróðbjartur
here	hér, hingað	Hrodbjart's (name)	hróðbjarts
heroes	bragna	hurrying	skynda
Herring-sound (place)	síldasund, síldasundi		
hers	hennar, henni, sinn, sinni, sínum		

I, i

English	Old Icelandic
herself	sér, sig, sjálf
hewed	hjó
hideous	ljótar
high	hár
high-born	tiginna
Hildigunn (name)	hildigunnar, hildigunnur

English	Old Icelandic
I	eg
Iceland (place)	íslandi
if	ef
immediately	þegar
in	á, að, er, í, inn
inconvenience	óhægindi

Word List (English to Old Icelandic)

English	*Old Icelandic*	English	*Old Icelandic*
increased	*æxti*	land-ruling	*landráða*
injury	*áverka*	lands	*landa, lands*
inlet	*vág*	lands-folk	*landsfólkinu*
inside	*innan*	lands-people	*landsmönnum*
intend	*ætla, ætlað*	latter	*síðara*
interaction	*samfarar*	launched	*skjót*
in-the-north	*norður*	lay	*lá, lagðist*
invited	*bað, biður, boðið*	laying-to	*lágu*
is	*er*	lean	*lér*
it	*að, hann, hún, það, þess*	leapt	*steig, stökk*
		learned	*spyrkat*
it-went	*fer*	leave	*láta*
		led	*leiddi, leiðir*

J, j

		left	*vinstri*
		less	*minna*
jaws	*kjafta*	let	*láta*
journey	*ferð, ferðar, för*	lied	*lygi*
journeyed	*færi*	life	*líf*
joyfully	*blíðlega*	life-less	*líflát*
		light	*ljós*

K, k

		lightly	*ljóslega*
		like	*líka*
killed	*drápu*	liked	*líkaði, líkar*
kin	*kindir*	likely	*líklegt*
kind	*háttar*	lineage	*ætt*
king	*konungr, konungs, konungur, þjóðar*	listen	*hlýða*
		little	*lítil, lítill, lítils, litla, lítt*
kingdom	*konungdóminn, ríki, ríkis*	lived	*bjó, lifði*
		locked	*læst*
kingdom's	*ríkustum*	long	*langa, langar, langir, langt, löng*
kinsmen	*frændur*		
knee	*kné*	longer	*lengi, lengra, lengur*
knew	*skildu, vissi, vita*	longships	*langskip*
know	*kunni, kunnigt, veit, vísir, vita*	look	*líta, sjá, sjáir*
		looking-forward	*hlökk*
knowing-much	*vitmikill*	loosed	*laust*
known	*kann, kunnigt*	loosened	*losnaði*
		lord	*herra*

L, l

		lose	*láta*
		lost	*misst*
lacking	*vantaði*	lot	*hlut*
laid	*leið, lögðu, lögðust*	love	*ástir, unna*
land	*land, landa, landi, landið*	luck	*gæfu, lykka*
		lying	*lá*

Word List (English to Old Icelandic)

English	Old Icelandic	English	Old Icelandic
		most-prolific	prúðlegsta
		most-valiant	snjallari
		mother	móðir, móður
		mound	haug
		mound-of-snow	hengiskafla
		mourned	harmaði
		mouth	munni
		much	mikið, mikil, mikill, mikinn, mikla, miklar, miklu, miklum, mjög, mjög

M, m

English	Old Icelandic
made	ger, gera, gerði, gerðr, gerðu, gerðust, gert
man	maðr, mann, manns
mannered	mannaðir
man's	manns
many	margir, margr, mart, mörg, mörgu
many-followers	fjölmenni
many-kinds-of	margskonar
many-men	fjölmenna
marriage	ráðahag
marriage-proposal	ráðahag
married	gift, kvongaður
marry	fá
mass	ógrynni
match	maki
matter	mál, máli
may	má, mætti, mættu, mega, megi, mundi
me	mér, mig
means	færi, tilföngum
meet	fund, hittast, mót, móts
meeting	móti
men	gumna, menn, mönnum, seggjum, virðar
merchant-voyages	kaupferðir
mercy	vægði
messengers	sendimenn
met	hittist
might	mátti
mind	hug
minds	huga
mine	minnar, mínum, mitt
missed	missa, misst
modestly	hæversklega
more	fleira, meir, meira, meiri
morning	morguninn
most	flestum, mesta, mesti, mestu, mjög
most-beautiful	fríðust

English	Old Icelandic
Muli (place)	múla
murder	morðráð
must	mun
my	mína, minnar, minni, mínu, mínum, mitt
myself	mig

N, n

English	Old Icelandic
named	heita, heitir, hét, nefnd, nefndur
near	hjá, nær
nearly	nálega
neck	hálsinn
need	þurfti
needed	þarf, þurfa
neither	hvorki
never	aldregi, aldrei
new	nýju
news	tíðinda, tíðindi, tíðindin, tíðindum
next	næst
night	nætur
no	ekki, engan, engi, nú
noble	göfga, göfugr
noble-like	göfuglegum
nobly	höfðinglega
none	eigi, engi
nor	né
not	eigi, ekki, engi
now	nú

O, o

Word List (English to Old Icelandic)

English	*Old Icelandic*	English	*Old Icelandic*
obey	*hlýða*		
obliged	*skyldari*		
obtained	*aflaði*		
Oddi (name)	*odda, oddi*		
Oddi's (name)	*odda*		
of	*á, að, af, er, í, of, og, þar*		
of-age	*aldurs*		
of-all	*öllum*		
off	*af*		
offered	*bauð*		
of-Goths	*gauta*		
of-him	*hans*		
of-marriage-grown	*gjafvaxta*		
often	*oft*		
of-the-Goths	*gauskrar*		
of-the-journey	*fararinnar*		
of-them	*þeirra*		
of-this	*þessa*		
of-you	*yður*		
old	*gamall*		
older	*eldri*		
on	*á, í*		
one	*annað, annar, einn, eins, einum, eitt, enn*		
one-day	*sinn*		
only	*eiga, eina, einn*		
or	*eða*		
or-else	*ella*		
other	*aðra, annars*		
others	*aðrir, öðru, önnur*		
otherwise	*annars, ella, ellegar*		
our	*vor*		
ours	*uns*		
out	*út, úti*		
out-from	*út*		
out-of	*úr*		
outrages	*illvirki*		
over	*of, ofan, yfir*		
overboard	*útbyrðis*		
overcome	*yfirkoma*		
over-going	*ofangöngunni*		
owned	*átt, eignaði*		
ownership	*eigu*		

P, p

English	*Old Icelandic*
particularly	*einkum*
parting	*skilnaður*
passed	*liðið*
passes	*leið*
path	*götuna, stíg*
peace	*friðaði*
people	*drótt, mannval, menn, mönnum, þjóða*
people-felled	*mannfall*
people-felling	*mannfallið*
person	*mann, manni*
place	*laut, stað, stóð*
placed	*staddur, staðið*
places	*staði*
planned	*stofnað*
poet	*skáld*
poetry	*kvæðinn*
poetry-making	*kveðskapurinn*
poet's-reward	*skáldskaparlaunum*
pointed-out	*vísaði*
possessions	*föng*
power	*föng, orku, vald*
praise	*lofsorð, mærði*
praised	*lofuðu*
precious	*dýrar*
preparation	*viðbúnaði*
preparations	*búið*
prepare	*búa*
prepared	*búa, búið, búins, skipuð*
presents	*presentur*
prestige	*tign*
prevail	*ráða*
princely	*tignar*
protection	*náð*
provisions	*liðskosti*

Q, q

English	*Old Icelandic*
queen	*drottningar*
quickly	*skjótast, skjótt, snarráðir*

Word List (English to Old Icelandic)

English	Old Icelandic
R, r	
rage	eiskranleg
raided	herjar
raiding	hernað, hernaði
raised	hafiður
ran	hljóp
rather	heldur, helst
reached	næðist
reaction	bregður
ready	búnir, greiða
realm	sýslu
recited	kveðið
redeem	kaupast
regarded	þykja
remarkable	merkilegasti
remembered	minntist, mundi
repay	launa
report	títt
respectable	sómasamlegri
responsibility	ábyrgð
retainers	hirð
returning	aftur
reward	launa
Reykjardal (place)	reykjardal
rich	ríkar
riches	auði
right	drótt, dróttar
rings	hringa
rode	riðu
rough	snarpri
roughly	snarpri
ruled	réð
ruler	jöfra
ruling	réð, stjórna
S, s	
said	játti, kvað, kvaðst, kváðu, sagði, sagðist, sagt, seggir, segir, segja, sögðu, taldi
sail	siglu
sail-danger	seglhættu
sake	sakir
same	sama
sat	sat, sett, settur
saw	sá, sæju, sáu, sjá
say	seggja, segja
saying	máli
search	leita
searching	leita
seaweed	þangi
see	líta, sjá, sjái
seek	sækja
seeking	leita
seem	þykja
seemed	sýndist, þætti, þótti, þóttist, þykir
seems	sýnist, þykir
seen	sá, séð, sén
sending-men	sendimenn
sent	sendi, sendir
separate	skiljast
set	sett, setti, settur, setur
shall	skal
shared	deili
sharply	snarpir
she	hana, henni, hér, hún
sheathed-sword	skeið
she-wolf's-head	ylgjarhöfuð
shield	skildi
shield-maiden	skjaldmær
shield-maidens	skjaldmeyja, skjaldmeyjar
shimmering	skjóma
ship	barð
ship-fleet	skipaflota, skipaflotann
ships	skip
ship's-course	skipaferðum
ship-steering-man	skipstjórnarmaður
shoe-thong	skóþvenginn, skóþvengur
short	skjóta
shortage	skorta, skorti
shorter	skemur, skjótara
should	mun, muni, skildi, skuluð, skyldi, skyldu

Word List (English to Old Icelandic)

English	Old Icelandic	English	Old Icelandic
show	*lýsa*	start	*hefjast*
sickness	*sótt, sóttin*	statements	*ráð*
side	*megin*	steered	*stýrði*
sides	*megin*	stem	*stofni*
sister	*systir*	stepped	*sté*
sit	*sitja*	stewards	*sýslumenn*
skills	*list*	stiff-footed	*stirður*
slayings	*vígaferði*	stood	*staddur, staðið, stóð, stóðu*
sleep	*svefni*		
slept	*sofnaði, sofnar*	storm	*hríðmál*
small-stones	*smágrjót*	straight	*drjúgt*
so	*sá, sem, sjá, slíku, sú, svo*	straightaway	*þegar*
		strain	*hneig*
so-as	*að*	strength	*afli, magni*
soft-bed-prepared	*umbúnaður*	stricken-sun	*hnigsólar*
sold	*seldur*	striking	*hjuggu*
some	*sumir*	striking-distance	*höggfæri*
someone	*nokkur*	strong	*sterkur*
something	*nokkuð, nokkur*	struck	*höggur*
some-time	*eitthvert, nokkuð*	subduing	*brýtur*
somewhat	*nokkuð, nokkur, nokkurs*	subjects	*þegnum*
		such	*slíka, slíks, slíku, slíkum, svo*
son	*son, sonar*		
son-of-Helgi (name)	*helgason*	such-like	*þvílíks*
Son-of-Hrodbjart (name)	*roðbjartssonr*	summoned	*kvatt*
		supervision	*umsjá*
soon	*brátt, snemma*	swooping	*svipan*
soonest	*skjótast*	sword	*hjörs, sverði, sverðinu*
sorcery	*fjölkynngi*	swords	*sverða*
sought	*leit, leitaðist, sækja*		
sound	*sundunum*		
speak	*talar*		
spear	*skafti*		

T, t

English	Old Icelandic
spear-guardian	*geirvaldr*
spears	*geiri, vigrum*
speech	*máli*
spite	*böls*
spoke	*kvað, kvaðst, mælt, mælti, mæltu*
spoken	*mælt*
stain	*áta*
standing	*staddir, standa*
star	*stjörnu*
Star-Oddi (name)	*stjörnu-odda, stjörnu-oddi*
stars	*stjörnur*

English	Old Icelandic
take	*taka, takast*
taken	*taka, tekinn*
takes	*tekst*
tall	*hátt*
teeth	*tönnum*
telling	*sagði, sögu*
temple	*hofs*
Temple-Head (place)	*höfða, hofshöfði*
tens	*tugum*
test	*reyna*
than	*en, í*
thanked	*þakkaði, þakkar*

Word List (English to Old Icelandic)

English	*Old Icelandic*	English	*Old Icelandic*
that	á, að, en, enn, er, hinn, hvað, sá, sem, það, þann, þar, þeirri, þetta, til	the-king	konung, konungi, konunginn, konunginum, konungr, konungs, konungsins, konungur, konungurinn, siklingi, siklingr
the	á, að, en, er, hið, hin, hina, hinn, hinni, hins, hinum, í, það, þau, þess, þessi, þetta		
the-assembly	þing	the-kingdom	ríki, ríkið, ríkinu, ríkis
the-battle	bardaga, bardaginn, orustunni	the-king's	konungs, konungsins, konungurinn, siklings
the-berserkers	berserkjanna, berserkjunum	the-king's-men	konungsmönnum
		the-king's-poet	konungsskáld
the-best	best	the-king's-ship	konungsskipið, konungsskipinu
the-blow	höggið		
the-bodies	hold	the-king's-sister	konungssystir
the-border	mörkinni	the-land	landi, landinu, lands, lönd
the-brothers	bræðir		
the-day	daginn	the-lands	lands
the-dream	draum, drauminn, drauminum	the-land's-people	landsfólkið
		them	þeim, þeir, þeirra
the-earl	jarl, jarli, jarls	the-matter	máli
the-earl's-daughter	jarlsdóttir	the-men	ljónar
the-evil-doers	illvirkjanna, illvirkjarnir	the-most	mest
the-feast	veisluna, veislunni	the-mound	hauginn, hauginum
the-fight	sameignar	themselves	sér, sig
the-firth	firrðist	then	á, að, en, hina, síðan, þá, það, þaðan, þann, þar, því
the-forest	skóginn		
the-goddesses	ásynju		
the-gods	véar	the-news	tíðindi
the-government	landstjórnin	the-night	nóttina
the-greatest	mestur	the-other	annar
the-guest	gesturinn	the-others	hinum
the-hand	handa	the-outlaw-men	útilegumannanna
the-helm	hjálmi	the-people	alþýða, mönnum
the-helmsman	hilmis	the-poem	kvæði, kvæðið, kvæðinu
the-highway	þjóðbrautinni		
the-hill	hólinn, hólinum	the-poet	skáld, skáldi, skáldinu, skálds
the-house	húsinu		
their	sín, sinna, sitt, þeirra	the-queen	drottning, drottningar, drottningin
theirs	sínum, þeira, þeirra		
		there	þangað, þar, þau, þeir, þeiri, þeirra
the-island	eyjarinnar		
the-journey	ferð, ferðinni	therefore	því
the-key	grafinn	the-ring	hringinn
		the-robbers	stigamönnunum
		the-robbing-men	stigamannanna

Word List (English to Old Icelandic)

English	*Old Icelandic*	English	*Old Icelandic*
the-saga	*sagan, sagði, söguna, sögunnar, sögunni*	throw	*skjóta*
		thrown	*varp*
the-sake-of	*sakir*	tied	*bindur*
the-same	*sæma, saman*	time	*tíma, tímar*
these	*þenna, þessa, þessar, þessi, þessir*	times	*sinni*
		t-look	*sjást*
the-sea	*sjár*	to	*á, að, af, en, í, svo, það, til, vit*
the-ship	*skipan, skipi*		
the-ships	*skipanna, skips*	to-be	*verða*
the-sound	*sundin, sundunum*	to-do	*gera*
the-stars	*stjörnum*	together	*saman, samför*
the-surf	*lágarða*	togetherness	*samför*
the-tables	*borðum*	to-have	*láta*
the-toast	*erfinu*	to-hear	*áheyrsla*
the-treasure	*féið*	to-her	*henni*
the-treasurer	*gunndjarfr*	to-him	*hann, honum*
the-truth	*satt*	to-know	*vita*
the-way	*gata*	told	*getið, sagðag, sagði, sagt, talað, töldu*
the-weather	*veðri*		
the-wedding	*brúðhlaup*	told-of	*getið*
the-wicked	*svikmenni*	to-me	*mér*
the-woman	*kvenna*	to-meet	*hitt*
they	*það, þær, þar, þau, þegar, þeim, þeir, þeirra*	too	*of*
		took	*leiðir, næmdu, nam, takast, tekur, tók, tókust*
they-are	*eru*		
they-were	*voru*	toothed	*tindótt*
things	*hluta, hluti, hlutum*	to-other	*öðrum*
think	*hugsað, hygg*	to-travel	*fara*
thinking	*hugur*	toughness	*harðfengi*
thirty	*þrítug*	to-you	*þér, yður*
this	*sú, það, þenna, þess, þessa, þessar, þessarar, þessari, þessi, þessu, þessum, þetta*	traditions	*sið*
		travel	*færi, far, fara, farandi, farar, fari, ferðina, fóru*
		travelled	*fara, fer, fór, fórst, fóru*
this-king	*konungurinn*		
thong	*þvenginn*	travelling	*farið, ferðina*
Thord (name)	*Þórður*	travel-weary	*farmóður*
though	*þó, þótt, þóttist*	treasure	*fé, fyrðar*
thought	*hug, hugði, hugðu, mundi, þætti, þótt, þótti, þóttist, þóttust, þyki*	treasured	*dýrmörum*
		trees	*börva, viður*
		trollish	*tröllslegt*
		trolls	*trölls*
three	*þrjú*	trust	*treysta*
throne	*stól*	truthful	*sannsögull*
through	*úr*	turned	*snýr*

Word List (English to Old Icelandic)

English	Old Icelandic
twelve	*tólf*
two	*tveggja, tveir, tvo*

U, u

English	Old Icelandic
un-alert	*ósnöfurmannlega*
un-courteous	*ólát*
under	*und, undan, undir*
unequal	*ójafnað, ójafnari*
unfolded	*rekka*
unheard-of	*endemi*
uninvited	*óboðið*
unlocked	*luku*
un-pleasant	*ódælli*
un-swinging	*ósvífr*
until	*uns*
unusual	*fáheyrður*
up	*upp*
upon	*á*
upright	*rekkum*
urged	*fýstu*
us	*oss*

V, v

English	Old Icelandic
valiant	*böðfrækn*
various	*ýmissa*
verse	*vísur*
verses	*vísur*
very	*einkar*
victory	*sigri, sigur*
victory-gift-gods	*sigrgöfgaðir*
viking	*víking*
viking-raids	*víking*
vikings	*víkinga, víkingar*
virtuous	*dyggir*
vision	*fyrirburður, víst*
visions	*fyrirburð*
visit	*vitja*
voyage	*ferðar*

W, w

English	Old Icelandic
wafting	*hvofta*
wake	*vakni*
wall	*vegg*
wanted-to	*vill*
war-clothes	*herklæðum*
war-company	*herliði*
warfare	*herför, vígroða*
warrior	*gramr*
warriors	*drengir, gramr, grams*
was	*enn, er, eru, sem, væri, var, varð, vera, voru*
was-heard	*spyrjast*
was-named	*hét*
waves	*bylgjur*
way	*leið, veg, venja*
ways	*vega*
wealth	*fé, fjár, fjárins*
wealthy-treasures	*auðæfum*
weaponed	*vopnaðir*
weapon-nimble	*vopnfimi*
weapons	*vopnum*
weapons-exchange	*vopnaskipti*
weight	*vægis*
well	*allvel, vel*
went	*færu, fór, för, fóru, gekk, gengu, gengur*
were	*er, væri, var, voru*
we-sailed	*sigldum*
what	*en, er, hvað, hverra*
when	*er*
where	*er, hvar*
which	*en, er, sem*
while	*hríð, meðan*
who	*er, hver*
whole	*heilum*
wide	*breiðan, víða*
widely	*víða*
wield	*valda*
wife	*eiginkonu, kona, konu*
wife-of	*kona*
will	*vil, vill*
willed	*vildi, vildu, vilja*
willing	*fúsastur*
will-you	*viltu*
windswept	*byrsóta*

Word List (English to Old Icelandic)

English	*Old Icelandic*
winters	*vetra*
wise	*fróður, vitrustum, vitur*
wisest	*vitrasta*
wish	*vil, vilji, viljið, vill*
wished	*vildi, vildu*
with	*að, enda, með, of, úr, við, víða*
within	*innan*
without	*utan*
woke	*vaknaði*
woken	*vaknað*
wolf	*heiðingja*
wolf's	*ylgjar*
woman	*kona, kvenna*
women	*konur*
won	*gagn*
wonder	*undrast, undur*
wonderful	*ágætum*
wonder-like	*undarlegt, undarlegur*
wood	*skíð, víði*
worded	*orð, ort*
words	*málma, orð, orða*
word-struggle	*orðahjaldur*
working-man	*verkmaður*
worth	*verður, virðing*
worthily	*virðulega*
worthiness	*virðing, virðingu*
worthy	*verða, virðing, virðulegri, virðulegur*
would	*mundi, mundu, muni*
would-be	*væri*
wounds	*sárum*
written	*ritnar*

Y, y

yet	*þó*
you	*þér, þig, þú, yður*
young	*ung, unga, ungur*
your	*yðvarrar, yðvarri*
yours	*þín*
yourself	*sjálfum*
youth	*æsku*

A Word Comparison of Old Norse and Old Icelandic Words

A Word Comparison of Old Norse and Old Icelandic Words

Old Norse	Old Icelandic	English	Old Norse	Old Icelandic	English
áðr	áður	after	boðit	boðið	invited
áðr	áður	before	borit	borið	bore
ærit	ærið	abundance	borit	borið	brought
ætlat	ætlað	intend	borit	borið	carried
aftr	aftur	back	brattr	brattur	broad
aftr	aftur	returning	Bregðr	bregður	reaction
ákafliga	ákaflega	extremely	brýtr	brýtur	subduing
aldri	aldrei	never	búit	búið	preparations
aldrigi	aldregi	never	búit	búið	prepared
aldrs	aldurs	of-age	bundit	bundið	bound
allbráðliga	allóráðlega	all-un-forethought	Dagfinnr	dagfinnur	Dagfinn (name)
allráðligt	allráðlegt	advisable	dreymði	dreymdi	dreamed
alþýðu	alþýða	the-people	dróttning	drottning	the-queen
alvápnuðu	alvopnuðu	all-weaponed	dróttningar	drottningar	queen
andaðr	andaður	died	dróttningar	drottningar	the-queen
Annarr	annar	one	dróttningin	drottningin	the-queen
annarr	annar	the-other	drukkit	drukkið	drank
annat	annað	another	drukkit	drukkið	drunk
Annat	annað	one	dýrðlig	dýrðleg	glorious
annathvárt	annaðhvort	another-either	dyrigætti	dyragætti	doorway
annathvárt	annaðhvort	either-way	eðr	eða	or
at	að	a	eiskranlig	eiskranleg	rage
at	að	in	ek	eg	I
at	að	it	ellifu	ellefu	eleven
at	að	of	elligar	ellegar	otherwise
at	að	so-as	erendi	erindi	errand
at	að	that	fá	fái	get
at	að	the	færi	færu	went
at	að	then	fáheyrðr	fáheyrður	unusual
at	að	to	fara	fari	travel
at	að	with	farit	farið	gone
atburðr	atburður	events	farit	farið	travelling
atburðr	atburður	happening	farmóðr	farmóður	travel-weary
aufúsa	öfúsa	gratitude	fátkaðist	fáttkaðist	few
austr	austur	east	feðr	föður	father
bar	þar	there	fegrst	fegurst	fairest
betr	betur	better	féit	féið	the-treasure
bezt	best	best	fekk	fékk	got
beztu	bestu	best	fell	féll	fell
beztum	bestum	best	fellu	féllu	fell
biðr	biður	invited	fengit	fengið	got
bindr	bindur	tied	ferr	fer	it-went
blíðliga	blíðlega	joyfully	ferr	fer	travelled

A Word Comparison of Old Norse and Old Icelandic Words

Old Norse	Old Icelandic	English	Old Norse	Old Icelandic	English
firrðisk	firrðist	the-firth	hezta	besta	best
flokkr	flokkur	flokk	heztum	bestum	best
forkunnliga	forkunnlega	exceedingly	Hildiguðr	hildigunnur	Hildigunn (name)
frægr	frægur	famous			
frændr	frændur	kinsmen	hingat	hingað	here
fremð	fremd	honour	hirðmaðr	hirðmaður	court-man
fróðr	fróður	wise	Hjörguðr	hjörgunnur	Hjorgunn (name)
fúsastr	fúsastur	willing			
fylgð	fylgd	follow	Hjörvarðr	hjörvarður	Hjorvard (name)
fylldir	fylltir	filled			
fyrða	fyrðar	treasure	Hléguðr	hlégunnur	Hlegunn (name)
fyrirburðr	fyrirburður	vision			
Garpr	garpur	Garp (name)	höfðingliga	höfðinglega	nobly
gauzkrar	gauskrar	of-the-Goths	höfuðit	höfuðið	head
Geirviðr	geirviður	Geirvid (name)	höggit	höggið	the-blow
			höggr	höggur	struck
gengit	gengið	gone	hógligr	hóglegur	comfortably
gengr	gengur	went	hon	hún	her
gerðisk	gerðist	came	hon	hún	it
gersamliga	gersamlega	completely	hon	hún	she
gerzt	gerst	done	Hróðbjartr	hróðbjartur	Hrodbjart (name)
gestrinn	gesturinn	the-guest			
getit	getið	told	hugr	hugur	thinking
getit	getið	told-of	Hugsat	hugsað	think
geysimikit	geysimikið	exceedingly-great	hulðu	huldu	covering
			hváfta	hvofta	wafting
glaðliga	glaðlega	gladly	hvárir	hvorir	each
glöggliga	glögglega	clearly	hvárki	hvorki	neither
göfugligum	göfuglegum	noble-like	hvárt	hvort	each
gótt	gott	good	hvárt	hvort	either
hægliga	hæglega	comfortable	hvárt	hvort	how
hættliga	hættlega	dangerously	hvártveggja	hvortveggja	each-way
hæverskliga	hæversklega	modestly	hvat	hvað	that
haf	hafa	had	hvat	hvað	what
hafiðr	hafiður	raised	hvé	hve	how
haukstóls	haukastóls	hawk-seat	hverr	hver	each
heðan	héðan	from-here	hverr	hver	who
hefr	hefir	had	in	hin	the
heitit	heitið	dominion	ina	hina	the
heldi	héldi	held	inn	hinn	the
heldr	heldur	rather	inni	hinni	the
helt	hélt	held	ins	hins	the
helzt	helst	rather	inum	hinum	the
herða	harða	hard	inum	hinum	the-others
heygðr	heygður	buried	it	hið	the
hezt	best	the-best			

369

A Word Comparison of Old Norse and Old Icelandic Words

Old Norse	Old Icelandic	English	Old Norse	Old Icelandic	English
Jöruskógr	*jöruskógur*	Battle-forest (place)	*maðr*	*maður*	man
			mætti	*mættu*	may
kallaðr	*kallaður*	called	*mála*	*málma*	words
kemr	*kemur*	came	*mannaðr*	*mannaður*	brought-up
koma	*komi*	come	*mannfallit*	*mannfallið*	people-felling
komit	*komið*	came	*Margt*	*mart*	many
komit	*komið*	come	*merkiligsti*	*merkilegasti*	remarkable
kómu	*komu*	came	*mestr*	*mestur*	the-greatest
konungr	*konungur*	king	*mik*	*mig*	me
konungr	*konungur*	the-king	*mik*	*mig*	myself
konungrinn	*konungurinn*	the-king	*mikit*	*mikið*	great
konungrinn	*konungurinn*	the-king's	*mikit*	*mikið*	greatly
konungrinn	*konungurinn*	this-king	*mikit*	*mikið*	much
konungsskipit	*konungsskipið*	the-king's-ship	*mjök*	*mjög*	most
			mjök	*mjög*	much
köru	*kjöru*	chose	*mjök*	*mjög*	much
kostat	*kostað*	earned	*morgininn*	*morguninn*	morning
kostr	*kostur*	choice	*munda*	*mundi*	would
kostrinn	*kosturinn*	choice	*nætr*	*nætur*	night
kostrinn	*kosturinn*	distinguished	*náliga*	*nálega*	almost
kunna	*kunni*	know	*náliga*	*nálega*	closely
kurteisliga	*kurteislega*	courtly	*náliga*	*nálega*	nearly
kvæða	*kvæði*	announced	*nát*	*náð*	protection
kvæðit	*kvæðið*	the-poem	*nefndr*	*nefndur*	named
kvánfang	*kvonfang*	a-match	*nökkur*	*nokkur*	something
kvánfangs	*kvonfangs*	a-match	*nökkur*	*nokkur*	somewhat
kvánföngin	*kvonföngin*	a-match	*nökkurr*	*nokkur*	someone
kvángaðr	*kvongaður*	married	*nökkurs*	*nokkurs*	somewhat
kveðit	*kveðið*	recited	*nökkut*	*nokkuð*	something
kveðskaprinn	*kveðskapurinn*	poetry-making	*nökkut*	*nokkuð*	some-time
			nökkut	*nokkuð*	somewhat
kveldit	*kveldið*	evening	*norðr*	*norður*	in-the-north
lagit	*lagið*	granted	*óboðit*	*óboðið*	uninvited
landit	*landið*	land	*of*	*um*	about
landsfólkit	*landsfólkið*	the-land's-people	*óhægendi*	*óhægindi*	inconvenience
landsstjórnin	*landstjórnin*	the-government	*ok*	*og*	also
			ok	*og*	and
lengr	*lengur*	longer	*ok*	*og*	of
liðit	*liðið*	passed	*ök*	*og*	and
líkligt	*líklegt*	likely	*ór*	*úr*	from
ljósliga	*ljóslega*	lightly	*ór*	*úr*	out-of
lokit	*lokið*	concluded	*ór*	*úr*	through
lokit	*lokið*	ended	*ór*	*úr*	with
lykðum	*lyktum*	completion	*orðahjaldr*	*orðahjaldur*	word-struggle
maðr	*maður*	a-man			

A Word Comparison of Old Norse and Old Icelandic Words

Old Norse	Old Icelandic	English	Old Norse	Old Icelandic	English
orrostu	orustu	battle	staðit	staðið	placed
orrostunni	orustunni	the-battle	staðit	staðið	stood
örvígr	ósvífr	un-swinging	sterkr	sterkur	strong
ósnöfrmannliga	ósnöfurmannlega	un-alert	stigamönnum	stigamönnunum	the-robbers
prúðligsta	prúðlegsta	most-prolific	stígr	stígur	climbed
ráðligt	ráðlegt	advice	stirðr	stirður	stiff-footed
ráðvandr	ráðvandur	honest	stofnat	stofnað	planned
reiknaðr	reiknaður	counted	stórmannliga	stórmannlega	great-man-like
ríkit	ríkið	the-kingdom	svá	svo	so
rjóðr	rjóður	clearing	svá	svo	such
sá	sáu	saw	svá	svo	to
sæi	sæju	saw	svát	svo	so
sæmð	sæmd	honour	Svipun	svipan	swooping
sæmði	sæmdi	honour	talat	talað	told
sæmiligar	sæmilegar	honourable	talði	taldi	said
safnat	safnað	gathered	tekr	tekur	took
sagðak	sagðag	told	þangat	þangað	from-there
sák	sá	saw	þangat	þangað	there
sé	séu	are	þat	það	it
seldr	seldur	sold	þat	það	that
sér	sért	are	Þat	það	the
sét	séð	seen	Þat	það	then
setr	setur	set	Þat	það	they
settr	settur	sat	þat	það	this
settr	settur	set	þat	það	to
sigr	sigur	victory	þeira	þeirra	of-them
sik	sig	herself	þeira	þeirra	their
sik	sig	himself	þeira	þeirra	theirs
sik	sig	his	þeira	þeirra	them
sik	sig	themselves	þeira	þeirra	there
sjá	sjái	see	þeira	þeirra	they
sjálfr	sjálfur	himself	þeiri	þeirri	that
skemr	skemur	shorter	þik	þig	you
skilði	skildi	should	þingat	þingað	assembled
skilðu	skildu	knew	Þórðr	þórður	Thord (name)
skilnaðr	skilnaður	parting	þvít	því	because
skipstjórnarmaðr	skipstjórnarmaður	ship-steering-man	þykki	þyki	thought
skor	skör	across	þykkir	þykir	seemed
skóþvengr	skóþvengur	shoe-thong	þykkir	þykir	seems
skyldi	skyldu	should	þykkja	þykja	regarded
sómasamligri	sómasamlegri	respectable	þykkja	þykja	seem
sonr	son	son	tíðenda	tíðinda	news
staddr	staddur	placed	tíðendi	tíðindi	news
staddr	staddur	stood	tíðendi	tíðindi	the-news

A Word Comparison of Old Norse and Old Icelandic Words

Old Norse	Old Icelandic	English
tíðendin	tíðindin	news
tíðendum	tíðindum	news
tíginna	tiginna	high-born
tígn	tign	prestige
tígnar	tignar	princely
tízka	tíska	fashion
tját	tjáð	expressed
tölðu	töldu	told
tröllsligt	tröllslegt	trollish
tryggðarmaðr	tryggðarmaður	faithful-man
tvá	tvo	two
umbúnaðr	umbúnaður	soft-bed-prepared
undarligr	undarlegur	extraordinary
undarligr	undarlegur	wonder-like
undarligt	undarlegt	wonder-like
undr	undur	wonder
ungr	ungur	young
unz	uns	ours
unz	uns	until
útan	utan	without
vá	vó	guarded
vaknat	vaknað	woken
ván	von	expected
ván	von	expecting
vanr	vanur	accustomed
vápnaðir	vopnaðir	weaponed
vápnaskipti	vopnaskipti	weapons-exchange
vápnfimi	vopnfimi	weapon-nimble
vápnum	vopnum	weapons
var	varð	was
vár	vor	our
várr	vor	our
várrar	vorrar	aware
Váru	voru	they-were
váru	voru	was
váru	voru	were
vaxit	vaxið	grown
vegligasta	veglegasta	greatest
veittr	veittur	given
veizla	veisla	feast
veizlu	veislu	feast
veizluna	veisluna	feast
veizluna	veisluna	the-feast
veizlunni	veislunni	the-feast
verðr	verður	became
verðr	verður	worth
verit	verið	been
verkmaðr	verkmaður	working-man
við	viður	trees
vildi	vildu	willed
vili	vilji	wish
vilið	viljið	wish
villtu	viltu	will-you
virðuliga	virðulega	worthily
virðuligr	virðulegur	worthy
virðuligri	virðulegri	worthy
virkðamönnum	virktamönnum	chosen-man
virkðavinum	virktavinum	friends
viss	vís	aware
vissir	vísir	know
vitr	vitur	wise
yðr	yður	of-you
yðr	yður	to-you
yðr	yður	you

www.ingramcontent.com/pod-product-compliance
Lightning Source LLC
Chambersburg PA
CBHW051359070526
44584CB00023B/3219